D0849582

Supply Chain Management and Advanced Planning

Concepts, Models, Software
and Case Studies

Springer
Berlin
Heidelberg
New York
Barcelona
Hong Kong
London
Milan
Paris
Singapore
Tokyo

Hartmut Stadtler · Christoph Kilger
Editors

Supply Chain Management and Advanced Planning

Concepts, Models, Software
and Case Studies

With 113 Figures
and 48 Tables

Springer

Prof. Dr. Hartmut Stadtler
Technische Universität Darmstadt
FB Rechts- und Wirtschaftswissenschaften
FG Fertigungs- und Materialwirtschaft
Hochschulstraße 1
D-64289 Darmstadt
Germany

Dr. Christoph Kilger
j&m Management Consulting GmbH
Kaiserringforum
Willy-Brandt-Platz 6
D-68161 Mannheim
Germany

ISBN 3-540-67682-1 Springer-Verlag Berlin Heidelberg New York

Library of Congress Cataloging-in-Publication Data
Die Deutsche Bibliothek – CIP-Einheitsaufnahme
Supply Chain Management and Advanced Planning: Concepts, Models, Software and Case Studies /
ed.: Hartmut Stadtler; Christoph Kilger. – Berlin; Heidelberg; New York; Barcelona; Hong Kong; London; Milan; Paris; Singapore; Tokyo: Springer, 2000
    ISBN 3-540-67682-1

Springer-Verlag Berlin Heidelberg New York
a member of BertelsmannSpringer Science+Business Media GmbH

© Springer-Verlag Berlin · Heidelberg 2000
Printed in Germany

Hardcover-Design: Erich Kirchner, Heidelberg

SPIN 10724876   42/2202-5 4 3 2 1 0 – Printed on acid-free paper

Preface

Hartmut Stadtler[1], Christoph Kilger[2]

[1] Darmstadt University of Technology, Institute of Business Administration, Department of Operations and Materials Management, Hochschulstraße 1, 64289 Darmstadt, Germany

[2] j & m Management Consulting GmbH, Kaiserringforum, Willy-Brandt-Platz 6, 68161 Mannheim, Germany

During the late 80s and throughout the 90s information technology changed modern manufacturing organizations dramatically. Enterprise Resource Planning (ERP) systems became the major backbone technology for nearly every type of transaction. Customer orders, purchase orders, receipts, invoices etc. are maintained and processed by ERP systems provided by software vendors – like Baan, J. D. Edwards, Oracle, SAP AG and many more. ERP systems integrate many processes, even those that span multiple functional areas in an organization, and provide a consistent database for corporate wide data. By that ERP systems help to integrate internal processes in an organization.

Mid of the 90s it became apparent that focussing on the integration of internal processes alone does not lead to a drastic improvement of business performance. While ERP systems are supporting the *standard* business workflows, the biggest impact on business performance is created by *exceptions* and *variability*, e. g. customers order more than expected, suppliers deliver later than promised, production capacity is reduced by an unforeseen breakdown of equipment etc. The correct reaction to exceptions like these can save a lot of money and increase the service level and will help to improve sales and profits. Furthermore, state-of-the-art *planning procedures* – for planning sales, internal operations and supply from the vendors well in advance – reduce the amount of exceptional situations, helping to keep business in a standard mode of operation and turning out to be more profitable than constantly dealing with exceptional situations.

This functionality – powerful planning procedures and methodologies as well as quick reactions to exceptions and variability – is provided by *Advanced Planning Systems*. An Advanced Planning System (APS) exploits the consistent database and integrated standard workflows provided by ERP systems to leverage high velocity in industry. Due to these recent developments, software vendors of APS boost a major breakthrough in enterprise wide planning and even collaborative planning between the partners along a supply chain.

Do APS hold the promises? What are the concepts underlying these new planning systems? How do APS and ERP systems interact, and how do APS supplement ERP systems? What are the current limits of APS and what is required to introduce an APS in a manufacturing organization successfully?

These were the questions we asked ourselves when we started our project on "Supply Chain Management and Advanced Planning" in summer 1998. Since we realized that there were many more interested in this new challenging field, the idea of publishing this book was born.

This book is the result of collaborative work done by members of four consultancy companies – aconis, j & m Management Consulting, KPMG and PRTM – and three universities – University of Augsburg, Darmstadt University of Technology and Georgia Institute of Technology. Our experiences stem from insights gained by utilizing, testing and implementing several modules of APS from i2 Technologies, J. D. Edwards and SAP AG. Tests and evaluations of modules have been conducted within several projects including students conducting their final thesis.

On the other hand, some members of the working group have been (and still are) involved in actual APS implementation projects in several European enterprises. The real-world experience gained from these projects has been merged with the results from the internal evaluation projects and provided valuable insights into the current performance of APS as well as guidelines how to setup and conduct an APS implementation project.

Since summer 1998 our group has spent much time gaining insights into this new fascinating field, working closely together with colleagues from academic research, vendors of APS and customers of APS vendors. However, we are aware of the fact that APS vendors are constantly improving their systems, that new areas come into focus – like supplier collaboration, internet fulfilment, customer relationship management – and that, because of the speed of developments, a *final* documentation will not be possible. Hence, we decided to publish this book as a report on the current state of APS, based on our current knowledge and findings, covering the major principles and concepts underlying state-of-the-art APS.

This book will be a valuable source for managers and consultants alike, initiating and conducting projects aiming at introducing an APS in industry. Furthermore, it will help actual users of an APS to understand and broaden their view of how an APS really works. Also, students attending postgraduate courses in Supply Chain Management and related fields will profit from the material provided.

Many people have contributed to this book. In fact, it is a "Joint Venture" of the acadamic world and consultancy firms, both being at the forefront of APS technology. Hans Kühn gave valuable input to Chap. 2, especially to the section on the SCOR-model. Daniel Fischer was involved in the writing of Chap. 8 on Demand Fulfilment and ATP. The ideas of the KPI profile and the Enabler-KPI-Value Network, described in Chap. 12, were strongly influenced by many discussions with Dr. Rupert Deger. Dr. Hans-Christian Humprecht and Christian Manß were so kind as to review our view of software modules of APS (Chap. 15). Dr. Uli Kalex was the main contributor to the design of the project solutions, on which the computer assembly case study (Chap. 18) and the semiconductor case study (Chap. 17) are based. Marja Blomqvist, Dr. Susanne Gröner, Bindu Kochugovindan, Helle Skott and Heinz Korbelius read parts of the book and helped to improve the style and contents. Furthermore, we profited a lot from several unnamed students who prepared their master thesis in the area of APS – most of them now being employed by companies implementing APS. Last but not least, we would like to mention Ulrich Höfling as well as the authors Jens Rohde and Christopher Sürie who took care of assembling the 24 chapters and preparing the index in a tireless effort throughout this project.

Many thanks to all!

We wish our readers a profitable reading and all the best for applying Advanced Planning Systems in practice successfully.

Hartmut Stadtler   Darmstadt, June 2000
Christoph Kilger   Mannheim, June 2000

Contents

Preface V
Hartmut Stadtler, Christoph Kilger

Introduction 1
Hartmut Stadtler
References 3

Part I. Basics of Supply Chain Management

1   Supply Chain Management – An Overview 7
Hartmut Stadtler
1.1   Definitions 7
1.2   Building Blocks 9
1.3   Origins 18
References 27

2   Supply Chain Analysis 29
Herbert Meyr, Jens Rohde, Hartmut Stadtler, Christopher Sürie
2.1   Performance Measurement 29
2.2   The SCOR-Model 36
2.3   A Supply Chain Typology 46
References 55

3   Advanced Planning 57
Bernhard Fleischmann, Herbert Meyr, Michael Wagner
3.1   What is Planning? 57
3.2   Planning Tasks along the Supply Chain 62
3.3   Example for Typical Planning Tasks in the Consumer Goods
      Industry 67
References 71

Part II. Concepts of Advanced Planning Systems

4   Structure of Advanced Planning Systems 75
Herbert Meyr, Michael Wagner, Jens Rohde
References 77

5   Strategic Network Planning 79
Marc Goetschalckx
5.1   A Verbal Formulation of the Strategic Network Design Problem . .   81
5.2   Successful Applications of Strategic Supply Chain Modelling-Based
      Design 89
5.3   Modelling Features in Current APS 90
5.4   Conclusions 92
References 94

6   Demand Planning 97
Michael Wagner
6.1   A Demand Planning Framework 97
6.2   Statistical Forecasting Techniques 101
6.3   Incorporation of Judgmental Factors 106
6.4   Additional Features 108
References 115

7   Master Planning 117
Jens Rohde, Michael Wagner
7.1   The Decision Situation 118
7.2   Model Building 124
7.3   Generating a Plan 131
References 133

8   Demand Fulfilment and ATP 135
Christoph Kilger, Lorenz Schneeweiss
8.1   Available-to-Promise (ATP) 136
8.2   Allocated ATP 140
8.3   Order Promising 144
References 148

9   Production Planning and Scheduling 149
Hartmut Stadtler
9.1   Description of the Decision Situation 149
9.2   How to Proceed from a Model to a Production Schedule 150
9.3   Model Building 153
9.4   Updating Production Schedules 158
9.5   Number of Planning Levels and Limitations 161
References 165

10   Distribution and Transport Planning 167
Bernhard Fleischmann
10.1 Planning Situations 167
10.2 Models 172
References 181

11   Coordination and Integration 183
Jens Rohde
11.1 Coordination of APS Modules 184
11.2 Integration of APS 186
11.3 Collaboration of Supply Chain Entities 191
References 194

Part III. Implementing Advanced Planning Systems

12   The Definition of a Supply Chain Project 197
Christoph Kilger
12.1 Supply Chain Review....................................... 198
12.2 Supply Chain Potential Analysis 207
12.3 Project Roadmap 211
References 216

13   The Selection Process 217
Christoph Kilger
13.1 Creation of a Short List.................................... 218
13.2 Functional Requirements................................... 221
13.3 Implementation and Integration 224
13.4 Post-Implementation 227
References 228

14   The Implementation Process 229
Ulrich Wetterauer
14.1 Focus.. 229
14.2 Design Conceptual Solution 235
14.3 Design Solution Details 236
14.4 Build and Test 237
14.5 Deploy 238
References 238

Part IV. Actual APS and Case Studies

15   Architecture of Selected APS 241
Herbert Meyr, Jens Rohde, Michael Wagner
15.1 i2 Technologies – i2 RHYTHM 241
15.2 J. D. Edwards – Active Supply Chain 244
15.3 SAP – APO 246
References 249

16   Scheduling of Synthetic Granulate 251
Marco Richter, Volker Stockrahm
16.1 Presentation of the Production Process 251
16.2 Special Planning Problems 253
16.3 Modelling the Production Process in APO PP/DS 253
16.4 Consequences and Benefits of the APO PP/DS Implementation .. 264
16.5 Outlook – Supply Network Planning with APO 265

17   Semiconductor Manufacturing 267
Lorenz Schneeweiss, Ulrich Wetterauer
17.1 Introduction... 267
17.2 The Modelling Concept of i2 RHYTHM Factory Planner........ 273
17.3 Modelling 276
17.4 Model Communication...................................... 279
17.5 Lessons Learned 280

18   Computer Assembly 281
Christoph Kilger
18.1 Description of the Supply Chain 281
18.2 Scope and Expected Benefits 285
18.3 Planning Processes in Detail 287
18.4 Integration of i2 with SAP R/3 294

19   Food and Beverages..................................... 297
Michael Wagner, Herbert Meyr
19.1 Description of the Supply Chain 297
19.2 The Architecture of the Planning System 300
19.3 Model Building in J. D. Edwards Enterprise Planning........... 303
19.4 The Master Planning Module............................... 306
19.5 Concluding Remarks 313
References 313

Part V. Conclusions and Outlook

20   Conclusions and Outlook................................ 317
Hartmut Stadtler
References 320

Part VI. Supplement

21   Forecast Methods 323
Herbert Meyr
21.1 Forecasting for Seasonality and Trend 323
21.2 Initialization of Trend and Seasonal Coefficients................. 329

References 333

22   Linear and Mixed Integer Programming 335
Hartmut Stadtler
22.1 Linear Programming 335
22.2 Pure Integer and Mixed Integer Programming 339
22.3 Remarks and Recommendations 343
References 344

23   Genetic Algorithms 345
Robert Klein
23.1 General Idea 345
23.2 Populations and Individuals 346
23.3 Evaluation and Selection of Individuals 348
23.4 Recombination and Mutation 350
23.5 Conclusions 351
References 352

24   Constraint Programming 353
Robert Klein
24.1 Overview and General Idea 353
24.2 Constraint Satisfaction Problems 354
24.3 Constraint Propagation 356
24.4 Search Algorithms 357
24.5 Concluding Remarks 358
References 359

Index 361
About Contributors 369

Introduction

Hartmut Stadtler

Darmstadt University of Technology, Institute of Business Administration, Department of Operations and Materials Management, Hochschulstraße 1, 64289 Darmstadt, Germany

Supply Chain Management - just another shortlived management philosophy? The gains that have been realized when adopting *Supply Chain Management* (SCM) and Advanced Planning are impressive:

- Hewlett-Packard cut deskjet printer supply costs by 25% with the help of inventory models analyzing the effect of different locations of inventories within its supply chain. This analysis convinced Hewlett-Packard to adopt a modular design and postponement for its deskjet printers (Lee and Billington, 1995).
- Campbell Soup reduced retailer inventories on average by 66% while maintaining or increasing average fill rates by improving forecasts and introducing simple inventory management rules (Cachon and Fisher, 1998).
- IBM applied its Asset Management Tool, consisting of analytical performance optimization and simulation, to its personal systems division, saving material costs and price-protection expenses of more than $750 million in 1998 (Lin et al., 2000).
- BASF introduced vendor managed inventory with five key customers in its textile colours division. With the help of an Advanced Planning System it has been possible to raise the fill rate of its customer's inventory to almost 100%. Customers profited from eliminating safety stocks while it allowed BASF to generate less costly transportation and production schedules (Grupp, 1998).

These impressive gains show the potential of coordinating organizational units and integrating information flows and planning efforts along a supply chain.

Which manager can afford not to present such substantial gains in improving competitiveness? Nowadays, these gains cannot be achieved by one company alone, because companies have attempted to concentrate their business on those activities which they know best – their core competence. As a result, all other activities have been outsourced to other firms, if possible. Consequently, the characteristics and the quality of a product or service sold to a customer largely depend on several firms involved in its creation. This brought about new challenges for the integration of legally separated firms and the coordination of materials, information and financial flows not experienced in this magnitude before. A new managerial philosophy was needed – Supply Chain Management.

As with many management philosophies, impressive gains reported from pilot studies are promised. Often a few principles build the main body of such a new management philosophy. Since there are usually many more facets involved in managing a company successfully, some factors neglected may give rise to improvements achievable by the next management philosophy highlighted a few years later. Still, each management philosophy usually contains some building blocks that are advantageous and will survive over a longer period of time.

No great phantasies are needed to forecast that Supply Chain Management will not be the ultimate managerial philosophy, although in our opinion it has many more facets than most of its predecessors. Since there are several facets to look at, Supply Chain Management is difficult to grasp as a whole. While being aware of the wide area covered by Supply Chain Management, this book will concentrate on recent developments in coordinating materials and information flows by means of the latest software products – named *Advanced Planning Systems* (APS). During the past ten years progress in information technology – like powerful database management systems – communication means – like *electronic data interchange* (EDI) via internet – as well as solution methods to solve large quantitative models – e. g. by mathematical programming – opened up new perspectives for planning and controlling flows along a supply chain. A customer's order, demand forecasts or market trends may be exploded into required activities and sent to all parties in the supply chain immediately. Accurate schedules are generated which secure order fulfilment in time. Roughly speaking – this is the task of APS. Unlike traditional *Enterprise Resource Planning* (ERP) these new systems try to find feasible, (near) optimal plans across the supply chain as a whole, while potential bottlenecks are considered explicitly.

It is our intention to provide insights into the principles and concepts underlying APS. Part I of the book introduces the basics of SCM starting with a definition of SCM and its building blocks. The origins of SCM can be traced back into the fifties, where Forrester (1958) already studied the dynamics of industrial production-distribution systems (see Chap. 1). As a first step of introducing APS in industry it seems wise to document and analyze the current state of the supply chain and its elements. Here, a graphical representation with different levels of aggreagation – known as the SCOR-model – is most valuable (Chap. 2). Key performance indicators – one suitable tool for analyzing weaknesses of the supply chain – are described, too. It will provide valuable insights and guidance for setting targets for a supply chain project. Although APS are designed to be applicable for a number of industries, decision problems may vary widely. A typology of supply chains will help the reader to identifiy which characteristics of a specific APS match the requirements of the supply chain at hand and which do not and thus can guide the selection process of an APS. Chapter 3 explains the basics of advanced planning by introducing (hierarchical) planning and describing the planning tasks along the supply chain.

Part II describes the general structure of APS (Chap. 4) and its modules in greater detail. However, Part II will not only concentrate on functions and modelling features currently available in APS, but it will also describe ideas we regard to be good Advanced Planning and thus should be included in future releases of an APS. The presentation of concepts underlying these modules starts with strategic plannning (Chap. 5) followed by operational planning tasks for production and distribution. The quality of decision support provided by an APS largely depends on an adequate model of the elements of a supply chain, the algorithms used for its solutions and the coordination of modules involved. Chapters 6 to 10 describe the many modelling features and mention solution procedures available to tackle different planning tasks without explicitly refering to specific APS. Although several modules have been identified, software vendors claim to offer a coherent, integrated software suite with close links to ERP-Systems. These linkages are the topic of Chap. 11.

Obviously, implementing an APS within a firm or supply chain requires a lot more than modelling. Hence, we describe the tasks necessary for introducing a SCM project (Chap. 12), the selection process of an APS (Chap. 13) and its implementation in industry (Chap. 14).

Recalling the general structure of APS (Chap. 4), Part IV now considers specific APS offered by i2 Technologies, J. D. Edwards and SAP AG. It starts by pointing out differences in architecture (Chap. 15), followed by several case studies. Here we demonstrate how concepts and ideas outlined in the preceding chapters are applied to industrial practice with the help of actual APS. Special emphasis has been given to show how to model supply chain elements.

Part V sums up our experiences and gives an outlook of potential future developments. Finally, a supplement (Part VI) provides a brief introduction to major algorithms used to solve the models mentioned in Parts II and IV and should enable the reader to better understand how APS work and where their limits are.

References

Forrester, J. W. (1958) *Industrial dynamics: A major breakthrough for decision makers*, Harvard Business Review, Vol. 36, No. 4, 37–66

Cachon, G.; Fisher, M. (1998) *Campbell Soup's continuous replenishment program: Evaluation and enhanced inventory decision rules*, in: Lee, H. L.; Ng, S. M. (Eds.) Global supply chain and technology management, POMS series in technology and operations management, Vol. 1, Miami, Florida, 130–140

Lee, H. L.; Billington, C. (1995) *The evolution of supply-chain-integration models in practice at Hewlett-Packard*, Interfaces, Vol. 25, No. 5, 42–63

Lin, G.; Ettl, M.; Buckley, S.; Yao, D. D.; Naccarato, B. L.; Allan, R.; Kim, K.; Koenig, L. (2000) *Extended-enterprise supply-chain management at IBM personal systems group and other divisions*, Interfaces, Vol. 30, No. 1, 7–25

Grupp, K. (1998) *Mit Supply Chain Management globale Transparenz in der Distribution*, PPS Management, Vol. 3, No. 2, 50–52

Part I

Basics of Supply Chain Management

1 Supply Chain Management – An Overview

Hartmut Stadtler

Darmstadt University of Technology, Institute of Business Administration,
Department of Operations and Materials Management, Hochschulstraße 1,
64289 Darmstadt, Germany

What is the essence of Supply Chain Management (SCM)? How does it relate
to Advanced Planning? In which sense are the underlying planning concepts
"advanced"? What are the origins of SCM? These as well as related questions
will be answered in this chapter.

1.1 Definitions

During the nineties several authors have tried to put the essence of SCM into
a single definition. Its constituents are

- the object of the management philosophy,
- the target group,
- the objective(s) and
- the broad means for achieving these objectives.

The object of SCM obviously is the *supply chain* which represents a "...net-
work of organizations that are involved, through upstream and downstream
linkages, in the different processes and activities that produce value in the
form of products and services in the hands of the ultimate customer" (Christopher, 1998, p. 15). In a broad sense a supply chain consists of two or more
legally separated organizations, being linked by materials, information and
financial flows. These organizations may be firms producing parts, components and end products, logistic service providers and even the (ultimate)
customer himself. So, the above definition of a supply chain also incorporates
the target group – the ultimate customer.

As Fig. 1.1 shows, a network usually will not only focus on flows within
a (single) chain, but usually will have to deal with divergent and convergent
flows within a complex network resulting from many different customer orders
to be handled in parallel. In order to ease complexity, a given organization
may concentrate only on a portion of the overall supply chain. As an example,
looking in the downstream direction the view of an organization may be
limited by the customers of its customers while it ends with the suppliers of
its suppliers in the upstream direction.

In a narrow sense the term supply chain is also applied to a large company
with several sites often located in different countries. Coordinating materials, information and financial flows for such a multinational company in an

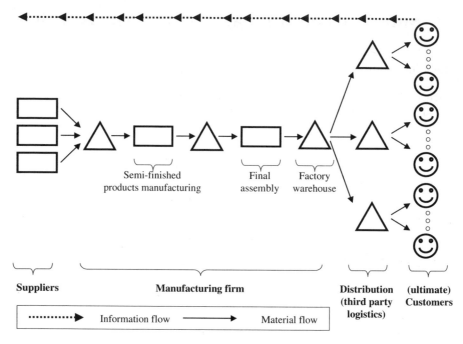

Fig. 1.1. Supply chain (example)

efficient manner is still a formidable task. However, decision-making should be easier, since these sites are part of one large organization with a single top management level. A supply chain in the broad sense is also named an *inter-organizational* supply chain, while the term *intra-organizational* relates to a supply chain in the narrow sense. Irrespective of this distinction, a close cooperation between the different functional units like marketing, production, procurement, logistics and finance is mandatory – a prerequisite being no matter of course in today's firms.

The objective governing all endeavours within a supply chain is seen as increasing competitiveness. This is because no single organizational unit now is solely responsible for the competitiveness of its products and services in the eyes of the ultimate customer, but the supply chain as a whole. Hence, competition has shifted from single companies to supply chains. Obviously, to convince an individual company to become a part of a supply chain requires a *win-win situation* for each participant in the long run, while this may not be the case for all entities in the short run. One generally accepted impediment for improving competitiveness is to provide superior customer service which will be discussed in greater detail below (Sect. 1.2). Alternatively, a firm may increase its competitiveness by fulfilling a prespecified, generally accepted customer service level at minimum costs.

There are two broad means for improving competitiveness of a supply chain. One is a closer *integration* of the organizations involved and the other is a better *coordination* of materials, information and financial flows (Lee and Ng, 1998, p. 1). Overcoming organizational barriers, aligning strategies and speeding up flows along the supply chain are common subjects in this respect.

We are now able to define the term *Supply Chain Management* as the task of integrating organizational units along a supply chain and coordinating materials, information and financial flows in order to fulfil (ultimate) customer demands with the aim of improving competitiveness of a supply chain as a whole.

1.2 Building Blocks

The *House of SCM* (see Fig. 1.2) illustrates the many facets of SCM. The roof stands for the ultimate goal of SCM – competitiveness – and the means – customer service. Competitiveness can be improved in many ways, e. g. by reducing costs, increasing flexibiltiy with respect to changes in customer demands or by providing superior quality of products and services.

The roof rests on two pillars representing the two main components of SCM, namely integration of a network of organizations and coordination of information, materials and financial flows. The figure also shows that there are many disciplines which have built the foundations of SCM.

The two main components which incur some degree of novelty, will now be broken down into their building blocks. Firstly, forming a supply chain requires the *choice of suitable partners* for a mid-term partnership. Secondly, to become an effective and successful *network organization*, consisting of legally separated organizations, calls for actually practising *inter-organizational collaboration*. Thirdly, for an inter-organizational supply chain, new concepts of *leadership* aligning strategies of the partners involved are important.

Coordination of flows along the supply chain can be executed efficiently by utilizing the latest developments in *information and communication technology*. These allow processes formerly executed manually to be automated. Especially, activities at the interface of two entities can be scrutinized and duplicate activities (like keying in the data of a consignment) can be reduced to a single activity. *Process orientation* thus often incorporates a redesign followed by a standardization of the new process.

For executing customer orders, the availability of materials, personnel, machinery and tools has to be planned. Although production and distribution planning as well as purchasing have been in use for several decades, these mostly have been isolated and limited in scope. Coordinating plans over several sites and several legally separated organizations represents a new challenge which is taken up by *Advanced Planning* (Systems).

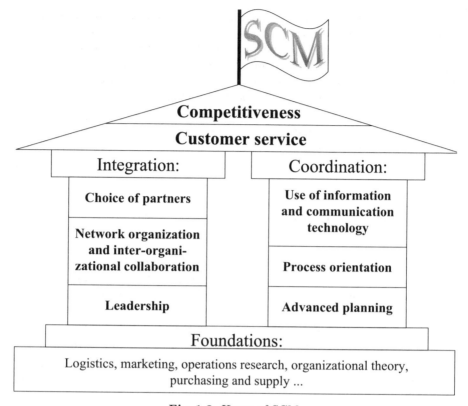

Fig. 1.2. House of SCM

Subsequently we will describe the house of SCM in greater detail, starting with the roof, followed by its two pillars and ending with some references to its foundations.

1.2.1 Customer Service

Customer service is a multi-dimensional notion. According to a survey conducted by LaLonde and Zinszer (cited in Christopher (1998, pp. 39)) there are three elements of customer service,

- pre-transaction,
- transaction and
- post-transaction elements.

Some of these elements will be illustrated in the following.

Pre-transactional elements relate to a company's activities preceding a contract. It concerns customer access to information regarding the products and services a firm offers, the existence of an adequate link between organizations involved. Obviously, for standard products ordered routinely (like screws), an impersonal purchase via internet may be sufficient. However, large projects (like a construction of a business building) will require several, intense personal links between the organization involved at different levels of the hierarchy. Finally, flexibility to meet individual customer requirements may be an important element for qualifying for and winning an order.

Transactional elements are all those which contribute to order fulfilment in the eyes of a customer. Availabililty of products (from stock) may be one option. If a product or service has to be made on demand, order cycle times play an important role. During delivery times a customer may be provided with information on the current status and location of an order. Delivery of goods can include several additional services, like an introduction into the use of a product, its maintenance etc.

Post-transactional elements mostly concern the service provided once the order is fulfilled. This includes elements like repairing or exchanging defective parts and maintenance, the way customer complaints are dealt with and product warranties (Christopher, 1998, pp. 41).

For measuring customer service and for setting targets, key performance indicators are used in practice, like e. g. the maximum order lead-time, the portion of orders delivered within x days, the portion of orders without rejects or the fill rate (for details see Sect. 2.1 and Silver et al. (1998, pp. 243)).

If a certain level or standard of customer service has been agreed upon, it must be broken down such that each entity of the supply chain knows how to contribute to its achievement. Consider order lead-times offered to customers as an example (Fig. 1.3).

Assuming a delivery time of nine days has to be offered to customers. Now, following each activity upstream in the supply chain with its expected lead-times for information and material flows, it becomes clear, where the *decoupling point* between the two options production-to-stock and production-to-order currently can be located. Since the actual lead-times for assembly totals 11 days, this would require to assemble-to-stock.

Stocks held at the decoupling point incur costs and increase overall throughput times. A decoupling point requires that no customized items or components have to be produced upstream. Ideally, items produced on stock have such a large degree of commonness that they can be used within several products. This will reduce the risk of holding the "wrong" stocks, if there is an unexpected shift in products' demand.

If accumulated lead-times of customer specific parts exceed expected delivery times, the supply chain as a whole – perhaps including key customers – has to look for either reducing lead-times for materials or for information flows (e. g. transferring orders by electronic means may save one day while a further day may be saved by advanced scheduling techniques at the assembly plant, thereby allowing to *assemble-to-order* while suppliers *manufacture-to-stock*).

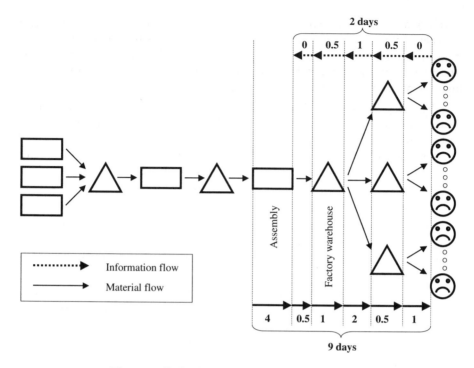

Fig. 1.3. Order lead-time and decoupling point

1.2.2   Integration

As has been stated above, a supply chain in the broad sense consists of several legally separated firms collaborating in the generation of a product or service with the aim of improving the competitiveness of a supply chain as a whole. Integration refers to the special building blocks that cause these firms to collaborate in the long-term, namely

- choice of partners,
- network organization and inter-organizational collaboration,
- leadership.

The *choice of partners* starts with analyzing the activities associated with generating a product or service for a certain market segment (see also Chap. 2). Firstly, activities will be assigned to existing members of a supply chain, if these relate to their core competencies. Secondly, activities relating to standard products and services widely available on the market and with no potential of differentiation in the eyes of the ultimate customers, will be bought from outside the supply chain. Thirdly, for all remaining activities, a partner to join the supply chain has to be looked for in the course of a make-or-buy decision procedure (Schneider and Bauer, 1994).

Selection criteria should not be based solely on costs, but on the future potential of a partner to support the competitivenes of the supply chain. A suitable organizational culture and a committment to contribute to the aims of the supply chain will be of great importance. A possible partner may bring in specialized know-how regarding a production process or know-how of products and its development. In case of a global supply chain, additional criteria have to be considered (like taxes, exchange rates etc. (see Chap. 5)).

The assignment of activities to those members within the supply chain who can perform them best as well as the ability to adapt the structure of a supply chain quickly according to market needs are seen as a major advantage compared with traditional hierarchies.

From the perspective of organizational theory, supply chains are a special form of a *network organization*. It consists of loosely coupled, independent actors with equal rights. Its organizational structure is adapted dynamically according to the tasks to be performed and the aims of the network organization as a whole (Sydow, 1992; Hilse et al., 1999, p. 30). A supply chain may be regarded as a single (virtual) entity by its customers. The term virtual firm, however, is used for a network of firms collaborating only in the short-term, sometimes only for fulfilling a single customer order.

Inter-organizational collaboration is a necessity for an effective supply chain. A supply chain is regarded as a cross between pure market interaction and a hierarchy. It tries to combine the best features of the two. Ideally, each entity within a supply chain will concentrate on its core competencies and will be relieved from stringent decision procedures and administrative routines attributed to a large hierarchy. Information and know-how is shared openly among members. Competition among members along the supply chain is substituted by the committment towards improving the competitiveness of the supply chain as a whole. However, a risk still remains that collaboration is cancelled at some time. These features are assumed to enhance innovativeness and flexibilty with respect to taking up new market trends (Burns and Stalker, 1961, pp. 121).

Although legally independent, entities within a supply chain are economically dependent on each other. Obviously, the structure of a supply chain will remain stable, only if there is a win-win situation for each member – at least in the long run. If this is not achieved in the short-term by usual price mechanisms, compensation schemes must be looked for. To enforce the coherence of supply chain members several types of bonds may be used. These are

- "technological bonds attached to the technologies applied by the firms,
- social bonds in the form of personal trust,
- administrative bonds resulting from adjustment of administrative routines and systems and
- legal bonds in the form of contracts between the firms" (Håkansson and Johanson, 1990).

A further bond may be introduced by exchanging contributions to capital. Bonds must be practised continuously to build up a certain degree of confidence – the basis of a long-term partnership. In the case of a global supply chain special attention has to be paid to intercultural business communicatons (Ulijn and Strother, 1995).

Leadership, being the third building block of integration, is a delicate theme in light of the ideal of self-organizing, poly-centric actors forming a supply chain. At least some decisions should be made for the supply chain as a whole, like the cancellation of a partnership or the integration of a new partner. Similarly aligning strategies among partners may require some form of leadership (as an example see Rockhold et al. (1998)).

In practice, leadership may be executed either by a focal company or a steering committee. A *focal company* is usually a member having the largest (financial) power, the best know-how of products and processes or has the greatest share of values created during order fulfilment. In some cases the focal company may be the founder of a supply chain, too. Due to these reasons, decisions made by the focal company will be accepted by all members. On the other hand, a *steering committee* may be introduced, consisting of representatives of all members of a supply chain. The rules of decision-making – like the number of votes per member – are subject to negotiations.

Despite the advantages attributed to a supply chain, one should bear in mind that its structure is vulnerable – the exit of one partner may jeopardize the survival of the supply chain as a whole. Also, a member may run the risk of becoming unattractive and to be substituted by a competitor once his know-how has been dispensed within the supply chain.

Last but not least, coordination of activities across organizations must not exceed comparable efforts within a hierarchy. In light of the latest developments in information and communication technology as well as software for planning material flows this requirement has now been fulfuilled to a large extent.

1.2.3   Coordination

Coordination of information, materials and financial flows – the second main component of SCM – comprise three building blocks

- utilization of information and communication technology,
- process orientation,
- advanced planning.

Advances in *information technology* (IT) made it possible to process information at different locations in the supply chain and thus enable the application of advanced planning. Cheap and large storage devices allow to store and retrieve historical mass data, like e. g. past sales. These Data Warehouses may now be used for a better analysis of customer habits as well as for more precise demand forecasts. Graphical user interfaces allow users to access and manipulate data more easily.

Communication via electronic data interchange (EDI) can be established via private and public nets, the most popular being the internet. Members within a supply chain can thus be informed instantaneously and cheaply. As an example, a sudden breakdown of a production-line can be distributed to all members of a supply chain concerned as a so-called alert.

Rigid standards formerly introduced for communcation in special lines of businesses (like ODETTE in the automotive industry) are now being substituted by more flexible meta-languages (like the extensible markup language (XML)).

Communication links can be differentiated according to the parties involved:

Business-to-business (B2B) communications allow companies to redesign processes, like that of purchasing. Manual tasks, e. g. placing an order for a standard item, can now be taken over by a computer. It then controls the whole process, from transmitting the order, order acceptance by the supplier and order execution, until the consignment is received and checked. Finally, the amount payable is transferred to the supplier's account automatically. Automated purchasing allowed the Ford Motor Company to reduce its staff in the purchasing function drastically (Hammer and Champy, 1993, pp. 57). Other advantages stem from increased speed and reduced errors. Furthermore, if standard items are ordered, firms can make use of auctions via the internet. Due to a global access to the internet, a strong competition and reduced purchasing prices may result. Large databases allow all parties involved to access the specifications of these standard products.

Business-to-consumer (B2C) communications aim at approaching the individual end user via the internet. Several new challenges have to be addressed here, like a user-friendly access to information regarding products and services, securing safety of payments and finally the transport of goods or services to the customer. B2C opens up a new marketing channel to end users and offers a means for incorporating end users within a supply chain.

The second building block, *process orientation*, aims at coordinating all the activities involved in customer order fulfilment in the most efficient way. It starts with an analysis of the existing supply chain, the current allocation of activities to its members. Key performance indicators can reveal weaknesses, bottlenecks and waste within a supply chain, especially at the interface between its members. A comparison with best practices may support this effort (for more details see Chap. 2). As a result, some activities will be subject to improvement efforts, while some others may be reallocated. The building block "process orientation" has much in common with business process reengineering (Hammer and Champy, 1993), however, it will not necessarily result in a radical redesign.

Advanced planning – the third building block – incorporates long-term, mid-term and short-term planning levels. Software products – called *Advanced Planning Systems* – are now available to support these planning tasks. Although an Advanced Planning System (APS) is separated into several modules, effective information flows between these modules should make it a coherent software suite. Customizing these modules according to the specific needs of a supply chain requires specific skills, e. g. in systems and data modelling, data processing and solution methods.

APS do not substitute but supplement existing *Enterprise Resources Planning* (ERP) systems. APS now take over the planning tasks, while an ERP system is still required as a transaction and execution system (for orders). The advantages of the new architecture have to be viewed in light of well-known deficiencies of traditional ERP systems with regard to planning (Drexl et al., 1994). In essence, an ERP system models the different planning tasks inadequately. Furthermore, these planning tasks are executed sequentially, without allowing for revisions to upper-level decisions. Some tasks – like bill-of-materials processing (BOMP) – do not consider capacities at all. Furthermore, lead-times are used as a fixed input for the BOMP, while it is common knowledge that lead-times are the result of planning. It is not surprising that users of ERP systems complain about long lead-times and many orders exceeding dead lines. Also, production planning and distribution planning are more or less separated systems. Last but not least the focus of ERP systems has been a single firm, while APS have been designed also for inter-organizational supply chains.

Although separated in several modules, APS are intended to remedy the defects of ERP systems through a closer integration of modules, adequate modelling of bottleneck capacities, a hierarchical planning concept and the use of the latest algorithmic developments. Since planning is now executed in a computer's core storage, plans may be updated easily and continuously (e. g. in the case of a break down of a production line).

Planning now has the capability to realize bottlenecks in advance and to make the best use of them. Alternative modes of operations may be evaluated, thus reducing costs and improving profits. Different scenarios of future developments can be planned for in order to identify a robust next step for the upcoming planning interval. Furthermore, it is no longer necessary to provide lead-time estimates as an input for planning. This should enable companies using APS to reduce planned lead-times drastically compared with those resulting from an ERP system.

A most favourable feature of APS is seen in its ability to check whether a (new) customer order with a given due date can be accepted (ATP, see Chap. 8). In case there are no sufficient stocks at hand, it is even possible to generate a tentative schedule, inserting the new customer order into a current machine schedule where it fits best. Obviously, these new features allow a supply chain to better comply with accepted due dates, to become more flexible and to operate more economically.

We would like to add that proposals for a better integration of organizational units cannot be separated from the notion of coordination of flows and vice versa. The choice of partners in a supply chain or the effectiveness of a postponement strategy can best be evaluated by advanced planning. On the other hand the structure of a network organization sets up the frame for optimizing flows within a supply chain.

1.2.4 Foundations

For operating a supply chain successfully, many more ingredients are needed which have been reported in the literature in recent years in subjects like

- logistics and transportation,
- marketing,
- operations research,
- organizational behaviour, industrial organization and transaction cost economics,
- purchasing and supply,
- ...

to name only a few (for a complete list see Croom et al. (2000, p. 70)).

Certainly there are strong links between SCM and logistics, as can be observed when looking at the five principles of logistics thinking (Pfohl, 1996, p. 182):

- Thinking in values and benefits,
- systems thinking,
- total cost thinking,
- service orientation,
- striving for efficiency.

Thinking in values and benefits implies that it is the (ultimate customer) who assigns a value to a product. The value and benefit of a product can be improved with its availability when and where it is actually needed. Systems thinking requires examination of all entities involved in the process of generating a product or service simultaneously. Optimal solutions are aimed at the process as whole, while being aware that optimal solutions for individual entities may turn out to be suboptimal. All activities are oriented towards a given service level. Service orientation is not limited towards the ultimate customer, but also applies to each entity receiving a product or service from a supplier. Efficiency comprises several dimensions. The technological dimension requires the choice of processes which result in a given output without wasting inputs. Furthermore, decision-making will be guided by economical goals, relating to current profits and future potentials. These two dimensions will be supplemented by a social and ecological dimension.

A further subject, operations research, has contributed to model building and model solving required for coordinating flows along the supply chain. The basics of model building have already been developed in the sixties and seventies. However, only with the rise of powerful computers, large in-core storage devices and the availability of adequate solutions methods – like mathematical programming and powerful meta-heuristics (e. g. genetic algorithms and tabu search) – these models now can be solved with reasonable computational efforts (see Part VI).

Note that the vast body of literature on SCM has concentrated so far on the *integration* of inter-organizational supply chains. However, with regard to the *coordination* of flows, efforts still concentrate on intra-organizational supply chains. While it will not be too difficult to apply APS to an inter-organizational supply chain with a central planning unit, new challenges arise in decentralized planning (like the availability of data required for planning, coordinating plans, compensation schemes etc.). Recalling that ERP systems only incorporate unconnected, insufficient analytical models (like for single level, uncapacitated lot-sizing), APS – even for intra-organizational supply chains – represent a great progress. So, the term *advanced* in APS has to be evaluated in view of the insufficient decision support offered by ERP systems until now.

For those interested in learning more about the first ideas and publications which have influenced our current view of SCM a chapter about its origins will follow.

1.3 Origins

The term SCM has been created by two consultants – Oliver and Webber – as early as 1982. The supply chain in their view lifts the mission of logistics to become a top management concern, since "...only top management can assure that conflicting functional objectives along the supply chain are reconciled and balanced ...and finally, that an integrated systems strategy that reduces the level of vulnerability is developed and implemented" (Oliver and Webber, 1992, p. 66). In their view, coordinating materials, information and financial flows within a large multi-national firm is a challenging and rewarding task. Obviously, forming a supply chain out of a group of individual companies such that it acts like a single entitiy is even harder.

Research into the integration and coordination of different functional units has started much earlier than the creation of the term SCM in 1982. These efforts can be traced back in such diverse fields as logistics, marketing, organizational theory, operations management and operations research. Selected focal contributions are briefly reviewed below without claiming completeness (for further information see Ganeshan et al. (1998)). These contributions are

- channel research (Alderson, 1957),
- collaboraton and cooperation (Bowersox, 1969),
- location and control of inventories in production-distribution networks (Hanssmann, 1959),
- bullwhip effect in production-distribution systems (Forrester, 1958),
- hierarchical production planning (Hax and Meal, 1975).

1.3.1 Channel Research

Alderson (1957) puts forward *channel research* as a special field of marketing research. He already argued that the principles of *postponement* require that "...changes in form and identity occur at the latest possible point in the marketing flow; and changes in inventory location occur at the latest possible point in time" (Alderson, 1957, p. 424). Postponement serves to reduce market risk, because the product will stay in an undifferentiated state as long as possible allowing to better cope with unexpected market shifts. Also postponement can reduce transportation costs, since products will be held back in the supply chain as far as possible (e. g. at the factory warehouse) until they are actually needed downstream (e. g. at a distribution centre) thereby reducing the need for a transport of goods between distribution centres in case of a shortage of goods and an imbalance in the distribution of stocks. Thirdly, when examining the postponability of a (production) step one might find out that it can be eliminated entirely, i. e. "...if a step is not performed prematurely, it may never have to be performed" (Alderson, 1957, p. 426). As an example Alderson reported on the elimination of bagging wheat in sacks. Instead, a truck with an open box body had been chosen.

The three principles of postponement are still applied today. With regard to elimination, we can see that customers pick their goods directly from pallets thus eliminating the need for the retailer to put the goods in shelves. Another example being the customers of IKEA performing the assembly of furniture by themselves.

However, one should bear in mind that postponement in product differentiation requires that a product has already been designed for it, i. e. modifying a product to become customer specific should both be possible technically and economically later on. The capability of assessing the effects of postponement in a supply chain wide context is the achievement of advanced planning today. Thus, the different alternatives of postponement have been analyzed and simulated before Hewlett Packard introduced postponement successfully for its desk jet printer lines (Lee and Billington, 1995).

1.3.2 Collaboration and Coordination

Bowersox (1969) described the state of knowlegde in marketing, physical distribution and systems thinking. There has already been an awareness that individual objectives of the different functional units within a firm may counteract overall efficiency. For example (Bowersox, 1969, p. 64),

- manufacturing traditionally desires long production runs and lowest procurement costs,
- marketing traditionally prefers finished goods inventory staging and broad assortments in forward markets,
- finance traditionally favours low inventories and
- physical distribution advocates total cost considerations relating to a firm's physical distribution mission.

Long production runs lower the setup costs per product unit while resulting in higher inventory holding costs. Similarly end product inventories allow short delivery times, but increase inventory holding costs. Furthermore, raw materials and parts used up in production of end products may no longer be used within other end products, thus limiting flexibility to cope with shifts in end product demands (see postponement).

Furthermore, Bowersox has criticized the fact that physical distribution systems mainly have been studied from the vantage of vertically integrated organizations. "A more useful viewpoint is that physical distribution activities and related activities seldom terminate when product ownership transfer occurs." (Bowersox, 1969, p. 65). If the interface between two or more physical distribution systems is not properly defined and synchronized, this "...may well lead to excessive cost generation and customer service impairment" (Bowersox, 1969, p. 67).

Although arguing from the viewpoint of physical distribution, Bowersox has already advocated a need for intra-organizational as well as inter-organizational *cooperation and coordination*.

1.3.3 Location and Control of Inventories in Production-Distribution Networks

Hanssmann (1959) was the first to publish an analytical model of interacting inventories in a supply chain with three serial inventory locations. At each location a periodic review, the order-up-to-level inventory system is used. There are positive lead-times which are integer multiples of the review period. Customer demands are assumed to be normally distributed. Decision support is provided for two cases: The location of inventory if only one single inventory location is allowed in the supply chain and the control of inventories if all three inventory locations may be used. Shortage costs and inventory holding costs are considered as well as revenues from sales which are assumed to be a function of delivery time. As a solution method, dynamic programming is proposed.

The location and allocation of inventories in serial, convergent and divergent supply chains is still an important topic of research today.

1.3.4   Bullwhip Effect in Production-Distribution Systems

The *bullwhip effect* describes the increasing amplification of orders occuring within a supply chain the more one moves upstream. Surprisingly, this phenomenon also occurs even if end item demand is fairly stable. This phenomenon will be explained more deeply, since it is regarded as a classic of SCM.

The dynamic behaviour of industrial production-distribution systems has already been analyzed by Forrester (1958). The simplest system studied is a supply chain made of a retailer, a distribution centre, a factory warehouse and a production site (Fig. 1.4). Each entity can make use only of locally available information when making its ordering decisions for coping with demands. Another important feature are time delays between decision-making (e. g. ordering) and its realization (e. g. receipt of the corresponding shipment). These delays are indicated in Fig. 1.4 as numbers on top of respective arcs resp. flows (measured in weeks). Assume a customer order comes in. Then the retailer requires one week to deliver it from stock. The lead-time between an incoming customer order until a decision to replenish inventory is made is three weeks (including processing the order), while order transmission to the distribution centre takes another half week. The distribution centre requires one week to process the order, while shipping the order to the retailer takes another week. Thus, five and a half weeks pass from an incoming customer order until the replenishment of the retailer's inventory (see Fig. 1.4: sum of bold numbers). Further lead-times for upstream entities can be derived in the same way from Fig. 1.4.

Forrester has shown the effects of a single, sudden 10% increase in retail sales on orders placed and inventory levels of each entitiy in the supply chain (see Fig. 1.5). He concludes (Forrester, 1961, p. 25) that "... orders at factory warehouse reach, at the 14th week, a peak of 34% above the previous December" and "... the factory output, delayed by a factory lead-time of six weeks, reaches a peak in the 21st week, an amount 45% above the previous December." Obviously, these amplified fluctuations in ordering and inventory levels result in avoidable inventory and shortage costs and an unstable system behaviour. Although the time unit of one week seems outdated nowadays, replacing it by a day may reflect current practices better and will not disturb the structure of the model. These so-called information-feedback systems have been studied extensively with the help of a simulation package (DYNAMO).

In order to show the relevance of the work of Forrester on todays topics in SCM we will add some newer findings here.

The introduction of the so-called *beer distribution game* by Sterman (1989) has drawn great attention from researchers and practitioners alike to study the bullwhip effect again. Looking at an industrial production-distribution system from the perspective of bounded human rationality, Sterman studied

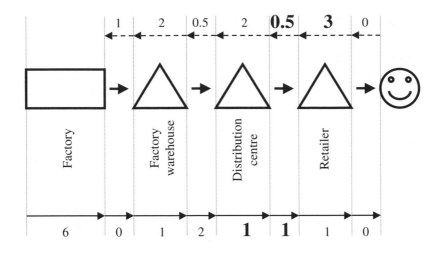

Fig. 1.4. Supply chain modelled by Forrester (1961, p. 22)

the ordering behaviour of individuals possessing only isolated, local information.

In such an environment, where an individual's knowledge is limited to its current inventory status, the actual amount ordered by its direct successors in the supply chain and knowledge about its past performance, a human being tends to overreact by an amplification of orders placed. Even worse, amplification and phase lags of ordering increase steadily the more one moves upstream the supply chain. This has to be interpreted in light of a given, nearly stable end item demand with just one (large) increase in demand levels in an early period of the game.

This behaviour which is far from optimal for the total supply chain, has been observed in many independent repetitions of the beer distribution game as well as in industrial practice. Actually the term bullwhip effect has been coined by managers of Procter & Gamble when examining the demand for Pampers disposal diapers (according to Lee et al., 1997).

Obviously, real world production-distribution systems are a lot more complex than those described above. However, examining behavioural patterns and policies often adopted by local managers, these may amplify fluctuations even further. Studying the causes of the bullwhip effect and its cures have become a very rich area of research in SCM. Recently, Lee et al. (1997) divided recommendations to counteract the bullwhip effect into four categories:

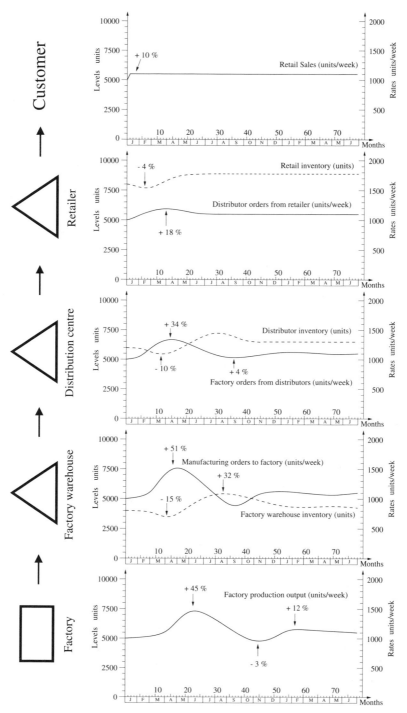

Fig. 1.5. The bullwhip effect (along the lines of Forrester (1961, p. 24))

- avoid multiple demand forecast updates,
- break order batches,
- stabilize prices,
- eliminate gaming in shortage situations.

Avoiding *multiple demand forecasts* means that ordering decisions should always be based on ultimate customer demand and not on the ordering behaviour of an immediate downstream partner, since the ordering behaviour of an immediate downstrem partner usually will show amplifications due to order batching and possible overreactions. With the advent of EDI and the capability to input sales made with the ultimate customer (point-of-sale (POS) data), accurate and timely data can be made available to each entity in the supply chain, thus also reducing the timelag in the feedback system drastically. If ultimate customer demands are not available, even simple forecasting techniques (see Chap. 6) will prevent human overreactions and smooth demand forecasts.

In a more radical approach one could change from decentralized decision-making to generating procurement plans centrally. Even the ultimate customer may be included in these procurement plans, as it is the case in *vendor managed inventory* (VMI). However, here the supply chain has to bear responsibility that the ultimate customer will not run out of stock. Finally, the downstream entity(s) could even be bypassed by executing sales directly with the ultimate customer (a well-known example being direct sales of Dell Computers).

Order batching is a common decision for cutting fixed costs incurred with placing an order. Ordering costs can be cut down drastically by using EDI for order transmission as well as a standardization of the (redesigned) ordering procedure. Transportation costs can be reduced if full truck loads are used. However, this should not be achieved by increasing batch sizes, but by asking distributors to order assortments of different products simultaneously. Likewise, the use of third-party logistics companies helps make small batch replenishments economical by consolidating loads from multiple suppliers located near each other and thereby achieving economies of scale resulting from full truck loads. Similarly, a third-party logistics company may use assortments to full truckloads when delivering goods. This may give rise to cutting replenishment intervals drastically, resulting in less safety stocks needed without sacrifycing service levels or increasing transportation costs.

Since marketing initiatives which try to influence demands by wholesale price discounting also contribute to the bullwhip effect, these should be abandoned. This understanding has moved companies to *stabilize prices* by guaranteeing its customers an every-day low price.

The fourth category for counteracting the bullwhip effect intends to *eliminate gaming* in shortage situations. Here, gaming means that customers order additional, non-required amounts, since they expect to receive only a portion of outstanding orders due to a shortage situation. This behaviour can be influenced by introducing more stringent cancellation policies, accepting only orders in proportion to past sales records and sharing of capacity and inventory information.

Many of the recommendations given above for counteracting the bullwhip effect profit from recent advances in communication technology and large database management systems containing accurate and timely information about the current and past state of each entity in the supply chain. Many time delays existing in productions-distributions systems either are reduced drastically or even no longer exist, thus reducing problems encountered in feedback systems. Furthermore, to overcome cognitive limitations, a mathematical model of the supply chain may be generated and used to support decision-making of individuals (Lanzenauer and Pilz-Glombig, 2000). This research also indicates that APS with its modelling features and state-of-the-art solution procedures, will be a means to end counteracting the bullwhip effect.

1.3.5 Hierarchical Production Planning

Although detailed mathematical models have been proposed for production planning much earlier, Hax and Meal (1975) have shown how to build hierarchically coordinated, solvable models which provide effective decision support for the different decision-making levels within a hierarchical organization. Although first presented as a decision support system for a real world tire manufacturing firm, the versatility of the approach soon became clear. Briefly, *hierarchical (production) planning* is based on the following five elements:

- decomposition and hierarchical structure,
- aggregation,
- hierarchical coordination,
- model building,
- model solving.

The overall decision problem is decomposed into two or more decision levels. Decisions to be made are assigned to each level such that the top level includes the most important, long-term decisions – i. e. those with the greatest impact on profitability and competitiveness. A separation into distinct decision levels is called *hierarchical*, if for each level a single upper level can be identified which is allowed to set the frame within which decisons of the subordinated level have to take place (with the exception of the top level of the hierarchy). Note there may be several separate decision units (e. g. production sites) within a given decision level coordinated by a single upper level.

Like decomposition, *aggregation* serves to reduce problem complexity. It also can diminish uncertainty (e. g. of demand forecasts). Aggregation is possible in three areas: Time, products and resources. As an example consider an upper level, where time may be aggregated into time buckets of one week, only main end products are taken into account – irrespective of its variants, while available capacities at a production site are viewed as a rough maximum (weekly) output rate.

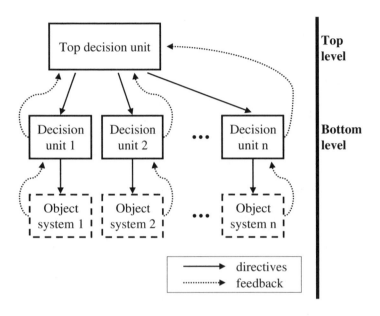

Fig. 1.6. Basic structure of a hierarchical planning system

Hierarchical coordination is achieved by directives and feedback. The most obvious directive is target setting by the upper level (e. g. setting a target inventory level for an end product at the planning horizon of the lower level). Another way is to provide prices for utilizing resources (e. g. a price for using additional personnel). A decision unit, on the other hand, may return a feedback to its upper level regarding the fulfilment of targets. These now allow the upper level to revise plans, to better coordinate lower-level decisions and to enable feasible plans at the lower level. These explanations are illustrated in Fig. 1.6. Here, the object system can be interpreted as the production process to be controlled.

For each decision unit a *model* is generated which adequately represents the decision situation and which anticipates lower level reactions on possible directives. It also links targets set by the upper level to detailed decisions to be made at the decision unit considered. Thereby the upper level plan will be disaggregated. If a mathematical model is chosen, solvability has to be taken into account, too.

Finally, a suitable *solution procedure* has to be chosen for each model. Here, not only optimum seeking algorithms may be employed, but also manual procedures or group decision-making may be possible.

Hierarchical planning has attracted many researchers and practitioners alike. Thus, a large amount of knowledge has been accumulated so far (for more details see Schneeweiss, 1999). Since hierarchical plannning represents an appealing approach to conquer complex decision problems, while incorporating the experience of human decision-makers at different levels of an organization, it is not surprising that todays APS are constructed along the principles of hierarchical planning (see Chap. 3 for more details).

References

Alderson, W. (1957) *Market behavior and executive action*, Homewood, Illinois

Bowersox, D. J. (1969) *Physical distribution development, current status, and potential*, Journal of Marketing, Vol. 33 (January), 63–70

Burns, T.; Stalker, G. M. (1961) *The management of innovation*, Oxford

Croom, S.; Romano, P.; Giannakis, M. (2000) *Supply chain management: An analytical frameword for critical literature review*, European Journal of Purchasing & Supply Management, Vol. 6, 67–83

Christopher, M. (1998) *Logistics and Supply Chain Management - strategegies for reducing cost and improving service*, 2nd ed., London et al.

Drexl, A.; Fleischmann, B.; Günther, H.-O.; Stadtler, H.; Tempelmeier, H. (1994) *Konzeptionelle Grundlagen kapazitätsorientierter PPS-Systeme*, Zeitschrift für betriebswirtschaftliche Forschung, Vol. 46, 1022–1045

Forrester, J. W. (1958) *Industrial dynamics: A major breakthrough for decision makers*, Harvard Business Review, Vol. 36, No. 4, 37–66

Forrester, J. W. (1961) *Industrial dynamics*, New York, London

Ganeshan, R.; Jack, E.; Magazine, M. J.; Stephens, P. (1998) *A taxonomic review of supply chain management research*, in: Tayur, S.; Ganeshan, R.; Magazine, M. (Eds.) Quantitative models for supply chain management, Dordrecht, The Netherlands, 839–879

Oliver, R. K.; Webber, M. D. (1992) *Supply-chain management: Logistics catches up with strategy (reprint fom Outlook (1982))*, in: Christopher, M. (Ed.) Logistics – The strategic issues, London et al., 63–75

Håkansson, H.; Johanson, J. (1990) *Formal and informal cooperation strategies in international networks*, in: Ford, D. (Ed.) Understanding business markets, London, 100–111

Hammer, M.; Champy, J. (1993) *Reenginieering the corporation*, New York

Hanssmann, F. (1959) *Optimal inventory location and control in production and distribution networks*, Management Science, Vol. 7, No. 4, 483–498

Hax, A. C.; Meal, H. C. (1975) *Hierarchical integration of production planning and scheduling*, in: Geisler, M. A. (Ed.) Studies in Management Science, Vol. I, Logistics, Amsterdam, 53–69

Hilse, H.; Götz, K.; Zapf, D. (1999) *Netzwerk contra Hierarchie: Die Abbildung organisationsstruktureller Widersprüche in einem neuartigen Potential für Rollenstress*, in: Götz, K. (Ed.) Führungskultur: Die organisationale Perspektive, München, 29–44

Lee, H. L.; Ng, S. M. (1998) *Preface to global supply chain and technology management*, in: Lee, H. L.; Ng, S. M. (Eds.) Global supply chain and technology management, POMS series in technology and operations management, Vol. 1, Miami, Florida, 1–3

Lee, H. L.; Billington, C. (1995) *The evolution of supply-chain-integration models in practice at Hewlett-Packard*, Interfaces, Vol. 25, No. 5, 42–63

Lee, H. L.; Padmanabhan, V.; Whang, S. (1995) *The bullwhip effect in supply chains*, Sloan Management Review, Spring, 93–102

Lanzenauer, C. Haehling von; Pilz-Glombig, K. (2000) *A supply chain optimization model for MIT's beer distribution game*, Zeitschrift für Betriebswirtschaftslehre, 70 Jg., H. 1, 101–116

Pfohl, H.-Chr. (1996) *Logistiksysteme. Betriebswirtschaftliche Grundlagen*, 5th ed., Berlin et al.

Rockhold, S.; Lee, H.; Hall, R. (1998) *Strategic alignment of a global supply chain for business success*, in: Lee, H. L.; Ng, S. M. (Eds.) Global supply chain and technology management, POMS series in technology and operations management, Vol. 1, Miami, Florida, 16–29

Schneeweiss, C. (1999) *Hierarchies in distributed decision making*, Berlin et al.

Schneider, D.; Bauer, C. (1994) *Re-Design der Wertkette durch make or buy*, Wiesbaden

Silver, E. A.; Pyke, D. F.; Peterson, R. (1998) *Inventory Management and Production Planning and Scheduling*, 3rd ed., New York et al.

Sterman, J. D. (1989) *Modeling managerial behavior: Misperceptions of feedback in a dynamic decision making experiment*, Management Science, Vol. 35., No. 3, 321–339

Sydow, J. (1992) *Strategische Netzwerke*, Wiesbaden

Ulijn, J. M.; Strother, J. B. (1995) *Communicating in business and technology: From psycholinguistic theory to international practice*, New York, Frankfurt

2 Supply Chain Analysis

Herbert Meyr[1], Jens Rohde, Hartmut Stadtler and Christopher Sürie[2]

[1] University of Augsburg, Department of Production and Logistics,
Universitätsstraße 16, 86135 Augsburg, Germany
[2] Darmstadt University of Technology, Institute of Business Administration,
Department of Operations and Materials Management, Hochschulstraße 1,
64289 Darmstadt, Germany

Before starting an improvement process one has to have a clear picture of the structure of the existing supply chain and the way it works. Consequently a detailed *analysis* of operations and processes constituting the supply chain is necessary. Therefore tools are needed that support an adequate evaluation, modelling and description of supply chains. In Sect. 2.1 (key) performance measures are presented. Section 2.2 adds the Supply Chain Operations Reference (SCOR)-model which introduces a standardized terminology, standardized process definitions, metrics and best practices for modelling and configuration of supply chains. A typology of supply chains that enables identification of necessary planning tasks will be discussed in Sect. 2.3.

2.1 Performance Measurement

Performance measures have two main effects and work in two directions. First of all they can be used as a good description of the as-is situation. In this context they are helpful to describe the past and the present of the process to be considered. On the other hand they can be used to set performance goals. This establishes a focus into the future. By fixing a will-be value or target of a performance measure it is possible to watch the progress in reaching the target and the success in achieving the target itself.

This is why performance measures are utilized in a wide range of operations. Their primary application is in *operational controlling*. Most controlling systems are based on performance measures (indicators, metrics) of any kind. It is hard to imagine a controlling system that does not make use of performance measures regularly. In fact, the utilization of a wide variety of measures as they are necessary to model all business processes of a company enables the company to run its business according to management-by-exception. While controlling uses performance measures on a regular, on-going basis, they are applied irregularly as well. As mentioned above they can be applied when changing processes or in other special projects.

2.1.1   Indicators and Systems of Indicators

Indicators are defined as numbers that inform about relevant criteria in a clearly defined way (see e. g. Horváth (1998) for a comprehensive introduction to indicators and systems of indicators). Both *absolute numbers* (e. g. net income, cash flow, number of employees) and *relative numbers* (ratios) are used as indicators, the latter being used commonly. Three types of ratios have to be distinguished. The first type links two different factors like operating profit and revenue to form an indicator named operating margin. The second type of ratios structures information. For example, if total liabilities comprise current and long-term liabilities, the division of current liabilities by total liabilities is such a measure, indicating to which extent liabilities are short-term financed and need to be paid back by short-term cash-flow. The third type of ratios are indices. Here one number operates as a fixed basis and does not vary over time (e. g. prices, exchange rates).

Indicators are advantageous for the *description* and *simplification* of complex systems. Changes in process outcomes over time can be observed with the help of indicators. Besides comparing the values of indicators at different times, they can be utilized to compare similar operations at a given point in time. Another characteristic of indicators is that they are highly operational. Moreover, three functions can be attributed to indicators:

Information. Their main purpose is to inform management. In this function, indicators are applied to support decision-making and to identify problem areas. Indicators can therefore be compared with standard or target values.

Steering. Indicators are the base for target setting. These targets guide those responsible for the process considered to accomplish the desired outcome.

Controlling. Indicators are well suited for the supervision of operations and processes.

The main disadvantage inherent to indicators is that they are only suited to describe *quantitative facts*. "Soft" facts are difficult to measure and likely to be neglected when indicators are introduced (e. g. motivation of personnel).

When using indicators, one key condition is the *correct interpretation* of their respective values. It is essential to keep in mind that variations observed by indicators have to be linked to a *causal model* of the underlying process or operation. A short example will illustrate this. To measure productivity of an operation the ratio of revenue divided by labour is assumed here as an appropriate indicator:

$$productivity = \frac{revenue[\$]}{labour[h]} \tag{2.1}$$

Revenue is measured in currency units (\$), whereas labour is measured in hours worked (per plant, machine or personnel), where the relevance of the different measures for labour depends on the specific product(s) considered. Supposed productivity is 500 $/h in period 1 and 600 $/h in period 2, there is definitely a huge difference. In fact, when calculating productivity a *causal link* between revenue and labour is assumed implicitly. On the other hand, there are many more rationales that could have caused the increase in productivity. These have to be examined too before a final conclusion can be derived. In this example price hikes, changes in product-mix, higher utilization of resources or decreased inventories can account for substantial portions of the observed increase in productivity.

Therefore, it is essential to find appropriate measures with clear links connecting the indicator and the causal model of the underlying process (root causes).

Often, not single indicators but systems of indicators are applied. *Systems of indicators* result from the coupling of different indicators. Three schemes of systems of indicators can be distinguished (Syska, 1990, pp. 30):

Calculation schemes. Any indicator that is part of a calculation scheme is related to other indicators by mathematical formulae. Calculation schemes often take the form of a pyramid with a primary indicator on top which is broken down to less aggregated, more operational indicators towards the bottom.

Rule schemes. Indicators that form a rule scheme are linked by mathematical formulae too. In addition they are connected with respect to the causal model of the process or operation described. Rule schemes aim to give a complete description of the process considered. An example for a system of indicators based on a rule scheme is the "Managerial Controls System" introduced by Tucker (1961).

Target schemes. Indicators of a target scheme are only linked loosely. They are obtained from the target set forth by the management of the company. Indicators which can be linked directly to these targets or which correlate with these targets are applied (see Chap. 12 for an example).

The most widely known system of indicators is the DuPont-System of Financial Control dating back to 1919 (see e.g. Horváth (1998, pp. 550)). It is based on a *calculation scheme* with the *return on investment* (ROI) as primary indicator on top of the pyramid.

$$
\begin{aligned}
ROI &= \frac{net\ income}{investment} = \\
&= \frac{net\ income}{revenue} \cdot \frac{revenue}{investment} = \\
&= return\ on\ revenue \cdot investment\ turnover
\end{aligned}
\tag{2.2}
$$

The primary indicator (ROI) is successively broken down into secondary indicators that are utilized to analyze changes of ROI. The first step leads to return on revenue and investment turnover as new indicators as shown above.

Further steps analyze the influence of the various cost drivers on return on revenue, whereas investment turnover is split to analyze current and fixed assets.

Traditionally indicators and systems of indicators have been based on *financial data*, as financial data have been widely available for a long time. Improvements in terms of superior financial performance that are caused by the successful application of SCM can be measured by these indicators. Nevertheless some additional, more appropriate measures of supply chain performance should be derived, since the focus of SCM is customer orientation, the integration of organizational units and their coordination.

The transition to incorporate non-financial measures in the evaluation of business performance is widely accepted, though. Kaplan and Norton (1992) introduced the concept of a balanced scorecard that received broad attention not only in scientific literature but also in practical application (see e. g. Kaplan and Norton (1993) and Meyer (1994)). In addition to financial measures the balanced scorecard comprises a customer perspective, an innovation and learning perspective and an internal business perspective. These perspectives integrate a set of measures into one management report that provides deep insight into a company's performance. The measures chosen depend on the individual situation faced by the company. Figure 2.1 gives an example for a balanced scorecard used by a global engineering and construction company.

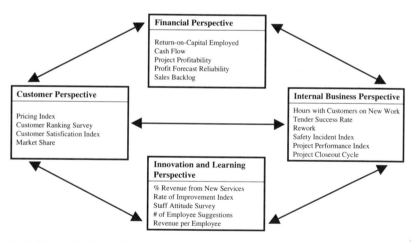

Fig. 2.1. Example for indicators used by a balanced scorecard (Kaplan and Norton, 1993, p. 136)

Non-financial measures have the advantage that they are often easier to quantify as there is no allocation of costs necessary for their calculation. Secondly, they turn attention to physical processes more directly.

2.1.2   Key Performance Indicators for Supply Chain Management

A valuable tool for analyzing supply chains is the SCOR-model (for details
see Sect. 2.2). It defines many measures for supply chain performance that
range from highly aggregated indicators to indicators on a very detailed operational level. The fundamental indicators describing supply chains utilized
by the SCOR-model on its highest level will be presented as *key performance
indicators* (KPIs). Since the metrics in correspondence to the model are hierarchical, these measures often comprise other more operational metrics.
This is why their definition sometimes addresses more an issue than gives an
exact definition of a metric on an operational level. Key performance indicators to be evaluated when considering supply chains are (along the lines of
Supply-Chain Council (2000b)):

Delivery Performance

As customer orientation is a key component constituting SCM, delivery performance is an essential measure for total supply chain performance. As
promised delivery dates may be too late in the eye of the customer, his
expectation or even request fixes the target. Therefore delivery performance
has to be measured in terms of actual delivery date compared to delivery
date requested by the customer. Two components of delivery performance
can therefore be identified. The first one is the *order fill rate* which is defined
as the percentage of ship-from-stock orders shipped within 24 hours. The
second component, named *on time delivery* is defined as the proportion of
orders delivered on or before the date requested by the customer.

Order Fulfilment Performance

Order fulfilment performance is closely related to delivery performance. It
also comprises two measures: *order fill rate* and *order fulfilment lead-times*.
The order fill rate is again the proportion of ship-from-stock orders shipped
within 24 hours. Order fulfilment lead-times measure the meantime from
the date the order is placed to the date the customer receives shipment of
the order from the customer's point of view. Not only short lead-times but
reliable lead-times will satisfy customers and lead to a strong relationship,
even though the two types of lead-times (shortest vs. reliable) have different
cost aspects.

Perfect Order Fulfilment

Perfect order fulfilment also relates to delivery performance, but represents
the strongest measure. Perfect order fulfilment is reached with the right product delivered to the right place at the right time. Only perfect order fulfilment
ensures customer satisfaction. An on-time shipment containing only 95% of
items requested will often not ensure 95% satisfaction with the customer.

Supply Chain Responsiveness

Supply chain responsiveness is defined as the ability of the complete supply chain to react according to changes in the marketplace. Supply chains have to react on significant changes within an appropriate time frame to ensure their competitiveness. Therefore, separate flexibility measures that range from *volume flexibility* to *product-mix flexibility* have to be introduced. These indicators measure the ability to change plans and even the entire supply chain network layout in specified areas.

Production Flexibility

Production flexibility is another important measure of over-all supply chain responsiveness. Production flexibility is defined in two directions taking into account an increase and decrease in production. For example, on an operational basis upside flexibility is determined by the number of days needed to absorb an unplanned lasting 20% growth in demand.

Total Logistics Management Cost

Logistics efficiency is essential for a successful supply chain, as several partners have to be integrated into just one process. The contribution of logistics management cost to total revenue has to be controlled, because it affects profitability in many ways. Hence, an integrated information system operating on a joint database and a mutual cost accounting system may prove to be a vital part of the supply chain.

Value-Added Employee Productivity

Productivity measures usually aim at the detection of cost drivers in the production process. Value-added employee productivity is calculated by the division of the difference between revenue and material cost by total employment (measured in (full time) equivalents of employees). Therefore it analyzes the value each employee adds to all products sold.

Warranty Cost

Superior product quality is not a typical supply chain feature, but a driving business principle in general. One possibility to measure product quality is to measure warranty cost, although warranty cost in addition includes how warranty processing is carried out. To decrease warranty cost, product quality has to be improved.

Cash-to-Cash Cycle Time

Cash-to-cash cycle time is the time it takes on average until a dollar spent (for raw materials) flows back to the company as revenue. It comprises the sum of the three components: inventory days of supply plus number of days sales outstanding minus the (favourable) average payment period for materials. The inventory days of supply are the main starting point for supply chain improvements.

Inventory Days of Supply

The inventory days of supply measure how fast inventory is produced and then sold to customers. An increase in inventory days of supply points out a build-up of inventory or a change in product-mix towards products with a longer production period. Slow inventory turnover affects liquidity and should therefore be monitored carefully.

Asset Turns

Asset turns is a financial activity indicator, defined by the division of revenue by total assets. Asset turns measure the effectiveness of a company in operating its assets. They specify sales per asset. Asset turns should be watched with caution as they vary sharply among different industries.

On an operational level more exact definitions for supply chain performance indicators are given (see Supply-Chain Council (2000c)). Precise definitions for performance indicators can also be found in the production management literature. For example regarding the different aspects of delivery performance various indicators named *service levels* are distinguished there (see e. g. Tempelmeier (1999, pp. 368)). The first one, α-service level, is an event oriented measure. It is defined as the probability that an incoming order can be fulfilled completely from stock. Usually, it is defined with respect to a predefined period (e.g. day, week or order cycle). Secondly, β-service level is quantity oriented. It is defined as the proportion of incoming order quantities that can be fulfilled from inventory on-hand. In contrast to α-service level, the β-service level takes into account the extent to which orders cannot be fulfilled. The γ-service level is a time and quantity oriented measure. It comprises two aspects: the quantity that cannot be met from stock and the time it takes to meet the demand. Therefore it adds the time information not considered by the β-service level to this measure. An exact definition is:

$$\gamma\text{-service level} = 1 - \frac{\text{mean demand not fulfilled by end of period}}{\text{mean demand per period}} \tag{2.3}$$

2.1.3   Issues Faced When Utilizing Indicators

Before and while utilizing performance indicators, several issues have to be addressed. First of all, the influence of non-financial indicators on the financial performance needs to be investigated. Second, non-quantitative targets which are not included in the set of indicators should be kept in mind. Third, indicators are primarily retrospective. Future developments (e. g. changes in customer behaviour) should be anticipated if possible. And fourth, target values should not be fulfilled as an end in itself, e. g. because they are rewarded with premiums, but because they contribute to over-all performance.

Besides these general issues arising when utilizing indicators, there are some more issues specific to supply chains:

Definition of indicators. As supply chains usually span over several companies or at least several entities within one company a *common definition* of all indicators is obligatory. Otherwise the comparison of indicators and their uniform application will be counterproductive.

Perspective on indicators. The view on indicators might be different considering the roles of the two supply chain partners, the supplier and the customer. A supplier might want to calculate the order fill rate based on the order receipt date and the order ship date, as these are the dates he is able to control. From the customer's point of view the basis would be the request date and the receipt date at customer's warehouse. If supplier's and customer's dates do not match, this will lead to different results with respect to an agreed order fill rate. This is why both have to agree on one *perspective*.

Capturing of data. Data needed to calculate the indicators should be captured in a consistent way throughout the supply chain. *Consistency* with respect to units of measurement and the availability of *current* data for the supply chain partners are essential. Furthermore, *completeness* of the used data is obligatory, i. e. all necessary data should be available in adequate systems and accessible by supply chain partners.

Confidentiality. Confidentiality is another major issue when more than one company forms the supply chain. As all partners are separate legal entities, they might not want to give complete information about their internal processes to their partners. Furthermore, there might be some targets which are not shared among partners.

Nevertheless, it is widely accepted that supply chain integration benefits from the utilization of key performance indicators. They support communication between supply chain partners and are a valuable tool for the coordination of their individual, but shared plans.

2.2   The SCOR-Model

The *Supply Chain Operations Reference* (SCOR)-model (current version is 3.1) is a tool for representing, analyzing and configuring supply chains. The

SCOR-model was developed by the *Supply-Chain Council* (SCC), founded in 1996 as a non-profit organization by the *Institute Advanced Manufacturing Research* (AMR) and the consulting firm *Pittiglio Rabin Todd & McGrath* (PRTM) as well as over 65 major companies (Supply-Chain Council, 2000a). SCC now has got over 650 members world-wide.

The SCOR-model is a reference model. Unlike optimizing models, no mathematical formal description of a supply chain and no optimal or heuristic methods for solving a problem are given. Instead, a terminology and processes are standardized (see Sects. 2.2.1 and 2.2.2) enabling a general description of supply chains. Configuring these processes, different entities of a supply chain can be modelled/depicted, and thus, be compared. Furthermore, by using common KPIs named *metrics*, supply chain entities are analyzed, and provided *best practices* allow performance improvements for single entities as well as for the supply chain as a whole (see Sect. 2.2.3). Before describing the elements of the SCOR-model, the following definitions for the terms used are given (Becker et al., 2000, pp. 4 and pp. 141):

Activity. An activity depicts a single step in fulfilling accomplishment.

Task. A task consists of several activities.

Process. A process is a completed sequence of activities for accomplishing economic objects with respect to content and time (e. g. customer order).

Business process. A business process is a special kind of a process that is shaped by business' top targets.

Core process. A core process is a process that directly refers to the business' product(s) and hence to value creation.

Support process. A support process is a process that is necessary to execute a core process, but does not directly add value. The separation between core and support processes is dependent on the economic purpose of the business.

Reference model. A reference model provides a general documentation of best practices within a special (business) domain.

Best practice. A recognized best management method and/or application for designing and performing a process (O'Dell and Grayson, 1998, p. 167).

2.2.1 Standard Terminology

Using a standardized terminology that defines and unifies the used terms, communication between entities of a supply chain is improved. Regularly, non-unified definitions of a single term lead to misconception in business relations. Lengthy coordination is necessary to avoid this misconception or wrong assumptions are made. The problems are the bigger, the less one knows about the different usages of a term. SCC has established a standard terminology for SCM. Within the SCOR-model about 100 terms, named *process terms*, are defined in a glossary (Supply-Chain Council, 2000c, pp. 171). Table 2.1 shows selected definitions as an example (the abbreviations in column four refer to SCOR processes that will be described in Sect. 2.2.2).

Table 2.1. Selected SCOR process terms (Supply-Chain Council, 2000c)

Term	Type	Definition	Process category #, Process element #, "From" Process Element or Term/ Acronym
Bill-of-materials (BOM)	Input/ output	The bill-of-materials is a structured list of all the materials or parts needed to produce a particular finished product, assembly, subassembly, manufactured part or purchased part.	EP.7
Deliver stocked product	Process category	The process of delivering a product which is maintained in a finished goods state prior to the receipt of a firm customer order.	D1
Plan and build loads	Process element	Transportation modes are selected and efficient loads are built.	D1.5, D2.5, D3.5

2.2.2   Levels of the SCOR-Model

The SCOR-model consists of a system of process definitions for standardizing processes relevant for SCM. SCC recommends to model a supply chain from the suppliers' suppliers to the customers' customers. Processes like customer interactions (order entry through paid invoice), physical material transactions (e. g. equipment, supplies, products, software) and market interactions (e. g. demand fulfilment) are supported. Sales and marketing (demand generation), product development, research and development and post-delivery customer support are not addressed within the SCOR-model (Supply-Chain Council, 2000c, p. 2). The standard processes are divided into three hierarchical levels: *process types*, *process categories* and *process elements* described in the following paragraphs (following Supply-Chain Council, 2000c).

Level 1 – Process Types

Level 1 consists of the three elementary process types: *source, make* and *deliver*, coordinated by the process type *plan* (see Fig. 2.2). These process types comprise operational as well as strategic activities (see Chap. 3). The description of the process types follows Supply-Chain Council (1999).

Plan. Processes for demand and supply planning/balancing. Strategic issues like make-or-buy decisions, configuration of the supply chain, long-term

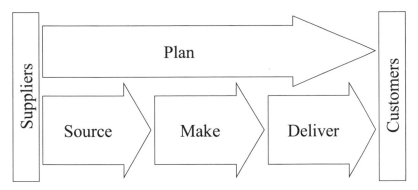

Fig. 2.2. SCOR-model's level 1

capacity and resource planning, product phase-in/phase-out etc. are contained. Supported operational issues are, e. g. aggregate and prioritize demand requirements as well as plan inventory, distribution requirements, production, material and rough-cut capacity for all products and channels.

Source. Processes required to procure products and services to meet planned and current demand. Contained strategic tasks are, e. g. vendor certification and feedback, vendor contracts and sourcing quality. Obtaining, receiving, inspecting, holding and issuing material are tasks of opertional character.

Make. Processes that transform material, intermediates and products in their next state, meeting planned and current demand. Strategic issues like engineering changes, facility location and facility equipment as well as tasks for production execution like requesting and receiving material, manufacturing products, testing products and packaging are included.

Deliver. Processes that provide the product(s) of the supply chain. These processes comprise order management processes like entering and maintaining orders, generating quotations for distribution centres and customers as well as credit collection and invoicing; warehouse management processes like picking, packing and shipping of products; and transportation management processes like product import/export.

Level 2 – Process Categories

The four process types of level 1 are divided into 17 *process categories* (see Fig. 2.3). At this level typical redundancies of established business, such as overlapping planning processes and duplicated purchasing, can be identified. Delayed customer orders indicate a need for integration of suppliers

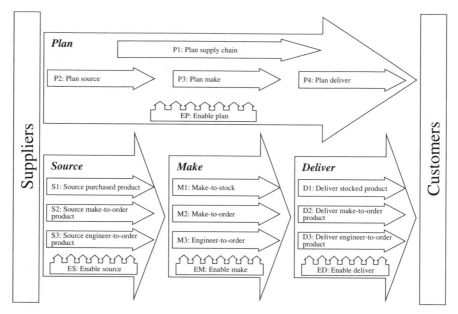

Fig. 2.3. SCOR-model's levels 1 and 2 (updated following Supply-Chain Council, 1999)

and customers. Each process category belongs to one of the types[1]: *planning*, *executing* and *enabling* (see Table 2.2).

Planning. Process categories of this type support the allocation of resources to the expected demand. They incorporate balancing of supply and demand in an adequate planning horizon. Regularly, these processes are executed periodically. They directly influence the supply chain's flexibility to changes in demand.

Executing. The type "executing" comprises process categories that are triggered by planned or current demand. Regularly, they incorporate scheduling and sequencing as well as transforming and/or transporting products. The process types source, make and deliver are divided with respect to the nature of customer orders (e.g. make-to-stock, make-to-order and engineer-to-order). Process categories of the type "executing" directly influence the time interval between incoming orders and delivery. They depict the core processes of a supply chain.

Enabling. Process categories of this type are support processes for process categories of the types "planning" and "executing". They prepare, preserve and control the flow of information and the relations between the other processes.

---

[1] To distinguish between these types of process categories and the process types of level 1, the terms *type(s)*, for the first one, and *process type(s)*, for the second one, will be used.

Table 2.2. Types of process categories

	Plan	Source	Make	Deliver
Planning	P1	P2	P3	P4
Executing		S1–S3	M1–M3	D1–D3
Enabling	EP	ES	EM	ED

Level 3 – Process Elements

At this level, the supply chain is tuned. The process categories are decomposed into *process elements*. Detailed metrics and best practices for these elements are part of the SCOR-model (see following Sect. 2.2.3). Process elements of the types "planning" and "executing" are represented in a logical sequence. Furthermore, most elements provide an *input* stream (information and material) and/or an *output* stream (also information and material). Figure 2.4 shows the third level of the "P1: Plan supply chain" process category. Supply-Chain Council (2000c, pp. 8–15) gives the following definitions for this process category and its process elements:

"**P1.** The development and establishment of courses of action over specified time periods that represent a projected appropriation of supply chain resources to meet supply chain requirements.

P1.1. The process of identifying, prioritizing and considering, as a whole with constituent parts, all sources of demand in the supply chain of a product or service.

P1.2. The process of identifying, evaluating, and considering, as a whole with constituent parts, all things that add value in the supply chain of a product or service.

P1.3. The process of developing a time-phased course of action that commits supply-chain resources to meet supply-chain requirements.

P1.4. The establishment of course of action over specified time periods that represent a projected appropriation of supply-chain requirements. "

The input and output streams of a process element are not linked to input and output streams of other process elements. However, the indication in brackets, depicts the corresponding supply chain partner, process type, process category or process element from where information or material comes. Thus, the process elements are references, not examples of possible sequences.

The process elements are decomposed on the fourth level. Companies implement their specific management practices at this level. Not being part of the SCOR-model, this step will not be subject of this book.

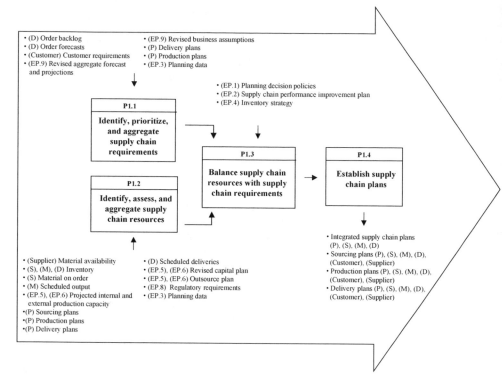

Fig. 2.4. Example of SCOR-model's level 3 (Supply-Chain Council, 2000c, p. 8)

2.2.3   Metrics and Best Practices

The SCOR-model supports performance measurement on each level. Level 1 metrics provide an overview of the supply chain to evaluate management (see Table 2.3 as well as Sect. 2.1.2). Levels 2 and 3 include more specific and detailed metrics corresponding to process categories and elements. Table 2.4 gives an example of level 2 metrics that are corresponding to the "P1: Plan supply chain" process category. More metrics are provided for each process category and level 3 process element, except for process elements of the type "enabling" (Supply-Chain Council, 2000b; Supply-Chain Council, 2000c).

The metrics are systematically divided into the four categories *reliability, flexibility and responsiveness, costs* and *assets*. Reliability as well as flexibility and responsiveness are external (customer driven), whereas costs and assets are internal points of view. All metrics are defined in the glossary of Supply-Chain Council (2000c, pp. 190).

In 1991 PRTM initiated the *Integrated Supply Chain Benchmarking Study* (now: Supply-Chain Management Benchmarking Series) for SCC members (PRTM, 1997). Within the scope of this study all level 1 metrics and selected metrics of levels 2 and 3 have been gathered. The information has been eval-

Table 2.3. SCOR's level 1 metrics (Supply-Chain Council, 2000b)

External, customer facing		Internal facing	
Reliability	Flexibility and responsiveness	Cost	Assets
Delivery performance	Supply chain responsiveness	Total logistics management cost	Cash-to-cash cycle time
Order fulfilment performance	Production flexibility	Value-added employee productivity	Inventory days of supply
Perfect order fulfilment		Warranty cost	Asset turns

Table 2.4. SCOR's level 2 metrics – example "P1: Plan Supply Chain" (Supply-Chain Council, 2000c)

Performance attributes	Metric
Reliability	Forecast acccuracy Delivery to customer request date Fill rate Product and process data acccuracy (BOMs, routings etc.)
Flexibility and responsiveness	Cumulative source/make delivery time Re-plan cycle time Cash-to-cash cycle time
Cost	Total order management cost Deliver/source planning cost Inventory carrying cost Value-added productivity Obsolete inventory
Assets	Return on assets Capacity utilization Total inventory days of supply

uated regarding different lines of business. Companies joining the Integrated Supply Chain Benchmarking Study are able to compare their metrics with the evaluated ones. Furthermore, associated best practices have been identified. Selected best practices, corresponding to process categories and process elements, are depicted in the following paragraph.

An example of an identified best practice for the "P1: Plan supply chain" process category is the high integration of the supply/demand process from gathering customer data to order receipt, through production to supplier request. SCC recommends performing this integrated process by using an APS with interfaces to all supply/demand resources. Moreover, the utilization of tools that support balanced decision-making (e. g. trade-off between service level and inventory investment) is identified as best practice (Supply-Chain Council, 2000c, p. 10). To perform process element "P1.3: Balance supply chain resources with supply chain requirements" (see Fig. 2.4) effectively, balancing of supply and demand to derive optimal combination of customer service and resource investment by using an APS, is recognized as best practice. A complete list of best practices for each process category and process element is given in Supply-Chain Council (2000c).

2.2.4   A Procedure for Application of the SCOR-Model

After having described the elements of the SCOR-model, a procedure for application will be outlined. This procedure corresponds to Supply-Chain Council (1999). It consists of four steps:

- Analyze the basis of competition.
- Configure the supply chain.
- Align performance levels, practices and systems.
- Implement supply chain processes and systems.

The first three steps correspond to the three levels of the SCOR-model. Step four depicts the implementation of gathered knowledge, and thus, is not part of the model.

The *analysis of basis of competition* is based on level 1 metrics of the SCOR-model (see Table 2.3). These metrics are entered in the so-called *Supply Chain Scorecard*. In column "actual" one enters the current performance. The columns "parity", "advantage" and "superior" allow to illustrate the different competitive positions to be achieved. Comparing the current with the aspired competitive position, a pre-selection for detailed modelling and analysis can be made.

Supply-Chain Council (1999) recommends an approach in seven steps for *configuring the supply chain.*

1. Define the business unit to be configured.
2. Geographically place entities that are involved in source, make and deliver process types. Not only locations of a single business, but also locations of suppliers (and suppliers' suppliers) and customers (and customers' customers) should be denoted.
3. Enter the major flows of materials as directed arcs between locations of entities (see Fig. 2.5).
4. Assign and link source, make and deliver processes to each location using second level's process categories.
5. Define partial process chains of the (modelled) supply chain. A partial process chain is a sequence of processes that are planned by a single "P1" planning process category.

6. Enter planning processes ("P1"–"P4") using dashed lines to illustrate the assignment between processes for "planning" and those for "executing" (see Fig. 2.5 and also Table 2.2).
7. Define a top-level "P1" planning process if possible, i. e. a planning process category that coordinates two or more partial process chains.

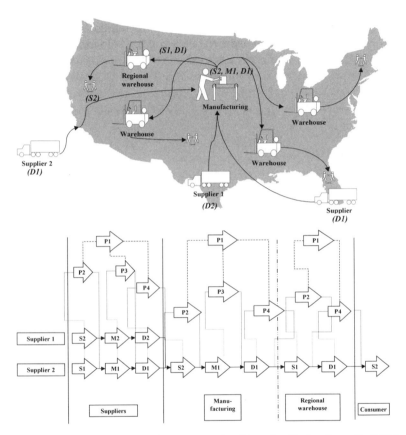

Fig. 2.5. Example results of steps 3 and 6 (Supply-Chain Council, 1999)

After analyzing the basis of competition and configuring the supply chain, *performance levels, practices and systems are aligned.* Critical process categories of level 2 can be detailed in level 3. At this level the most differentiated metrics and best practices are available. Thus, detailed analysis and improvements on process elements are supported.

The *implementation of supply chain processes and systems* is, as already mentioned, not part of the SCOR-model. However, it is recommended to continue to use the metrics of the SCOR-model. They provide data for internal and external benchmarking studies to measure and document consequences of change processes within a supply chain.

2.3   A Supply Chain Typology

The SCOR-model is an excellent tool to analyze, visualize and discuss the structure of the supply chain and to reveal redundancies and weaknesses. It enables the formulation of structural changes and strategies to improve the performance of the supply chain as a whole. When it comes to planning, a typology of planning tasks will help to identify the type of decision problems facing the supply chain and guide the selection of standard or specialized modules, models and algorithms for decision support. Such a typology will be discussed in the following supporting the SCOR-model at level 2.

2.3.1   Motivation and Basics

In the early days of production planning and control a single concept and software system has been applied in industry – material requirements planning (MRP) – irrespective of the many different requirements existing in such diverse areas like the production of foods or automobiles. On the other hand, if a production manager was asked whether the production system he manages is unique and requires special purpose decision-making tools, the answer probably will be "yes". As regards the type of decisions to be made, the truth lies somewhere in the middle of these two extremes. Abstracting from minor specialities usually reveals that there are common features in today's production and distribution systems which require similar decision support and thus can be supported by the same software modules.

APS are much more versatile than MRP and ERP systems due to their modelling capabilities and different solution procedures (even for one module). Modules offered by a software vendor may still be more suited for a certain type of supply chain than for another. So, it is our aim to outline a *supply chain typology* which allows to describe a given supply chain by a set of attributes which we feel might be important for decision-making and the selection of an APS. Attributes may have nominal properties (e. g. a product is storable or not), ordinal properties (e. g. an entity's power or impact on decision-making is regarded higher or lower than average) or cardinal properties (i. e. the attribute can be counted, like the number of legally separated entities within a supply chain).

Attributes with a similar focus will be grouped into a peculiar category to better reveal the structure of our typology (see Tables 2.5 and 2.6). We will discriminate functional attributes to be applied to each organization, entity, member, or location of a supply chain as well as attributes describing the structure of relations among its entities (structural attributes).

2.3.2 Functional Attributes

Functional attributes (see Tab. 2.5) of an entity are grouped into the four categories

- procurement type,
- production type,
- distribution type and
- sales type.

Table 2.5. Functional attributes of a supply chain typology

Functional attributes	
Categories	Attributes
Procurement type	products procured
	sourcing type
	flexibility of suppliers
Production type	organization of the production process
	repetition of operations
	etc.
Distribution types	distribution structure
	pattern of delivery
	deployment of transportation means
	loading restrictions
Sales type	relation to customers
	availability of future demands
	products life cycle
	products sold
	portion of service operations

The *procurement type* relates to the *products* to be procured, ranging from standard products to highly specific products, requiring special product know-how or production process know-how (or equipment). The second attribute depicts the *sourcing type*, better known by its properties: single sourcing, double sourcing and multiple sourcing. Single sourcing exists, if there is a unique supplier for a certain product to be procured. In double sourcing there are two suppliers, each fulfilling a portion of demand for the product to be procured (e. g. 60% of the demand is fulfilled by the main supplier, 40 % by the second supplier). Sourcing contracts with suppliers are usually valid in the medium-term (e. g. a product's life cycle). Otherwise, products can be sourced from multiple suppliers, alternately. Thirdly, the *flexibility of suppliers* with respect to the amounts to be supplied may be important. Amounts may either be fixed, have a lower or upper bound due to given contracts with suppliers or may be freely available.

The *production type* is formed by several attributes. The two most prominent attributes are the organization of the production process and the repetition of operations. Process organization and flow lines represent well-known properties of the production process. Process organization requires that all resources capable of performing a special task (like drilling) are located in the same area (a shop). Usually a product has to pass through several shops until it is finished. A flow shop exists, if all products pass the shops in the same order, otherwise it is a job shop. A flow line exists in case resources are arranged next to each other corresponding to the sequence of operations required by the products to be manufactured on it. Usually capacities within a flow line are synchronized and intermediate inventories are not possible. Hence, for planning purposes a flow line can be regarded as a single entity.

The attribute *repetition of operations* has three broad properties, mass production, batch production and making one-of-a-kind products. In mass production, the same product is generated constantly over a long period of time. In batch production several units of a given operation are grouped together to form a batch (or lot) and are executed one after the other. Several batches are loaded on a resource sequentially. At the start of a batch a setup is required, incurring some setup costs or setup time. When making one-of-a-kind products which are specific to a (customer) order, special care is needed to time phase the many operations usually belonging to a (customer) order (for further specifications of a product type see Schneeweiss (1999, pp. 10) and Silver et al. (1998, pp. 36)).

The *distribution type* is made of the distribution structure, the pattern of delivery, the deployment of transportation means and possible loading restrictions. The *distribution structure* describes the network of links between the factory (warehouse) and the customer(s). A one-stage distribution structure exists, if there are only direct links between a factory (warehouse) and its customers. In case the distribution network has one intermediate layer (e. g. either central warehouses (CW) or regional warehouses (RW)) a two stage distribution structure is given. A three stage distribution structure incorporates an additional layer (e. g. CW *and* RW).

The *pattern of delivery* is either cyclic or dynamic. In a cyclic pattern, goods are transported at fixed intervals of time (e. g. round-the-world ship departures). A dynamic pattern is given if delivery is made depending on demand (for transportation). As regards the *deployment of transportation means* one can distinguish the deployment of vehicles on routes (either standard routes or variable routes depending on demand) and simply a given transportation capacity on individual links in the distribution network. It may even be possible to assume unlimited transportation capacities and to consider only a given cost function (e. g. based on a contract with a large third-party service provider). *Loading restrictions* (like the requirement of a full truck load) may form a further requirement.

The *sales type* of an entity in the supply chain largely depends on the *relation to its customers*. One extreme may be a downstream entity in the supply chain (with some kind of "agreement" regarding expected demands and an open information flow) while the other extreme may be a pure market relation with many competitors (e. g. auctions via internet conducted by the purchasing departments of a large company). This attribute is closely related to the *availability of future demands*. These may be known (by contract) or have to be forecasted. The existence of (reliable) demand forecasts, is best described by the length of the forecast horizon. The typical length and the current stage of a *product's life cycle* largely influences appropriate marketing, production planning and financial strategies. As regards the *products* to be sold one should discriminate the range from standard products to highly specific products (in accordance to the products procured). Apart from selling tangible goods the *portion of service operations* is constantly growing (e. g. the training of a customer's personnel).

2.3.3 Structural Attributes

Structural attributes (see Table 2.6) of a supply chain are grouped into the two categories

- topography of a supply chain and
- integration and coordination.

Table 2.6. Structural attributes of a supply chain typology

Structural attributes	
Categories	Attributes
Topography of a supply chain	network structure degree of globalization location of decoupling point(s)
Integration and coordination	legal position balance of power direction of coordination type of information exchanged

As regards the *topography of a supply chain* the attribute *network structure* describes the material flows from upstream to downstream entities which are either serial, convergent, divergent or a mixture of the three. Note that the network structure often coincides with the products' structure. The *degree of globalization* ranges from supply chains operating in a single country to those with entities in several continents. Global supply chains not only have to take into account tariffs and impediments to trade as well as exchange rates varying over time but also can profit from it. Also, the *location of the decoupling point(s)* within the supply chain has to be mentioned. It is the first stage (or location) in the flow of materials, where a further processing step or a change in the location of a product will only be executed with respect to a customer order (see also Sect. 1.2). Note, the decoupling point may differ between product groups. Starting with the most upstream location of a decoupling point we have engineer-to-order (with no make-to-stock at all), followed by manufacture-to-order of parts, then assemble-to-order and deliver-to-order. In a vendor managed inventory system a supplier even has to deliver-to-stock, since there are no orders from the buyer to replenish inventories.

Integration and coordination concerns the attributes legal position, balance of power, direction of coordination and type of information exchanged. The *legal position* of entities has already been mentioned. In case entities are legally separated, an inter-organizational supply chain exists, otherwise it is called intra-organizational. For intra-organizational supply chains it will be much easier to coordinate flows centrally than for inter-organizational supply chains. Also the *balance of power* within an inter-organizational supply chain plays a vital role for decision-making. A dominant member in the supply chain can act as a focal firm. On the other hand we have a supply chain of equals, named a polycentric supply chain.

As regards information flows several attributes may be considered. As an example consider the *direction of coordination*. It may be purely vertical or purely horizontal or a mixture of both. Vertical information flows comply with hierarchical planning. On the other hand horizontal flows may exist between two adjacent entities within the supply chain which can easily and quickly make use of local information (e. g. to overcome the effects of a breakdown of a machine). Also the *type of information exchanged* between members influences planning (e. g. some entities may hesitate to reveal its manufacturing costs but are willing to provide information about available capacities).

While attributes describing a production type are generally accepted and validated today, a typology of the service sector is still in its infancy (for a state-of-the-art survey see Cook et al. (1999)). Also, the aforementioned attributes only provide a basis for a rough grouping of decision problems which may be refined further according to the needs of a given SCM project. For this, special purpose typologies can be of help (e. g. for production processes concerning cutting and packing (Dyckhoff and Finke, 1992)). In some cases, this will also indicate that special purpose solution procedures may be needed, currently not provided by APS.

In order to reduce the burden associated with an (extensive) typology, one should bear in mind its aim. Since decision-making and decision support is of interest here, one might concentrate on activities to be performed on those products and services regarded most important (e. g. "A" products in an ABC-classification based on the annual turnover, see Silver et al. (1998, pp. 32)). Furthermore, attention can be focused on those activities which either have to be performed on potential bottlenecks along the supply chain or which affect critical performance criteria considerably (e. g. order lead-time).

Once a list of functional attributes has been established for each entity of a supply chain, it will show the degree of diversity existing in the supply chain. For partners having similar properties the choice of an appropriate decision-making tool (or module of an APS) can be made jointly, saving costs and time. In order to demonstrate the applicability of the above typology it will be used in the following section and in our case studies (Part IV).

2.3.4   Example for the Consumer Goods Industry

Here and now the typology will be applied for supply chains where consumer goods are produced and sold. Functional attributes are presented for the consumer goods manufacturing entity only. Structural attributes consider the supply chain as a whole comprising both manufacturers and retailers. Some attributes of our typology are not used within the example, because they play only a minor role in supply chains of the consumer goods type. This kind of supply chain is considered again in Chap. 19. Therefore, our description is rather detailed and affects additional proprietary attributes not mentioned explicitly in the above (universal) typology.

Table 2.7 summarizes the characteristics of the consumer goods supply chain. Since the products to be sold are the determining factor of our example, we start illustrating the *sales type* category.

Sales Type In the remainder, we concentrate on the subset of consumer goods that comprises standard products with a low volume, weight and value per item (e. g. food, beverages, office supplies or low tech electronics). A typical consumer goods manufacturer offers several hundreds of final items that are technologically related.

The final customer expects to find his preferred brand in the shelf of a grocery or electronics store. If the desired product is not available, he probably changes his mind and buys a comparable product of another manufacturer. This behaviour is due to the low degree of product differentiation predominant in the consumer goods industry. Therefore, consumer goods manufacturers are forced to produce on stock by means of demand estimates.

Since the product life cycle of standard products typically extends over several years, a solid data basis for forecasting is available. However, demand for some products may be subject to seasonal influences (e. g. for ice cream or bulbs) or price promotions.

Table 2.7. Supply chain typology for the consumer goods industry

Functional attributes	
Attributes	Contents
products procured	standard (raw materials)
sourcing type	multiple
organization of the production process	flow line
repetition of operations	batch production
distribution structure	three stages
pattern of delivery	dynamic
deployment of transportation means	unlimited, routes (3rd stage)
availability of future demands	forecasted
products life cycle	several years
products sold	standard
portion of service operations	tangible goods
Structural attributes	
Attributes	Contents
network structure	mixture
degree of globalization	several countries
location of decoupling point(s)	deliver to order
legal position	intra-organizational
direction of coordination	mixture
type of information exchanged	merely unlimited

When consumer goods are standardized, the emphasis of marketing has to be set on service level and price. Altogether, a strictly competitive market is given.

Distribution Type Consumer goods are distributed via wholesalers and/or retailers to the final customers. The distribution network of a consumer goods manufacturer quite often comprises three distribution stages (see Fleischmann (1998) and Fig. 2.6).

The product programme of the manufacturer is supplied by one or a few factories. Thereby, some product types may be produced in more than one site. The finished goods can temporarily be stored in a few CWs, each of them offering the whole range of products. Large orders of the manufacturer's customers (i.e. wholesalers, retailers or department stores) can be delivered directly from the factory or CW to the respective unloading point.

Since most orders are of rather small size and have to be transported over long distances, a further distribution stage consisting of RWs or stock-less

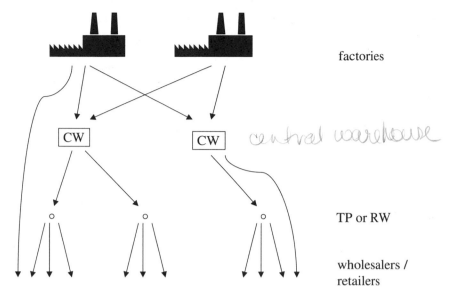

factories

CW   CW   *central warehouse*

TP or RW

wholesalers / retailers

Fig. 2.6. Three-stage distribution system

transshipment points (TP) is often used. The customers in the vicinity (at most 100 km radius) of such a RW/TP are supplied in one-day tours starting from this RW/TP. Over the (typically) long distance between the CW and the RW/TP all orders of the respective region are bundled (typically by third-party service providers) so that a high transport utilization is achieved.

As opposite to RWs, no stock is held in TPs, thus causing lower inventory holding, but higher transportation costs due to the higher delivery frequency. A similar distribution structure may be applied by major sales chains which replenish their (large number of) department stores from their own retail CWs.

Production Type Production of consumer goods often comprises only one or two production stages, e. g. manufacturing and packaging. On each production stage one or a few parallel (continuous) production lines (flow lines) are organized in a flow shop. A line executes various operations. But since these operations are strictly coordinated, each line may be planned as a single unit. The lines show a high degree of automation and are very capital intensive. Because of this automation, however, short and reliable lead-times can be achieved.

The capacity of the production lines is limited and they are usually highly utilized. Therefore, they represent potential bottlenecks. For the handling of the lines, few but well-trained operators are necessary. A short-term expansion of working time is normally not possible. The working time of the whole team supervising a line has to be determined on a mid-term time range. However, in many companies lines are already operating seven days a week, 24 hours a day.

As mentioned above, there are a lot of final items. But these are often technologically related and can be assigned to a few *setup families*. Changeovers between items of the same family are negligible. But changeovers between items of different families cause high setup costs and setup times. Therefore, batch production is inevitable. The degree of these costs and times may vary notably with respect to the family produced last on the same line (*sequence dependent* setup times and costs).

Procurement Type Consumer goods frequently have a rather simple bill-of-materials. In these cases only few suppliers have to be coordinated. As long as unsophisticated components, but mainly standard products (e. g. raw materials) are needed, procurement is not really a problem. Mid- and long-term contracts and cooperations ensure the desired flow of raw materials from the suppliers to the manufacturer.

Topography of the Supply Chain The production network (eventually several sites producing the same product), the distribution network of the manufacturer and possibly the distribution network of large wholesalers/retailers contain both divergent and convergent elements thus forming a network structure of the mixture type. Production and distribution networks usually extend over several countries, eventually even over multiple continents. Since products are made to stock, the decoupling point is settled in CWs or RWs, from which goods are delivered to order.

Integration and Coordination As regards the consumer goods manufacturing entity, there is a strong need for intra-organizational coordination. Several organizational units of the same company (e. g. order management, sales, manufacturing, procurement) have to exchange information horizontally. Furthermore, the central planning unit has to coordinate the bulk of decentral units by sending directives and gathering feedback, thus inducing heavy vertical information traffic. Since all of these units belong to the same company, information should be freely available.

In addition, new logistical concepts of SCM result in special emphasis on inter-organizational relations within the supply chain, particularly on the interface between consumer goods manufacturers and large retailers. Current trends can be outlined as follows:

- The flow of information between the manufacturers and retailers is improved by EDI or WWW connections.
- Short delivery cycles (with rather small quantities) are established in order to closely connect the material flow with the demand of final customers (*Continuous Replenishment / Efficient Consumer Response*).

- Traditional responsibilities are changed. Large retailers abstain more and more from sending orders to their suppliers, i. e. the consumer goods manufacturers. They instead install consignation stores whose contents are owned by their suppliers until the goods are extracted by the retailer. A supplier is responsible for filling up his inventory to an extend which is convenient for both the supplier and the retailer. As already mentioned, such an agreement is called *vendor managed inventory* (VMI).

References

Becker, J.; Kugeler, M.; Rosemann, M. (2000) *Prozessmanagement: Ein Leitfaden zur prozessorientierten Organisationsgestaltung*, Berlin et al.

Cook, D. P.; Goh, C.-H.; Chung, C. H. (1999) *Service typologies: A state of the art survey*, Production and Operations Management, Vol. 8, No. 3, 318-338

Dyckhoff, H.; Finke, U. (1992) *Cutting and packing in production and distribution: A typology and bibliography*, Heidelberg

Fleischmann, B. (1998) *Design of freight traffic networks* in: Fleischmann, B.; Nunen, J.A.E.E. van; Speranza, M. G.; Stähly, P. (Eds.) *Advances in Distribution Logistics*. Lecture Notes in Economics and Mathematical Systems, Vol. 460, Berlin et al., 55–81

Horváth, P. (1998) *Controlling*, 7th ed., München

Kaplan, R. S.; Norton, D. P. (1992) *The balanced scorecard - Measures that drive performance*, Harvard Business Review, Vol. 70, No. 1, 71–79

Kaplan, R. S.; Norton, D. P. (1993) *Putting the balanced scorecard to work*, Harvard Business Review, Vol. 71, No. 5, 134–142

Meyer, C. (1994) *How the right measures help teams excel*, Harvard Business Review, Vol. 72, No. 3, 95–103

PRTM (1997) *Introduction to the 1997 Integrated Supply-Chain Benchmarking Study*, URL: http://www.supply-chain.org/members/html/presentations.cfm, State: June 9, 2000

O'Dell, C.; Grayson, C. J. (1998) *If only we knew what we know: The transfer of internal knowledge and best practice*, New York

Schneeweiss, C. (1999) *Einführung in die Produktionswirtschaft*, 7th ed., Berlin et al.

Silver, E. A.; Pyke, D. F.; Petersen, R. (1998) *Inventory management and production planning and scheduling*, 3rd ed., New York et al.

Supply-Chain Council (1999) *Supply Chain Council & Supply chain operations reference (SCOR) model overview*, URL: http://www.supply-chain.org/html/scor_overview.cfm, State: June 9, 2000

Supply-Chain Council (2000a) *Homepage*, URL: http://www.supply-chain.org, State: June 9, 2000

Supply-Chain Council (2000b) *SCOR metrics level 1 primer*, Tech. Paper, Pittsburgh, URL: http://www.supply-chain.org/members/html/wpaper.cfm, State: June 9, 2000

Supply-Chain Council (2000c) *Supply chain operations reference-model – Version 3.1*, Tech. Paper, Pittsburgh, URL: http://www.supply-chain.org/members/html/scormodel.cfm, State: June 9, 2000

Syska, A. (1990) *Kennzahlen für die Logistik*, Berlin et al.

Tucker, S. A. (1961) *Successful managerial control by ratio-analysis*, New York et al.

3 Advanced Planning

Bernhard Fleischmann, Herbert Meyr, Michael Wagner

University of Augsburg, Department of Production and Logistics,
Universitätsstraße 16, 86135 Augsburg, Germany

3.1 What is Planning?

Why planning? Along a supply chain hundreds and thousands of individual decisions have to be made and coordinated every minute. These decisions are of different importance. They comprise the rather simple question *"Which job has to be scheduled next on a respective machine?"* as well as the very serious task whether to open or close a factory. The more important a decision is, the better it has to be prepared.

This preparation is the job of *planning*. Planning supports decision-making by identifying alternatives of future activities and selecting some good ones or even the best one. Planning can be subdivided into the phases (see Domschke and Scholl (2000), pp. 29)

- *recognition* and *analysis* of a decision problem,
- definition of *objectives*,
- *forecasting* of future developments,
- *identification* and *evaluation* of feasible activities (*solutions*) and finally
- *selection* of good solutions.

Supply chains are very complex. Not every detail that has to be dealt with in reality can and should be respected in a plan and during the planning process. Therefore, it is always necessary to abstract from reality and to use a simplified copy of reality, a so-called *model*, as a basis for establishing a plan. The "art of model building" is to represent reality as simple as possible but as detailed as necessary, i. e. without ignoring any serious real world constraints.

Forecasting and *simulation models* try to predict future developments and to explain relationships between input and output of complex systems. However, they do not support the selection of one or a few solutions that are good in terms of predefined criteria from a large set of feasible activities. This is the purpose of *optimization models* which differ from the former ones by an additional *objective function* that is to be minimized or maximized.

Plans are not made for eternity. The validity of a plan is restricted to a predefined *planning horizon*. When reaching the planning horizon, at the latest, a new plan has to be made that reflects the current status of the supply chain. According to the length of the planning horizon and the importance of the decision to be made, planning tasks are usually classified into three different planning levels (see Anthony (1965)):

Long-term planning: Decisions of this level are called *strategic decisions* and should create the prerequisites for the development of an enterprise/supply chain in the future. They typically concern the design and structure of a supply chain and have long-term effects, noticeable over several years.

Mid-term planning: Within the scope of the strategic decisions, mid-term planning determines an outline of the regular operations, in particular rough quantities and times for the flows and resources in the given supply chain. The planning horizon ranges from 6 to 24 months, enabling the consideration of seasonal developments, e. g. of demand.

Short-term planning: The lowest planning level has to specify all activities as detailed instructions for immediate execution and control. Therefore, short-term planning models require the highest degree of detail and accuracy. The planning horizon is between a few days and three months. Short-term planning is restricted by the decisions on structure and quantitative scope from the upper levels. Nevertheless, it is an important factor for the actual performance of the supply chain, e. g. concerning lead-times, delays, customer service and other strategic issues.

The last two planning levels are called *operational*. Some authors call the second level *tactical* (e. g. Silver et al. (1998), Chap. 13.2), but as this notion has several contradictory meanings in literature, it is not used in this book.

A naive way of planning is to look at the alternatives, to compare them with respect to the given criteria and to select the best one. Unfortunately, this simple procedure encounters, in most cases, three major difficulties:

First, there are often several criteria which imply conflicting objectives and ambiguous preferences between alternatives. For example, customer service ought to be as high as possible while – at the same time – inventories are to be minimized. In this case no "optimal" solution (accomplishing both objectives to the highest possible degree) exists. A common way to deal with this *multi-objective decision problem* is to set a minimum or maximum satisfaction level for each objective except for one that will be optimized. In the above example one may try to minimize inventories while guaranteeing a minimum customer service level. Another useful way to handle multiple objectives consists in pricing all objectives monetarily by revenues or costs and maximizing the resulting *marginal profit*. However, not every objective can be expressed in monetary values, e. g. the customer service. A more general way is to define scale values or scores for every objective and to aggregate them into a weighted sum. A danger of this procedure is that it yields pretended "optimal" solutions which strongly depend on the arbitrary weights. An APS supports each of these procedures in principle. The case studies in Part IV give examples for some relevant modeling features of the *i2, J. D. Edwards* and *SAP* systems.

The second difficulty is caused by the huge number of alternatives that are predominant in supply chain planning. In case of continuous decision variables, e. g. order sizes or starting times of a job, the set of alternatives is actually infinite. But also for discrete decisions, e. g. the sequence of several jobs on a machine, the number of alternatives may be combinatorially large. In these cases it is impossible to find an optimal solution by enumeration of all alternatives, and even a feasible solution may be difficult to find. In this situation, mathematical methods of *operations research (OR)* should support the planning process. Some methods are able to determine an exact optimal solution, e. g. Linear Programming (LP) or network flow algorithms, but for most combinatorial problems only near-optimal solutions can be computed by *heuristics*, e. g. local search. The success of these methods also depends on the way a problem is modeled. The capabilities of OR methods for some important types of optimization models are exemplarily shown in the Supplement (Part VI).

The third and probably hardest difficulty is dealing with uncertainty. Planning anticipates future activities and is based on data about future developments. The data may be estimated by forecast models, but there will be a more or less important forecast error. This error reduces the availability of products and therefore reduces the customer service a company offers. For improvement of the service safety stocks can be utilized which buffer against demands differing from the forecast. However, that is not the only way to tackle uncertainty.

Nearly always, reality will deviate from the plan. The deviation has to be controlled and the plan has to be revised if the discrepancy is too large. Planning on a *rolling horizon basis* is an implementation of this plan-control-revision interaction. The planning horizon (e. g. one year) is divided into periods (e. g. months). At the beginning of January a plan is made that covers January to December. But only the first period, the so-called *frozen period*, is actually put into practice. At the beginning of the second period (February) a new plan is made considering the actual developments during the first period and updated forecasts for the future periods. The new planning horizon overlaps with the previous one, but reaches one period further (until the end of January of the next year; see Fig. 3.1) and so on.

This procedure is a common way of coping with uncertainty in operational planning both in classical planning systems and in APS. A more efficient way of updating the plans is *event-oriented planning*: A new plan is not drawn up in regular intervals but in case of an important event, e. g. unexpected sales, major changes in customer orders, breakdown of a machine etc. This procedure requires that all data which are necessary for planning, e. g. stocks, progress of work etc., are updated continuously so that they are available at any arbitrary event time. This is the case for an APS which is based on data from an Enterprise Resource Planning (ERP) system.

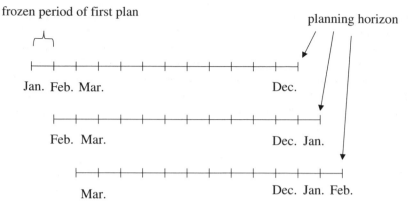

Fig. 3.1. Planning on a rolling horizon basis

There are three main characteristics of APS:

- *Integral planning* of the entire supply chain, at least from the suppliers up to the customers of a single enterprise, or even of a more comprehensive network of enterprises;
- *true optimization* by properly defining alternatives, objectives and constraints for the various planning problems and by using optimizing planning methods, either exact ones or heuristics;
- *a hierarchical planning system* (see Schneeweiss (1999) and Chap. 1) which is the only framework permitting the combination of the two preceding properties: Optimal planning of an entire supply chain is neither possible in form of a monolithic system that performs all planning tasks *simultaneously* – this would be completely impracticable – nor by performing the various planning tasks successively – this would miss optimality. Hierarchical planning is a compromise between practicability and the consideration of the interdependencies between the planning tasks.

Note that the traditional material requirements planning (MRP) concept (see Orlicky (1975)) which is implemented in nearly all ERP systems does not have any of the above properties: It is restricted to the production and procurement area, does not optimize and in most cases even not consider an objective function, and it is a successive planning system.

The main idea of hierarchical planning is to decompose the total planning task into *planning modules*, i. e. partial plans, assigned to different levels, where every level covers the complete supply chain but the tasks differ from level to level: On the upmost level, there is only one module, the development of an enterprise wide, long-term but very rough plan. The lower the levels are, the more restricted are the supply chain sections covered by one plan, the shorter is the horizon and the more detailed is the plan. Plans for different supply chain sections on one level are coordinated by a more comprehensive plan on the next upper level in a hierarchical structure (see Fig 3.2).

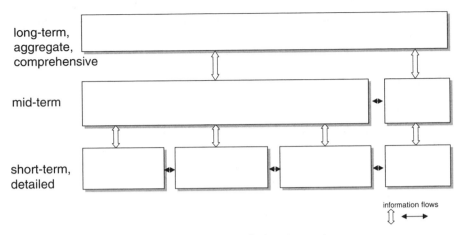

long-term,
aggregate,
comprehensive

mid-term

short-term,
detailed

information flows

Fig. 3.2. Hierarchy of planning tasks

The increasing (resp. decreasing) degree of detail is achieved by disaggregating (resp. aggregating) data and results when going down (resp. up) in the hierarchy. *Aggregation* concerns

- products, aggregated into groups,
- resources, aggregated into capacity groups and
- time: periods, aggregated into longer ones.

The modules are linked by vertical and horizontal information flows. In particular, the result of a higher planning module sets restrictions for the subordinate plans, and the results of the latter yield feedback information on performance (e. g. costs, lead-times, utilization) to the higher level. The design of a *hierarchical planning system* (HPS) requires a careful definition of the modular structure, the assignment of planning tasks to the modules and the specification of the information flows between. Usually, an HPS works with a rolling horizon, where sophisticated coordinations of the planning intervals and horizons on the different levels have been suggested in literature (e. g. Hax and Meal (1975), Stadtler (1986)). However, event-oriented planning simplifies the use of an HPS and makes it more flexible. A prerequisite is a communication system that leads alerts (see Chap. 11) on "events" to the relevant planning levels and tasks. Moreover, the result of one planning task can generate alerts for other plans.

APS try to "computerize" planning. This might incur some problems for many human planners because they are afraid of being substituted by machines. This fear is based upon three major advantages of APS: they visualize information, reduce planning time and allow an easy application of optimization methods. However, modeling is always a relaxation of reality. Therefore, human knowledge, experience and skill is yet required to bridge the gap between model and reality. Planning systems, no matter how *advanced* they might be, remain decision support systems, i. e. they support human decision-makers. Also, in event-oriented planning it is usually the human planner who decides, whether a plan is to be revised. Finally, each planning module requires a human "owner", who is responsible for its function, data and results.

3.2   Planning Tasks along the Supply Chain

The whole Supply Chain Network can be split into internal supply chains for every partner in the network, each consisting of four main supply chain processes with substantially different planning tasks. *Procurement* includes all subprocesses which provide resources (e. g. materials, personnel etc.) necessary for production. The limited capacity of resources is the input to the *production* process which may consist of various subprocesses. The *distribution* bridges the distance between the production site and the customers, either retailers or other enterprises processing the products further. All of the above logistical processes are driven by demand and order figures determined by the *sales* process.

Supply Chain Planning Matrix

The *Supply Chain Planning Matrix* (SCP-Matrix, see Rohde et al. (2000)) classifies the planning tasks in the two dimensions "planning horizon" and "supply chain process". Fig. 3.3 shows typical tasks which occur in most supply chain types, but with various contents in the particular businesses. In Fig. 3.3 the long-term tasks are shown in a single box to illustrate the comprehensive character of strategic planning. The other boxes represent the matrix entries, but do not correspond exactly to the planning modules of an HPS. The latter may contain only parts of a box – e. g. on the short-term level, the planning tasks can be decomposed according to further dimensions like factory sites or product groups – or combine tasks of several boxes. This is a question of the design of the HPS as mentioned in Sect. 3.1. The SCP-Matrix is also used by most APS providers to position their *software modules* so that the matrix is well covered (see Chap. 4). The construction of an HPS from the software modules of an APS is discussed in Part IV.

Long-term Planning Tasks

Product Programme and Strategic Sales Planning The decision about the product programme a firm wants to offer should be based on a long-range forecast which shows the possible sales of the whole product range. Such a forecast includes dependencies between existing product lines and future product developments and also the potential of new sales regions. It is

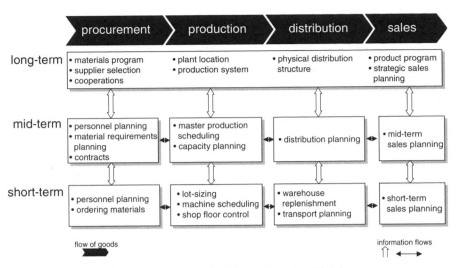

Fig. 3.3. The Supply Chain Planning Matrix

often necessary to create different scenarios depending on the product programme decision. Long-range forecasts consider information on product-life-cycles and economical, political and competitive factors. As it is not possible to estimate long-range sales figures for each item, the products need to be aggregated into groups of items sharing common sales and production characteristics. Marginal profits of potential sales and fixed costs for assets have to be considered in the objective function of the product programme optimization problem.

Physical Distribution Structure As more and more companies concentrate their production capacities because of high investments in machining, the distance between the production facility and customers and the respective distribution costs increase. Such trends and a changing environment require a reorganization of the distribution system. The physical structure comprises the number and size of warehouses and cross docking points including the necessary transportation links.

Typical input for the decision is the product programme and the sales forecast, the planned production capacity in each plant and the underlying cost structure. The objective is to minimize the long-term costs for transportation, inventory, handling and investments in assets (e.g. warehouses, handling facilities etc.). The question, whether the transports are performed by an own fleet of vehicles or a third-party carrier is very closely related to the decision on the physical distribution system. For this reason, the two decision types should be integrated into one model.

Plant Location and Production System Long-term changes in product programmes or sales figures require to review the existing production capacities and locations. Furthermore, the continuous improvement of production technologies leads to new prerequisites. Therefore, the production and decision systems need to be verified. Usually, decisions on plant locations and the distribution structure are made together. They are based on long-term forecasts and production capacities available (without consideration of single machines). Planning the production system means organizing a single production plant, i. e. designing the layout of the plant and the resulting material flows between the machines.

Materials Programme and Supplier Selection The materials programme is often directly connected to the product programme, because the final products consist of some predefined components and raw materials. Sometimes different materials could be used alternatively for the same purpose. In order to select one of them for the materials programme one should consider price (including possible quantity discounts), quality and availability.

As A-class materials (see e. g. Silver et al. (1998) for an introduction to the ABC-analysis) cause the biggest part of procurement costs, it is reasonable to source those parts through special supply channels. Therefore, the suppliers should be rated according to quality, service and procurement costs.

Cooperations Further reduction of procurement costs is often achieved by strategic cooperations with suppliers of A-class items. The planning and evaluation of collaboration concepts gains importance, because no longer companies but whole supply chains compete against each other. These concepts include simultaneous reduction of inventories and backorders using concepts like *vendor managed inventories (VMI)*, *EDLP (every-day-low-price strategies)* and *JIT (just-in-time)* supply. While the above cooperation concepts concern day-to-day operations, *simultaneous engineering* and *consolidation centres* set strategic frames for the daily procurement processes.

Mid-term Planning Tasks

Mid-term Sales Planning The main task in mid-term sales planning is forecasting the potential sales for product groups in specific regions. As the forecasts are input to master production scheduling, the products are grouped according to their production characteristics (e. g. preferred resources, changeover times etc.). The forecast is usually calculated on a weekly or monthly basis for one year or less. It includes the effects of mid-term marketing events and promotions on sales. The necessary safety stocks for finished products are mainly determined by the quality of the forecast. Therefore, it is reasonable to set them on the basis of the forecast error which has to be calculated in the forecasting procedure.

Distribution Planning Mid-term distribution planning comprises the planning of transports between the warehouses and determination of the necessary stock levels. A feasible plan fulfils the estimated demand (forecasts) and considers the available transportation and storage capacities while minimizing the relevant costs. Inventory holding and transportation costs are elements of the objective function. The planning horizon consists of weekly or monthly buckets. Therefore, the underlying model only considers aggregated capacities (e. g. available truck capacity and not single trucks). The distribution plan could also state the usage of the own fleet and the necessary capacity which must be bought from a third-party carrier.

Master Production Scheduling and Capacity Planning The result of this planning task shows how to use the available production capacity of one or more facilities in a cost efficient manner. Master production scheduling (MPS) has to deal with seasonal fluctuations of demand and to calculate a frame for necessary amounts of overtime. As the plan is based on families of products and weekly or monthly time buckets, it does not consider single production processes. The objective is to balance the cost of capacity against the cost of (seasonal) inventories. If more than one production facility is considered, the transportation costs between the locations have to be included in the objective function.

Personnel Planning Capacity planning provides a rough cut overview on the necessary working time for finished products. Personnel planning has to calculate the personnel capacity for components and other production stages which have to be passed before the final assembly of the products. This planning step considers the specific know how of personnel groups and their availability according to labour contracts. If not enough employees are available to fulfil the work load, personnel planning shows the necessary amount of additional part time employees.

Material Requirements Planning As MPS plans only finished products and critical materials (concentration on bottlenecks), material requirements planning (MRP) has to calculate the production and order quantities for all remaining items. This could be done by the traditional MRP-concept (see Orlicky (1975)) which is available in most ERP-systems or by stochastic inventory control systems. Whereas the MRP-concept is suitable for rather critical materials and A-class components, stochastic inventory systems are adequate for C-class items. The calculation of material requirements should support lot-sizing decisions for every item in the bill-of-materials (BOM) and consider the dependencies between the lots on different levels of the BOM. Mid-term planning sets frames for weekly or monthly order quantities and safety stock levels (if stochastic inventory systems are given) which ensure the desired service level for production.

Contracts On basis of the weekly or monthly requirements obtained from MRP, basic agreements with A-class suppliers can be made. Such contracts set the price, the total amount and other conditions for the materials to be delivered during the next planning horizon.

Short-term Planning Tasks

Short-term Sales Planning In make-to-stock environments the short-term sales planning comprises the fulfilment of customer orders from stocks. Therefore, the stock on hand can be partitioned in committed stocks and the *available-to-promise* (ATP) quantity. If a customer requests a product, the sales person checks online whether the quantity could be fulfilled from ATP and turns the requested amount in committed stock. For customer inquiries on the availability of products in future periods the ATP quantity is calculated by adding stock on hand and planned production quantities. The capable-to-promise (CTP) functionality is an extension of the traditional ATP task which has the additional option of creating new production orders.

Warehouse Replenishment, Transport Planning While the mid-term distribution planning suggests weekly or monthly transportation quantities for product families, the short-term warehouse replenishment particularizes this plan in daily quantities for single products. This time-phased deployment schedule considers detailed transportation capacities (e. g. available trucks) and actual customer orders or short-term forecasts. Planned or actual production quantities set the frame for the transportation plan and also restrict the possible degree of customer service. Every day the planned truck loads have to be deployed to customer locations according to a cost-minimizing routing.

Transports occur not only in the distribution process, but also as part of the procurement and may be controlled by either the supplier or the receiver. In the latter case, transport planning is necessary on the procurement side as well, and the transport processes have to be considered also in the mid-term and long-term levels of procurement planning.

Lot-sizing and Machine Scheduling, Shop Floor Control Short-term production planning comprises the determination of lot-sizes and the sequences of the lots on the machines. Lot-sizing has to balance the costs of changeovers and stock holding with respect to dependencies between different products. These lots are scheduled according to their due dates and the available capacity with minutely accuracy. Both tasks can independently be executed if the changeovers are not dependent on the sequence of the products. As interruptions or delays are common in complex production environments, the shop floor has to be controlled actively and orders have to be rescheduled appropriately.

Short-term Personnel Planning, Ordering Materials The short-term production schedule determines the appropriate personnel of the shop floor with respect to the knowledge and capability. Short-term personnel planning determines the detailed schedule of the staff with consideration of employment agreements and labour costs. As some amount of material might already have been committed by mid-term contracting, the short-term task of filling the commitments in a cost efficient manner still remains.

Coordination and Integration

As already mentioned the planning modules in an HPS need to be connected by information flows. Typical contents of these flows are discussed in the following.

Horizontal Information Flows The main horizontal flows go upstream, consisting of customer orders, sales forecasts, internal orders for warehouse replenishment and for production in the various departments as well as purchasing orders to the suppliers. This way, the whole supply chain is driven by the customers. However, the exchange of additional information in both directions and not only between neighbored modules, can improve the supply chain performance significantly (see bullwhip effect, Chap. 1). This concerns in particular actual stocks, available capacity lead-times and point-of-sales data.

Vertical Information Flows Downwards flows coordinate subordinate plans by means of the results of a higher level plan. Typical informations are aggregate quantities, allocated to production sites, departments or processes. The timing of quantities is better expressed in form of projected final stocks at the end of the lower level planning horizon, because this includes the information about the longer planning horizon on the upper level and provides more flexibility on the lower level. Coordination is also achieved by allocation of capacities and by setting due dates.

Upwards flows provide the upper level with more detailed data on the performance of the supply chain, e. g. actual costs, production rates and utilization of the equipment, lead-times etc. This information can be used in the upper level planning for anticipating the consequences for the more detailed processes on the lower level.

3.3 Example for Typical Planning Tasks in the Consumer Goods Industry

In the following typical planning tasks of a consumer goods supply chain – as described in Chap. 2 – are explained.

Long-term Planning Tasks Typically a consumer goods supply chain consists of some critical suppliers, a few production sites and various stock points which are all connected by the flow of material or products. This network has to be overhauled regularly because changes in demand and competition influence the optimal location and capacity of sites and warehouses.

The decision on the structure of the supply chain has to consider demand forecasts for 2, 3 or more years. Therefore, the life-cycles of the products and the availability of competitive or substitutive products play an important role. As the planning of the physical distribution structure and the planning of the facility location are connected by dependent flows of products, it is advisable to integrate these tasks in one module.

Quite a lot of producers of consumer goods have close contact to key suppliers which could influence the location of production sites. Therefore, such suppliers need to be considered in a planning model concerning the network structure.

Master Production Scheduling, Capacity Planning and Mid-term Distribution Planning As consumer goods manufacturers often face seasonal or strong fluctuating demand it is necessary to smooth those effects by pre-production in periods with less customer orders. Here, master production scheduling has to trade off the costs for seasonal stocks due to pre-production and the costs for capacity, especially the additional expenditure for working overtime in periods with peak demand. As more and more labour agreements permit flexible working times in the consumer goods industry, sophisticated planning methods could lead to lower costs by effective utilization of the additional freedom.

Furthermore, quite a lot of consumer goods companies use more than one site for producing the same product. Thus, the above planning task is getting more complex, as capacity problems could be balanced by shifting production quantities from one site to another. Therefore, the costs for transports to the demand point are relevant and have to be considered, too, during the decision process. This extension of master production scheduling leads to a planning model (in general: master planning) which includes both the tasks of mid-term production planning and mid-term distribution planning.

Usually, the main result of master planning in the consumer goods area is *not* the production quantity, because the demand or forecast might change in the short run. Therefore, short-term scheduling needs to plan with updated demand data. So, the necessary capacity (esp. working time, shift pattern and overtime), the quantity which has to be pre-build (seasonal stock) and the transport capacity on each link are the decisions aided by master planning.

Mid-term and Short-term Sales Planning Forecasting is often the crucial point in consumer goods industries because inventory of finished products is quite expensive and lost sales or backlogs reduce the customer's trust in the company. These effects are sometimes amplified by depreciations which arise because of the low shelf-lifes of the products. Therefore, it is necessary to include the seasonal influences and the additional demand which is caused by promotions and marketing activities.

In mid-term forecasting usually aggregated product groups are considered and the time buckets comprise one week or more. The total planning horizon should at least include one complete seasonal cycle. Usually, the planning task consists of two steps. The first involves statistical forecasting under consideration of trends and seasonal effects. For that purpose the time series of past demand are analyzed and extrapolated into the future. In a second step the additional demand which is caused by planned marketing activities is added to the base forecast.

The short-term forecasting procedure then considers all products and a more detailed time grid (usually daily buckets). As the sales personnel has exact information on promotions for each time bucket (day), it is advisable to compose the short-term forecast figures by adding a statistical base forecast, the additional demand resulting from promotions and the change in demand caused by seasonal fluctuations. The information on seasonal effects has to be considered as add-on to the base forecast, because the short horizon comprises not a complete cycle which is necessary for a seasonal planning model.

Lot-sizing and Machine Scheduling Production Planning in consumer goods industries seems simple as the production process only consists of one or two stages. But in practice one of the hardest planning problems occurs because of high sequence dependent setup costs. This dependence enforces the simultaneous determination of lot-sizes and sequences as changes in the sequence of lots cause alterations in setup costs which influence the lot-sizing decision. But the sequencing decision in turn is based on known lot-sizes.

Distribution Planning, Warehouse Replenishment A further crucial task in consumer goods industries is to balance the inventories in the multi-stage distribution network. The make-to-stock environment requires safety stocks to avoid stock-outs at the most downstream stage (before customer delivery). For risk pooling purposes it is often reasonable to hold a part of the safety stocks at warehouses upstream (e. g. central warehouses etc.). The cost efficient deployment of safety stocks among the different stock points could prevent from high investments while maintaining the required customer service level.

In the short run warehouse replenishment decisions have to take into account the preset minimum stock levels which are based on the safety stock levels.

Coordination and Integration This section should provide some insight into the complex task of integrating the operational part of a planning concept

for the consumer goods industries. As this line of business has quite a lot of
different faces, it is not possible to provide a single solution which fits to all
companies. The planning concept (see Fig. 3.4) is based on an organizational

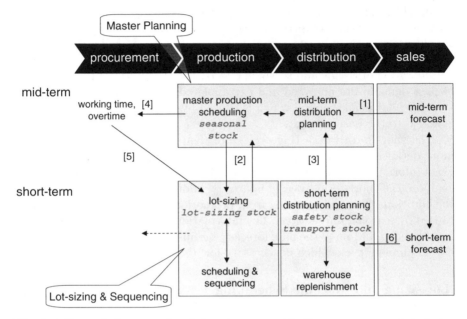

Fig. 3.4. Example for operational planning concept in the consumer goods industry

structure which is quite common in the following fields: foods and beverages,
detergents and some electronic appliances.

As already stated above, the mid-term production and distribution planning parts are usually integrated into one master planning model. The dynamic data input comprises the available capacity and the demand estimates
for every master planning planning bucket which is retrieved from the sales
planning model (see Fig. 3.4, flow [1]). As the available production capacity is
mainly determined by machine maintenance or investment in new technology,
it is obvious that this information is provided by the production sites.

An important issue in integrating planning tasks is the consideration of
different inventory types for finished products. For detailed inventory planning one needs to know where a single inventory type is planned, where it is
considered as a minimum stock level and where it must be approximated. As
the seasonal stock is optimized in master planning, for example, it is considered to be the minimum stock level in the subsequent lot-sizing & sequencing
model (see Fig. 3.4, flow [2]). These stock levels have to be disaggregated as
mid-term planning is done on the basis of product groups and aggregated
capacity. But, in turn, the lot-sizing stock results from the optimization of
inventory holding costs and changeover costs and, for reasons of complexity,

cannot be determined in master planning. Because of this lack, approximated lot-sizing stocks have to be added to minimum stock levels in master planning. These estimations are adjusted based on lot-sizing & sequencing plans which consider changeovers.

Furthermore the capacity requirements (e. g. necessary working time and overtime) are planned in master planning and are input to the lot-sizing & sequencing task. As those rough "times" need to be refined according to shift patterns and individual time accounts, usually an additional step is necessary. This is done decentrally at the plant and calculates capacity plans for short-term planning (see Fig. 3.4, flows [4] and [5]).

While the production and distribution decisions are integrated in master planning for mid-term planning, the short-term distribution planning does not consider lot-sizing & sequencing. Distribution planning is coordinated with master planning by transit stocks and available truck capacity (see Fig. 3.4, flow [3]). As in mid-term planning only aggregated capacities per link are considered, in the short run every truck and its availability are included. Therefore, the mid-term distribution planning uses estimated transit stocks which are the result of the detailed short-term shipment plan. Further, short-term demand forecasts which are integrated in one model together with the mid-term forecasting are input to distribution planning (see Fig. 3.4, flow [6]). The result of distribution planning is a shipment/ replenishment plan prepared for immediate execution. The net requirements from distribution planning bridge the interface between production and distribution.

References

Anthony, R. N. (1965) *Planning and control systems: A framework for analysis*, Cambridge/Mass.

Domschke, W.; Scholl, A. (2000) *Grundlagen der Betriebswirtschaftslehre*, Berlin et al.

Fleischmann, B. (1998) *Design of freight traffic networks*, in: Fleischmann et al. (Eds.) Advances in distribution logistics, Berlin et al., 55–81

Hax, A. C.; Meal, H. C. (1975) *Hierarchical integration of production planning and scheduling*, in: Geisler, M. A. (Ed.) Logistics: TIMS Studies in management sciences Vol. 1, Amsterdam, 53–69

Orlicky, J. A. (1975) *Material requirements planning*, New York et al.

Rohde, J.; Meyr, H.; Wagner, M. (2000) *Die Supply Chain Planning Matrix*, in: PPS-Management, Vol. 5, No. 1, Berlin, 10–15

Schneeweiss, C. (1999) *Hierarchies in distributed decision making*, Berlin et al.

Silver, E. A.; Pyke, D. F.; Peterson, R. (1998) *Inventory management and production planning and scheduling*, 3rd ed., New York et al.

Stadtler, H. (1986) *Hierarchical production planning: Tuning aggregate planning with sequencing and scheduling*, in: Axsäter S.; Schneeweiß, C. et al. (Eds.) Multistage production planning and inventory control, Berlin et al., 197–226

Part II

Concepts of Advanced Planning Systems

4 Structure of Advanced Planning Systems

Herbert Meyr, Michael Wagner[1] and Jens Rohde[2]

[1] University of Augsburg, Department of Production and Logistics,
   Universitätsstraße 16, 86135 Augsburg, Germany
[2] Darmstadt University of Technology, Institute of Business Administration,
   Department of Operations and Materials Management, Hochschulstraße 1,
   64289 Darmstadt, Germany

APS have independently been launched by different software companies at
different points in time. Nevertheless, a common structure underlying most
of the APS can be identified. An APS typically consists of several *software
modules* (eventually again comprising several software components), each of
them covering a certain range of planning tasks (see Rohde et al. (2000)).

In Sect. 3.2 the most important tasks of supply chain planning have been
introduced and classified in the two dimensions *planning horizon* and *supply
chain process* by use of the SCP-Matrix (Fig. 3.3). As Fig. 4.1 shows, certain
planning sections of the SCP-Matrix, e. g. mid-term procurement, production
and distribution, are typically covered by a respective software module. The
names of the modules vary from APS provider to APS provider, but the
planning tasks that are supported are basically the same. In Fig. 4.1 supplier-
independent names have been chosen that try to characterize the underlying
planning tasks of the respective software modules.

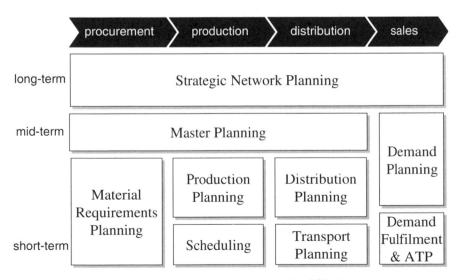

Fig. 4.1. Software modules covering the SCP-Matrix

APS typically do not support all of the planning tasks that have been identified in Sect. 3.2. In the remainder of the book it will be shown which tasks are actually considered (Part II), how to select and implement APS (Part III), how to build models using software modules (Part IV) and which solution methods are commonly used (Part VI). Here and now, only an overview of the structure of the software modules and the planning tasks concerned is given:

- **Strategic Network Planning** covers all four long-term planning sections, especially the tasks *plant location* and the design of the *physical distribution structure*. Some questions that arise in *strategic sales planning* (e. g. which products to place in certain markets) can be considered, too. Basically, the design of the supply chain and the elementary material flows between suppliers and customers are determined.

- Further tasks of *strategic sales planning* (e. g. long-term demand estimates) and the *mid-term sales planning* are usually supported by a module for **Demand Planning**.

- Most APS providers offer **Demand Fulfilment & ATP** components which comprise the *short-term sales planning*.

- **Master Planning** coordinates procurement, production and distribution on a mid-term time level. The tasks *distribution, capacity* and *mid-term personnel planning* are often considered simultaneously. Furthermore, *master production scheduling* is supported.

- If there are two separate software modules for **Production Planning** and **Scheduling** the first one is responsible for *lot-sizing* whereas the second one is used for *machine scheduling* and *shop floor control*. Quite often, however, all three tasks are supported by a single software module.

- The short-term **Transport Planning** is covered by a corresponding software module. Sometimes an additional **Distribution Planning** module deals with material flows in a more detailed manner than it can usually be done by Master Planning.

- The planning tasks *BOM explosion* and *ordering of materials* are often left to the ERP systems which traditionally supply these functionalities and are needed as transaction systems, anyway. Only seldom APS providers launch a special software module **Material Requirements Planning** that supports the (mid- to) short-term procurement directly. For these reasons the Material Requirements Planning module will not be discussed in further detail.

Planning tasks of different types of industries/supply chains may vary substantially. APS providers are increasingly getting aware of this situation. Therefore, they offer several software components or even modules covering the same planning tasks, but respecting the peculiarities of the particular type of supply chain considered. So actually a third dimension *supply chain type* should be added to Fig. 4.1. For sake of clarity, however, we abstain from this further visualization.

Software modules can be seen as some sort of "planning kit". The users buy, install and integrate only those modules which are essential for their business. In most cases not all modules of an APS provider are installed. Sometimes, but not often components of different APS providers are combined.

The other way round is also possible. Some APS providers do not cover all planning sections by their software modules. However, APS suppliers seem to be highly interested in offering complete solutions.

Sometimes software modules are utilized for planning tasks they originally have not been designed for. For example, a Master Planning module can be used for Distribution Planning. This happens if modelling features of the modules are quite similar and the same solution method can be applied to different types of problems. Since APS users have to pay for each software component individually, such a situation will particularly occur if "competing" modules of the same APS provider exist.

Besides the already proposed software modules, frequently additional software components are supplied which support the integration of different software modules, e. g. the aggregation of data and disaggregation of results of different planning levels (see Chap. 11).

Also often tools for the integration (mostly per Internet) of different supply chain partners operating in different locations are offered. These software components provide the necessary data for a supply chain-wide, long- and mid-term planning and communicate the outcome of the central planning process to the respective decentral units. In most cases an alert system supports the interaction between central and decentral planning (see Sect. 3.1). Since Internet technology can be applied for various purposes, APS suppliers more and more offer additional e-business tools, e. g. for the opening of virtual markets in order to purchase raw materials etc.

References

Rohde, J.; Meyr, H.; Wagner, M. (2000) *Die Supply Chain Planning Matrix*, in: PPS-Management, Vol. 5, No. 1, Berlin, 10–15

5 Strategic Network Planning

Marc Goetschalckx

Georgia Institute of Technology, School of Industrial and Systems Engineering, 765 Ferst Drive, Atlanta, Georgia 30332-0205

In this chapter we will focus on the long term, strategic planning and design of the supply chain. During the strategic planning, an organization attempts to design a supply chain which will enable this organization to maximize its economic performance over an extended period of time. Together with product research and development and marketing, the supply chain is one of the essential tools for a company to achieve their strategic business goals and practices. During the strategic planning process, companies identify their key products, customer markets for these products, core manufacturing processes and suppliers of raw and intermediate materials. Virtually all organizations must redesign their supply chain from time to time to respond to changing market conditions, but the recent wave of mergers and acquisitions and the globalization of the economy have made this process even more frequent and important. For example, a company may wish to expand into a new geographical area where no infrastructure is currently in place, such as the expansion by electronics manufacturing companies into Eastern Europe after those countries adopted a market economy. Another company may wish to consolidate the duplicate distribution systems created by a merger or acquisition. Finally, strategic planning is not only used for expansion but also for retraction, such as when the United States Armed Forces developed a strategic plan for the base closings associated with the withdrawal from Western Europe.

Typically, the planning horizon for strategic planning ranges from three to ten years and the decisions involve the definition of customer and product zones, the definition of the stages in the manufacturing process, the establishment or closure of manufacturing and distribution facilities and the installation of major manufacturing lines. The objectives are most often financial objectives such as *profit maximization* or *cost minimization*, subject to customer service and budget constraints. The consequences of these decisions are manufacturing and distribution capacity and allocation of these capacities to products and customer zones. These capacities and allocations then become constraints in the master planning process. The master planning in turn determines the more detailed material flows and material storage for a number of smaller seasonal time periods.

Clearly, the decisions made during the strategic network planning have a major impact on the long term profitability and competitive position of a corporation. But such far-reaching decisions typically have to be made based on data generated by very aggregate forecasts and economic trends. Demand for consumer goods in the developing nations of South America depends on the population data for that region, the global and local economic condition and the profitability of serving that demand depends on the exchange rates during the planning period. As a consequence, corporations have become very much interested not only in the economic efficiency of their supply chain for the projected conditions, but also in the robustness and flexibility of their supply chain to adapt to changing and unanticipated conditions. Solution algorithms for design systems when the data is not known with certainty belong to the class of *stochastic optimization* models and algorithms.

Planning models and decisions of the strategic network design have both an interrelated spatial and temporal characteristic. For example, during an expansion into a new geographical area a company may decide to manufacture its products during the first two years in existing manufacturing facilities and to transport them to the new customer area. But starting in year three when demand has grown sufficiently, the most economic production-distribution strategy may be to manufacture the products locally. This implies that the construction of the new manufacturing plant has to be started immediately. Many of the decisions made during strategic planning are of the go/no-go type. For example, the decision may be either to build a manufacturing plant in year three or not, but it is not possible to build half a plant. This type of decision is modelled with binary (integer) variables. The optimal solutions to these integer models are notoriously and provably hard to find. The solution algorithms and techniques to solve the models either to optimality or within a prescribed gap from optimal belong to the class of *Mixed Integer Programming* (MIP) algorithms.

Finally, the strategic planning process is complicated by the fact that organizations execute strategic planning infrequently. A typical frequency may be during the creation of the next five-year plan. As a consequence, the people that performed the previous strategic planning have been promoted or left for other organizations. This implies that the new design team may have very little experience in model building and model solving.

Clearly, the proper execution of strategic planning effort is a very challenging task. The decision support models must be comprehensive and cover both engineering and financial constraints, and often they are company or industry specific. The models require a large quantity and variety of data which often must be forecasted with large degrees of uncertainty. The decisions are binary and thus even the deterministic MIP models would be very difficult to solve to optimality. But the data are typically not known with certainty which indicates the use of stochastic optimization. And the infrequent planning effort implies that the organization cannot develop and maintain a level of experience and that transferring experience from another corporation or industry group may be difficult.

The remainder of this chapter will first present a verbal formulation of the strategic network planning problem. It will then identify some of the major features of formulations published in the literature and identify modelling challenges for the future formulations. Next several successful strategic network planning cases will be discussed, followed by a discussion of modelling features of current APS. Finally, conclusions and future directions will be presented.

5.1   A Verbal Formulation of the Strategic Network Design Problem

The main objects in a strategic network design project are related to the different countries, planning periods, products, customers, vendors and suppliers, manufacturing and distribution facilities and transportation assets. Decisions are the status of a particular facility or relationship during a specific planning period and the product flows and storage in the supply chain during a planning period. For example, if the binary variable y_{jlt} equals one may indicate that a facility of type l is established at location or site j during time period t. Similarly, the continuous variable x_{ijmpt} may indicate the product flow of product p from facility i to facility j using transportation channel m during time period t. The relationships between the different variables are usually fairly simple and typically linear. A supplier capacity relation will sum all the outgoing flows of a product to the different destination facilities and over all outgoing transportation channels to ensure it does not exceed the capacity of the supplier for that product during that period. While each decision variable and each constraint in itself is simple, the number of variables and constraints creates a significant problem for model formulation, data collection and model solution. The comprehensive strategic supply chain models may contain thousands of the binary variables and millions of the continuous variables in tens of thousands of constraints. Consider the following hypothetical supply chain model of relatively modest size with 20 product groups, 30 possible facilities and facility technologies, 50 customer groups, 3 alternative transportation channels between the facilities and the customer groups and 5 planning periods. The number of continuous flow variables would be approximately $20 \cdot 30 \cdot 50 \cdot 3 \cdot 5 = 450,000$. The number of binary decision variables would be approximately $30 \cdot 5 = 150$. The number of conservation of flow, demand and supply constraints would at least $20 \cdot 80 \cdot 5 = 8,000$. The number of linkage constraints between material flow and facility status would range from $20 \cdot 80 = 1,600$ for a "loose" formulation to $450,000$ for a very tight formulation with a small integrality gap (see section 22.3 for an explanation). If the logistic system was sufficiently stationary to be modelled as a single planning period, the number of continuous variables, binary variables, flow constraints and linkage constraints for the weak and strong formulation would $90,000$, 30, 1600, 1600 and $90,000$ respectively. A schematic representation of a single period logistics systems is given in Fig. 5.1. Multiple periods would have a similar structure for each period, with inventory arcs connecting warehouses in subsequent periods.

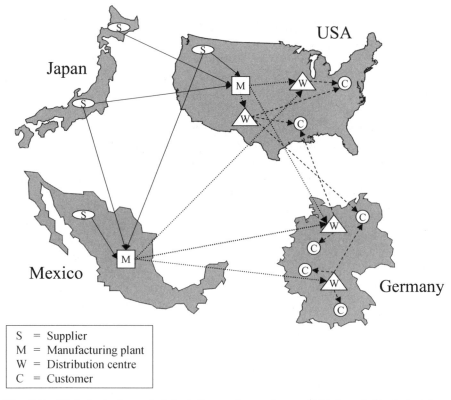

S	=	Supplier
M	=	Manufacturing plant
W	=	Distribution centre
C	=	Customer

Fig. 5.1. Global single-period logistics system schema (Vidal and Goetschalckx, 1997a)

Even the very compact mathematically formulation of the models may extend over many pages and the necessary notation may obscure the fundamental structure of a capacitated, *multi-period, multi-echelon, multicommodity* network flow problem where the capacity of nodes or arcs depends on binary status variables. We choose instead to give one possible verbal formulation of the global strategic network design problem.

5.1.1 MODEL GSCF (Global Supply Chain Formulation)

Maximise   sum of the global after-tax discounted yearly profits in the reference currency of the corporation

Subject to: For every planning period:

- Expressions for the net income before taxes of the activities of the corporation
- Expressions for the after tax profit in each country
- Suppliers' capacity
- Production capacity at manufacturing plants and distribution centres
- Transportation capacity of the transportation channels and modes
- Customer demand constraints
- Bill-of-materials and flow balance constraints at the facilities, for manufacturing lines and in the transportation channels
- Minimum profit for subsidiaries on a country basis
- Linkage constraints between manufacturing lines and facilities and between material flows and facilities and transportation channels
- Bounds on transfer prices and general bounds on decision variables

The net income before taxes consists of the difference between the sales price to either the final customer or a downstream subsidiary minus the total cost which includes operating and acquisition costs. The total cost on a country and planning period basis is defined as:

Total Cost =   Supply cost +

Fixed manufacturing cost +
Variable manufacturing cost +

Fixed facility operating cost +
Variable facility operating cost +
Warehousing cost +

Cycle inventory cost at the facilities +
Pipeline inventory cost +

Inventory carry-over cost between periods +
Transportation cost

5.1.2   Review of Models in the Literature

A comprehensive review of all the models available or used in the design of supply chain systems is not possible within the confines of a single chapter. There exist several excellent reference books focussing on inventory models, Silver et al. (1998), on the inventory and transportation interactions, Tayur et al. (1999), and on the interactions between production planning and inventory, Graves et al. (1993). The focus in this chapter will be on features included in models for the strategic design of integrated supply chain systems. Tables 5.1 and 5.2 summarize the features in the supply chain models for single-country or domestic models and Table 5.3 summarizes the features for international models. Fundamentally, international models have the same characteristics, variables and constraints as single-country models but, in addition, they model exchange rates, tax rates, duties, tariffs and local content laws. The tables are an update and extension of the tables of strategic models for the design of domestic and global supply chain systems given in Vidal and Goetschalckx (1997b).

Ballou and Masters (1993) surveyed developers and practitioners in the industry to determine the most important characteristics and the state of the art in decision support systems for supply chain design. They found that model features and user friendliness were the most important features of the models and design packages. Ballou and Masters (1999) repeated the survey six years later and observed that advances in computer hardware and software had allowed real-world strategic supply chain systems design projects to be completed using mathematical models incorporated in commercial software packages. They reported that specialized and efficient algorithms have been developed to solve the spatial or geographical location aspect of supply chain systems, but that specialized or general-purpose simulation models are used for the temporal aspects such as tactical inventory and production planning. Few models combine or integrate the spatial and temporal aspects of the supply chain. Based on a survey of active models and software packages, they found that the models are becoming more comprehensive and are beginning to include some tactical aspects. Global characteristics such as taxes, duties and tariffs as well as exchange rates are included in only a few models. They report that Linear Programming (LP), MIP and heuristics are the most commonly used techniques to find solutions. The practitioners responded with a large majority that modelling was used to configure their supply chain. In contrast with the 1993 result, in 1999 the practitioners ranked optimality of the solution as the most important characteristic of the software. The best features of the models were their ability to represent the real-world system and to find an effective configuration. The worst features were difficulty in obtaining the necessary data, the complexity of using the model and the poor treatment of inventory costs, especially in connection to customer service levels. The authors also observed that a consolidation trend is reducing the number of models and software packages available on the market.

Table 5.1. Main characteristics of selected MIP strategic production-distribution models

MODEL CHARACTERISTICS	[1]	[2]	[3]	[4]	[5]	[6]	[7]	[8]
STOCHASTIC FEATURES								
• Material requirements								
• Material supply lead-times								
• Demands of products and parts								
• Transportation times								
• Exchange rates						X		
• Reliability of vendors								
DYNAMIC CHARACTERISTICS								
• Static model (single-period)	X	X	X	X	X			
• Multi-period model						X	X	X
• Dynamic demand only								
STATUS OF FACILITIES								
• Fixed number, status and location of facilities (flow optimization)				X	X	X		
• Fixed location of facilities (discrete location)	X	X	X				X	X
• Continuous facility location								
CAPACITIES								
• Production capacity at plants	X	X	X	X	X	X	X	X
• Supply capacity of vendors					X	X	X	X
• Capacity of transportation channels								X
• Distribution Centre (DC) capacities	X	X					X	X
• Manufacturing line capacity								X
• Other capacities					X			
MULTICOMMODITY MODEL	X	X	X	X	X	X	X	X
SINGLE SOURCING								
• Customers from DC	X							X
• Customers per commodity		X						X
• DC per commodity								X
• Manufacturing plants from vendors								X
OBJECTIVE FUNCTION								
• Minimization of costs	X	X	X				X	X
• Maximization of profits				X	X	X		
• Multi-objective function								

References considered in Table 5.1 and Table 5.2:

[1] Geoffrion and Graves (1974)
[2] Geoffrion et al. (1978)
[3] Brown et al. (1987)
[4] Cohen and Lee (1989)
[5] Cohen et al. (1989)
[6] Cohen and Moon (1991)
[7] Arntzen et al. (1995)
[8] Dogan and Goetschalckx (1999)

Table 5.2. Main characteristics of selected MIP strategic production-distribution models (continued)

MODEL CHARACTERISTICS	[1]	[2]	[3]	[4]	[5]	[6]	[7]	[8]
NONLINEAR COSTS CONSIDERED								
• Nonlinear DC costs	X	X						
• Concave production costs						X		
• Nonlinear transportation costs								
• Nonlinear purchasing costs								
NUMBER OF ECHELONS	1	1	0	1	0	0	N/C	N/C
FIXED COSTS INCLUDED								
• Fixed production costs			X	X	X	X	X	
• Fixed facility costs	X	X	X	X				X
• Vendor fixed costs				X	X			X
• Fixed transportation channel costs								
• Manufacturing line costs							X	X
SIDE CONSTRAINTS INCLUDED								
• Bill of Materials				X	X	X	X	
• Bounds on the No. of open facilities	X	X	X					X
• Other side constraints				X		X		
CUSTOMER SERVICE FEATURES								
• Customer demand satisfaction	X	X	X	X	X	X	X	X
• Maximum time (distance) to serve customers	X							X
• % of orders satisfied from on-hand inventory								
INVENTORY CHARACTERISTICS								
• Pipeline inventory		X					X	X
• Cyclic inventory in facilities							X	X
• Safety stock:								
o Proportional to throughput								
o Stochastic (Level of Service)								
INTERNATIONAL FEATURES								
• Taxes and duties				X	X		X	
• Offset requirements				X			X	
• Local content					X		X	
METHODS OF SOLUTION APPLIED								
• Benders Decomposition	X	X						X
• Decomposition with goal constraints			X					
• A variant of Benders Decomposition						X		X
• Factorization							X	
• A heuristic method				X				
• Commercial MIP solver								X
• LP solution by fixing binary variables				X				
0 – 1 VARIABLES AND CPU TIME								
• Maximum number of 0-1 variables	513	N/C	N/C	N/C	N/C	60	(1)	102
• Maximum number of constraints	8441	N/C	19841	3000	N/C	N/C	6000	1000
• Reported computational time (CPU sec.)	191	±1800	64	N/C	N/C	58	±60	154

N/C: Not clearly statet in the paper or not applicable

Table 5.3. Main international issues in selected global supply chain models

INTERNATIONAL ISSUE	[1]	[2]	[3]	[4]	[5]	[6]	[7]
STOCHASTIC FEATURES							
• Exchange rate fluctuation	X	X		X		X	
• Suppliers' reliability							X
• Reliability of transportation channels							
• Lead-times				X			
• Stochastic facility fixed costs	X						
• Stochastic demand			X				
• Uncertainty of market prices	X	X	X				
• Political environment							
• Stochastic customer service level							
TAXES AND DUTIES							
• Taxes and duties	X	X	X	X	X	X	X
• Modelling of profit repatriation issues							X
• Duty drawback and duty relief				X			
• Modelling of transfer prices	X	X					X
GENERAL FACTORS							
• Selection of manufacturing technology				X			
• Product differentiation by country							X
• Bill of Materials (BOM constraints)	X	X		X	X	X	
• Impact of economies of scale	X	X					
• Excess capacity determination							
• Financial decisions	X			X			X
• Infrastructure modelling			X				
• Cash flow modelling				X			X
• Information flow modelling							
• Global supply chain coordination				X			
• Modelling of competitors' actions				X			X
• Modelling of alliances							
TRADE BARRIERS							
• Quotas		X					
• Local content		X		X			
• Offset requirements			X	X			
• Subsidies		X					

References considered in Table 5.3:

[1] Hodder and Dincer (1986)
[2] Cohen et al. (1989)
[3] Cohen and Lee (1989)
[4] Cohen and Kleindorfer (1993)

[5] Arntzen et al. (1995)
[6] Vidal and Goetschalckx (2000)
[7] Vidal and Goetschalckx (1997b)

5.1.3   Strategic Supply Chain Modelling Challenges

A comprehensive model for strategic supply chain design must tie together the relevant decision variables and constraints related to the countries, periods, products, facilities, transportation channels, product flows and inventories. Inherently, these models will be very large which represents a significant challenge in itself and increases the difficulty of the other challenges identified below. In addition, the binary decision variables related to the status of facilities require the use of MIP solution algorithms which are not nearly as robust or efficient as LP or network flow algorithms.

At the current time three factors continue to make models for the design of global supply chains complex and very difficult to solve to optimality. The first factor includes all the complications created by taxation, duties, tariffs and local content rules and regulations in a global model which create a non-homogeneous domain for the supply chain. For example, a realized profit may not have the same value because of different tax rates, or the value of an otherwise identical product may be different depending on its country of origin. Models for these global supply chains will require more variables to keep track of the products that are now differentiated by their complete production history. Corporations in the short run can only respond to these regulations by varying either the materials flows in the supply chain or by changing the transfer prices. Incorporating transfer prices leads to non-linear (bilinear) models that are much harder to solve than the corresponding linear mixed integer models.

The second factor are the increasing velocity of the products in the supply chain and the accelerating life cycle of the products which have become even more constraining because of the inherent greater length in distance and time of global supply chains. A product may go from introduction, to demand exceeding capacity, to being phased out in a time span of six months. This implies that supply chain models have to decrease the length of a single planning period and have to incorporate more and more tactical and even operational features. The most important among them is the incorporation of pipeline, cycle and safety inventory. Typically strategic supply chain models restrict themselves to so-called linear safety inventory policies, where the safety inventory for a product is proportional to the average demand with the proportionality factor being determined by the customer service constraints, demand variation and replenishment lead-time. Including time-to-market and maximum-total-flow-time constraints in the supply chain models changes the formulation from the more common *arc-based formulations* to an origin-destination *path-based formulations*. This again increases significantly the number of variables for multi-echelon supply chain models.

The difference between arc-based and path-based formulations can best be illustrated with the following example. When modelling the flow of a product from supplier A, through distribution centre B, to the customer C, an arc-based formulation would have arcs from A to B and from B to C and *conservation of flow* constraints for the interior facility B. A path-based formulation would have a single path from A through B to C and would not need conservation of flow constraints, but in the full model there would be many more paths than arcs.

The third factor is the requirement that global supply chains at the same time should be efficient for the current set of economic conditions but also flexible and robust enough so that the chain can resist sudden shocks and changes and can adapt to constantly changing products, customers and suppliers. The facilities in a supply chain may have a useful economic life of twenty years, but the products flowing through the supply chain may completely change every few years. So the physical infrastructure must be efficiently enough to serve the current product needs but also generic enough to be able to serve different products in the future. A model to determine the best supply chain for a number of *scenarios*, each with a certain probability of occurrence, must include variables and constraints for each scenario. This again will increase the number of variables and constraints by a factor equal to the number of scenarios.

Models that incorporate all the features identified above will tend to be very large, complex and will no longer have the standard linear mixed integer structure. Specialized solution algorithms and heuristics will have to be developed to solve these models in a reasonable amount of computing time. At the same time corporations have come to realize that small deviations from optimality can result in significant financial consequences and are demanding more and more optimal solutions.

The increasing complexity of the models, the demand for near-optimal solutions and the complexity of the solution algorithms to achieve acceptable solution times, all require a high level of technical expertise in model development and solution algorithm execution. Even the ever increasing processing speeds and growing memory capacity of computers will not be sufficient to allow the use of standard non-specialized solution techniques. Very few organizations will have the technical expertise to build and solve their own models, but most will rely on third parties to provide them with this service.

5.2   Successful Applications of Strategic Supply Chain Modelling-Based Design

Arntzen et al. (1995) present a global supply chain model which minimizes a weighted combination of activity time and total system cost. The total system cost includes, in addition to the traditional cost components, the cost for major manufacturing styles and duties and duty drawbacks. The constraints include, in addition to the normal capacity, linkage constraints, material flow balance constraints and constraints on local content and offset trade. This model combines the spatial and temporal aspects of supply chain design. All production and transportation related costs considered in the objective function are weighted by a factor α. The objective function also contains production time and transportation time terms weighted by a factor $(1 - \alpha)$. They describe several large applications of the model to streamline the operations of the Digital Equipment Corporation with savings in the hundreds of millions of dollars. The authors stress the continuous improvement process of model building, application to case studies and increasing the level of sophistication and capabilities of the model.

Vidal and Goetschalckx (1997b) formulated a bilinear programming model to maximize the after tax profits for a multinational company by optimizing the *transfer prices* and the material flows in the supply chain. The model includes the traditional domestic costs and constraints and uses deterministic exchange rates. They developed a heuristic iterative procedure that alternates between optimizing the transfer prices and the material flows until a local optimum has been reached. A case-dependent upper bound and optimality gap are computed. Numerical experiments show that the computational effort and the after tax profit improvements over hierarchical heuristics increase with the size of the allowable range of the transfer prices. One of the main results was that the hierarchical design process where the transfer prices are first determined based on the tax rates and then the optimal product flows are determined can be significantly less profitable than an heuristic, integrated approach where both decisions are made simultaneously.

Dogan and Goetschalckx (1999) applied *Benders Decomposition* to solve a large, seasonal multi-period supply chain formulation very efficiently as compared to standard branch-and-bound with LP relaxation (see section 22.2 for an explanation). The main benefit of integrating the strategic network configuration with the tactical master planning was that the company decided to install less manufacturing capacity and to produce to inventory in the slower demand periods which yielded significant cost savings. Geoffrion and Powers (1995) observe that the large-scale models for strategic supply chain design have proven to be extremely difficult to solve to optimality without the application of Benders decomposition or factorization methods. They identify the problems whose structure is more tractable by applying Benders Decomposition methods, such as those with single sourcing of customer-specific product groups, bounds on the shipments of a given product at a given facility and piecewise linear approximations to nonlinear warehousing costs. However, they report that Benders decomposition is now being removed from the optimizers because of the level of technical resources and implementation effort that it requires to perform well.

The common thread among these and other successful applications of model-based strategic supply chain design is the sustained effort of a group of highly specialized designers, who exploited the structure of the problem to generate a formulation of acceptable size and degree of realism and a solution algorithm that had an acceptable computation time.

5.3   Modelling Features in Current APS

Some further definitions are required, to identify the features currently present in APS. An alternative-generating solution algorithm creates itself "feasible" solutions. An alternative-selecting algorithm selects the solution of the highest quality from a set of feasible candidate solutions provided to it as input parameters.

A prominent example in the design of supply chain systems of an alternative generating algorithm is the *location-allocation* problem, where the location of a given number of distribution facilities and the allocation of customers to these distribution facilities is to be determined. The decision space is the continuous area where the customers are located. Several optimal (single facility) or heuristic algorithms exist that will generate the location of the distribution facilities, see Domschke and Drexl (1996). However, even the optimal location derived from the model may be infeasible for the real-world system. Because the algorithm has to describe the cost of the configuration in mathematical expressions, exceptions to cost or constraints can be difficult to incorporate. In addition, since the algorithm determines the solution, a method must be developed to evaluate all possible solution configurations. This typically implies that simplified and approximated cost functions will be used. All of these factors combined indicate that the application of alternative generating algorithms is usually reserved for problems that have a simple cost and constraint structure.

On the other hand, alternative-selecting algorithms select a solution configuration from among a set of possible and feasible configurations. This implies that there exists an external mechanism to generate feasible configurations and evaluate the cost of these configurations. Typically this is a person or separate algorithm which is an expert for the problem domain. The solution of the alternative-generating phase may be used to narrow down the search for the candidate locations of the alternative-selecting phase.

The following review of modelling features in APS is based on Stadtler (2000) and discusses the Supply Network Planning modules of two APS vendors. Note that the features of the two APS vendors were not differentiated but rather a combined list of currently available features is given. So, some modelling features may not be available in a given APS (e. g. multi-period models).

The APS support multi-echelon and both single- and multi-period models. Note that only multi-period models allow modelling of the dynamics of markets and changes in the structure of a supply chain over time. Models can incorporate finite capacities for transportation channels and distribution and production facilities, while uncapacitated models may identify an extreme "blue sky" alternative. The facility status can either be determined by the algorithm or fixed by the designer and the optimal product flows are then determined by the algorithm. *Single sourcing* for all commodities combined as well as single sourcing by commodity from a vendor to a manufacturing plant or from a distribution centre to a customer can be modelled. Both profit and cost oriented *objective functions* can be modelled. *Non-linear costs* may be approximated by *piecewise linear* cost functions, e. g. representing different transportation modes (trucks, ship etc.) or economies of scale encountered in capacity expansion plans. Decreasing cost rates in the function of volume typically require the use of binary variables in the model, while increasing tax rates in function of profit do not require these additional binary variables. The additional binary variables can make the model significantly more difficult to solve. *Side constraints* and *inventory constraints* are possible, if modelled as purely linear expressions on material flows or facility status.

APS vendors expect users to develop scenarios e. g. describing the best, worst and expected case of future conditions. For each case a model is solved and may be analyzed and compared by the decision-maker. A single solution will then be implemented. However, this might not be an adequate way to cope with *stochastic features* and risks, since the best decisions in a stochastic environment will only by chance coincide with that of a certain scenario, see Eppen et al. (1989). On the other hand, building a stochastic formulation will increase the model size drastically and hence is not possible in APS today.

Standard solution algorithms and solvers for Linear and Mixed Integer Programming are used by APS within Strategic Network Planning. However, only a subset of the modelling features and algorithm tuning parameters available for standard MIP software has been selected for Strategic Network Planning, since it was regarded to be adequate for this module by an APS vendor. The advantage being that modelling features, data flows, storage and retrieval of solutions as well as powerful graphical representations of solutions have already been specified and are easy to use. Furthermore, some intelligent LP rounding heuristics which are not part of standard solvers have been included. Finally, special purpose alternative-generating solution algorithms have been implemented (Domschke and Drexl, 1996).

A complete redesign of a supply chain with the problem dimensions described in section 5.1 may require excessive computational times when using current APS if it can be modelled at all. However, an evaluation of a given supply chain structure and the allocation of resultant (optimal) material flows can be solved quickly for even the largest industrial cases. So, great expertise and care is needed to build realistic and solvable models utilizing the modelling features provided by the APS module Strategic Network Planning.

5.4   Conclusions

There will always exist a tradeoff between model solvability and model realism. The more realistic the model is, the more resources have to be allocated for model development and validation, data collection and validation, model maintenance and model solving. Since all models involve some level of abstraction, approximations and assumptions, the results of the models should always be interpreted carefully with common (engineering) sense. Different models with different levels of detail and realism are appropriate and useful at different stages of the design process. Systematically increasing the level of model complexity for the same problem and evaluating their solutions and their consistency provides a way to, at least partially, validate the models.

The more complex the real world system is, the more approximate any model will become. Models used to assist in strategic decision making are infamous for not capturing many of the real world factors and subjective influences (Vidal and Goetschalckx, 1996). Such strategic models should only be used as decision support tools for the design team. A healthy skepticism with respect to the results of any model is required. Just because a computer model specifies a particular decision does not imply that this is the best decision for the real world system.

To remain competitive global corporations need a methodology to evaluate and efficiently configure global logistics systems in a short amount of time. While at the current time, there exist several comprehensive models and solution algorithms for the design of single-country or domestic logistics systems, such methodology does not appear to exist for global logistics systems.

For domestic logistics systems, comprehensive and multi-period design models have been developed. The models are capable of determining the optimal configuration of the logistics system, including which manufacturing lines should be located in which facilities. They can also determine the production and inventory schedule for systems with seasonal demands. Computation times are in the order of tens of minutes for realistically sized problems. The simultaneous decision on facilities, manufacturing lines, production and inventory schedules can yield significant savings compared to the sequential decision process where first the facilities are located during the strategic network design phase and then the tactical production-distribution-inventory flows are determined during the master planning phase.

One of the most significant issues in global logistics systems is the incorporation of taxation, tariffs and duty relief effects. Since they are within the control of a corporation, determination of the transfer prices between subsidiaries of the global corporation will yield the most immediate benefits with minimal investment cost. Tax authorities have limited the flexibility to set these transfer prices, but at the current time, the prices can still be set within a prescribed interval. Making the decisions on transfer prices and material flows simultaneously may yield significant after tax profit increases for the corporation when compared to the most sophisticated sequential decision processes.

At the current time, the research trend is towards an integration and combination of the features of the domestic and global models which will allow the simultaneous optimization of facilities and production-distribution-inventory flows in a global logistics system. A second trend is towards the design of flexible and robust supply chains that are based on possible scenarios and stochastic data. It is clear that such a model and solution methodology can yield significant savings for a corporation interested in expanding globally. Significant challenges exist with respect to determining near-optimal solutions for these models.

A drawback of the newer models and solution algorithms is the significant level of technical expertise required to achieve the fast solution times. A very important area of future research is the standardization and technology transfer process of these solution methodologies so that they can be more widely applied. Global corporations implement ERP systems and Business Data Warehouses at ever increasing rates, providing APS and decision-makers with the basic data and information necessary for Supply Network Planning. It can be expected that models and methodologies currently available in APS will become more versatile in the near future and incorporate some of the features currently only discussed in the academic literature. This will allow these global corporations to use this information in a timely fashion to significantly increase their profits and to remain competitive.

References

Arntzen, B. C., Brown, G. G., Harrison, T. P., Trafton, L. L. (1995) *Global supply chain management at Digital Equipment Corporation*, Interfaces, Vol. 25, No. 1, 69–93

Ballou, R. H., Masters, J. M. (1993) *Commercial software for locating warehouses and other facilities*, Journal of Business Logistics, Vol. 14, No. 2, 71–107

Ballou, R. H., Masters, J. M. (1999) *Facility location commercial software survey*, Journal of Business Logistics, Vol. 20, No. 1, 215–233

Brown, G. G., Graves, G. W., Honczarenko, M. D. (1987) *Design and operation of a multicommodity production/distribution system using primal goal decomposition*, Management Science, Vol. 33, No. 11, 1469–1480

Cohen, M. A., Fisher, M., Jaikumar, R. (1989) *International manufacturing and distribution networks: A normative model framework*, in: Ferdows, K. (Ed.), Managing international manufacturing, Amsterdam, 67–93

Cohen, M. A., Kleindorfer, P. R. (1993) *Creating value through operations: The legacy of Elwood S. Buffa*, in: Sarin, R. K. (Ed.), Perspectives in Operations Management (Essay in Honor of S. Buffa), Boston, 3–21

Cohen, M. A., Lee, H. L. (1989) *Resource deployment analysis of global manufacturing and distribution networks*, Journal of Manufacturing Operations Management, Vol. 2, 81–104

Cohen, M. A., Moon, S. (1991) *An integrated plant loading model with economies of scale and scope*, European Journal of Operational Research, Vol. 50, 266–279

Domschke, W., Drexl, A. (1996) *Logistik: Standorte*, 4th ed., München, Wien

Dogan, K., Goetschalckx, M. (1999) *A primal decomposition method for the integrated design of multi-period production-distribution systems*, Research Report, IIE Transactions, Vol. 31, No. 11, 1027–1036

Eppen, G. D., Martin, R. K., Schrage, L. (1989) *A scenario approach to capacity planning*, Operations Research, Vol. 37, No. 4, 517–527

Geoffrion, A. M., Graves, G. W. (1974) *Multicommodity distribution system design by Benders decomposition*, Management Science, Vol. 20, No. 5, 822–844

Geoffrion, A. M., Powers, R. F. (1995) *20 years of strategic system design: an evolutionary perspective*, Interfaces, Vol. 25, No. 5, 105–127

Geoffrion, A. M., Graves, G. W., Lee, S. J. (1978) *Strategic distribution system planning: A status report*, Chapter 7 in: Hax, A. C. (Ed.), Studies in operations management, Amsterdam, 179–204

Graves, S. C., Rinnooy Kan, A. H. G., Zipkin, P. H. (Eds.) (1993) *Handbook in Operations Research and Management Science, 4: Logistics of production and inventory*, Amsterdam

Hodder, J. E., Dincer, M. C. (1986) *A multifactor model for international plant location and financing under uncertainty*, Computer & Operations Research, Vol. 13, No. 5, 601–609

Silver, E., Pyke, D., Peterson, R. (1998) *Inventory management and production planning and scheduling*, 3rd ed., New York

Stadtler, H. (2000), Personal communication, *Modelling features in two APS systems*

Tayur, S., Ganeshan, R., Magazine, M. (Eds.) (1999) *Quantitative models for supply chain management*, Boston, Massachusetts

Vidal, C. J., Goetschalckx, M. (1996) *The role and limitations of quantitative techniques in the strategic design of global logistics systems*, CIBER Research Report 96-023, Georgia Institute of Technology. Accepted for publication in the Special Issue on manufacturing in a global economy of the *Journal of Technology and Forecasting and Social Change*

Vidal, C. J., Goetschalckx, M. (1997a) *Strategic production-distribution models: A critical review with emphasis on global supply chain models*, European Journal of Operational Research, Vol. 98, 1–18

Vidal, C. J., Goetschalckx, M. (1997b) *A Global supply chain model with transfer pricing and transportation cost allocation*, School of Industrial and Systems Engineering Research Report, Georgia Institute of Technology. Accepted for publication in the *European Journal of Operational Research*

Vidal, C. J., Goetschalckx, M. (2000) *Modeling the impact of uncertainties on global logistics systems*, Journal of Business Logistics, Vol. 21, No. 1, 95–120

6 Demand Planning

Michael Wagner

University of Augsburg, Department of Production and Logistics,
Universitätsstraße 16, 86135 Augsburg, Germany

Large benefits which are achieved by Supply Chain Management are accredited to the reduction of inventories, esp. to the decrement of safety stocks. While safety stocks are mainly influenced by uncertainty, it is appealing that most effort should be spent on the reduction of uncertainty. Two sources of uncertainty are known in supply chains:

- process uncertainty (e. g. unreliable production processes, fluctuating lead-times etc.)
- demand uncertainty (difference in planned or estimated demand and actual sales)

The purpose of Demand Planning is to improve decisions affecting demand accuracy and the calculation of buffer or safety stocks to reach a predefined service level. All decisions in the whole supply chain should be based on already fixed (accepted) customer orders *and* planned sales or forecasts, the latter ones are determined in the Demand Planning process. Therefore, the performance of each supply chain entity depends on the quality of the demand plan. This also implies that these figures need to be the result of a collaborative effort.

The next section explains the different tasks of a demand planning process and shows which of the tasks should be supported by an APS.

6.1 A Demand Planning Framework

What are the results of Demand Planning and who needs it? This should be the first question in a Demand Planning implementation. Figure 6.1 shows all Demand Planning tasks and its planning horizon using the output of Demand Planning. For example, mid-term Master Planning will require demand forecasts for every product group, sales region and week and the safety stocks (as minimum stock levels) for every distribution centre or plant location. On the other hand, short-term replenishment decisions for finished products are based on daily forecasts for every product. Therefore, it is necessary to define the requirements of all planning tasks before deciding on Demand Planning tasks and their application. The structure of the forecasting part of Demand Planning depends heavily on the results one wants to get from it. Additionally the selection of forecasting methods requires knowledge of the corresponding forecasting horizon and the level of detail.

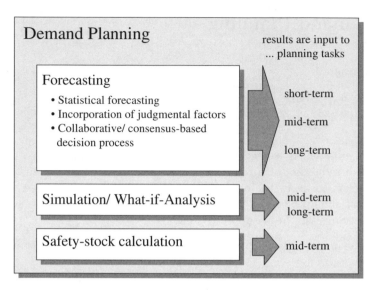

Fig. 6.1. Demand Planning tasks

The forecasting module of Demand Planning comprises the following three planning tools:

- Statistical forecasting uses sophisticated methods to create forecasts for a lot of items automatically. This might be the first step in the Demand Planning process and captures the main characteristics of the time series. A few statistical forecasting methods are described in the following Section.
- The second step uses the statistical forecasts and adds information to the time series which was not respected by the previous step. This input comprises information on promotions, marketing campaigns, change in the number of stores etc. and can be considered by manual corrections of the forecast or with the aid of the software tool. Here, the user provides the information on when the factor influences the forecast (e. g. promotion in sales region 3 in week 4) and the Demand Planning module calculates the corresponding quantities from former causal influences.
- As described above, the forecasting process has to be supported by a lot of supply chain members from different functional areas (sales, production, procurement etc.). Therefore, an efficient collaboration process is necessary to obtain a result which is accepted by all participants. The outcome of this process is a consensus-based forecast that is used for every planning step in the whole supply chain.

Forecasting, as described above, is not a real planning or decision process as it "only" aims at predicting the future as accurately as possible. But it does not influence the demand and therefore, for example, views the decisions on promotions as being given. Hence, changing demand requires an additional module: simulation/what-if-analysis. This tool enables the user to view the consequences of different scenarios. This allows to plan promotions (when and where?), the shape of the life-cycle curve or decide on the point in time at which a new product will be launched.

So far, forecasting appears to be quite easy and seems to be a reliable tool to create reliable input to the processes distribution, production and procurement. But, as Nahmias (1997) argues in his textbook, the main characteristic of forecasts is that they are usually wrong! Therefore, each planning step which is based on Demand Planning data contains uncertainty to some extent. The difference between the production or distribution quantity (result of planning based on forecasts) and actual sales (customer orders) influences the service level of the whole supply chain. As this service level usually can not reach 100%, safety stocks are an adequate tool for improving customer service. The amount of safety stock required for reaching a desired service level is closely linked to forecasting, as the forecast error is input to the calculation.

Demand Planning means predicting future sales; therefore, it is necessary to incorporate all information available in a supply chain which could be relevant. But this information is often only specific and stored decentrally. For example, a sales person may "only" provide input to the forecasting process of the products and the sales region he/she is responsible for. All information pieces finally should add to a forecast which covers the whole demand being served by the supply chain. On the other hand one must be able to retrieve forecasts aggregated for special purposes, like demand figures aggregated to product groups and weeks for Master Planning. Therefore, the database of Demand Planning has to support at least the following three dimensions (see also Fig. 6.2) of aggregations and disaggregations:

- product dimension: product → product group → product family → product line
- geographic dimension: customer → sales region → DC region/location
- time dimension: different bucket size (days → weeks → years) and horizon

The product dimension is structured in a hierarchy, relating products to product groups, groups to families, families to product lines etc. The product hierarchy ranges from the top level representing all products to the lowest product level on which a forecast is created. The geographic dimension is also hierarchically structured. It represents the structure of the market, for example regions, countries, industry branches, key accounts etc. The third dimension of forecasting is time. The time dimension is normally structured by years, quarters and months. In some cases it is necessary to go down to the week or even day. Forecast quantities can be attached to any intersection of product, geography and time.

Such three-dimensional databases grow very fast even for mid-sized companies. State-of-the-art database technology, as efficient relational systems

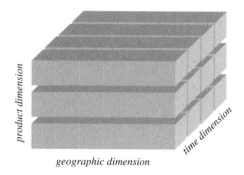

product dimension

time dimension

geographic dimension

Fig. 6.2. Three-dimensional structure of demand planning data

or Data Warehouses plus modern OLAP (online analytical processing) tools, build the bottom line of a high-performance Demand Planning solution.

But, as many people work on one forecast it is evident that all this subjective information could be contradictory. This contradiction is either resolved by a hierarchical structure of forecast responsibilities or by a collaboration process among the concerned planners.

Responsibilities for demand planning tasks can be organized in process chains. For each process the characteristics (e. g. frequency of the process, peculiarities of the three dimensions) need to be defined during the implementation. Typical process chains for mid-term forecasting in the computer industry and in the food industry are described in the following:

Computer Industry

Sales forecast (dimensions: regions, finished product groups, months)
  The sales force builds the sales forecast which estimates the quantities for the sales region they serve. This forecast is aggregated to product groups (e. g. high-end business PC), because the product which will be offered is determined afterwards.
Headquarter forecast (dimensions: all regions, finished products, months)
  In the headquarter the sales forecast for the distinct regions is added up and refined according to single products. This is possible since the headquarter forecast is a collaborative process of representatives from sales, marketing, material management etc.
Component forecast (dimensions: all regions, components, months)
  The forecast for the components which have to be procured from suppliers is not computed by applying the bill-of-materials (BOM) to the finished product forecast. This is not possible, since the BOM change very fast, because the life-cycle of certain components (e. g. hard disks) is shorter than the life-cycle of the computer. Therefore, the planner forecasts the percentage to which a specific component is build in a finished product and deviates the component forecast there from.

Food Industry

Sales forecast (dimensions: regions, finished products, weeks)
  In the food industry the sales forecast is already detailed to single products and weeks. It also comprises additional demand which is expected to result from promotional activities (e.g. special prices for specific customers) in the sales regions.
Collaborative forecast (dimensions: all regions, finished products, weeks)
  The sum of the sales forecasts is the basis for the collaborative forecast. It considers additional information on marketing activities (e.g. TV-sport), the launch of new products and the activities of competitors. The collaborative forecast is made by managers from sales, production, marketing and procurement.
Procurement forecast (dimensions: all regions, components, weeks)
  The procurement forecast in the food industry can be calculated easily by applying the BOM to the collaborative forecast.

6.2   Statistical Forecasting Techniques

Forecasting methods were developed since the 1950's for business forecasting and at the same time for econometric purposes (e.g. unemployment rates etc.). The application in software modules makes it possible to create forecasts for a lot of items in a few seconds. Therefore, all leading APS vendors incorporate statistical forecasting procedures in their demand planning solution. Each of these methods tries to incorporate information on the history of a product/item in the forecasting process for future figures. But, there exist two different basic approaches – time-series-analysis and causal models. The so-called *time-series-analysis* assumes that the demand follows a specific pattern. Therefore, the task of a forecasting method is to estimate the pattern from the history of observations. Future forecasts can then be calculated from using this estimated pattern. The advantage of those methods is that they only require past observations of demand. The following demand patterns are most common in time-series-analysis (see Silver et al. (1998) and also Fig. 6.3):

1. Level model: The demand x_t in a specific period t consists of the level a and random noise u_t which cannot be estimated by a forecasting method.

$$x_t = a + u_t \qquad (6.1)$$

2. Trend model: The linear trend b is added to the level model's equation.

$$x_t = a + b \cdot t + u_t \qquad (6.2)$$

3. Seasonal model: It is assumed that a fixed pattern repeats every T periods (cycle). Depending on the extent of cyclic oscillations a multiplicative or an additive relationship can be considered.

$$x_t = (a + b \cdot t) + c_t + u_t \quad \text{additive model,} \tag{6.3a}$$

$$x_t = (a + b \cdot t) \cdot c_t + u_t \quad \text{multiplicative model} \tag{6.3b}$$

where $c_t = c_{t-T} = c_{t-2T} = \ldots$ are seasonal indices (coefficients).

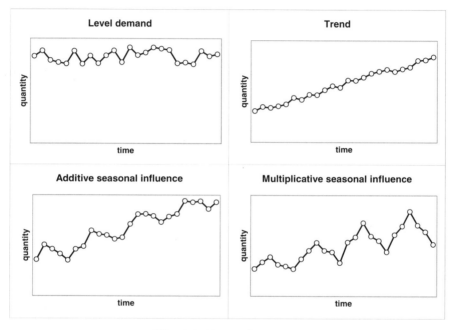

Fig. 6.3. Demand patterns

The second approach to statistical forecasting are *causal models*. They assume that the demand process is determined by some known factors. For example, the sales of ice cream might depend on the weather or temperature on a specific day. Therefore, the temperature is the so-called leading indicator for ice cream sales. If enough observations of sales and temperature are available for the item considered, then the underlying model can be estimated. For this example, the model might consist of some amount of independent demand z_0 and the temperature factor $z^1(t)$

$$x_t = z^0 + z^1(t) \cdot w_t + u_t \tag{6.4}$$

where w_t is the temperature on day t.

As for parameter estimation in causal models the demand history and one or more time-series with indicators are needed, the data requirements are much higher than for time-series analysis. Furthermore, practical experience shows that simple time-series models often produce better forecasts than complex causal models (see e.g. Silver et al. (1998, pp. 130)). These tend to interpret stochastic fluctuations (noise) as "structure" and therefore, introduce a systematic error in the model.

In the following three paragraphs the characteristics and the approach of the most frequently used forecasting methods are described. The first part introduces the forecasting techniques used for time-series models.

6.2.1   Moving Average and Smoothing Methods

As each demand history is distorted by random noise u_t, the accurate estimation of parameters for the model is a crucial task. Also, the parameters are not fix and might change over time. Therefore, it is necessary to estimate under consideration of actual observations *and* to incorporate enough past values to eliminate random fluctuations (conflicting goals!).

Simple Moving Average   The simple moving average (MA) is used for forecasting items with level demand (see Sect. 6.1). The parameter estimate for the level $\hat{a}$ is calculated by averaging the past n demand observations. This parameter serves as a forecast for all future periods, since the forecast $\hat{x}_t$ is independent of time. According to simple statistics, the accuracy of the forecast will increase with the length n of the time-series considered, because the random deviations get less weight. But this is no more applicable if the level changes with time. Therefore, values between three and ten often lead to reasonable results for practical demand series. But the information provided by all former demands is lost according to this procedure.

Exponential Smoothing   The need to cut the time-series is avoided by the exponential smoothing method, because it assigns different weights to all (!) observed demand data and incorporates them into the forecast. The weight for the observations is exponentially decreasing with the latest demand getting the highest weight. Therefore it is possible to stay abreast of changes in the demand pattern and to keep the information which was provided by older values. For the case of level demand the forecast for period $t + 1$ will be calculated according to the following equation:

$$\hat{x}_{t+1} = \hat{a}_t = \alpha \cdot x_t + \alpha(1 - \alpha) \cdot x_{t-1} + \alpha(1 - \alpha)^2 \cdot x_{t-2} + \ldots \qquad (6.5)$$

The parameter α is the smoothing constant, to which values between 0 and 1 can be assigned. For $\alpha = 0.2$ the weights in Table 6.1 are being used, if the forecast has to be made for period 1. Furthermore it is not necessary to

Table 6.1. Weights of past observations in exponential smoothing for $\alpha = 0.2$

period	0	-1	-2	-3	-4	...
weight	0.2	0.16	0.13	0.10	0.08	...

store the whole history of an item as (6.5) can be simplified. The only data which needs to be kept in the database are the latest forecast and the latest demand value.

Exponential smoothing for level demand patterns is easy to apply and requires little storage capacity. Therefore, it provides good forecasts for this kind of model and it also calculates reasonable forecasts for items which are influenced by high random fluctuations (Silver et al., 1998).

The exponential smoothing procedure for level demand can be extended for trend models and multiplicative seasonal models (see (6.2) and (6.3b)). The method for the trend model is known as Holt's procedure (see e. g. Nahmias (1997)). It smoothes both terms of the model, the level a and the trend component b with different smoothing constants α and β.

Winters introduced the seasonal model with exponential smoothing. A lot of lines of business are facing seasonal patterns, but don't incorporate it in forecasting procedures. For example, consider the manager of a shoe store, who wants to forecast sales for the next two weeks in daily buckets. As sales are usually higher on Saturdays than on Mondays, he has to take the weekly "season" into account. Winters method is an efficient tool to forecast seasonal patterns, because it smoothes the estimates for the three parameters a, b and c. In contrast to the former two models the seasonal method needs far more data to initialize the parameters. For reliable estimates for the seasonal coefficients it is necessary to consider at least two cycles of demand history (e. g. two years). For more details on Winters model see Chap. 21.

6.2.2   Regression Analysis

Where significant influence of some known factors is present, it seems to be straightforward to use causal models in the forecasting process. Regression analysis is the standard method for estimation of parameter values in causal models. Usually linear dependencies between the dependent variable x_t (e. g. the demand) and the leading factors (independent variables; e. g. temperature, expenditures for promotions etc.) are considered. Therefore, a multiple regression model can be formulated as follows (see e. g. Hanke and Reitsch (1995)):

$$x_t = z_0 + z_1 \cdot w_{1t} + z_2 \cdot w_{2t} + \dots \qquad (6.6)$$

The ice cream model in (6.4) is called the simple regression model, as it only considers one leading indicator. Multiple linear regression uses the method of least squares to estimate model parameters $z_0, z_1, z_2, \dots$. This procedure minimizes the sum of the squared difference between the actual demand and the forecast the model would produce. While exponential smoothing can consider all past observations, the regression method is applied to a predefined set of data. The drawbacks of such a procedure are the same as for the moving average model. Further, the weight of all considered values equals one and therefore the model cannot react flexibly to changes in the demand pattern.

As the data requirements of linear regression models are much higher than for simple time-series models, it is obvious that this effort is only paid back, if the models are used for aggregate mid-term or long-term forecasts or for a few important end products.

The following example shows the application of linear regression for the ice cream model: Assuming that the ice cream retailer observed the following demands and temperatures (°C) over 10 days (Table 6.2) the linear regression

Table 6.2. Demand and temperature data for the ice cream example

period	1	2	3	4	5	6	7	8	9	10
actual demand	43	45	54	52	54	55	43	33	52	51
temperature (°C)	15	17	19	16	21	22	18	15	19	18

will calculate the equation

$$\text{demand } x_t = 8.24 + 2.22 \cdot w_{1t} \tag{6.7}$$

with w_{1t} being the temperature on day t. Using (6.7) one can determine the forecasts (model value) which the model would have produced (see Table 6.3). But, for this it is necessary to be able to estimate the temperature reliably. Figure 6.4 shows the data and the resulting forecasts for the ice cream model.

Table 6.3. Example forecasts using the linear regression model

period	1	2	3	4	5	6	7	8	9	10
model value	42	46	50	44	55	57	48	42	50	48

6.2.3 ARIMA/Box-Jenkins-method

While both model-types described above assume statistical independence of demand values in different periods, the autoregressive integrated moving-average (ARIMA) models explicitly consider dependent demands. Therefore, these methods don't make assumptions about the underlying demand pattern, but compose a function from different building-blocks which fits the

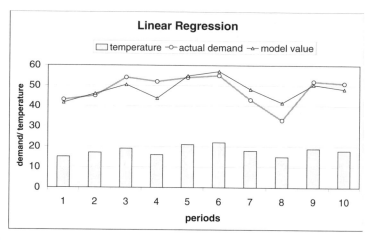

Fig. 6.4. Linear regression: results for the ice cream model

observed data best. The model function is found by iteratively executing the following three steps (see Hanke and Reitsch (1995)):

1. *Model identification:* An appropriate ARIMA model is selected by comparing the autocorrelation of the theoretical distributions and the observed autocorrelation. Autocorrelation states the existence of correlation between the actual demand and observations somewhere back in time.
2. *Model estimation:* As in regression models the parameters of the forecasting function have to be estimated in ARIMA models. Therefore, the procedure searches for values which minimize the mean squared error of the model.
3. *Testing of the model:* If the error term is purely random and independent, then the model is assumed to be reliable.

As one can imagine from the above procedure, the Box-Jenkins-method requires much experience and significant input from the demand planner. Further, the initial estimation of the model should be based on at least 50 observations of demand. Therefore, ARIMA models might be suitable only for some important A-class items or for mid-term aggregate forecasts. But, if ARIMA models are utilized, the quality should be better than for simple time-series models or even causal models.

6.3 Incorporation of Judgmental Factors

Implementing an efficient demand planning process usually comes along with supporting the human planner with software tools. When it comes to statistical methods and their application one typical question arises: How is the software able to make better forecasts than a human planner with years of experience in demand planning? The simple answer is that mathematical methods are unbiased. Empirical studies (see e. g. Makridakis et al. (1997)) give evidence, that bias is the main reason why myopic statistical methods often produce better result. But that's only half of the truth, because information on specific events or changes (e. g. promotional activities, customer feedback on new products etc.) can lead to significant changes in demand patterns which might not be considered in standard time-series models. Therefore, it is necessary to combine the advantages of both worlds in an integrated demand planning process.

For example, consider the demand planning process of a company selling mineral water. In such an environment the regular demand can be forecasted by a seasonal time-series model quite accurately. But, the demand series are distorted by occasional additional demand due to promotional activities in some retail outlets. This effect can be estimated by the sales force responsible for the promotion, while the base line is forecasted by a fitting statistical model.

Integration of statistical and judgmental forecasting is only reasonable, if information inherent in a statistical forecast is not considered in the judgmental process. In this case the information would be double counted and therefore the demand would be overestimated.

In the following we describe some methods on how to integrate statistical forecasting and *structured* judgment. Non-structured judgment is often applied by demand planners, if they check the figures produced by a decision-support tool and "tune" the values using their sure instinct. But, for integration purposes it is necessary to structure judgment. Detailed process definitions and guidelines create a framework for such a structured judgment. Armstrong and Collopy in Wright and Goodwin (1998) describe the following five procedures for the integration:

- revised judgmental forecasts:
  The first step in this procedure is made by demand planners, who create judgmental forecasts based on the knowledge of relevant data (e. g. historical data, causal factors etc.). Afterwards they are confronted with forecasts which are calculated using statistical methods. Then the planners have the possibility to revise their initial estimate incorporating the new information. But, there is no predefined percentage to which extent each of the components has to be considered in the final forecast. This procedure often leads to more accurate forecasts than simple judgment not aided by statistical methods. Furthermore, it has the advantage that it leaves the control over the demand planning process to the human planner.
- combined forecasts:
  As the above procedure assigned variable weights to the two forecasts, it is evident that these values are often biased or influenced by political

means. A more formal procedure is assured by combining the two values according to a predefined weighting scheme. Even if equal weights are assigned to judgmental forecasts and statistical forecasts, better results are possible.

- revised extrapolation forecasts:
  Modifying statistical forecasts manually to take specific domain knowledge of the planner into account is common practice in a lot of companies. But, the revision process has to be structured accordingly. This means that the judgmental modification has to be based on predefined triggers (e. g. promotions, weather etc.).
- rule-based forecasts:
  Rule-based forecasts are also based on statistical forecasts. But, the selection or combination of different forecasting methods is supported by structured judgments of experts. The rules used for the selection are derived from the specific knowledge of the experts or on past research. They are based on characteristics of time-series or on causal factors. Rule-based forecasting improves simple extrapolation methods especially, if the series have low variability and low uncertainty.
- econometric forecasts:
  Regression models are referred to as econometric forecasting methods, if the model selection process and the definition of causal variables is provided by structured judgment. Improvements are reported especially, if this procedure is applied to long-range forecasts. As bias could have much impact on the result of econometric forecasts, it is advisable to give the judgmental process a very rigid structure.

Structured judgment needs to be supported by detailed feedback mechanisms which show the planner the quality of his input. Therefore, error reports have to differentiate between the quality of (automatic) statistical forecasting and judgmental forecasts.

6.4   Additional Features

The implementation of demand planning needs to address the specific requirements of the partners working together in the supply chain. Therefore, it is essential to understand the time-series under consideration. Depending on the characteristics of the series and the dimensions (time, product, geography) of the forecast different forecasting procedures have to be utilized. Some of the implementation issues which have to be taken into account are described in the following paragraphs. In the last part of this Section additional functionality for specific demand planning tasks is introduced. These are not necessary in each branch of business, but they would be helpful if those problems are present.

6.4.1 Sporadic Demand

We call a time-series sporadic (intermittent), if no demand is observed in quite a lot of periods. Those demand patterns especially occur for replacement parts or if only a small part of the demand quantity is forecasted; for example the demand for jeans in a specific size on one day in a specific store might be sporadic. The usage of common statistical forecasting methods would produce large errors for those items. Additional judgmental forecasting would not increase the quality, because the occurrence of periods with no demand is usually pure random and therefore not predictable. Furthermore, sporadic demand often occurs for a large amount of C-class items, for which it would be appreciable to get forecasts with low costs and low time effort for human planners.

Therefore, efficient procedures for automatic calculation of forecasts for sporadic demand items were developed. These methods try to forecast the two components "occurrence of period with positive demand" and "quantity of demand" separately. For example, Croston's method (see Silver et al. (1998) or Tempelmeier (1999)) determines the time between two transactions (demand periods) and the amount of the transaction. The update of the components can then be done by simple exponential smoothing methods. Significant reduction of the observed error is possible, if the sporadic demand process has no specific influence which causes the intermittent demand pattern. For example, the frequent occurrence of stockouts in a retail outlet could produce a time-series that implies sporadic demand.

6.4.2 Lost Sales vs. Backorders

Forecasts are usually based on the demand history of an item. But, while industrial customers (B2B) often accept backorders, if the product is not available, the consumer (B2C) won't. Therefore, the amount of observed sales equals the amount of demand in the backorder case, but in the lost-sales case the sales figures might underestimate the real demand. For forecasting purposes the demand time-series is needed and therefore, must be calculated from the observed sales figures. This problem frequently occurs, if forecasts for the point-of-sales (retailers, outlets) should be calculated.

There are two generally different solution approaches for the problem of forecasting in presence of lost sales: The first one tries to calculate a virtual demand history which is based on the sales history and the information on stock-outs. The forecasts can then be computed on the basis of the virtual demand history. This approach delivers good results, if the number of stock-outs is quite low. An alternative solution to the lost-sales problem is the usage of sophisticated statistical methods which consider the observed sales as a censored sample of the demand sample (see e.g. Nahmias (1997)). For these methods it is necessary to know the inventory management processes which were/are applied for the products under consideration.

6.4.3   Measuring Forecast Accuracy and Triggering Exceptions

Why do we measure forecast accuracy? First of all, it is *not* a tool for the controller to check the quality of the demand planner's work. It is rather a building block in the demand planning process. The demand planner might check whether the statistical method is appropriate for the time-series, whether additional human judgment pays back or wether it is useful to incorporate information on promotions. In all cases a criterion is needed for the evaluation of his decisions. But, there are many ways to get the appropriate forecast accuracy.

All accuracy measures are based on the forecast error e_t. It is defined as the difference between the forecasted quantity $\hat{x}_t$ and the actual quantity x_t: $e_t = \hat{x}_t - x_t$. This value of the forecast error is influenced by the following parameters:

- The time delta between forecast and actuals: Forecasting is aiming at providing information about future shipments, sales etc. Normally, it is easier to tell the nearer future than the future that is far away. Thus, the forecast accuracy strongly depends on the time between the forecast creation and the time period that is being forecasted. For example, consider a forecast for the sales volume in June this year. The sales forecast for the month of June that has been created in March normally has a lower accuracy than the forecast that has been created in May.
- The forecast granularity: The level of aggregation also has a strong impact on the forecast accuracy. Take sales forecast again as an example: It is easier to forecast the total sales volume for all products, for all geographic areas and for a complete fiscal year, than to forecast on a weekly basis low level product groups for all sales regions individually. Thus, the forecast accuracy normally decreases if the forecast granularity increases.

There are many methods to compute the forecast accuracy, based on the forecasting error e_t. Each measure is calculated for a fixed horizon n (in the past) which has to be defined by the planner. If the horizon is short, then the value reacts fast to deviations from the average, but then it also might fluctuate heavily due to random demand variations. The following three measures (see e. g. Silver et al. (1998)) are most common in practice and also in demand planning software:

$$\text{mean squared error (MSE)} = \frac{1}{n} \sum_{i=1}^{n} e_i^2 \qquad (6.8)$$

$$\text{mean absolute deviation (MAD)} = \frac{1}{n} \sum_{i=1}^{n} |e_i| \qquad (6.9)$$

$$\text{mean absolute percentage error (MAPE)} = \left[\frac{1}{n} \sum_{i=1}^{n} \left| \frac{e_i}{x_i} \right| \right] \cdot 100 \qquad (6.10)$$

The MSE is the variance of the forecast error in the time horizon under consideration. In the Linear Regression forecasting procedure the MSE is used as the objective function which is minimized. As the error is squared in the formula, large deviations are weighted more heavily than small errors. Whereas the MAD uses linear weights for the calculation of the forecast accuracy. Further, the meaning of the MAD is easier to interpret, as it can be compared with the demand quantity observed. The main drawback of the two measures above is the lack of comparability. The values of MSE and MAD are absolute quantities and therefore, cannot be benchmarked against other products with higher or lower average demand. But, the computation of the MAPE standardizes the value based on the observed demand quantities x_i. The result is a percentage-value for the forecast accuracy which is comparable to other products.

The measures described above allow detailed analysis of the past, but they need to be discussed from the beginning each time they are calculated. In demand planning tools for some 100 or 1000 items one wants an automatic "interpretation" of the forecast error and therefore, might need an alert or triggering system. This system should raise an alert, if the statistical forecasting procedure no more fits to the time-series or if the sales office didn't provide the information on a sales promotion. Such an alert system can be triggered by thresholds which are based on one of the measures for the forecast accuracy. These thresholds are defined by the demand planner and updated under his responsibility. Besides the threshold technique some other triggering mechanisms have been developed which all are based on the forecast accuracy measured by MSE or MAD.

6.4.4   Model Selection and Parameter Estimation

The selection of a forecasting model and the estimation of necessary parameters[1] are issues which are raised in the implementation phase of demand planning or during the update of forecasting parameters. This update should be made more or less regularly (e.g. every year) but not too often, as this would result in too much nervousness. APS often provide some kind of automatic model selection and parameter estimation. Thereto, the user only has to define the time-horizon on which the calculation should be based. The system then searches all available statistical forecasting procedures and parameter combinations and selects the one which produces the best forecast accuracy in the specified time-segment. As a result the user gets a list with the forecasting method and the corresponding parameters for each product/item he should implement. Therefore the demand planner doesn't have to check if a model fits the time-series under consideration (e.g. "Are the sales figures really seasonal or does the system only interpret random fluctuations?") and can use the toolset of statistical methods like a black box.

---

[1] so-called pick-the-best option

But, practical experience shows that the long-term performance is better and more robust, if only 1-3 forecasting methods with equal parameter settings for a group of products are applied. This follows from the following drawbacks of the described automatic selection:

- The time-horizon should cover enough periods to get statistically significant results. But often the history of time-series is relatively short when demand planning is introduced first.
- The criterion for the evaluation is mostly one of the forecast accuracy measures described above. However, those values don't tell you anything about the robustness of the models' results.
- For the selection procedure three distinct time-segments are necessary:
  - In the first segment the models components are initialized. For example for Winters seasonal model 2-3 full seasonal cycles (e. g. years) are necessary to calculate initial values for the seasonal coefficients.
  - The second segment of the time-series history is used to optimize the parameter values. Therefore, the parameters are changed stepwise in the corresponding range (grid-search) and the forecast accuracy is measured.
  - The optimized parameters are used to get forecasts for the third time-segment which is also evaluated using the forecast accuracy. This accuracy value is then the criterion for the selection of the best forecasting model.

  The setting of the length of each of the time-segments has significant influence on the result of the model selection. Mostly the user has no possibility to change those settings or even can not view the settings in the software.

Therefore, the automatic model selection can guide an experienced demand planner while searching for the appropriate proceeding. But, it is not suggestive to use it as a black box.

6.4.5   Life-Cycle-Management and Phase-in/Phase-out

In quite a lot of innovative businesses, like the computer industry, the life-cycles of certain components or products were reduced to less than a year. For example, high-tech firms offer up to three generations of a hard-disk every year. As common statistical forecasting procedures require significant demand history, it would take the whole life-cycle until useful results are gathered. But, since new products replace old products with almost the same functionality, it is plausible to reuse some information on the demand curve for the next generation.

Two main approaches are known in practice: The first one indexes the complete time-series and determines the life-cycle-factor which has to be multiplied with the average demand to get the quantity for a specific period in the life-cycle (*life-cycle-management*). This method is able to stay abreast of arbitrary types of life-cycles. The only information needed for the application for new products is the length of the cycle and the estimated average demand. These two values are adapted continuously when observed demand data gets available during the "life" of the product.

The second approach (*phasing method*) divides the whole life-cycle in three phases. The "phase-in" describes the launch of a new product and is characterized by the increase of the demand according to a certain percentage (linear growth). Afterwards the series follows a constant demand pattern, as considered for the statistical forecasting procedures. During the "phase-out" the demand decrease along a specific percentage until the end of the life-cycle of the product. The only data necessary for the phasing model are the lengths of the phases and the in-/decrease-percentages.

For successful application of the above models it is necessary that the APS provides the functionality to build a "model library". In this database life-cycles or phasing models are stored for each product group under consideration. Mostly only one life-cycle exists for the whole product group and this model is updated every time a life-cycle ends.

6.4.6 Safety Stocks

Most APS-providers complement their Demand Planning module with the functionality for safety stock calculation. This is intuitive since the forecast error is one of the major factors influencing the amount of stock which is necessary to reach a specific service level. The calculation of safety stocks is quite complex, as there exist many different formulas each for a specific problem setting. The demand planner's task hereby is to check whether the prerequisites are met in his application. While this Chapter cannot provide a fully detailed overview on safety stocks and inventory management, we want to focus on the functionality which can be found in most APS-systems. For further information the reader is referred to one of the inventory management books by Silver et al. (1998) or Nahmias (1997).

Most software tools offer safety stock calculations for "single-stage inventory systems". This means that it is assumed that there exists only one single stocking point from which the demand is served. Multi-stage or multi-echelon systems (e. g. distribution chains with DC- and retailer-inventories) on the other hand have the possibility to store safety stocks on more than one stage.

For single-stage systems the amount of necessary safety stock ss is generally determined by the product of the standard deviation of the forecast error during the risk time σ_R and the safety factor k:

$$\text{safety stock } ss = k \cdot \sigma_R \tag{6.11}$$

Assuming that the variance of the forecast error in the future is the same as in the past, σ_R can be calculated by multiplying the standard deviation of the forecast error[2] σ_e with the square root of the risk time $\sqrt{R}$. The length of the risk time depends on the inventory management system. The following two systems have to be distinguished:

- periodic review system:
  In such an environment the inventory position is reviewed only every t time periods (review interval). Each time the inventory is reviewed, an order is triggered and sent to the supplying entity (e. g. the production department, the supplier). The delivery is assumed to be available after the replenishment lead-time L. Therefore, the risk time equals the sum of the review interval and the replenishment lead-time: $R = L + t$.
- continuous review system:
  In continuous review systems the point in time at which an order is released is triggered by a predefined reorder point. If the inventory position falls below the reorder point, an order of a specific quantity q is released. The risk time in a continuous review system equals only the replenishment lead-time L: $R = L$.

But that is only half of the safety stock formula. The safety factor k represents all other determinants of the safety stock. In the following the determinants and some of their values are explained:

- service level:
  For the service level quite a lot of definitions exist. The most common ones are the following:
  - cycle- or α-service level:
    α is defined as the fraction of periods in which no stock-out occurs. Therefore, the safety stock has to ensure the probability (which fits the companies business objectives) of no stock-out during the replenishment cycle.
  - fill rate (β-service level): The fill rate is the order quantity of a product which can be met directly from stock.
  - order fill rate: While the fill rate considers the smallest unit of measurement of a product, the order fill rate counts *complete* customer orders served from stock.
- review interval or order quantity:
  In periodic review systems the review interval is fixed and the order quantities depend on the estimated demand in an order cycle. For continuous review systems the opposite applies, as the order quantity is fixed and the length of the order cycle depends on the demand. But, if the demand is approximately level, both parameters can be converted in each other by the simple relation:
  order quantity $q =$ demand $d\cdot$ cycle length t.
  The required parameter can be calculated by minimizing the ordering

---

[2] calculated from past time-series

costs and the holding costs for the lot-sizing stock. This computation can be made by applying the well-known economic order quantity (EOQ)-formula (e. g. Silver et al. (1998)).

- demand distribution function:
  The distribution function of the observed demand is usually approximated by a standard distribution known ¿from statistics. One of the most common distribution functions is the normal distribution. The distribution parameters (mean and variance) can easily be calculated from a sample of demands from the historic time-series.

All these parameters have to be combined in a formula which stays abreast the requirements of the business under consideration. Now, it should be clear that an APS-tool can only provide safety stock calculations if specific assumptions are met. But, if all parameters are user-definable the software can cover a wide range of different settings. Therefore, it is necessary to transfer the inventory management rules which are applied in the company to the standard parameters which are needed in the software. And that is the challenge of the demand planner.

As the above part on safety stock calculation should only give a short impression on the complexity of inventory management, the inspired reader can gather more information in one of the inventory management books listed at the end of this Chapter.

References

Hanke, J. E.; Reitsch, A. G. (1995) *Business forecasting*, 5th ed., Englewood Cliffs et al.

Makridakis, S. G.; Wheelwright, S. C.; Hyndman, R. J. (1997) *Forecasting: methods and applications*, 3rd ed., New York et al.

Nahmias, S. (1997) *Production and operations analysis*, 3rd ed., Chicago et al.

Silver, E. A.; Pyke, D. F.; Peterson, R. (1998) *Inventory management and production planning and scheduling*, 3rd ed., New York et al.

Tempelmeier, H. (1999) *Material-Logistik: Modelle und Algorithmen für die Produktionsplanung und -steuerung und das Supply Chain Management*, 4th ed., Berlin et al.

Wright, G.; Goodwin, P. (1998) *Forecasting with judgment*, New York et al.

7 Master Planning

Jens Rohde[1] and Michael Wagner[2]

[1] Darmstadt University of Technology, Institute of Business Administration,
Department of Operations and Materials Management, Hochschulstraße 1,
64289 Darmstadt, Germany

[2] University of Augsburg, Department of Production and Logistics,
Universitätsstraße 16, 86135 Augsburg, Germany

The main purpose of *Master Planning* is to synchronize the flow of materials along the complete supply chain. It supports the mid-term decisions on effective utilization of production, transportation, supply capacities, seasonal stock (along the lines of Anthony (1965)) and balancing of supply and demand. As a result of this synchronization, production and distribution entities are able to reduce inventory levels. This reduction is mainly founded in the redundancy of buffers between entities to enable a durable flow of material, caused by decentral decision processes. Due to decreasing variance of production and distribution quantities by coordinated plans, safety stocks can be reduced.

To synchronize the flow of materials effectively it is important to decide on the use of capacities of each entity of the supply chain, e. g. regular and overtime shifts. As Master Planning covers mid-term decisions (see Chap. 3) it is necessary to consider at least one seasonal cycle to be able to balance all demand peaks. The decisions on production and transportation quantities need to be addressed simultaneously while minimizing total costs for inventory, overtime, production and transportation.

The results of Master Planning are targets (directives) for Production Planning and Scheduling, Distribution and Transport Planning as well as Material Requirements Planning. For example, Production Planning and Scheduling (module) has to consider the amount of planned stock at the end of each master planning period and the reserved capacity up to the planning horizon. The use of specific transportation lines and capacities are examples of directives for Distribution and Transport Planning. Section 7.1 will illustrate the Master Planning decisions and results in detail.

However, it is not possible and even not reasonable to perform optimization on detailed data. An aggregation of products and materials to product groups and material groups, respectively and concentration on bottleneck resources is necessary. Not only a reduction in data can be achieved, but also the uncertainty in mid-term data and the model's complexity can be reduced. Model building including the aggregation and disaggregation processes is discussed in Sect. 7.2.

A master plan should be generated centrally and updated periodically. These tasks can be divided into several steps. The steps and how the results are used in further steps are described in Sect. 7.3.

7.1   The Decision Situation

Based on demand data from the Demand Planning module, Master Planning has to create an aggregated production and distribution plan for all supply chain entities. It is important that this is done with respect to available capacity and dependencies between the different production and distribution stages. Such a capacitated plan for the whole supply chain leads to a synchronized flow of materials without creating large buffers between these entities.

To make use of the Master Planning module it is necessary that production and transportation quantities can be divided and be produced in different periods. Furthermore, intermediates and products should be stockable (at least for several periods) to be able to balance capacities by building up inventories. At least, the production process should not have large output variations, otherwise deterministic planning like it is done in Master Planning will not make sense.

The following options have to be evaluated, if bottlenecks on production resources occur:

- produce in earlier periods while increasing seasonal stock,
- produce in alternative sites with higher production and/or transportation costs,
- produce in alternative production modes with higher production costs,
- buy products from a vendor with higher costs than own manufacturing costs,
- work overtime to fulfil the given demand with increasing production costs and possible additional fixed costs.

It is also possible that a bottleneck occurs in transportation lines. In this case the following alternatives have to be taken into consideration:

- produce and ship in earlier periods while increasing seasonal stock in a distribution centre,
- distribute products using alternative transportation modes with different capacities and costs,
- deliver to customers from another distribution centre.

The only way to solve these problems optimally is to consider the supply chain as a whole and to generate a solution with a centralized view while considering all relevant costs and constraints. Otherwise decentral approaches lead to bottlenecks in other locations and suboptimal solutions.

To generate feasible targets, a concept of anticipation is necessary. This concept should predict the (aggregate) outcomes of lower levels' decision-making procedures resulting from given targets as precisely as possible within the context of Master Planning. Furthermore, it should be less complex than performing complete planning runs at the lower planning levels. A simple example for anticipation is to reduce the periods' production capacity by a fixed amount to consider setup times expected from lot wise production. However, in production processes with large varying setup times, dependent on product mix, this concept may not be accurate enough and more appropriate solutions for anticipating setup decisions have to be found (for further information see Schneeweiss (1999) and Stadtler (1998)).

The following paragraphs introduce a short example to depict this decision situation. It will be used in this chapter to illustrate the decisions of Master Planning and to show the effects, results and the data used.

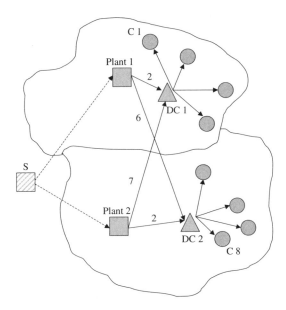

Fig. 7.1. Example of a supply chain

The supply chain in Fig. 7.1 has two production sites (Plant 1 and Plant 2) with one distribution centre each (DC 1 and DC 2). Two different products are produced in a single-stage process in each plant. The customers are served from their local *distribution centre* (DC) which usually receives products from the nearest production site. However, it is possible for a distribution centre to receive products from the plant in the other area, but this leads to higher transportation costs. Products can only be stored in the DCs. The regular production capacity of each production unit is 80 hours per week (two shifts, five days). It is possible to extend this capacity by working overtime.

A third production unit (supplier S) leads to a multi-stage production problem and – in this example – to a common capacity restriction for the production of parts. In the remainder of this chapter the third production unit is not regarded.

7.1.1   Planning Horizon and Periods

The planning horizon is characterized by the interval of time for which plans are generated. All data in this horizon is known with certainty. It is important to select a planning horizon that covers at least one seasonal cycle or an integer multiple. Otherwise it is not possible to balance capacities throughout a season, and hence, peaks in demand are possibly not covered. If e. g. demand peaks occur in the last quarter of a year and only half a year is considered, it is not possible to balance this peak during planning of the second half (see following simplified example, Tables 7.1–7.3). Often the planning horizon for Master Planning covers twelve months.

Table 7.1. Seasonal demand peak

Quarter	1	2	3	4
Demand	12	13	10	**45**
Capacity available	20	20	20	20

Table 7.1 shows the quarterly demand and the available capacity. Producing one part takes one capacity unit. If it is not possible to extend capacity, a plan with a horizon of two quarters leads to the infeasible plan shown in Table 7.2. While considering a whole seasonal cycle (in this case four quarters) a feasible plan can be derived (see Table 7.3).

Table 7.2. Infeasible solution

Quarter	1	2	3	4
Demand	12	13	10	45
Capacity available	20	20	20	20
Capacity used	12	13	20	**35**

Table 7.3. Feasible solution

Quarter	1	2	3	4
Demand	12	13	10	45
Capacity available	20	20	20	20
Capacity used	20	20	20	20

As we have already seen in the previous example, the planning horizon is divided into several periods, so-called *time buckets*. The length of these periods must be chosen carefully with respect to the lead-times on every stage of the supply chain (often a week or month). In *bucket-oriented* Master Planning, the lead-time of each process[1] that uses potential bottleneck resources is usually defined as one time bucket or an integer multiple. A potential bottleneck resource might cause delays (waiting times) due to a high utilization rate. It is also possible that one might neglect the lead-time of some activities performed on non-bottleneck resources. Then a part has to be produced in the same bucket as its predecessor and successor, respectively. This imprecision may lead to directives that may not be disaggregated into feasible schedules at the lower planning levels, but shorter planned lead-times. The other possibility with one bucket or an integer multiple is that it regularly leads to more appropriate directives, but extends the planned lead-times artificially caused by modelling.

Shorter time buckets result in a more accurate representation of the decision situation and the lead-time modelling, but imply a higher complexity for the planning problem. Higher complexity, inaccuracy of data in future periods and the increasing expenditure for collecting data support the trade-off between accuracy and complexity. Furthermore, it is possible only via big time buckets to plan in quantities and not with individual orders or product units.

Another possibility is the use of varying lengths for different periods. That is, the first periods represent shorter time buckets to enable more exact planning on current data. The more one reaches the planning horizon the bigger the chosen time buckets are. However, this approach poses problems with modelling of lead-time offsets between production and distribution stages (see also Chap. 3).

To work on current data, it is necessary to update the Master Plan in discrete intervals of time. By updating, new reliable demand forecasts and known customer orders are considered in the new plan. During the *frozen horizon* (see also Chap. 3) the master plan is implemented. The look ahead of several periods is necessary to be able to balance capacities as already mentioned.

7.1.2 Decisions

There is a trade-off between costs for inventories, production, transports and capacity extension. The corresponding quantities which are produced, moved or stored need to be determined by the master planning process.

Production quantities (for each time bucket and product group) are mainly determined through the production costs and the available capacity. But these

---

[1] Here, a process is an aggregation of several successive production and transportation activities (see also Sect. 7.2.3).

quantities also depend on whether the capacity is extended by additional shifts which has to be modelled as a decision variable in Master Planning. Not only production capacity, but also transportation capacity (e. g. capacity of available transportation means) on the links between plants, warehouses and customers needs to be planned by the Master Planning model. Decisions on setups and changeovers are taken into account in Master Planning only if a lot usually covers more than a period's demand. Otherwise the decision is left to Production Planning and Scheduling and setup times are anticipated through flat reduction of available capacity in Master Planning.

While the transportation capacities set only a frame for the quantities which could be carried from A to B, the decision on the transportation quantity (for every product group and time bucket) needs to be addressed, too. Since most often linear transportation costs are considered in mid-term planning, it is possible only to determine the quantities and not the detailed loading of single trucks.

If production and transportation quantities are determined, the stock levels are known. Furthermore, inventory variables are used to account for inventory holding costs.

Decision variables in the *example* are:

- production quantities for every product, period and plant,
- transportation quantities for every transportation link plant – DC, every product and period,
- ending inventory level for every product, period and DC,
- overtime for every plant in every period.

7.1.3   Objectives

As described in the previous section a model for Master Planning has to respect several restrictions when *minimizing total costs*. The costs affecting the objective function depend on the decision situation. Within Master Planning they do not have to be as precise as within e. g. accounting systems, they are only incorporated to find out the most economical decision(s). A single example may clarifiy the point. When there are two products sharing the common bottleneck as in the previous example, it would only be needed to know which of the two products has the least inventory cost per capacity unit used. This will be the product to stock first, irrespective of "correct costs", as long as the relation between the costs remains valid.

In most master planning settings products can be stored at each production site and DC, respectively. Therefore, the inventory holding costs (e. g. for working capital, handling) have to be part of the objective function. Furthermore, the ability of extending capacity by additional shifts or transportation means has to be taken into account. Therefore, the corresponding costs need to be considered in the objective function. Also, variable production costs may differ between production sites, and thus, are part of the master planning process. If lot-sizing decisions should be made in Master Planning, it is necessary to incorporate costs for setups as well.

Sometimes Master Planning models are extended to optimize supply decisions which means that the different prices of the suppliers also have to be considered in the objective function.

Every stage of the production-distribution network is connected to other parts of the supply chain by transportation links which are associated with transportation costs. Usually only variable linear cost rates for each transportation link and an adequate lead-time offset are considered in mid-term Master Planning.

The objective function of the *example* minimizes to the sum of

- production costs (variable cost rate · production quantity),
- inventory holding costs (cost rate · inventory level),
- additional costs for using overtime (cost rate · amount of overtime),
- transportation costs (cost rate on a link · transportation quantity).

7.1.4 Data

The data for Master Planning are received from different systems and modules. The forecast data which describe the demand of each product and product group, respectively, in each period in the planning horizon are a result of Demand Planning.

Capacities need to be incorporated for each potential bottleneck resource (e. g. machines, warehouses, transportation). If the company gives transportation orders to third-party carriers with 100% availability, then it would not be necessary to put transportation capacities into the model. But if capacity extensions for higher cost rates are possible, then this additional amount of capacity has to be considered with the respective cost rates. For the calculation of necessary capacity, production efficiency and production coefficients have to be put into the model. While a Master Planning model often abstracts from changeovers, it is advisable to reduce the available capacity by a certain percentage.

The BOMs of all products (groups) form the basis of the material flows within the model and provide the information on input-output coefficients. For every storage node (e. g. warehouse, work-in-process inventory) minimum (e. g. safety stocks and estimated lot-sizing stocks) and maximum stock levels need to be defined for each product (group) which the model has to consider during the planning procedure.

Additionally all cost elements which where noted in the above section are input to the model.

Data for the *example* are:

- forecasts for each sales region and product in every period,
- available regular capacity for each plant (machine) and period,
- maximum overtime in each plant,
- the production efficiency of products produced in specific plants (in tons of finished products per hour),
- the minimum stock levels at each DC and for every product (e. g. safety stocks).

7.1.5 Results

The results of Master Planning are the optimized values of decision variables which are sent to other planning modules as targets. Some decision variables even have only planning character and are never put into practice, as they are determined in other modules in more detail (e. g. production quantities are planned in Production Planning and Scheduling).

Therefore, the most important results are the planned capacities (in each bucket for every resource (group) and transportation link) and the amount of seasonal stock at the end of each time bucket. Both cannot be determined in the short-term planning modules, because they need to be calculated under consideration of the complete seasonal cycle. Production capacities are input to Production Planning and Scheduling and seasonal stock (eventually plus additional other stock targets) at the end of each Master Planning bucket is set as a minimum stock level in detailed scheduling.

Capacity extensions like overtime, additional shifts or additional trucks need to be put into practice for the frozen period, as they often cannot be influenced afterwards. The same applies to procurement decisions for special materials with long lead-times or those which are purchased on the basis of a basic agreement.

Results in the *example* are:

- seasonal stock which is the difference between the minimum stock and the planned inventory level for every product, period and DC,
- amount of overtime for every plant in every period which should be reserved.

7.2 Model Building

In most APS Master Planning is described by a *Linear Programming* (LP) model. However, some constraints (including binary and integer variables, respectively) imply to convert the LP model to a more complex *mixed integer programming* (MIP) model. Regularly, MIP models cannot be solved in an economic time (see Chap. 22). In this section we will illustrate the steps of building a Master Planning model and how complexity depends on modelled decisions. Furthermore, it is explained how complexity can be reduced by aggregation and how penalty costs should be used for finding (feasible) solutions.

Though it is not possible to give a comprehensive survey of all possible decisions, this chapter will show the dependence between complexity and most common decisions. In contrast to perfect reproduction of reality, Master Planning needs a degree of standardization (i. e. constraints to be modelled, objectives etc.), at least for a line of business. Thus, it is possible to use a Master Planning module that fits after adjusting parameters (i. e. costs, BOMs and routings, regular capacities etc.) and not after building new mathematical models and implementing new solvers.

7.2.1 Modelling Approach

Figure 7.2 shows a general approach for building a supply chain model which can be applied to most APS.

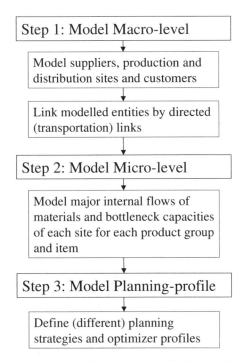

Fig. 7.2. Building a supply chain model

Step 1: Model Macro-level

In the first step key-customers, key-suppliers and production and distribution sites of the supply chain are modelled. These entities are connected by directed transportation links. In some APS, transportation links are modelled as entities and not as directed connections[2]. Result of this step is a general network of supply chain entities.

For our example (Fig. 7.1) in this step the two plants (Plant 1 and Plant 2) and the distribution centres (DC 1 and DC 2) are modelled. That is, their locations and eventually their types (e. g. production entity and distribution entity) are determined. Afterwards, the key-supplier (S) and the key-customers (C 1, ..., C 8) are specified. The supplier (S) does not represent a potential bottleneck, hence, he should not be modelled explicitly in this step. The customers represent the demand of products for the supply chain. Finally, the transportation links are modelled. These can be used for a simple lead-time offset of production decisions or for modelling of capacitated transportation constraints.

Step 2: Model Micro-level

Each entity of the supply chain can be modelled in more detail in the second step if required. All resource groups that could turn out to become a bottleneck should be modelled for each entity and transportation line. The internal flows of materials and capacities of potential bottlenecks are defined for each product group and item (group). The dependence between product and item groups is mapped via input and output materials for each process. Table 7.4 shows selected features which can be modelled in APS.

For our example capacities and costs are modelled for each entity and transportation link. Plant 1 has a regular capacity of 80 units per time bucket. Each unit of overtime costs 5 monetary units (MU) without fixed costs and producing one part of Product 1 or Product 2 has linear costs 4 of MU. Plant 2 has nearly the same structure except for linear production costs of 5 MU for each produced unit. Then, the internal structure of each distribution centre is modelled. The storage of each distribution centre is uncapacitated. DC 1 has linear storage costs for Product 1 of 3 MU per product unit per time bucket and for Product 2 of 2 MU per product unit per time bucket. DC 2 has linear storage costs of 4 and 3 MU for one unit of product 1 and 2, respectively, per time bucket. Finally, the transportation links are modelled on the micro-level. All transportation links are uncapacitated. Transportation costs from Plant 1 to DC 1 are linear with 2 MU per unit of both Products 1 and 2 and to DC 2 a costs 3 MU per product unit is incurred. The transport from Plant 2 to DC 1 and 2 costs 5 and 2 MU per product unit, respectively. Transportation from the distribution centres to customers is not relevant.

---

[2] For example i2 Technologies' Supply Chain Planner (see also Chaps. 15, 17 and 18).

Table 7.4. Selected model features of Master Planning in APS

Process	Parameter	Characteristic
Procurement	purchase costs	linear
		piecewise linear
Production	production costs	linear
		piecewise linear
	production quantities	continuous
		semi-continuous
	capacity	regular capacity
		enhanced capacity with linear costs per extra unit
	capacity requirement	fixed or linear
Storage	inventory costs	linear
	capacity	regular capacity
		enhanced capacity with linear costs per extra unit
Distribution	transport costs	linear
		piecewise linear
	transport quantities	integer
		partially integer
	capacity	regular capacity
		enhanced capacity with linear costs per extra unit
Sales	lateness	maximum lateness
		linear penalty costs
	not fulfilled	linear penalty costs

Step 3: Model Planning-profile

The last step is to define a planning-profile. Defining the planning-profile includes the definition of resource calendars, planning strategies for heuristic approaches and profiles for optimizers. Planning strategies could include how a first feasible solutions is generated and how improvements are obtained. Optimizer profiles could include different weights for parts of the objective function (e. g. inventory costs and transportation costs). For example, an optimizer profile that forces production output could be chosen within a growing market.

The example of this chapter should be solved by Linear Programming. The only objective is to minimize total costs (see also Chap. 22). A planning-profile would instruct the Master Planning module to use an LP-solver without special weights for different parts of the objective function.

7.2.2 Model Complexity

Model complexity and optimization run time are (strongly) correlated. For this reason, it is important to ask which decisions lead to which complexity of the model. Thus, it is possible to decide on the trade-off between accuracy and run time. The more accurate a model should be, the more are the decisions to be mapped. But this implies increased run time and expenditure for collecting data. This section will show the correlation between decisions described in this chapter and a model's complexity.

The main *quantity decisions* that have to be taken into consideration in a Master Planning model are production and transport quantities. For these quantities integer values are mostly negligible at this aggregation level. Mainly, they are used to reserve capacity for potential bottleneck resources. Because they are rough capacity bookings it is justifiable to abstract from integer values. If different production or transportation modes can be used partially, additional quantity decisions for each mode, product and period are neccessary. Other important quantity decisions are stock levels. They result from corresponding production and transportation quantities and stock levels of the previous period.

Capacity decisions occur only if it is possible not to utilize complete regular capacity or to enhance capacity of certain supply chain entities. One aspect of enhancing regular capacity is by working overtime. This implies a new decision about the amount of overtime in each period for each resource. Additional costs have to be gathered. If it is only possible to introduce complete extra shifts the problem is much harder. Binary decisions have to be made if extra shifts are introduced in certain periods (and for certain resources) to take fixed costs for a shift (e. g. personnel costs for a complete shift) into account. Performance adjustments of machines usually lead to non-linear optimization models. Computational efforts, and thus, solvability of such models decrease sharply.

Decisions concerning production and transportation processes are e. g. decisions about the usage of alternative routings. This possibility will increase the model's complexity by new decisions and more data. However, if it is not possible to split production and transportation quantities to different resources – e. g. deliver customers from not more than one distribution centre – the processes are concerned. In contrast to the quantity decision for different modes described above, additional binary decisions about the chosen mode have to be made.

7.2.3   Aggregation and Disaggregation

Another way to reduce complexity of the model is *aggregation*. Aggregation refers to a reasonable grouping and consolidation of time, decision variables and data to achieve complexity reduction for model and data volume (Stadtler, 1988, p. 80). Data basis' accuracy can be enhanced by less variance within an aggregated group and higher planning levels are unburdened from detailed information.

Furthermore, inaccuracy increases in future periods. This inaccuracy, e. g. in case of demand of product groups, can be balanced by reasonable aggregation if forecast errors of products within a group are not totally correlated. Therefore, capacity requirements for aggregated product groups (as a result of Master Planning) are more accurate, even for future periods.

Aggregation of time, decision variables and data will be depicted in the following. Regularly, these alternatives are used simultaneously.

Aggregation of Time

This is the consolidation of several smaller periods to one large period. It is unreasonable to perform Master Planning e. g. in daily time buckets. To collect data in an adequate accuracy for such small time buckets for one year in the future which is mostly the planning horizon in mid-term planning is nearly inoperable. Therefore, Master Planning is regularly performed in weekly or monthly time buckets. If different intervals of time buckets are used on different planning levels, the disaggregation process raises the problem of giving targets for periods in the dependent planning level that do not correspond to the end of a time bucket in the upper level. To solve this problem, varying planning horizons of lower planning levels can be chosen (see Fig. 7.3).

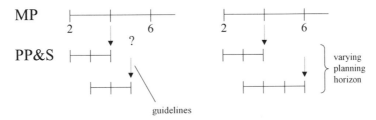

Fig. 7.3. Aggregation of time

Aggregation of Decision Variables

Generally, aggregation of decision variables refers to the consolidation of production quantities. In the case of Master Planning, transportation quantities have to be aggregated, too. Bitran et al. (1982) suggest aggregating products with similar production costs, inventory costs and seasonal demand to product types. Products with similar setup costs and *identical* BOMs are aggregated to product families. A main problem for Master Planning that is not regarded by the authors is the aggregation of products in a multi-stage production environment with *non-identical* BOMs. The similarity of BOMs and also transportation lines is highly important. But the question of what similarity means remains unanswered. Figure 7.4 illustrates the problem of aggregating BOMs. Products P 1 and P 2 are aggregated to product type

P 1/2 where the average quotas of demand of P 1/2 are $\frac{1}{4}$ for P 1 and $\frac{3}{4}$ for P 2. The parts A and B are aggregated to part type AB. The aggregated BOM for P 1/2 shows that one part of P 1/2 needs one part of type AB and $\frac{1}{4}$ part of part C (caused by average quota for demand). Producing one part of type AB means producing one part A and two parts B. The problem is to determine a coefficient for the need of type AB in product P 3 (an aggregation procedure for a sequence of operations in discussed in Stadtler (1996) and Stadtler (1998)). Shapiro (1999) remarks with his 80/20-rule that in most

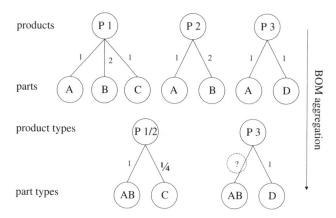

Fig. 7.4. BOM aggregation (following Stadtler (1988, p. 90))

practical cases about 20% of the products with the lowest revenues regularly make the main product variety. This products can be aggregated to fewer groups while those with high revenues should be aggregated very carefully and selectively. However, it is important to perform an aggregation with respect to the decisions that have to be made. If setup costs are negligible for a certain supply chain, it does not make sense to build product groups via similar setup costs. No product characteristic, important for a Master Planning decision, should be lost within the aggregation process.

Aggregation of Data

Aggregation of data is the grouping of e. g. production, transportation and inventory capacities, purchasing bounds and demand data. Demand data are derived as directives from Demand Planning module and have to be aggregated with respect to aggregation of products. Particularly, aggregating resources to resource groups cannot be done without considering product aggregation. There should be as few interdependencies as possible between combinations of products and resources. Especially in Master Planning, transportation capacities have to be considered in addition to production and inventory capacities. Due to the various interdependencies between decision variables and data, these aggregations should be done simultaneously.

7.2.4 Using Penalty Costs

A model's solution is guided by the costs chosen within the objective function. By introducing certain costs that exceed the relevant costs for decisions (see Sect. 7.1.3), these decisions are penalized. Normally, relevant costs for decisions differ from costs used for accounting, e. g. only variable production costs are considered without depreciations on resources or apportionments of indirect costs. *Penalty costs* are used to represent constraints that are not explicitly modelled. Master Planning has to fulfil all demand requests in time. To avoid infeasible plans it can be necessary to penalize unfulfilled demand. Similarly, if setup times are not explicitly considered, the loss of time on a bottleneck resource can be penalized by costs correlated to this loss of time.

To be able to interpret the cost value derived from the objective function correctly, it is important to separate the costs taken from accounting and penalty costs. Regularly, penalty costs exceed other costs by a very high amount. To obtain the "regular" costs of a master plan and not only the penalized costs of a solution this separation is indispensable. Among others, the following penalties can be inserted in the objective function:

- setup costs to penalize the loss of time on bottleneck resources (if not explicitly modelled),
- costs for unfulfilled demand and late deliveries of finished products and parts,
- costs for enhancing capacity (especially overtime) to penalize its use explicitly,
- additional production costs for certain sites to penalize e. g. minor quality,
- penalty costs for excessive inventory of customer specific products.

7.3 Generating a Plan

This section will illustrate which different steps have to be performed to generate a Master Plan and how to use Master Planning effectively. Figure 7.5 shows these steps in an overview.

As already mentioned, the Master Plan is incrementally updated e. g. in weeks or months. By this update, new and accurate information like actual stock levels and new demand data are taken into consideration. Before a planning run can be performed it is necessary to gather all relevant data (see Sect. 7.1). This can be a hard task, as data are mostly kept in different systems throughout the supply chain. However, to obtain accurate plans this task should be done very seriously. To minimize expenditure in gathering data, this process should be done with a high degree of automation. For the

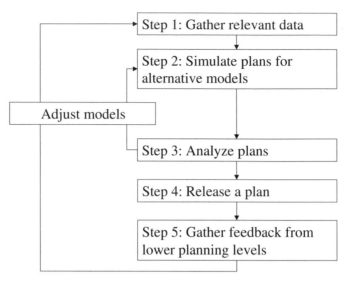

Fig. 7.5. Steps in Master Planning

Table 7.5. Demand data

Period		1	2	3	4	5
Product 1	Sales region 1	20	30	30	50	40
Product 2	Sales region 1	50	40	60	40	50
Product 1	Sales region 2	40	30	30	40	40
Product 2	Sales region 2	50	40	50	60	50

previous example, the paramters described in Sect. 7.2.1 and the demand
data shown in Table 7.5 are gathered.

Most APS provide the possibility to simulate alternatives. Several models
can be built to verify e. g. different supply chain configurations or samples
for shifts. Furthermore, this simulation can be used to reduce the number of
decisions that have to be made. For example, *dual values* of decision variables
can be used after analyzing the plans to derive actions for enhancing regular
capacity (see Chap. 22).

In the next step the "best" plan is chosen. That is, one has to decide which
plan of simulated alternatives should be implemented. If this is done manually, subjective estimations influence decisions. On the other hand, influences
of not explicitly modelled knowledge (e. g. about important customers) are
prevented by an automatic decision. Table 7.6 shows the planned production
quantities for the example. The transportation quantities correspond to the
production quantities, except for transport of Product 1 from Plant 1 to the
DCs in the first period. 20 units of Product 1 produced in Plant 1 are delivered to DC 1, 10 are delivered to DC 2 to meet the demand of Sales region 2,

Table 7.6. Production quantities

Period		1	2	3	4	5
Product 1	Plant 1	30	30	30	50	40
Product 2	Plant 1	50	50	50	40	50
Product 1	Plant 2	30	30	30	40	40
Product 2	Plant 2	50	40	50	60	50

though transportation costs are higher. Seasonal stock is only built in the second period for Product 2 in DC 2, amounting to 10 product units. Overtime is necessary for both plants in periods four and five. Plant 1 utilizes 10 time units of overtime each, Plant 2 utilizes 20 and 10 time units, respectively. The costs for the five periods planning horizon are shown in Table 7.7.

Table 7.7. Costs for five periods

Production	3,780.00
Transportation	250.00
Inventory	1,690.00
Overtime	20.00

After the master plan's directives are forwarded to the decentral decision units, detailed plans are generated. The results of these have to be gathered to derive important hints for model adjustments. For example, if setups considered by a fixed estimate per period result in infeasible plans, it is necessary to change this amount. Once an adequate master plan has been generated, decisions of the first period(s) are frozen and the process of rolling schedules is continued.

References

Anthony, R. N. (1965) *Planning and control systems: A framework for analysis*, Cambridge

Bitran, G. R.; Haas, E. A.; Hax, A. C. (1982) *Hierarchical production planning: a two-stage system*, in: Operations Research, Vol. 30, 232–251

Schneeweiss, C. (1999) *Hierarchies in distributed decision making*, Berlin et al.

Shapiro, J. F. (1999) *Bottom-up vs. top-down approaches to supply chain modeling*, in: Tayur, S.; Ganeshan, R.; Magazine, M. (Eds.) Quantitative models for supply chain management, Dordrecht, The Netherlands, 737–760

Stadtler, H. (1988) *Hierarchische Produktionsplanung bei losweiser Fertigung*, Heidelberg

Stadtler, H. (1996) *Mixed integer programming model formulations for dynamic multi-item multi-level capacitated lotsizing*, in: European Journal of Operational Research, Vol. 94, 561–581

Stadtler, H. (1998) *Hauptproduktionsprogrammplanung in einem kapazitätsorientierten PPS-System*, in: Wildemann, H. (Ed.) *Innovationen in der Produktionswirtschaft – Produkte, Prozesse, Planung und Steuerung*, München, 163–192

Tempelmeier, H. (1999) *Material-Logistik: Modelle und Algorithmen für die Produktionsplanung und -steuerung und das Supply Chain Management*, 4th ed., Berlin et al.

8 Demand Fulfilment and ATP

Christoph Kilger[1] and Lorenz Schneeweiss[2]

[1] j & m Management Consulting GmbH, Kaiserringforum, Willy-Brandt-Platz 6, 68161 Mannheim, Germany
[2] KPMG Consulting GmbH, Olof-Palme-Straße 31, 60439 Frankfurt a.M., Germany

The planning process that determines how the actual customer demand is fulfilled is called *demand fulfilment*. The demand fulfilment process determines the first promise date for customer orders and – thus – strongly influences the order lead-time and the on time delivery.[1] In today's competitive markets it is important to generate fast and reliable order promises in order to retain the customers and increase market share. This holds particularly true in an eBusiness environment: Orders are entered online in the eBusiness frontend, and the customer expects within a short time period to receive a reliable due date. Further, eBusiness solutions have to support online inquiries where the customer requests a reliable due date without committing the order.

The fast generation of reliable order promises gets more complex

- as the number of products increase,
- the average product life cycles get shorter,
- the number of customers increase,
- flexible pricing policies are being introduced and
- demand variations increase and get less predictable.

The traditional approach of order promising is to search for inventory and to quote orders against it; if there is no inventory available, orders are quoted against the production lead-time. This procedure may result in non-feasible quotes, because a quote against the supply lead-time may violate other constraints, e. g. available capacity or material supply.

Modern demand fulfilment solutions based on the planning capabilities of APS employ more sophisticated order promising procedures, in order

1. to improve the on time delivery by generating reliable quotes,
2. to reduce the number of missed business opportunities by searching more effectively for a feasible quote and
3. to increase revenue and profitability by increasing the average sales price.

In the following section, the principles of APS-based demand fulfilment solutions are described and the basic notion of ATP (available-to-promise) is

---

[1] In the following, we use the terms *order promising* and *order quoting* synonymously, as well as the terms *promise* and *quote*.

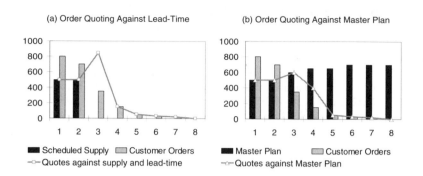

Fig. 8.1. Demand wave beyond the standard lead-time

introduced. Section 8.2 introduces the concept of allocation planning, resulting in allocated ATP (AATP). Section 8.3 illustrates the AATP-based order promising process by means of examples.

8.1 Available-to-Promise (ATP)

8.1.1 The Role of Master Planning

The main target of the demand fulfilment process is to generate fast and reliable order promises. The quality of the order promises is measured by the on time delivery KPI as introduced in Chap. 2. Using the traditional approach – quoting orders against inventory and supply lead-time – often will result in order promises that are not feasible, decreasing the on time delivery.

Figure 8.1 illustrates this by means of a simple example. Consider a material constrained industry like the high-tech industry, and let us assume that a specific component has a standard lead-time of two weeks. There are receipts from the suppliers scheduled for the next two weeks and – as we assume a material constrained industry – no additional supply will be available for the next two weeks. The volume of the orders on hand for week 1 and week 2 is exceeding the volume of the scheduled receipts. Figure 8.1 (a) illustrates this situation. Standard MRP logic is to schedule all orders against the scheduled receipts and – if not all orders can be satisfied by that – against the standard lead-time (in our example two weeks). In other words, MRP assumes infinite supply beyond the standard lead-time and creates supply recommendations based on the order backlog. The grey line in Fig. 8.1 (a) shows the quotes created by the MRP logic. In week 3 (i.e. after the standard lead-time) all orders are scheduled that cannot be quoted against the scheduled receipts. It is quite clear that the fulfilment of this "demand wave" will not be feasible,

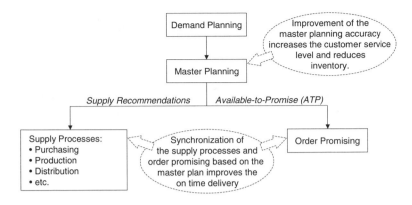

Fig. 8.2. Master Planning as the common basis of supply chain processes and order promising

as the available supply will most probably not increase by 100% from one week to the next week.

The master planning process (see Chap. 7) has the task to create a plan for the complete supply chain, including purchasing decisions. Thus, master planning creates a plan for future supply from the suppliers even beyond the already existing scheduled receipts.[2] The idea of APS-based demand fulfilment is to use this information to create reliable order quotes. Figure 8.1 (b) shows the master plan and the orders quoted against the master plan. For week 3 the master plan reflects the constraints of the suppliers, anticipating a slight increase of the supply volume that is considered to be feasible. As orders are quoted against the master plan the unrealistic assumption of infinite supply beyond the standard lead-time is obsolete – resulting in more reliable order promises.

In most APS – and also ERP systems – the master plan quantities that form the basis for order promising are called *Available-to-Promise (ATP)*. ATP is bucketized, typically in weeks.

Figure 8.2 summarizes the role of master planning. The master planning process is based on the demand plan that reflects the capability of the market to create demand. During the master planning process all material, capacity and lead-time constraints of the supply chain are applied to the demand plan, resulting in a feasible master plan. This plan is the common basis for the supply processes (supply recommendations for purchasing, production and distribution) and the order promising process (available-to-promise quantities). By that, supply is synchronized with order promising, resulting in reliable order quotes. As a consequence the on time delivery is improved.

---

[2] For week 1 and 2 the master plan reflects the scheduled receipts.

Please note that the accuracy of the master plan has – within certain bounds – no direct impact on the on time delivery. If the master plan does not mirror future orders very well the supply is not aligned with the orders at hand *and* orders receive a late, but reliable promise. However, the accuracy of the master plan does affect the customer service level (e. g. the order lead-time) and the inventory level. If orders come in as planned by the master plan the supply matches the demand, the number of inventory turns increases and orders receive a good promise within a short lead-time.

8.1.2 Granularity of ATP

Granularity of ATP Along the Product Dimension

In a make-to-stock environment (see Chap. 2) the standard way to represent ATP is on finished goods level (actual products that are to be sold). This requires an accurate forecast on finished goods level, as the forecast is the basis for ATP. Note, as products are produced driven by the forecast, the forecast accuracy must be high in a make-to-stock environment. The order lead-time is usually smaller than the production lead-time if products are made to stock. Orders consume directly from the corresponding ATP. While in a make-to-stock environment forecast on finished goods level is available (this follows from the definition of make-to-stock: pre-build finished goods according to the forecast prior to order entry), this is not the case in other manufacturing environments.

In a make-to-order environment (see Chap. 2) ATP is maintained on component level or intermediate product level. Consider the computer industry as an example for a make-to-order environment (see Chap. 18 for further details). From a limited number of components – e. g. disk drives, processors, controllers, memory – a huge number of configurations can be made. Hence, it is not feasible to create a forecast on finished goods level in the computer industry. Instead, the forecast is represented on product group level and on component level. Note that the production lead-time in a make-to-order environment is smaller than the order lead-time.[3] ATP is maintained on component level or on intermediate product level, e.g. base configurations or system boards. If an order is entered it consumes from multiple ATP sources according to its configuration. For example, an order might consume ATP from a specific base configuration, a specific processor, disk drive and memory. The latest ATP in terms of ATP time buckets that can be found determines the quote for the order; all ATP consumptions are synchronized according to the quote.

---

[3] But the supplier lead-time in the computer industry is much longer than the order lead-time; because of that purchasing decisions are driven by the component forecast (see Chap. 18).

The third manufacturing environment is configure-to-order. The main characteristics of a configure-to-order environment are a complex production process with long production lead-time and complex products that are difficult to forecast. Only a rough-cut forecast and master plan are created on product group level, and from that plan ATP on capacity and raw material level is determined. If an order is entered the bill-of-materials and the corresponding routings are exploded. The required raw material and capacity is determined, and ATP for raw material and capacity is searched. Alternate resources and alternate parts are considered in order to create a good quote. The concept of ATP applied to a configure-to-order environment is also called *capable-to-promise* (CTP).

In make-to-order and configure-to-order environments ATP may be represented on different stages of the production process. The production lead-time has to be taken into account in order to determine the time interval between the order promise and the corresponding ATP consumption date. Table 8.1 summarizes the ATP granularity of the three manufacturing enironments.

Table 8.1. ATP granularity of different manufacturing environments

Manufacturing environm.	Order lead-time	ATP granularity
make-to-stock	< production lead-time	product groups / finished goods
make-to-order	> production lead-time	product groups / components / intermediate products
configure-to-order	> production lead-time	capacity / raw material

Granularity of ATP Along the Time Dimension

ATP is maintained in discrete time buckets. These correspond to the time buckets of the forecasting process. Usually, the customer demand is forecasted based on weekly buckets or monthly buckets, and ATP is maintained in weekly or in monthly buckets, respectively. Orders are quoted by consuming ATP from a particular time bucket.

However, note that the ATP is generated by the master planning process. The master plan represents the planned supply fulfilling the forecasted demand. Thus, the master plan contains more detailed information than the bucketized ATP including the scheduled dates of the supply. This information is used to *detail* a promise that has been generated by consuming ATP from a particular ATP time bucket; the customer receives a promise that is detailed down to the level of detail of the master plan, e.g. on a daily basis.

ATP can be viewed as a *control instance* constraining the access to the detailed master plan. Figure 8.3 illustrates the control functionality of ATP.

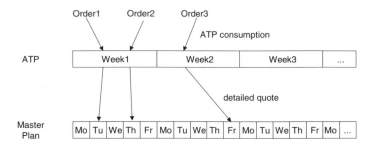

Fig. 8.3. ATP controls the access to the detailed master plan

8.2 Allocated ATP

8.2.1 Motivation

A supply chain (or a part of a supply chain) operates either in the supply constrained mode or in the demand constrained mode. If material and/or capacity are bottlenecks, then there is "open" demand that cannot be fulfilled. The supply chain supplies less finished goods than the customers request and operates in the *supply constrained mode*. If demand is the bottleneck, then all demand can be matched by supply. The supply chain operates in the *demand constrained mode*.

In the demand constrained mode the supply chain is able to generate excess supply that is not requested and will – most probably – not be consumed by the customers. The capability of a supply chain to produce excess supply is an indicator for inefficiencies in the supply chain (refer to Chap. 12). A supply chain is working more profitable if it is "operated on the edge" (Sharma, 1997) by removing all inefficiencies, e.g. excess capacity, excess assets and excess expenses. Thus, even in the demand constrained mode, supply should be limited in order to make the supply chain more profitable. As a consequence the supply chain moves towards the supply constrained mode. To summarize, a supply chain is either in the supply constrained mode or should move towards the edge of this mode.

In the supply constrained mode, if orders are promised on a *first-come-first-served policy* all orders are treated the same without taking the profitability of the order, the importance of the customer and the fact whether the order was forecasted or not, into account. As a consequence the profitability of the business, the relationship to the customers and the performance of the supply chain may be jeopardized.

A good example of how business can be optimized by using more sophisticated order promising policies is given by the international airlines. Airlines keep a specific fraction of the business and the first class seats open even if more economy customers are requesting seats than the total number of economy seats. For each flight, some of the business class and first class seats are *allocated* to the business and first class passengers based on the forecasted passenger numbers for that flight. Only a short time before the flight departs the allocations are released and passengers are "upgraded" to the next higher class. By that, airlines achieve a higher average sales price for the available seats and strengthen the relationship to their important customers, the business class and first class passengers.

APS apply the same principle by allocating ATP quantities to customer groups or sales channels in order to optimize the overall business performance. A classification scheme is defined that is used to classify customer orders. Typically, the order classes are structured in a hierarchy. The ATP quantities are allocated to the order classes according to predefined business rules. These allocations represent the right to consume ATP. When an order is entered, the order promising process checks the allocations for the corresponding order class. If allocated ATP is available, ATP can be consumed and the order is quoted accordingly. Otherwise, the order promising process searches for other options to satisfy the order, e.g. by checking ATP in earlier time buckets, by consuming ATP from other order classes (if that is allowed by the business rules defined) or by looking for ATP on alternate products.

The allocation of ATP to order classes can be exploited to increase the revenue and profitability of the business. For example, the average selling price may be increased by allocating supply to customers that are willing to pay premium prices, instead of giving supply away to any customer on a first-come-first-served basis. Traditional ATP mechanisms without allocation rules have to break committments that have been given to other customers in order to be able to quote an order of a key customer or an order with a higher margin. It is obvious that this business policy has a negative impact on the on time delivery and deteriorates the relationship to other customers.

The concept of allocated ATP in the context of APS has been developed by i2 Technologies. Subsequently, allocation planning is explained along the lines of i2 Technologies (1996) and i2 Technologies (2000).

8.2.2   The Customer Hierarchy

In order to allocate supply to customers a *model of the customer structure* and a *forecast of the future customer demand* is required. The model of the customer structure should be aligned with the geographic dimension in demand planning (see Chap. 6), as demand planning is structuring the forecast in terms of the geographic dimension. Hence, the customer structure forms a hierarchy similar to the geographic dimension in demand planning. Figure 8.4 shows an example of a customer hierarchy.

In the first step the forecast quantities for each customer (or customer group, resp.) are aggregated to the root of the hierarchy. This number gives the total forecast for that specific product (or product group). The total forecast is transferred to master planning, and master planning checks whether it is feasible to fulfil the total forecast considering the supply constraints. In

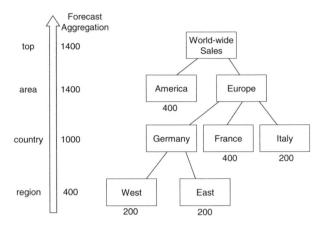

Fig. 8.4. Sales forecast aggregated along the customer hierarchy

our example, the total forecast is 1400, and we assume that master planning can confirm only 1200 to be feasible.

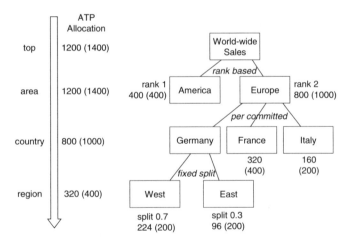

Fig. 8.5. Allocation of ATP in the customer hierarchy

In the second step the total feasible quantity according to the master plan is allocated from the top down to the leaves of the customer hierarchy. This allocation process for our example is visualized in Fig. 8.5 (the quantities in parantheses indicate the original forecast for this customer group). The allocation of the master plan quantities to the nodes of the customer hierarchy is controlled by allocation rules. In our example we have used three different allocation rules:

- *Rank based*: U.S. customers receive a higher priority (rank 1) compared to customers in Europe (rank 2). Thus, the available quantity for the U.S. and European customers is allocated to the U.S. first up to the original forecast for that area. A rank-based allocation policy may be helpful to support sales to a specific market, e. g. if the development of that market is in an early stage.
- *Per committed*: The available quantity is allocated to the nodes of the customer hierarchy according to the forecast the customers have committed to. In our example Germany and France have forecasted 400 each, and Italy has forecasted 200, making 1000 in total. However, for this group of customers, only 800 is available. The quantity of 800 is split appropriate to the fraction of the original forecast, i.e. Germany and France receive 40% each (320), and Italy receives 20% (160). The per committed allocation policy is well suited if each customer group shall get a fair share allocation according to what has been forecasted by that customer group.
- *Fixed split*: The fixed split allocation policy applies predefined split factors to distribute the feasible quantity to the customer groups. In our example, the customers in the Western part of Germany receive 70% of the available quantity, the customers in East Germany 30%. Please note that the resulting quantities are independent of the individual forecast of the customer groups. (But it does dependent on the total forecast of these customer groups.)

In addition to these allocation rules a portion of the available quantity can be retained at every level of the customer hierarchy. These retained quantities are consumed based on a first-come-first-served policy. Retained ATP can be used to account for potential variations of the actual demand related to the forecasted demand. For example, if 25% of the total quantity available for European customers is retained at the customer group Europe, 200 would be available on a first-come-first-served basis for all European customers, and only 600 would be allocated to German, French and Italian customers as defined by the corresponding allocation rules.

The allocations are the basis for generating order quotes. Thus, the allocations are an important information for the sales force before making commitments to their customers. Futher, the APS keeps track of the consumptions due to already quoted orders. The total allocated quantities and the already consumed quantities give a good indication whether the order volume matches the forecast. If orders and forecast do not match, some allocations are being over-consumed, whereas others remain unconsumed. This can be given as an early warning to the supply chain that the market behaves different as it has been forecasted – and appropriate action can be taken. For example, sales can setup a sales push initiative to generate additional demand to consume the planned ATP, and the supply operations can adjust production plans accordingly.

8.2.3   Allocation Planning

The process that assigns the overall ATP quantities received from master planning to the nodes of the customer hierarchy is called *allocation planning*. Allocation planning is executed directly after a new master plan is created – which takes place normally once a week. Thus, once a week the adjusted forecast is transformed into ATP by master planning and allocated to the customer hierarchy.

In addition to that, the allocations are updated on a daily basis in order to reflect changes in the constraints of the supply chain. For example if the supplier of some key component announces a delay of a scheduled delivery this may impact the capability of the supply chain to fulfil orders and – because of that – should be reflected in the ATP as soon as the information is available in the APS.

The planning horizon of allocation planning cannot be longer than the planning horizon of master planning, as no ATP is available beyond the master planning horizon. The master planning process covers usually six to twelve months. However, in many cases it is not necessary to maintain allocations over six months or more. For example, in the computer industry, 90% of the orders are placed three weeks prior to the customer requested delivery date. Thus, dependent on the lead-time from order entry date to the customer requested delivery date a shorter planning horizon for allocation planning can be chosen compared to master planning. In the computer industry for example, a three-months horizon for allocation planning is sufficient.

8.3   Order Promising

Order promising is the core of the demand fulfilment process. The goal is to create reliable promises for the customer orders in a short time. The quality of the order promising process is measured by the on time delivery and the order promising lead-time.

The *on time delivery* KPI is described in detail in Chap. 2; it measures the percentage of the orders that are fulfilled as promised (based on the first promise given). Thus, to achieve a high on time delivery it is important to generate reliable promises. A promise is *reliable* if the customer can trust the ability of the supply chain to fulfil the order as promised, i.e. if the customer receives the promised product in the promised quantity at the promised date. A supply chain that is able to consistently generate reliable promises over a long time period gets a competitive advantage over supply chains with a lower on time delivery.

Besides the on time delivery, the actual order promising lead-time is an important aspect of the customer service level. In recent times a large variety of order entry paths have been created – and more are evolving. For example, in the computer industry, customers can order products at an authorized dealer, at a reseller, in department stores and consumer markets or directly at the manufacturer by telephone or via the Internet. By that, the probability that peak situations occur where large number of orders are entered at the same time, increases. A typical value in the computer industry is 1000 orders per hour in peak load situations. Thus, the order promising process must be able to generate (reliable) quotes for individual orders in a very short time, e.g. down to milliseconds. Otherwise, customers wait for their promises and – while waiting – may change their mind and order online over the Internet or by telephone at a competitor.

8.3.1 ATP Search Procedure

The general ATP-based order promising process works as follows: First, the order promising process searches for ATP according to a set of search rules that are described below. If ATP is found, it is reduced accordingly and a quote for the order is generated. If no ATP can be found, no quote is generated, and the order must be either rejected or confirmed manually at the end of the allocation planning horizon. Note that if no ATP can be found for an order, the supply chain will not be able to fulfil the order within the allocation planning horizon.

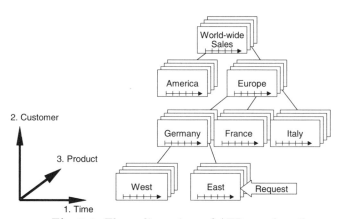

Fig. 8.6. Three dimensions of ATP search paths

ATP is searched along three dimensions: the time dimension, the customer dimension and the product dimension. Figure 8.6 illustrates the three dimensions of the ATP search paths. The following *search rules* are applied (for simplicity we assume that the ATP is on finished goods level; the search rules are similar for ATP on product group level and component level):

1. The leaf node in the customer hierarchy, to which the customer belongs, the product being requested by the order and the time bucket containing the customer requested date are determined. The ATP at this point is consumed – if available.

2. If ATP is not sufficient, then the time dimension is searched back in time for additional ATP (still at the leaf node in the customer hierarchy and at the product requested by the order); all ATP found up to a predefined number of time buckets back in time is consumed. Note that if ATP is consumed from time buckets earlier than the time bucket containing the customer requested date, the order is pre-build, and inventory is created.
3. If ATP is still not sufficient, steps 1. and 2. are repeated for the next higher node (parent node) in the customer hierarchy, then for the next higher and so on up to the root of the customer hierarchy.
4. If ATP is still not sufficient, steps 1. to 3. are repeated for all alternate products that may substitute the original product requested by the order.
5. If ATP is still not sufficient, steps 1. to 4. are repeated, but instead searching backward in time, ATP is searched forward in time, up to a predefined number of time buckets. Note that by searching ATP forward in time, the order is made late.

In the following, we illustrate the ATP search procedure by means of a simple example.

8.3.2   ATP Consumption By Example

Let us assume an order is received for 300 units from a customer in East Germany, with a customer requested date in week 4. The ATP situation for East Germany is depicted in Fig. 8.7. First, the ATP is checked for the customer group East Germany for week 4, then for week 3 and for week 2. (We assume that the ATP search procedure is allowed to consume ATP 2 weeks back in time.) The ATP that is found along that search path is 10 in week 4, 60 in week 3 and 50 in week 2, 120 in total (see Fig. 8.7).

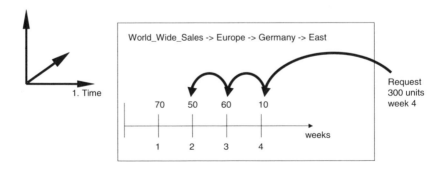

Fig. 8.7. Consumption of ATP along the time dimension

As the ATP search procedure may not consume ATP from a time bucket that is more than two weeks prior to the customer requested date, 180 units of the requested quantity is still open after the first step. In the second step, ATP is searched along the customer dimension. We assume for this example that there is ATP in the next higher node in the customer hierarchy that is Germany as shown in Fig. 8.8, but no ATP in the next higher nodes, i.e. Europe and World-wide Sales. From the ATP allocated at Germany, another 120 units can be consumed in weeks 4, 3 and 2, resulting in a total promised quantity of 240. 60 units are still open, as the requested quantity is 300 units.

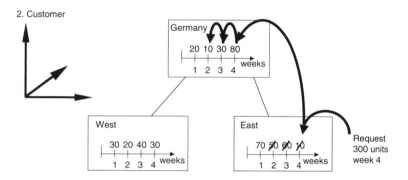

Fig. 8.8. Consumption of ATP along the customer dimension

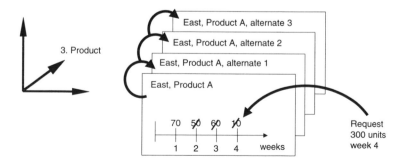

Fig. 8.9. Consumption of ATP along the product dimension

In the next step, the ATP search algorithm looks for alternate products as shown in Fig. 8.9. The alternates are sorted by priority. First, the alternate with the highest priority is considered, and the same steps are applied as for the original product, i.e. first search back in time and second search up the customer hierarchy. Then, these steps are applied to the alternate with second highest priority and so on.

References

i2 Technologies (1996) *RHYTHM Supply Chain Planner Concept Manual*, Irving, Texas

i2 Technologies (2000) *RHYTHM Demand Fulfillment Concept Manual*, Part No. 4.2.1-DOC-ITM-DFCM-ALL, Irving, Texas

Sharma, K. (1997) *Operating on the Edge*, private conversation

9 Production Planning and Scheduling

Hartmut Stadtler

Darmstadt University of Technology, Institute of Business Administration, Department of Operations and Materials Management, Hochschulstraße 1, 64289 Darmstadt, Germany

Assuming that the master plan has been generated, we can now derive detailed plans for the different plants and production units. In the following we will describe the underlying decision situation (9.1) and outline how to proceed from a model to a solution (9.2). Some of these steps will be presented in greater detail, namely model building (9.3) and updating a production schedule (9.4). Whether Production Planning and Scheduling should be done by a single planning level or by a two-level planning hierarchy largely depends on the production type of the shop floor. This issue will be discussed together with limitations of solution methods in Sect. 9.5.

9.1 Description of the Decision Situation

Production Planning and Scheduling aims at generating detailed production schedules for the shop floor over a relatively short interval of time. A *production schedule* indicates for each order to be executed within the planning interval its start and completion times on the resources required for processing. Hence, a production schedule also specifies the sequence of orders on a given resource. A production schedule may be visualized by a gantt-chart (see Fig. 9.4).

The *planning interval* for Production Planning and Scheduling varies from one day to a few weeks depending on the industrial sector. Its "correct" length depends on several factors: On the one hand it should at least cover an interval of time corresponding to the largest flow time of an order within the production unit. On the other hand the planning interval is limited by the availability of known customer orders or reliable demand forecasts. Obviously, sequencing orders on individual resources is useful only if these plans are "reasonably" stable, i.e. if they are not subject to frequent changes due to unexpected events like changing order quantities or disruptions.

For some production types (like a job shop) Production Planning and Scheduling requires sequencing and scheduling of orders on potential bottlenecks. For other production types (like group technology) an automated, bucket-oriented capacity check for a set of orders to be processed by a group within the next time bucket(s) will suffice. Sequencing of orders may then be performed manually by the group itself.

Planning tasks can and should be done decentrally, utilizing the expertise of the staff at each location and its current knowledge of the state of the shop floor (e. g. the availability of personnel).

The master plan sets the frame within which Production Planning and Scheduling at the decentralized decision units can be performed. Corresponding directives usually are:

- the amount of overtime or additional shifts to be used,
- the availability of items from upstream units in the supply chain at different points in time,
- purchase agreements concerning input materials from suppliers – not being part of our supply chain.

Furthermore, directives will be given by the master plan due to its extended view over the supply chain and the longer planning interval. As directives we might have

- the amount of seasonal stock of different items to be built up by the end of the planning horizon (for production units facing a make-to-stock policy),
- given due dates for orders to be delivered to the next downstream unit in the supply chain (which may be the subsequent production stage, a shipper or the final customer).

9.2   How to Proceed from a Model to a Production Schedule

The general procedure leading from a model of the shop floor to a production schedule will be described briefly by the following six steps (see Fig. 9.1).

Step 1: Model building

A model of the shop floor has to capture the specific properties of the production process and the corresponding flows of materials in a detail that allows to generate feasible plans at minimum costs.

Only a subset of all existing resources on the shop floor – namely those which might turn out to become a bottleneck – will have to be modelled explicitly, since the output rate of a system is limited only by these potential bottlenecks. Details on model building are presented in Sect. 9.3.

Step 2: Extracting required data

Production Planning and Scheduling utilizes data from

- an ERP system,

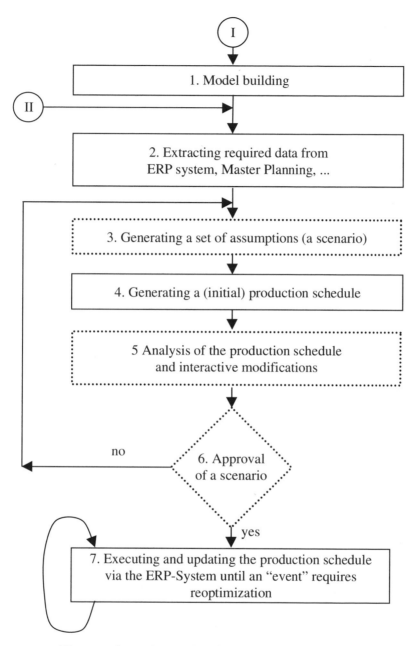

Fig. 9.1. General procedure for production scheduling

- Master Planning and
- Demand Planning.

Only a subset of the data available in these modules will be used in Production Planning and Scheduling. Therefore, it is necessary to specify which data will actually be required to model a given production unit (see step 2 in Fig. 9.1).

Step 3: Generating a set of assumptions (a scenario)

In addition to the data received from sources like the ERP system, Master Planning and Demand Planning the decision-maker at the plant or production unit level may have some further knowledge or expectations about the current and future situation on the shop floor not available in other places (software modules). Also, there may be several options with respect to available capacity (e. g. due to flexible shift arrangements).

Therefore, the decision-maker must have the ability to modify data and thereby to set up a certain scenario (step 3, Fig. 9.1: A dotted frame indicates that this step has to be performed by the decision-maker and is optional).

Step 4: Generating a (initial) production schedule

Next, a (initial) production schedule will be generated for a given scenario, automatically (step 4, Fig. 9.1). This may be done either by a two-level planning hierarchy or in one step (for more details see Sect. 9.4).

Step 5: Analysis of the production schedule and interactive modifications

If there is a bucket-oriented upper planning level then this production plan may be analyzed first before a detailed schedule is generated (step 5, Fig. 9.1). Especially, if the production plan is infeasible, the decision-maker may indicate some course of action interactively to balance capacities (like the introduction of overtime or the specification of a different routing). This may be easier than modifying a detailed sequence of operations on individual resources (lower planning level). Infeasibilities – like exceeding an order's due date or an overload of a resource – are shown as *alerts* (see Sect. 11.3.1).

Also, a solution generated for a scenario may be improved by incorporating the experience and knowledge of the decision-maker, interactively. However, to provide real decision support, the number of necessary modifications should be limited.

Step 6: Approval of a scenario

Once the decision-maker is sure of having evaluated all available alternatives, he / she will choose the production schedule representing the most attractive scenario for execution.

Step 7: Executing and updating the production schedule

The production schedule selected will be transferred to

- the MRP module to explode the plan,
- the ERP system to execute the plan and
- the Transportat Planning module for finding vehicle loadings once customer orders have been completed.

The MRP module performs the explosion of all planned activities on bottleneck resources to those materials that are produced on non-bottleneck resources or those to be delivered from suppliers. Furthermore, required materials will be reserved for certain orders.

The schedule will be executed up to a point in time where an event signals that a revision of the production schedule seems advisable (loop II; Fig. 9.1). This may be an event like a new order coming in, a breakdown of a machine or a certain point in time where a given part of the schedule has been executed (for more details on updating a production schedule see Sect. 9.4).

Changing the model of the plant is less frequent (loop I; Fig. 9.1). If the structure remains unaltered and only quantities are affected (like the number of machines within a machine group or some new variants of known products), then the model can be updated automatically via the data that is downloaded from the ERP system. However, for major changes, like the introduction of a new production stage with new properties, a manual adaptation of the model by an expert is advisable.

We will now describe the task of modelling the production process on a shop floor in greater detail.

9.3   Model Building

A *model* of the shop floor has to incorporate all the necessary details of the production process for determining (customer) order completion times, the input required from materials and from potential bottleneck resources. The time grid of a production schedule is either very small (e. g. hours) or even continuous.

9.3.1   Level of Detail

The model can be restricted to operations to be performed on (potential) bottlenecks, since only these restrict the output of the shop floor.

Since Production Planning and Scheduling is (currently) not intended for controlling the shop floor (which is left to the ERP system) some details of the shop floor – like control points monitoring the current status of orders – can be omitted.

All processing steps to be executed on non-bottleneck resources in between two consecutive activities modelled explicitly are only represented by a *fixed lead-time offset.* This recommendation is no contradiction to the well-known statement that Advanced Planning yields lead-times as a *result of planning* and not as an a priori given constant. Here, the lead-time offset will consist of only processing and transportation times on preceding non-bottleneck resources, since waiting times would not exist.

The model can be defined by the associated data. We discriminate between structural data and situation-dependent data.

Structural data consists of

- locations,
- parts,
- bill-of-materials,
- routings and associated operating instructions,
- (production) resources,
- specification of suppliers,
- setup matrices and
- timetables (calendars).

In a large supply chain with many plants at different locations it may be advantageous to attribute all the data to a specific location. Consequently, a part can be discriminated by its production location even if it is the same in the eyes of the customer.

The bill-of-materials is usually described on a single-level basis (stored in a materials file). There, each part number is linked only to the part numbers of its immediate predecessor components. A complete bill-of-materials for a given part may be constructed easily on a computer by connecting the single-level representations.

The resource consumption per item can be obtained from the routings and operating instructions. Both the number of items per order as well as the resource consumption per item are required for sequencing and scheduling of individual orders. Hence, a combination of the two representations called *Production Process Model* (abbreviated by PPM) concept is appealing.

As an example the PPMs in Fig. 9.2 describe the two-stage production of ketchup bottles of a specific size and brand. The first PPM represents production of the liquid – including cleaning the tub, stirring the ingredients and waiting to be filled up in bottles. Once the liquid is ready it has to be bottled within the next 24 hours. The liquid can be used in bottles of different sizes. For each size there will be an individual PPM. Also the liquid ketchup can be used up for different bottle sizes simultaneously.

A PPM is made up of at least one *operation* while each operation consists of one or several *activities*. An operation is always associated with one primary resource (like a tub). Secondary resources – like personnel – can also be attributed to an activity.

Activities may require some input material and can yield some material as an output. Surely, it has to be specified, at which point in time an input

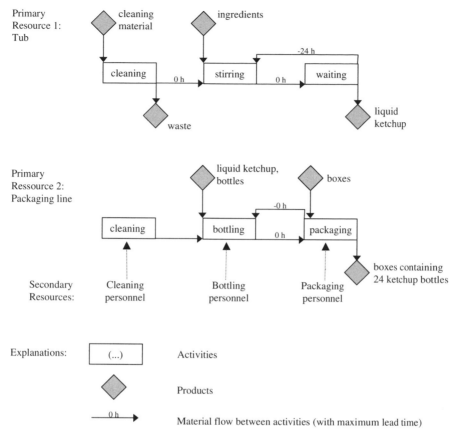

Fig. 9.2. A Production Process Model (PPM) for a two stage ketchup production

material is needed and when an output material is available. The technical sequence of activities within an operation – also called precedence relationships – can be represented by arcs. Like in project planning activities can be linked by

- end-start, end-end, start-end and start-start relationships together with
- maximal and minimal time distances.

This allows a very precise modelling of timing restrictions between activities including the parallel execution of activities (overlapping activities).

   The timing as well as the resource and material requirements of a (customer) order may be derived by linking the associated PPMs by the so-called *pegging arcs* (bolt and dotted arcs in Fig. 9.3). Pegging arcs connect the output material (node) of one PPM with the respective input material (node) of the successor PPM. Consequently, exploding an order (see order C505X in Fig. 9.3) and the corresponding PPMs, starting with the final production

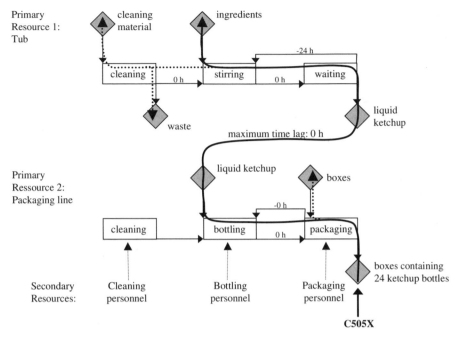

Fig. 9.3. Pegging: Linking two Production Process Models (PPMs)

stage, yields information about resource and material consumption within respective time windows. These time windows may be used directly when generating a feasible schedule (see also Vollmann et al. (1997, pp. 804)).

The (factory) calendar indicates breaks and other interruptions of working hours of resources. Another information included will be whether a plant (or resource) is operated in one, two or three shifts. Usually Advanced Planning Systems offer several typical calendars to choose from.

Situation-dependent data varies with the current situation on the shop floor. It consists of

- initial inventories, including work-in-process,
- setup state of resources and
- set of orders to be processed within a given interval of time.

Operational procedures to be specified by the user may consist of

- lot-sizing rules,
- priority rules or
- choice of routings.

Although rules for building lot-sizes should ideally be based on the actual production situation – like utilization of resources and associated costs –

Advanced Planning Systems often require to input some (simple) rules a priori. Such rules may be a fixed lot-size, a minimum lot-size or a lot-size with a given time between orders. Software packages might either offer to pick a rule from a given set of rules or to programme it in a high level programming language. Rules for determining sequences of orders on a certain resource are handled in a similar fashion (for more details on priority rules see Silver et al. (1998, pp. 676)).

If alternative routings to perform a production order exists then one should expect that the system chooses the best one in the course of generating a production schedule. However, we experienced that the user has to pick one "preferred" routing. Sometimes alternative routings are input as a ranked list. Only if a preferred routing leads to infeasibilities the solver will try the second best routing, then the third best etc.

9.3.2 Objectives

Last but not least objectives will have to be specified. These guide the search for a good – hopefully near optimal – solution. As objectives to choose from within Production Planning and Scheduling we observed mainly time oriented objectives like minimizing the

- makespan,
- sum of lateness,
- maximum lateness,
- sum of flow times and
- sum of setup times.

Three objectives referring to costs should be mentioned, too, namely the minimization of the sum of

- variable production costs,
- setup costs and
- penalty costs.

Although the degree of freedom to influence costs at this planning level is rather limited one can imagine that the choice of different routings, e. g. declaring an order to be a standard or a rush order, should be evaluated in monetary terms, too.

Penalty costs may be included in the objective function, if *soft constraints* have been modelled (e. g. fulfilling a planned due date for a make-to-stock order).

If the decision-maker wants to pursue several of the above objectives, an "ideal" solution, where each objective is at its optimum, usually does not exist. Then a compromise solution is looked for. One such approach is to build a weighted sum of the above individual objectives. This combined objective function can be handled like a single objective, and hence, the same solution methods can be applied (for more details on multi-objective programming see Tamiz (1996)).

9.3.3   Representation of Solutions

There are several options for representing a model's solution, namely the detailed production schedule. It may simply be a list of activities with its start and completion times on the resources assigned to it. This may be appropriate for transferring results to other modules.

A decision-maker usually prefers a *gantt-chart* of the production schedule (see Fig. 9.4). This can be accomplished by a gantt-chart showing all the resources of the plant in parallel over a certain interval of time. Alternatively one might concentrate on a specific customer order and its schedule over respective production stages. Likewise, one can focus attention on one single resource and its schedule over time.

If the decision-maker is allowed to change the production schedule interactively – e. g. by shifting an operation to another (alternative) resource – a gantt-chart with all resources in parallel is the most appropriate.

Now we will point our attention to the options of updating an existing production schedule.

9.4   Updating Production Schedules

Production Planning and Scheduling assumes that all data is known with certainty, i.e. the decision situation is deterministic. Although this is an ideal assumption, it may be justified for a certain interval of time. To cope with uncertainty – like unplanned variations of production rates or unexpected downtimes of resources – software tools allow monitoring deviations from our assumptions taking place on the shop floor immediately, resulting in updated expected completion times of the orders. Whether these changes are that large that a reoptimized schedule is required will be based on the decision-maker's judgement. Current software tools will enhance this judgement by providing extensive generation and testing facilities of alternative scenarios (also called *simulation*) before a schedule is actually delivered to the shop floor (see also steps three to five; Fig. 9.1).

Another feature to be mentioned here is a two step planning procedure – also called *incremental planning*. Assume that a new order comes in. If it falls into the planning horizon of Production Planning and Scheduling the activities of this new customer order may be inserted into the *given sequence* of orders on the required resources. Time gaps are searched for in the existing schedule such that only minor adjustments in the timing of orders result. If feasibility of the schedule can be maintained a planned due date for the new customer order can be derived and sent back to the customer.

Since this (preliminary) schedule may be improved by a different sequence of orders, reoptimization is considered from time to time, aiming at new sequences with reduced costs.

The following example will illustrate this case. Assume there are four orders that have to be scheduled on a certain machine with given due dates and the objective is to minimize the sum of sequence dependent setup times. Then the optimal sequence will be A-B-C-D (see Fig. 9.4). The actual time is 100 (time units). Processing times for all orders are identical (one time unit). Sequence dependent setup times are either 0, 1/3, 2/3 or 1 time unit.

After having started processing order A, we are asked to check whether a new order E can be accepted with due date 107. Assuming that *preemption* is not allowed (i. e. interrupting the execution of an order already started in order to produce another (rush) order), we can check the insertion of job E in the existing sequence directly after finishing orders A, B, C or D (see Fig. 9.5). Since there is a positive setup time between order A and E this sub-sequence will not be feasible since it violates the due date of order B. Three feasible schedules can be identified, where alternative c has the least sum of setup times. Hence, a due date for order E of 107 can be accepted (assuming that order E is worth the additional setup time of one time unit).

Once reoptimization of the sequence can be executed, a new feasible schedule – including order E – will be generated reducing the sum of setup times by 1/3 (see Fig. 9.6).

Table 9.1. Data: Due dates

Order	A	B	C	D
Due Dates	102	104	107	108

Table 9.2. Data: Matrix of setup times

to	A	B	C	D	E
A	1	0	1	1	1
B	1	1	0	1	$\frac{2}{3}$
C	1	1	1	0	$\frac{1}{3}$
D	1	1	$\frac{1}{3}$	1	1
E	1	1	$\frac{2}{3}$	1	1

Generating new sequences of orders is time consuming and usually will result in some *nervousness*. We discriminate nervousness due to changes regarding the start times of operations as well as changes in the amount to be produced when comparing an actual plan with the previous one. Nervousness can lead to additional efforts on the shop floor – e. g. earlier deliveries of some

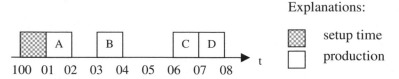

Fig. 9.4. Gantt-chart for four orders on one machine with due dates and sequence dependent setup times

Alternative a)

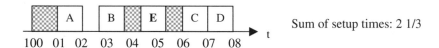

Sum of setup times: 2 1/3

Alternative b)

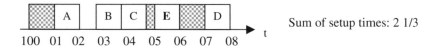

Sum of setup times: 2 1/3

Alternative c)

Sum of setup times: 2

Fig. 9.5. Generating a due date for the new customer order E

Sum of setup times: 1 2/3

Fig. 9.6. Reoptimized schedule

input materials may be necessary which has to be checked with suppliers. In order to reduce nervousness usually the "next few orders" on a resource may be *firmed* or *fixed*, i.e. their schedule is fixed and will not be part of the re-optimization. All orders with a start time falling within a given interval of time – named *frozen horizon* – will be firmed.

9.5 Number of Planning Levels and Limitations

9.5.1 Planning Levels for Production Planning and Scheduling

As has been stated above, software modules for Production Planning and Scheduling allow to generate production schedules either within a single planning level or by a two-level planning hierarchy. Subsequently, we will discuss the pros and cons of these two approaches.

Drexl et al. (1994) advocate that the question of decomposing of Production Planning and Scheduling depends on the production type given by the production process and the repetition of operations (see Sect. 2.3 for a definition). There may be several production units within one plant each corresponding to a specific production type to best serve the needs of the supply chain. Two well-known production types are process organization and flow lines.

In *process organization* there are a great number of machines of similar functionality within a shop and there are usually many alternative routings for a given order. An end product usually requires many operations in a multi-stage production process. Demands for certain operations may be combined to a lot-size in order to reduce setup costs and setup times. Usually many lot-sizes (orders) have to be processed within the planning interval (e. g. the next eight to sixteen) weeks.

In order to reduce the computational burden and to provide effective decision support the overall decision problem is divided into two (hierarchical) planning levels. The upper planning level is based on time buckets of days or weeks, while resources of similar functionality are grouped in resource groups. These big time buckets allow to refrain from sequencing. Consequently, lot-size decisions and capacity loading will be much easier. Given the structure of the solution provided by the upper planning level, the lower planning level will perform the assignment of orders to individual resources (e. g. machines) belonging to a resource group as well as the sequencing. The separation of the planning task into two planning levels requires some slack capacity or flexibility with respect to the routing of orders.

For (automated) *flow lines* with sequence dependent setup times a separation into two planning levels is inadequate. On the one hand a planning level utilizing big time buckets is not suited to model sequence dependent setup costs and times. On the other hand sequencing and lot-sizing decisions cannot be separated here, because the utilization of flow lines usually is very high and different products (lot-sizes) have to compete for the scarce resource. Luckily, there are usually only one to three production stages and only a few dozen products (or product families) to consider, so Production Planning and Scheduling can be executed in a single planning level.

In the following some definitions and examples illustrating the pros and cons of the two approaches will be provided.

A *time bucket* is called *big*, if an operation started within a time bucket has to be finished by the end of the time bucket. The corresponding model is named a big bucket model. Hence, the planning logic assumes that the setup state of a resource is not preserved from one period to the next. Usually, more than one setup will take place within a big time bucket of a resource (see Fig. 9.7).

In a model with *small* time buckets the setup state of a resource can be preserved. Hence, the solution of a model with small time buckets may incur less setup times and costs than the solution of a model with big time buckets (see operation B in Fig. 9.8). Usually, at most one setup can take place within a small time bucket of a resource (a further example is given by Haase (1994, p. 20)).

An aggregation of resources to resource groups automatically leads to a big bucket model, because the setup state of an individual resource as well as the assignment of operations to individual resources is no longer known.

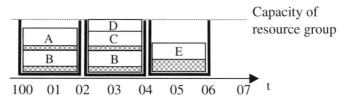

Fig. 9.7. A big bucket model

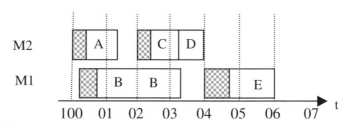

Fig. 9.8. Gantt-chart: A small bucket model (Time buckets of one time unit and two resources M1 and M2)

However, although a feasible big bucket oriented production plan exists, there may be no feasible disaggregation into a production schedule on respective resources. This can occur in cases such as

- sequence dependent setup times,
- loading of resource groups,
- a lead-time offset of zero time units between two successive operations.

Sequence dependent setup times cannot be represented properly within a big bucket model, since the loading of a time bucket is done without sequencing. Usually a certain portion of the available capacity is reserved for setup times. However, the portion may either be too large or too small. The former leads to unnecessarily large *planned* flow times of orders while the latter may result in an infeasible schedule. Whether the portion of setup times has been chosen correctly is not known before the disaggregation into a schedule has been performed.

Another situation where a feasible disaggregation may not exist is related to *resource groups*. As an example (see Fig. 9.9), assume that two resources have been aggregated to a resource group, the time bucket size is three time units, thus the capacity of the resource group is six time units. Each operation requires a setup of one time unit and a processing time of one time unit. Then the loading of all three operations within one big time bucket is possible. However, no feasible disaggregation exists, because a split of one operation such that it is performed on both machines requires an additional setup of one time unit exceeding the period's capacity of one machine. To overcome this dilemma one could reduce the capacity of the resource group to five time units (resulting in a slack of one time unit for the lower planning level). Then only two out of the three operations can be loaded within one time bucket. However, one should bear in mind that this usually will lengthen the planned flow time of an order.

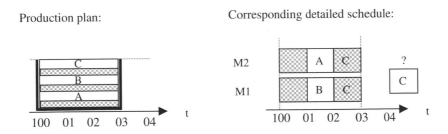

Fig. 9.9. An example of no feasible schedule when resource groups are loaded

For a multi-stage production system with several potential bottlenecks on different production stages, a feasible schedule might not exist if an order requiring two successive operations is loaded in the same big time bucket. As an example (see Fig. 9.9) depicting a two-stage production system with operation B being the successor of operation A each with a processing time of nine hours. A production stage is equipped with one machine (M1 and M2 respectively). A time bucket size of 16 hours (one working day) has been introduced. Although the capacity of one time bucket is sufficient for each operation individually, no feasible schedule exists that allows both operations to be performed in the same time bucket (assuming that overlapping operations are prohibited).

Fig. 9.10. An example of no feasible schedule in multi-stage production with lead-time offset zero

A feasible disaggregation can be secured if a fixed *lead-time offset* corresponding to the length of one big time bucket is modelled. Again this may incur larger planned flow times than necessary (32 hours instead of 18 hours in our example).

Consequently, it has to be considered carefully which of the above aggregations makes sense in a given situation. Usually, the answer will depend on the production type. Surely, an intermediate bucket oriented planning level can reduce the amount of detail and data to be handled simultaneously, but may also require some planned slack to work properly leading to larger planned flow times than necessary.

In order to combine the advantages of both the big and the small bucket model a third approach – a big time bucket with linked lot-sizes – has been proposed.

Here, several lots may be processed within a time bucket without considering its sequence (hence a big bucket model). However, a "last" lot within a time bucket is chosen which can be linked with a "first" lot in the next time bucket. If these two lots concern the same product a setup will be saved.

While this effect may only seem to be marginally at first sight, it also allows to model the production of a lot-size extending over two or more time buckets with only one initial setup – like in a small bucket model.

Last but not least a fourth approach has to be mentioned which does not use time buckets at all, instead a continous time axis is considered. Although this is the most exact model possible it usually will result in the greatest computational effort.

9.5.2   Limitations Due to Computational Efforts

For finding the best production schedule one has to bear in mind that there are usually many alternatives for sequencing orders on a resource (of which only a subset may be feasible). Theoretically, one has to evaluate $n!$ different sequences for n orders to be processed on one resource. While this can be accomplished for five orders quickly by complete enumeration ($5! = 120$), it takes some time for ten orders ($10! > 3.6$ m) and cannot be executed within reasonable time limits for 20 orders ($20! > 2.4 \cdot 10^{18}$). Furthermore, if one has the additional choice among parallel resources, the number of possible sequences again rises sharply. Although powerful solution algorithms have been developed that reduce the number of solutions to be evaluated for finding *good* solutions (see Chaps. 23 and 24), computational efforts still increase sharply with the number of orders in the schedule.

Fortunately, there is usually no need to generate a production schedule from scratch, because a portion of the previous schedule may have been fixed (e. g. orders falling in the frozen horizon) . Similarly, decomposing Production Planning and Scheduling into two planning levels reduces the number of feasible sequences to be generated at the lower planning level, due to the assignment of orders to big time buckets at the upper level.

Also, incremental planning or a reoptimization of partial sequences specified by the decision-maker will restrict computational efforts.

Further details regarding the use of Production Planning and Scheduling are presented in two case studies (Chaps. 16 and 17) as well as in Kolisch et al. (2000).

References

Drexl, A.; Fleischmann, B.; Günther, H.-O.; Stadtler, H.; Tempelmeier, H. (1994) *Konzeptionelle Grundlagen kapazitätsorientierter PPS-Systeme*, Zeitschrift für betriebswirtschaftliche Forschung, Vol. 46, 1022–1045

Haase, K. (1994) *Lotsizing and scheduling for production planning*, Lecture Notes in economics and mathematical systems, Vol. 408, Berlin et al.

Reeves, C. R. (1993) *Modern heuristic techniques for combinatorial problems*, Oxford

Kolisch, R.; Brandenburg, M.; Krüger, C. (2000) *Numetrix /3 Production Scheduling*, OR Spektrum, Vol. 22, No. 3 (in print)

Silver, E. A.; Pyke, D. F.; Petersen, R. (1998) *Inventory management and production planning and scheduling*, 3rd ed., New York et al.

Tamiz, M. (1996) *Multi-objective programming and goal programming, theories and applications* , Lecture Notes in economics and mathematical systems, Vol. 164, Berlin et al.

Vollman, T. E.; Berry, W. L.; Whybark, D. C. (1997) *Manufacturing planning and control systems*, 4th ed., New York et al.

10 Distribution and Transport Planning

Bernhard Fleischmann

University of Augsburg, Department of Production and Logistics,
Universitätsstraße 16, 86135 Augsburg, Germany

10.1 Planning Situations

10.1.1 Overview

Transport processes are essential parts of the supply chain. They perform the flow of materials that connects an enterprise with its suppliers and with its customers. The integrated view of transport, production and inventory holding processes is characteristic of the modern SCM concept.

The appropriate structure of a transport system mainly depends on the size of the single shipments: Large shipments can go directly from the source to the destination in full transport units, e.g. trucks or containers. Small shipments have to be consolidated in a transport network, where a single shipment is transshipped once or several times and the transport is broken at *transshipment points (TPs)*. A particularly effective consolidation of small shipments is achieved by a *logistics service provider (LSP)*, who can combine the transports from many senders.

The consolidation of transport flows decreases the transport cost. As the cost of a single trip of a certain vehicle on a certain route is nearly independent of the load, a high utilization of the loading capacity is advantageous. Moreover, the relative cost per loading capacity decreases with increasing size of the vehicles. But even with a strong consolidation of shipments to full loads, e.g. by an LSP, the smaller shipments cause relatively higher cost, because the consolidation requires detours to different loading places, additional stops and transshipment (see Fleischmann (1998, pp. 65)).

The following transport processes occur in a supply chain:

- The *supply of materials* from external suppliers or from an own remote factory to a production site (Sect. 10.1.3). Note that both cases are identical from a viewpoint of logistics.
- The *distribution of products* from a factory to the customers (Sect. 10.1.2). It may decompose into the replenishment of the stocks at regional distribution centres (DCs) and from there to the customers.

The processes in the network of an LSP overlap with the above processes, but may involve additional flows of goods that are not part of the supply chain under consideration. Usually, it is not practical to include the flows of all clients of an LSP into advanced planning. The additional flows can be taken into account implicitly by appropriate transport cost functions which should show economies of scale with respect to the shipment sizes, as explained above.

In this chapter, only planning tasks below the Master Planning level are considered. Strategic Network Planning and Master Planning both take care of the integration of transportation into advanced planning and yield the following data for the mid-term and short-term transportation planning:

Strategic Network Planning (see Chap. 5) determines the structure of the transport network, i.e.

- the locations of factories, suppliers, DCs and TPs,
- the transport modes and potential paths,
- the allocation of suppliers and customers to areas and of areas to factories, DCs, TPs and
- the use of LSPs.

Master Planning (see Chap. 7) determines

- aggregate quantities to be shipped on every transport lane,
- the transport mode and
- the increase and decrease of seasonal stocks at the factory warehouses and the DCs.

The aggregate quantities from Master Planning should not serve as strict instructions to the short-term transport planning in order to keep the latter flexible. The main purpose of that quantity calculation is to provide appropriate resources and capacities. However, in case of multiple sources – e.g. if a material can be ordered from several suppliers, a product is produced in several factories or a customer can be supplied from several DCs – the aggregate quantities reflect the global view of Master Planning. Then they represent important guidelines for short-term transportation which could be used, for instance, as percentages of transports from the different sources.

Also *Demand Planning* (see Chap. 6) provides essential data for transport planning:

- customer orders to be delivered,
- forecast of demand at the DCs and
- safety stocks at the DCs.

A key factor for the cost of regular transports, both in distribution and in procurement, is the *frequency* of the shipments which affects the inventory as well. To optimize the balance of transport and inventory cost, a mid-term planning of the shipment frequencies is required. So far, this kind of planning is not supported by APS modules. Planning models are discussed in Sect. 10.2.1.

10.1.2 Planning Tasks in Distribution

Distribution comprises the flow of products from the production sites to the customers. The distribution processes and the planning tasks differ remarkably in the various types of supply chains, depending on the following factors:

Type of Products *Investment goods*, e.g. machines or equipment for industrial customers, are shipped only once or seldom on a certain transport relation. *Materials for production* are also shipped to industrial customers, but regularly and frequently on the same path. These transports are often controlled by the customer, e.g. in the automotive industry, and are then subject of the procurement planning of the customer (see Sect. 10.1.3). *Consumer goods* are shipped to wholesalers or retailers, often in very small order sizes (with an average below 100 kg in some businesses), requiring a consolidation of the transports.

Decoupling Point If the decoupling point between forecast-driven and order-driven operations lies before the completion of the product, e.g. in a *make-to-order* or *assemble-to-order* situation, there is no motivation for stocks in the distribution system, so that the transport is carried out without intermediate warehousing. Standard products *made to stock* may be shipped first to regional DCs on forecast, i.e. the decoupling point is shifted into the distribution system. Finally, in the vendor managed inventory (VMI) concept, the customer's warehouse has the same function as a DC, i.e. the decoupling point is at the extreme down-stream position. The planning of VMI supply is therefore similar to the DC replenishment. In both cases, a combined planning of transports and inventory is necessary.

Distribution Paths Shipments may go *directly* from the factory or from a DC to the customer, with a single order. This simplest form of distribution is only efficient for large orders using up the vehicle. Smaller orders can be shipped jointly *in tours* starting from the factory or DC and calling at several customers. A stronger bundling of small shipments is achieved by a joint transport from the factory to a *transshipment* point and delivery in short distance tours from there. Figure 10.1 illustrates the different distribution paths. The selection of the appropriate path for every shipment is an important planning task.

Responsibility for the Transport Process The manufacturer can distribute his products in *own vehicles* or use an *external LSP*. In the latter case, a large part of transport planning is done by the LSP, as explained below, who has to consider the additional flows of all his clients.

Deployment comprises the short-term tasks of dispatching the transports to the customers and, in case of make-to-stock, the replenishment of the DCs by transports from the factories. Usually, this is to be done daily with a short horizon of one or a few days. Orders released for the delivery to customers have to be assigned to sources, if multiple sources are available, to distribution paths and to vehicles. These decisions mostly follow general

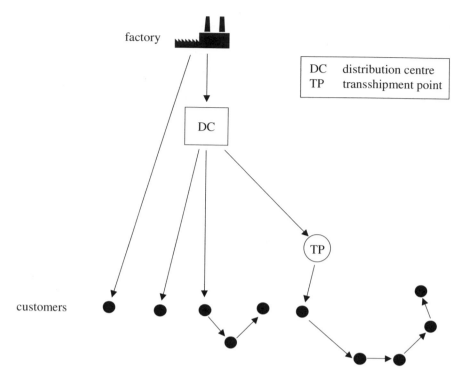

Fig. 10.1. Distribution paths

rules which are fixed on a longer term planning level. For instance, multiple sources like different factories or DCs, have fixed delivery areas resulting from Strategic Network Planning, so that for any order the relevant source follows immediately from the customer's postal code. The distribution path is selected according to the order size, e.g. up to 30 kg by a parcel service, up to 1000 kg from DC via transshipment at a TP, up to 3000 kg directly from DC and larger orders directly from factory. The assignment of orders to vehicles is part of the vehicle scheduling task discussed below.

The *replenishment of DCs* and, similarly, of the warehouse of a *VMI customer*, requires decisions on the quantity of every product to be shipped on the current day. These decisions can again be based on a longer term planning of the frequencies of shipments for every DC and VMI customer. If the vehicle supplies exclusively the considered DC, it is one objective in determining the shipment quantities to use up the vehicle capacity as well as possible. This is the *subject of vehicle loading*.

The deployment function for products made to stock is closely related to the *ATP function* (see Chap. 8): The customers expect their orders to be delivered from stock within a short agreed lead-time, mostly between 24 and 72 hours, necessary for order picking, loading and transportation. If the incoming orders of the current day in total exceed the available stock of a certain item, the orders cannot be released according to the standard rules. Instead, some of the following measures have to be decided on:

- shipping some orders from an alternative source,
- substituting the item by an available product, if the customer accepts it,
- reducing the quantities for DC replenishment which are in competition with the customer orders to be shipped from factory and
- reducing some customer orders in size, delay or canceling them: This most undesired decision is usually not completely unavoidable. Even if it is only necessary for a very small percentage of all orders, the concerned orders must be selected carefully.

All these decisions are part of the daily deployment function.
Vehicle scheduling comprises two different tasks:

- scheduling the short distance tours for delivering small orders from a TP in smaller vans and
- scheduling the trunk haulage from the factory to the DCs, from DCs to TPs and the direct delivery tours from a factory or a DC to customers.

These decisions can again be prestructured by longer term planning of fixed areas for the short distance tours and a regular line schedule for the circulation of trucks between factories, DCs and TPs (see Sect. 10.2.2). However, except for the case, where the vehicles are used exclusively for the supply chain under consideration, vehicle scheduling is typically the task of the LSPs in charge. As the network of an LSP may overlap with the supply chain only partially and he has to take orders of additional clients into account, the integration of vehicle scheduling into advanced planning will make little sense in most cases.

10.1.3   Planning Tasks in Procurement

This section deals with the case, where regular transports of materials from suppliers to a factory are controlled by the receiver, as it is usual e.g. in the automotive industry. Then, transport planning is part of the procurement process of the receiver. The various concepts of procurement logistics differ in the structure of the transportation network and in the frequency of the shipments. They may occur in parallel for different classes of materials for the same receiving factory. *Cyclical procurement* in intervals of a few days up to weeks permits to bundle the transport flow into larger shipments, but generates cycle stock at the receiving factory. In this case, transport planning has to balance the trade-off between transport and inventory cost. *JIT procurement* with at least daily shipments avoids the inbound material passing through the warehouse. Instead, it can be put on a buffer area for a short time. If the arrivals are even *synchronized with the production sequence*, the material can be put immediately to the production line where it is consumed. The latter case is called *synchronized procurement* in the following.

The following transport concepts exist for procurement:

- *Direct transports* from the supplier are suitable for cyclical supply and, if the demand is sufficiently large, also for daily supply. Only if the distance is very short, direct transports may be used for synchronized procurement.
- A *regional LSP* collects the materials in tours from all suppliers in his defined area, consolidates them at a TP and ships them in full trucks to the receiving factory. This concept permits frequent supply, up to daily, even from remote suppliers with low volume. The trunk haulage can also be carried out by rail, if there are suitable connections.
- An *LSP warehouse* close to the factory suits for synchronized procurement: The LSP is responsible for satisfying the short-term calls for the receiver by synchronized shipments. The suppliers have to keep the stock in the warehouse between agreed minimum and maximum levels by appropriate shipments, like in the VMI concept.

The choice among these concepts for different classes of materials is part of the Strategic Network Planning. The short-term planning task consists in generating the calls for material daily, i.e. specifying the quantity per item for orders from the suppliers. In case of cyclical supply, a longer term planning of the frequency for every supplier is useful.

10.2   Models

10.2.1   Transportation and Inventory

Transportation is a discontinuous process. It is carried out in single shipments of a partial or full load - e.g. of a truck, a van, a wagon or a container which take a certain transportation time. In a supply chain, transportation links various supply, production and consumption processes. At the interface of these processes, the inflows and outflows have to be balanced by inventories, except for the case, where a complete synchronization is possible and efficient. In addition, transportation causes transit stock.

In the following, some generic cases of inventories due to transportation are explained. A review of combined transportation and inventory planning is given by Bertazzi and Speranza (1999). First, only the transit stock and the inventory required for balancing asynchronous, but deterministic flows, i.e. production and/or transportation lot-sizing stocks, are considered. In general, additional safety stocks are to be held, as discussed at the end of this section.

Single Link, Single Product

The simplest case is a transportation process linking a production process of a certain product at location A with a consumption process at location B. Both production and demand are continuous with a steady rate. In this case, the optimal transportation scheme consists in regular shipments of the same quantity. Figure 10.2 depicts the cumulative curves of production, departure

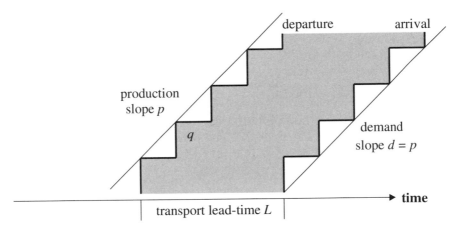

Fig. 10.2. Independent and synchronized schedules

from A, arrival in B and consumption. The vertical distances between these curves represent the development of the stock in A, in transit and in B. With the notations

p	production rate (units per day)
$d = p$	demand rate
Q	maximum load per shipment
L	transport lead-time
t	cycle time
$q = d \cdot t$	shipment quantity
h	inventory holding cost (per unit and day)
$T(q)$	cost of a shipment of quantity $q \leq Q$

the following relationships are obvious: The average lot-sizing stock is $L \cdot d$. As it does not depend on the transport schedule, it can be neglected in transport planning, as long as the transportation time is fixed. Therefore, $L = 0$ can be assumed in the following. However, the transit stock is an important factor in the overall supply chain planning as explained later on. The total cost per day due to transportation is

$$hq + T(q)d/q. \tag{10.1}$$

As the transport cost usually shows economies of scale, i.e. $T(q)/q$ is decreasing with increasing q, there is a tradeoff between inventory and transport cost which can be optimized by the choice of q. If $T(q) = F$ is fixed for $0 < q \leq Q$, i.e. the shipment is exclusive for the quantity q, the optimal q is obtained from the usual EOQ formula (see Silver et al. (1998, Chap. 5.2)) with two modifications: The factor $\frac{1}{2}$ of the holding cost h is missing and q must not exceed Q, i.e.

$$q* = min(Q, \sqrt{Fd/h}). \tag{10.2}$$

However, in most cases, the transportation costs are dominant, so that the transport in full loads $q* = Q$ is optimal.

Single Link, Several Products

Now, several products i are produced in A and consumed in B, each with a steady rate d_i and holding cost h_i. If the transport cost F per shipment is fixed again, it is optimal to ship always all products together, i.e. with a common cycle time t and quantities $q_i = d_i t$ (see Fleischmann (1999)). The optimal cycle time is

$$t^* = min(Q/\sum_i d_i, \sqrt{F/\sum_i h_i d_i}). \tag{10.3}$$

Even if demand fluctuates, it is optimal, at a certain shipment, to ship all products with positive net demand in the following cycle. Rules for determining shipment quantities in this case are discussed in Sect. 10.2.2.

General Case

The above assumption of steady demand may be realistic in case of consumer goods, whereas the consumption of materials by production and the output from production mostly take place in lots. Blumenfeld et al. (1991) and Hall (1996) investigate the influence of production and transport scheduling on inventories in various supply networks and underline the difference between *independent* and *synchronized schedules*. Synchronization of transports and the consumption of materials is the basic idea of JIT procurement. Synchronization of production and distribution is the rule in a make-to-order or assemble-to-order situation, because then both the completion of the production and the shipment to the customer follow his order with respect to the quantity and due date. Production to stock is by its nature not synchronized with shipments on customer orders.

But shipments from a factory to remote DCs or to VMI customers can be synchronized with production to stock. However, in case of many items produced cyclically on common lines and distributed to several destinations,

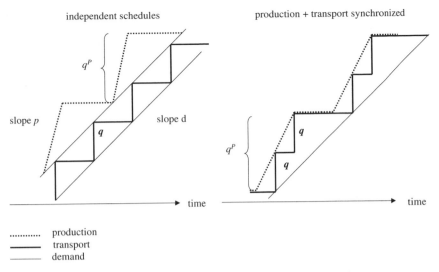

independent schedules   production + transport synchronized

.... production
————— transport
————— demand

Fig. 10.3. Independent and synchronized schedules

the synchronization may become very difficult or impractical. Figure 10.3 depicts the cumulative production, transportation and demand curves for a single product and a single destination in case of independent and of synchronized schedules. In the latter case the production lot-size q^P is an integer multiple of the shipment quantity q. Note that the production rate p is now greater than the demand rate d, because the production line has to produce other items in the intervals between the depicted lots. Obviously, synchronization reduces the average stock level which is in total (at the factory and at the DC)

$$I = \frac{1}{2}q^P(1 - d/p) + q \quad \text{for independent schedules} \qquad (10.4)$$

$$I^S = \frac{1}{2}q^P(1 - d/p) + qd/p \quad \text{for synchronized schedules} \qquad (10.5)$$

(see Blumenfeld et al. (1991)). But the difference is less than the shipment size q which is often small compared with the production lot size q^P. Note that in the case of independent schedules production and transportation scheduling are decomposed by a demand line, which is left-shifted from the true demand line by the transport cycle time (plus the transit time which is not shown in Fig. 10.3). Production has to satisfy this demand line, whereas transportation planning assumes this line as continuous supply like in the single cases considered above.

Routing and Inventory

Scheduling tours for collecting or delivering smaller quantities also influences inventory. In particular, this is true for the tours of a regional LSP collecting materials from several suppliers, but also for delivery tours to several VMI customers. In these cases, the *frequencies* in which the suppliers (or the customers) are visited are decision variables (which may differ from supplier to supplier) and influence both the inventory at the factory and the locations to be visited at a certain day, hence the transportation cost. Again, there is a tradeoff between low inventory (high frequencies) and low transportation costs (low frequencies). Models for combined vehicle routing and inventory planning have been developed only recently. Reviews are given by Baita et al. (1998) and Bertazzi and Speranza (1999).

Transportation and Safety Stocks

In a distribution system for products made to stock, the safety stocks that are necessary for guaranteeing a certain service level, depend on the strategy of the transports between the factory and the DCs (see Silver et al. (1998, Chap. 12.4)): In a strong *push system* any production lot is distributed immediately to the DCs. A modification consists in retaining some central safety stock at the factory warehouse which is distributed in case of imminent stockout at some DC. In a *pull system*, transports are triggered by the local stock at every DC, when it reaches a defined reorder point. In a push system, global information on the demand and stock situation at every DC is required for the central control. But also in a pull system, global information can improve the central allocation of stock in case of a bottleneck. In an APS, such global information should be available for the whole supply chain.

The push system corresponds to the case of synchronized production and distribution and thus requires less cycle stock, but in general higher total safety stock or more cross shipments between the DCs. The local safety stock at a DC has to cover the local demand uncertainty during the transport lead-time and cycle time, the total system safety stock the total demand uncertainty during the production lead-time and cycle time. In a consumer goods distribution system, the transport cycle time is usually very short, as a DC is usually replenished daily, but the production cycle time may last weeks to months, if many products share a production line. Therefore, the system safety stock calculation should be based on a periodic review model with the review period equal to the production cycle.

Transport Planning and Advanced Planning

Mid-term transport planning has to decide on the transport strategies, as discussed above, and the *transport frequencies* for the procurement from suppliers, the replenishment of DCs and the deliveries for VMI customers. By negotiation with other customers, it might even be possible to influence their order frequencies. These decisions imply target stocks of materials and of finished products, composed of transport cycle stock, transit stock and safety stock which are to be considered in the Master Planning as well as in the short-term scheduling of operations.

Short-term transport planning has to determine the quantities to be shipped within a short horizon, usually the next day. This task is considered in more detail in the following section.

10.2.2   Deployment

The general task of deployment is to match the short-term demand with available stock for the next day or few days. As the *source locations* (factories, suppliers), where stock is available, are in general different from the demand locations (DCs, customers), it has to be decided how much to ship from which source location to which demand location.

A Network Flow Model

This task can be formulated as a network flow problem with the data

source locations S_i with available stock a_i $(i = 1, .., m)$,

demand locations D_j with demand d_j $(j = 1, .., n)$,

transport cost c_{ij} per unit from S_i to D_j,

and the decision variables

shipment quantities x_{ij} from S_i to D_j

as follows:

minimize $\sum_{i,j} c_{ij} \cdot x_{ij}$, subject to

$$\sum_j x_{ij} \leq a_i \qquad \text{for every source location } S_i$$

$$\sum_i x_{ij} = d_j \qquad \text{for every demand location } D_j$$

$$x_{ij} \geq 0 \qquad \text{for all } i, j.$$

This is a special LP problem which can be extended to the case of several products and restricted transport capacity. It is in fact an extract from the Master Planning LP for the entire supply chain (see Chap. 7), restricted to transport processes and to a shorter horizon. It is therefore easy to integrate into an APS as it is offered by most APS suppliers. However, the benefit of such a short-term model is questionable, except for supply networks with many remote sources for the same products or materials. The shipment decisions are predetermined by the decisions *where to produce* and *how much to supply* which are typical medium-term Master Planning decisions. *In the normal case*, the short-term sourcing decisions follow single-source rules specified for a longer horizon. Only *in case of shortfall*, deviations have to be decided on, considering the impact on single customer orders and on the service level at DCs. These aspects which cannot be included into a LP model, are discussed in the following.

Delivering Known Customer Orders

In a make-to-order situation, the completion of the orders in due time is the responsibility of production planning and scheduling. Deployment can only deal with completed orders ready for delivery, and the shipment size is fixed by the customer order.

In a make-to-stock situation, many customer orders may compete for the same stock. If the stock at every source is sufficient for the normal allocation of orders, again, all order quantities can be released for delivery.

Otherwise ATP decisions have to be taken as explained in Sect. 10.1.2. If there are several sources with sufficient stock in total, reallocations can be made, either by transshipments from source to source or by directly reallocating certain customer orders from their normal source to an exceptional one. The latter measure is both faster and cheaper, in particular if customers are selected near the border between the delivery areas of the concerned sources. While this is difficult in conventional distribution systems with local control within the areas, it is no problem in an APS with global information and central control of deployment.

Decisions on reducing order sizes or canceling order lines usually consider customer priorities, the service level history by customer and the size of the order line. It is obvious that the mostly used service level, the order line fill rate (see Sect. 6.4), is maximized, if a few of the largest order lines are canceled instead of many small ones.

Replenishment of DCs and VMI Customers and Procurement

Shipment quantities for replenishment and procurement are not determined by customer orders but have to be derived from Demand Planning. Moreover, the calculation requires the prior specification of a certain *transport cycle time* (or of the transport frequency) for every relation, as explained in Sect. 10.2.1. The *net demand* for a shipment is then

d^N = demand forecast at the destination

during the following transport cycle and the transport lead-time

+ safety stock of the destination

./. available stock at the destination.

In a *pull system* the shipment quantity is set equal to d^N, if there is sufficient stock at the source *for all destinations*. The quantities may be modified by a vehicle loading procedure, as explained below. If the stock at the source is not sufficient, it is allocated to the destinations using a *"Fair Shares" rule* which takes into account the demand and stock situation of every destination and therefore requires global information and central control (see Silver et al. (1998, Chap. 12.4.3)). The basic idea of fair shares is to balance the stock at various demand locations so that the expected service level until the arrival of a new supply at the source (e.g. by a production lot) is equal at all locations. If the local stocks are included into the allocation procedure, it may result that, for some destination, the allocation is lower than the available stock, indicating that stock has to be transferred by lateral shipments.

In a *push system*, every supply arriving in the source is immediately distributed to the destinations according to fair shares. In case of short transport lead-times and long supply cycles for the source, it is advantageous to retain some central safety stock at the source which is distributed later according to updated fair shares.

Vehicle Loading

The previous calculations of shipment demand are carried out separately for every product and do not consider joint shipments of many products or transport units (e.g. whole pallets). This is the task of vehicle loading which starts from those shipment quantities and modifies them. As far as the quantities represent net demand, they can only be increased, but in general, the demand calculation can specify minimum quantities below the proposed quantities. An upper bound is given by the stock which is ready for shipment. Vehicle loading comprises the following steps:

- round up or down the shipment quantity of every product to whole transport units,
- adjust the size of the joint shipment, i.e. the sum of the single product quantities, to a full vehicle capacity, where the vehicle is eventually selected from a given fleet.

Both steps have to consider the minimum quantities and the available stock, the second step should try, within these bounds, to balance the percentages of increase (or decrease) over the products. Note that in the long run rounding of shipments to full vehicle loads will only be feasible, if the frequency of shipments is consistent with the average total demand.

Vehicle Scheduling

Vehicle scheduling is the task of the LSP. As far as he uses the vehicles for clients outside the considered supply chain – and this is a source of efficiency of the transport processes – vehicle scheduling cannot be integrated into advanced planning. This only makes sense, if the vehicles are used exclusively in the supply chain, in particular for own vehicles of a manufacturer.

In view of the huge body of literature, models and algorithms for vehicle scheduling and the limited importance for advanced planning, this subject is not dealt with here. Instead, the reader is referred to the following review articles.

Most literature concerns scheduling round trips of vehicles starting and ending at a single depot. This case is relevant for delivering small orders to customers from a TP and for collecting small orders for materials from suppliers by a regional LSP. A recent survey is Laporte (1998).

Vehicle scheduling for trunk haulage, as it occurs on the relations factory – DC, DC – TP, for direct deliveries to customers and in procurement transports, has been investigated only recently (see Stumpf (1998)).

10.2.3   APS Modules

This section is based on the documents of i2 Technologies (1998), Numetrix (1998) and SAP (1999).

The mid-term decisions on transport strategies and frequencies as explained in Sect. 10.2.1, are not supported directly in current APS. Rather, the results are input to the short-term deployment modules. However, the simulative use of the latter modules may be useful for that purpose.

The deployment functions explained in Sect. 10.2.2 are well covered in APS in particular by the following modules:

Deployment optimization with LP. According to the nature of LP models, this function is flexible with respect to a medium or short-term horizon. It is offered either as a separate module or as a subfunction of a Master Planning module for the whole supply chain. In any case, this function overlaps to a large amount with Master Planning, as already emphasized in Sect. 10.2.2.

ATP rules. A wide range of measures dealing with shortfalls of stock for delivering customer orders is supported, considering customer priorities.

Short-term deployment quantities. The shipment quantities can be calculated for push and pull strategies including fair shares rules. These modules can be used for DC replenishment, VMI customers modelled as supply network locations and for procurement.

Vehicle loading. The adjustment of shipment quantities to transport units and full vehicle loads is always available.

Vehicle scheduling. In spite of the weak relation with advanced planning, APS usually contain vehicle scheduling modules. Some systems even contain comprehensive transport management modules which suit for operations planning in an LSP network with many terminals and hubs, including routing and vehicle round trips for trunk haulage. Such modules are in any case useful for an LSP and could be linked by data flows with several APS of separate supply chains.

References

Baita, F.; Ukovich, W.; Pesenti, R.; Favaretto, D. (1998) *Dynamic routing-and-inventory problems: A review*, in: Transportation Research A, Vol. 32, No. 8, 585–598

Bertazzi, L.; Speranza, M.G. (1999) *Models and algorithms for the minimization of inventory and transportation costs: A survey*, in: Speranza, M.G.; Stähly, P. (Eds.), New trends in distribution logistics, Berlin et al., 137–157

Blumenfeld, D.E.; Burns, L.D.; Daganzo, C.F. (1991) *Synchronizing production and transportation schedules*, in: Transportation Research B, Vol. 25B, No. 1, 23–37

Fleischmann, B. (1998) *Design of freight traffic networks*, in: Fleischmann, B.; Nunen, J.A.E.E. van; Speranza, M.G.; Stähly, P. (Eds.), Advances in distribution logistics, Berlin et al., 55–81

Fleischmann, B. (1999) *Transport and inventory planning with discrete shipment times*, in: Speranza, M.G.; Stähly, P. (Eds.), New trends in distribution logistics, Berlin et al., 159–178

Hall, R. (1996) *On the integration of production and distribution: economic order and production quantity implications*, in: Transportation Research B, Vol. 30, No. 5, 87–403

i2 Technologies Inc. (1998) *i2 global footprint training*

Laporte, G. (1998) *Recent advances in routing algorithms*, in: Labbé, M.; Laporte, G.; Tanczos, K.; Toint, P. (Eds.), Operations research and decision aid methodologies in traffic and transportation management, Berlin et al.

Numetrix Inc. (1998) *3D 2.0 User's guide*, Toronto et al.

SAP AG (1999) *Supply network planning and deployment: functions in detail*, December 1999

Silver, E.A.; Pyke, D.F.; Peterson, R. (1998) *Inventory management and production planning and scheduling*, 3rd ed., New York et al.

Stumpf, P. (1998) *Vehicle routing and scheduling for trunk haulage*, in: Fleischmann, B.; Nunen, J.A.E.E. van; Speranza, M.G.; Stähly, P. (Eds.), Advances in distribution logistics, Berlin et al., 341–371

11 Coordination and Integration

Jens Rohde

Darmstadt University of Technology, Institute of Business Administration, Department of Operations and Materials Management, Hochschulstraße 1, 64289 Darmstadt, Germany

A strong *coordination* (i. e. the configuration of data flows and the division of planning tasks to modules) of APS modules is a prerequisite to achieve consistent plans for the different planning levels and for each entity of the supply chain. The same data should be used for each decentralized planning task and decision. APS can be seen as "add-ons" to existing ERP systems with the focus on planning tasks and not on transactional tasks. In most cases an ERP system will be a kind of "leading system" where the main transactional data are kept and maintained. The data basis of APS is incrementally updated and changes are made in the ERP system. This task will be called *integration* of APS with ERP systems. To enable an effective *collaboration* within the organizational units of a supply chain, data and also plans have to be shared. Each entity must do its business on current and consistent information. More and more internet technology is used by APS to achieve a common visibility and current information sharing for the supply chain as a whole and even external customers and suppliers.

The coordination between the different modules described in Part II of this book is very important to derive dovetailed detailed plans for each supply chain entity. Section 11.1 will show which guidelines are given, which data are shared and how feedback is organized. Furthermore, one can see which modules are normally used centrally and decentrally, respectively.

As we have already seen in Chap. 4, some decisions and tasks are left to the ERP system. These tasks and data which are used by APS but are kept in ERP systems are described in Sect. 11.2. The definition of the interface between ERP and APS has to determine which ERP data are used in APS and which data are returned. Moreover, *Data Warehouses* which keep important historical data and are mainly used by Demand Planning build interfaces to APS (see also Chap. 6).

Modules of APS supporting collaboration of supply chain entities as well as external customers and suppliers are part of Sect. 11.3. These modules enable working on current data and propagate alerts throughout the supply chain. Internet technology is used more and more by e-business applications which provide a faster way of communication between businesses and its customers and suppliers.

11.1 Coordination of APS Modules

A general structure for coordination of the different modules cannot be suggested. Several architectures can be found between individual planning modules which can be used as stand alone systems and fully integrated planning modules. A fully integrated system regularly has the advantage of an identical look-and-feel for all modules and accessibility to all modules by a single user interface. Furthermore, a single database provides data needed by every module and avoids redundancies and inconsistencies in the planning data caused by multiple databases. Different modules can interact via sending messages and exchanging data directly. In contrast, individual modules mostly do not have an identical look-and-feel and regularly no common data basis. An advantage of this architecture is that modules can easily be combined and chosen (if not all modules are needed) for a specific line of business. Most APS providers with such architectures provide special integration modules that enable controlled data and information exchange within the system (see also Chap. 15).

The following paragraphs describe which guidelines are given and how feedback is organized to generate the different plans for a supply chain as a whole. Figure 11.1 gives a general view of the main interactions. The data flows are exemplified, as they can be different from one supply chain to another (see Sect. 2.3 and Chap. 3). The main feedback is derived by periodic updates of plans while considering current data. Chapters 5–10 illustrate the interactions between APS modules in more detail.

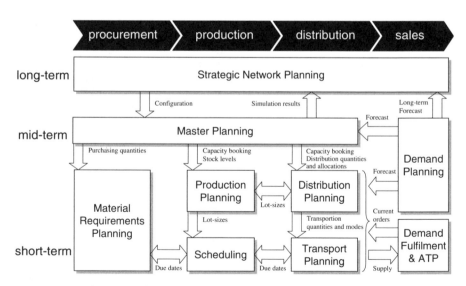

Fig. 11.1. Coordination and data flows of APS modules

Strategic Network Planning Strategic Network Planning determines the configuration of the supply chain. This configuration consists mainly of locations for each supply chain entity and possible distribution channels. Long-term Demand Planning gives input about trends in future demand. Simulated master plans can provide useful hints for capacity enhancements. However, the strategic goals of a supply chain (i. e. market position, expanding in new regions and markets etc.) specify the framework for this module.

Demand Planning Demand Planning provides demand data for mid-term Master Planning as well as for short-term Production and Distribution Planning. The forecast for end products of a supply chain is input for Master Planning. The short-term planning modules use current, more accurate short-term forecasts from Demand Planning. Furthermore, decentralized Demand Planning modules provide demand data for products not planned in Master Planning (e. g. non-critical components).

Master Planning Master Planning determines a production, distribution and purchasing plan for the supply chain as a whole with given demand from Demand Planning. Therefore, this task should be done centrally. The results provide purchasing guidelines for the decentral Material Requirements Planning – like purchasing quantities from external suppliers, production guidelines for the decentral Production Planning and Scheduling – like capacity booking for potential bottlenecks and stock levels at the end of each period and distribution guidelines – like distribution channel chosen and distribution quantities for decentral Distribution and Transport Planning. Feedback from short-term modules is derived by current stock levels, updated forecasts and current capacity usage. The average realization of given guidelines from short-term modules should be used for model adjustment in Master Planning.

Demand Fulfilment and ATP For Demand Fulfilment and ATP demand data from Demand Planning, production quantities for disaggregated products and intermediates, due dates from Production Planning and Scheduling, distribution plans and detailed vehicle routes from Distribution and Transport Planning and purchasing due dates from Material Requirements Planning are used (supply). Furthermore, current inventory levels at each production and distribution stage are needed as input. To be able to influence production and distribution plans, unused capacity bookings have to be known, too.

Production Planning and Scheduling The main guidelines from Master Planning are capacity bookings and stock levels for each period for the decentral units. Production Planning and Scheduling requires detailed, disaggregated information. Furthermore, current (short-term) forecasts and availability of production resources update the guidelines from Master Planning.

Lot-sizes and due dates from this module are exchanged with Distribution and Transport Planning to coordinate production and transport lot-sizes as well as with Material Requirements Planning to coordinate purchasing lot-sizes and due dates in a more detailed way than it is done by Master Planning.

Distribution and Transport Planning The coordination of Distribution and Transport Planning is similar to Production Planning and Scheduling. The short-term coordination by lot-sizes and due dates enables accurate production-distribution plans. The real production quantities provide main input for the transportation plans. Furthermore, time windows from customer orders are additional constraints for building and routing vehicle loads.

11.2   Integration of APS

To use an APS effectively, it has to be integrated in existing IT systems (see Fig. 11.2). The main interactions exist between APS and *online transaction processing* (OLTP) systems, e. g. ERP and legacy systems. Another important but mostly not yet implemented system is a *Data Warehouse* (DW). This "warehouse" stores major historical data of a business and supply chain, respectively. The next subsection will illustrate the integration of APS with OLTP systems. Afterwards, the integration with Data Warehouses is described. The integration of OLTP and Data Warehouses will not be subject of this book.

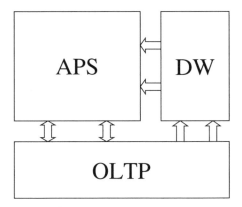

Fig. 11.2. APS integration

11.2.1   Integration with OLTP

An APS does not replace an existing ERP or legacy system. On the contrary, APS extend them by additional planning tasks. Transactional data are kept and maintained in the OLTP system. An APS is only responsible for its specific data, more exactly, all data that are needed but are not part of the OLTP system's data basis.

As Fig. 11.3 shows, an APS regularly communicates with several OLTP systems of different supply chain entities. Furthermore, planning tasks like BOM explosion for non-critical materials and ordering of materials are mostly left to ERP systems (see Chaps. 3 and 4). The *integration model* defines which objects are exchanged, where they come from and which planning tasks are performed on which system. The *data exchange model* specifies how the flow of data and information between the systems is organized.

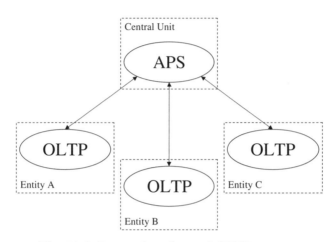

Fig. 11.3. Integration of several OLTP systems

Most APS provide a *macro-language* to define these models and enable an automatic exchange of data. While OLTP systems are regularly older systems, the adjustment has to be done by APS. That is, an APS has to be able to match data items from the OLTP system to its implicit structure and to handle different import and export formats[1], because it is mostly not possible to do all adjustments needed on the OLTP system. It must also be possible to maintain specific data like penalty costs and aggregation rules (see Chap. 7) within the APS.

Integration Model

Within the integration model, objects which are exchanged between OLTP and APS are defined. If, like it is done in most cases, not all products are planned in APS, the integration model has to define which products and

---

[1] At least an ASCII format with fixed field size or a predefined separator is necessary.

materials are critical. Also, the potential bottleneck resources have to be defined. These objects are e. g.:

- BOMs,
- routings,
- inventory levels and
- customer orders.

Furthermore, the integration model has to define which data are exchanged with which OLTP system. A supply chain consists of several entities with local systems. The right data have to be exchanged with the right system. This assignment can be done by modelling different sites with their flows of materials in the Master Planning module (see Chap. 7).

The integration model also defines which results are returned to the OLTP system and the planning tasks done by an APS or ERP system (e. g. performing BOM explosion of non-critical components in local ERP systems). By defining several integration models it is possible to simulate different alternatives of a division of labour between APS and ERP system.

Data Exchange Model

Data *which* have to be exchanged between OLTP and APS are mainly defined by the integration model. The data exchange model defines *how* these data are exchanged. The data transfer between OLTP and APS is executed in two steps (see Fig. 11.4).

The first step is the *initial data transfer*. During this step data needed for building the Master Planning, Production Planning and Scheduling and Distribution and Transport Planning model are transferred from OLTP to APS (e. g. the BOM and routings of critical products, properties of potential bottleneck resources, regular capacities etc.). After the models are generated "automatically", it is necessary to maintain the APS specific data like optimizer profiles, penalty costs and aggregation rules.

In the second step, data are transferred *incrementally* between the systems. The OLTP system should only transfer changes that have been made on the data to the APS and vice versa (*netchange*). The data exchanged are divided into *master data* and *transactional data*. Changes on master data require a model adjustment in the APS. For example, this could be the purchase of a new production resource or the long-term introduction of a second or third shift. Transactional data are transferred to and from APS as a result of planning tasks. For example, the following transactional data are sent incrementally to an APS:

- current inventories,
- current orders,
- availability of resources,
- planned production quantities and stock levels, respectively.

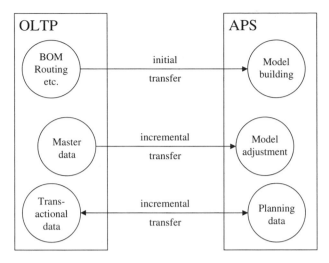

Fig. 11.4. Transferring data between OLTP and APS

Current inventories are needed for every APS module. For Master Planning they can be regarded as a feedback in an incremental planning process, the ATP module uses this data to perform online-promises, while in Distribution Planning it is necessary to calculate the real distribution quantities etc. Current orders are used to match planned orders. Those planned orders are a result of the Production Planning and Scheduling module if this planning task is performed on forecasts. All short-term planning modules have to consider the availability of resources like machines, trucks etc. to generate feasible plans. Planned production quantities and stock levels are for instance needed to perform BOM explosions for non-critical components in local ERP systems.

However, the separated data basis for APS modules poses problems of redundancies and inconsistencies. These problems have to be controlled by the data exchange model. Even though redundancy of data enables the APS to simulate different plans without affecting OLTP systems, it is very difficult to ensure that all systems have the correct data. Changes in each system have to be propagated to avoid an inconsistent data basis. That is, every modification has to be recorded and sent to the relevant systems. If too many changes are made, too many data are transferred between systems and data updates paralyze the APS. The trade-off between 100%–consistency and paralyzation of the APS has to be considered during the implementation process (see Chap. 14). That is to say, it is possible to perform updates in predefined time intervals to avoid trashing by data transfer but with a reduction in consistency.

11.2.2   Integration with Data Warehouses

While OLTP systems depict the current state of a supply chain entity a *Data Warehouse* is its "memory". Nearly all data are available – but not information. The goal of a Data Warehouse is to provide *the right information at the right time*. The Data Warehouse has to bring together disparate data from throughout an organization or supply chain for decision support purposes (Berry and Linoff, 1997, p. 360).

The terms *knowledge discovery in databases* (KDD) and *data mining* keep arising in combination with Data Warehouses. The term KDD is proposed to be employed to describe the whole process of extraction of knowledge from data. Data mining should be used exclusively for the discovery stage of this process (Adriaans and Zantinge, 1996, p. 5).

The interaction between APS and the Data Warehouse is a read-only process – the Data Warehouse is updated incrementally by transactional data from OLTP systems. The main use of Data Warehouses is in Demand Planning which uses historical data regularly to find patterns in demand and sales data and to analyze those time-series with statistical tools (see Chaps. 6 and 21). KDD, especially data mining, provides important input for every step in model building for all modules of an APS. While data mining tools have the focus in *finding patterns* in data, in contrast, *online analytical processing* (OLAP) tools are fast and powerful tools for *reporting* on data. OLAP tools provide a fast way for APS to access data of the Data Warehouse. The conventional way by queries (esp. SQL) is also possible to access data (see Fig. 11.5).

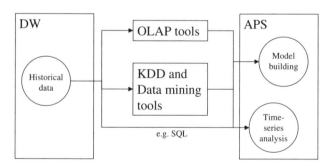

Fig. 11.5. Integration of Data Warehouse

SCM is a new challenge for the design of Data Warehouses. Not only have the data of a single company to be collected, but also supply chain wide transactional data have to be brought together in a consistent way to enable decision support for the supply chain as a whole.

11.3   Collaboration of Supply Chain Entities

After having described more internal and technical details of coordination and integration of APS, this section will take a look at the collaboration of entities of a supply chain as well as external suppliers and customers.

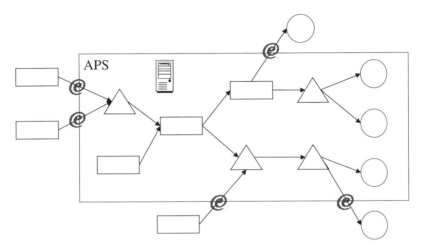

Fig. 11.6. Collaboration of entities

Figure 11.6 shows an example supply chain with one central APS and some external units. Supply chain entities within the rectangle share a single common data basis (not necessarily a single database) with a common visibility. One aspect of collaboration is the synchronization of the flows of materials by Master Planning. Its guidelines enable detailed plans to be generated almost decentrally and autonomously without a loss of coordination of plans. However, it is not reasonable to react on short-term stochastic influences or unpredictable problems (e. g. machine breakdowns) by performing new planning iterations – e. g. Master Planning – Production Planning – Master Planning – and so on. To solve these problems almost decentrally without time intensive loops a common visibility of current and first of all *relevant* information is essential. Relevant means that information has to be filtered and has to reach the right and responsible units at the right time. Some of the information shared among entities of a supply chain are:

- point-of-sale (POS) data,
- inventories and
- forecasts.

Several software modules in APS support information exchange processes within a supply chain as well as with external units. The following paragraphs will briefly depict three important concepts underlying these modules.

11.3.1 Alert Monitor

The alert monitor depicts the concept of *management-by-exception*. Management-by-exception is a technique to control guidelines. It differentiates between *normal cases* and *exceptional cases*. Here, the decision whether a situation is an exceptional case or not is delegated to the APS. The prerequisites for this concept are detailed information about tolerances for normal cases, exact definitions for reporting and delegation of decisions (along the lines of e. g. Silver et al. (1998) and Ulrich and Fluri (1995)).

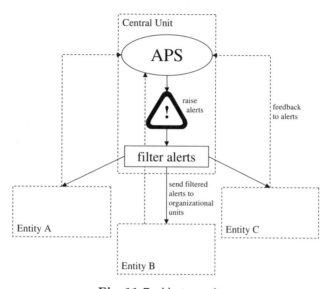

Fig. 11.7. Alert monitor

The APS raises alerts if problems and infeasibilities occur (see Fig. 11.7). To pass the right alerts to the right organizational units within a supply chain, it is necessary to filter these alerts first. Afterwards, filtered alerts are sent to the responsible organizational unit of a supply chain entity. Specifying these responsibilities is part of an implementation project (see Chap. 14). Finally, these alerts have to be sent physically, e. g. by e-mail or an internet based application.

The responsible units react on alerts by generating new plans, moving orders, using spare men etc. The new or adjusted plans are then sent back to the APS. The APS has to process the changes made and propagate them to each unit affected by the changes.

11.3.2 Vendor Managed Inventory

Vendor managed inventory (VMI) is a special service provided by several suppliers. The supplier plans the requirements of his own products within his customer's company. No more orders with information time-lags are sent to the vendor. The customer provides his inventory and demand data. With respect to this information the vendor plans his own and the warehouse replenishment of his customer. Modern EDI-techniques support a fast and current information service.

To control his own inventory and his customer's inventory simultaneously the vendor has to be able to access his customer's major inventory levels and forecasts and has to plan with respect to a system-wide inventory. This could be done by using the so-called *base-stock-system* (e. g. Tempelmeier (1999)).

11.3.3   e-Business

Alert monitor and VMI are concepts for collaboration within a supply chain. However, a supply chain has to be able to communicate and collaborate with external suppliers and customers that are not entities of itself (see Fig. 11.6). The internet technology and modern EDI concepts like XML provide a fast and cheap way of communication and collaboration between different companies and IT systems. Dependent on the parties involved, e-business can usually be divided into:

- business-to-business (B2B),
- business-to-consumer (B2C),
- business-to-administration (B2A) and
- consumer-to-administration (C2A).

APS e-business modules regularly support B2B and B2C applications. Especially in the field of B2B enormous cost savings are possible. Shorter lead-times in processing orders by a high degree of automation are only one potential. Orders can be registered via internet and processed automatically in OLTP systems. Another way is, to generate purchase orders automatically and send them to suppliers with e-business applications. Furthermore, *virtual markets* provide a global communication platform for business activities like offering, selling and purchasing products. While virtual markets provide a short-term, transaction oriented collaboration, APS use them mainly for purchasing processes with external suppliers. However, virtual markets can also be used for supporting B2C activities with external customers. In every case, one has to prove which products are suited for selling and purchasing by e-business applications. Mainly, standard and non-critical products, components and raw materials without high requirements in explanation meet the criteria to be sold and purchased here. Again, this selection has to be done carefully during the implementation process of an SCM project.

References

Adriaans, P.; Zantinge, D. (1996) *Data mining*, Harlow et al.

Berry, M. J. A.; Linoff, G. (1997) *Data mining techniques: For marketing, sales, and customes support*, New York et al.

Silver, E. A.; Pyke, D. F.; Peterson, R. (1998) *Inventory management and production planning and scheduling*, 3rd ed., New York et al.

Tempelmeier, H. (1999) *Material-Logistik: Modelle und Algorithmen für die Produktionsplanung und -steuerung und das Supply Chain Management*, 4th ed., Berlin et al.

Ulrich, P.; Fluri, E. (1995) *Management*, 7th ed., Bern

Part III

Implementing Advanced Planning Systems

12 The Definition of a Supply Chain Project

Christoph Kilger

j & m Management Consulting GmbH, Kaiserringforum, Willy-Brandt-Platz 6, 68161 Mannheim, Germany

Supply chain management projects range from specific improvements on a functional level to large-scale change programmes, involving the redefinition of the business strategy and redesign of business processes. Here, we focus on Advanced Planning System implementation projects, targeting to improve the performance of a supply chain by means of an APS. The starting point of an APS implementation project is "the realization that some kind of significant change is required" (KPMG, 1995). The drivers for the change may be perceived negatively as *pains* or positively as *potentials* – in any case it is apparent to the organization that business must be done differently in the future.

APS implementation projects focus on (i) the planning processes and (ii) the relationships to the partners in the supply chain, i. e. suppliers, customers and sub-contractors. As described in Chap. 3 planning processes create a plan of future business operations, e. g. demand planning, master planning, production scheduling etc. The initial phase of an APS implementation project must deliver a thorough understanding of

- the business model applied and the strategic alignment of the planning processes with the business model,
- the structure of the planning processes and the interaction between the planning processes,
- the planning systems currently employed to support the planning processes,
- the internal relationships and cooperation modes between departments involved in planning tasks, including purchasing, production, order management etc.,
- the current collaboration mode with the supply chain partners, in particular customers and suppliers, but also to some extent competitors and
- the current performance of the supply chain measured by key performance indicators like due date performance and inventory levels, and best practice business models and processes to compare with (see also Chap. 2).

The next section gives an overview of functional areas in a supply chain that have to be examined in order to make an initial assessment of potential improvement areas. This review of the current performance of the supply chain answers the question *Where are we today?*

Based on that review of the current performance of the supply chain the actual improvements that are targeted must be quantified. Section 12.2 focuses on the financial performance criteria of an APS implementation project. In particular, *external factors* influencing the financial performance criteria can be optimized by implementing an APS, as APS functionality enables a business to quickly react to external changes. This gives an answer to the question *Where do we want to go?*

The last step in the definition of an APS implementation project is to build a bridge from the financial performance criteria to the functions and features of Advanced Planning Systems. This bridge is built by logistical *key performance indicators* (KPIs) . KPIs relate functions and features of an APS – so-called *enablers* – to the financial performance criteria. The total scope of the APS implementation project is broken down into smaller sub-projects, each of those having a specific business objective. Section 12.3 shows how a project roadmap consisting of a sequence of sub-projects can be created – answering the question *How do we get there?*

12.1 Supply Chain Review

According to the perception that business performance must be improved, the initial phase of an APS implementation project is the review of the current processes. A common context and understanding within the organization about the structure of the supply chain, the improvement areas and the scope of the envisioned APS implementation project has to be developed. Involving the people that are executing the planning processes as well as management from the beginning of a change programme creates a common understanding of the goals and the scope of the change programme and helps to ensure that all further project activities strive towards consistent objectives (KPMG, 1995).

The following paragraphs discuss topics that have to be clarified with the various functional entities in an organization before entering an APS implementation project. Figure 12.1 summarizes the functional areas involved in the interviews prior to an APS implementation project.

12.1.1 Executive Management

Executive management is an important information source related to strategic issues, cross-functional change programmes and the right target levels of the supply chain.

An example for a strategic decision related to supply chain management is the creation of a new e-business sales channel in parallel to the existing sales channels (Kilger, 2000). This decision will clearly influence the existing sales channels – direct sales via sales representatives as well as indirect sales via channel partners – and hence, has to be managed from the top.

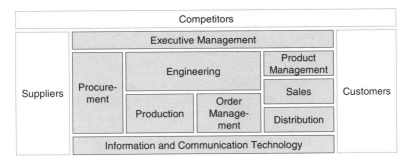

Fig. 12.1. Interview areas prior to an APS implementation project

Another example is the question whether to enter an electronic marketplace on either side of the supply chain – suppliers and customers. In particular, if some marketplace is open to other companies, it is possible that competitors will participate as well in the marketplace. Thus, this decision must be aligned with the strategic differentiation from competition and the targeted collaboration level with suppliers and customers, respectively.

Strategic decisions are long lasting decisions and have a big impact on all aspects of the business. They should be taken before entering a change programme, as they influence the general direction and the scope of the change programme. Furthermore, strategic decisions in a supply chain should be centered around a common vision of the supply chain participants (Poirier, 1999).

The second role of executive management is to enable the change of procedures across multiple functional areas and departments. Most planning processes stretch across multiple functional areas. The interviewer must investigate how these planning processes are done currently and how management is enforcing the collaboration between the departments. Examples for cross-functional planning processes are demand planning and master planning:

- Demand planning is jointly done by sales, marketing and product management.
- Procurement, production, distribution and order management have to create a joint master plan.

Executive management must break barriers between the departments, bridge gaps in understanding and enforce collaboration between the functional areas.

The third role of executive management is to set the target levels for the functional areas and the departments. In many cases, the target definitions of the departments are not consistent or even contradictory. For example, procurement is responsible for keeping inventory levels low, order management has to guarantee a high due date performance and production must ensure a high utilization rate of the production equipment. All three have to collaborate in the master planning process and thus have to agree on uniform goals and targets for the master planning process. Executive management must approve the common master planning targets and make sure that all three departments work towards these targets. Conflicting targets are even more likely to occur if the APS project includes multiple partners in the supply chain, e. g. suppliers and customers.

12.1.2   Sales

The sales force is closest to the customers and thus can give input about behaviour of the customers, the market segments, the demand patterns per segment etc. Sales should be the owner of the demand planning process, resulting in the demand plan that forecasts the future market demand. Important aspects to investigate are the planning frequency, the planning cycle time, the planning accuracy, the structure of the forecast (along the three forecasting dimensions product, geography and time) and issues like seasonal demand patterns, product cannibalism etc. (for details on the demand planning process see Chap. 6). Also the basic questions *What is being forecasted?* and *Who is giving input to the forecast* must be clarified. Often there is no common understanding of the definition of the forecast – which is a prerequisite for measuring the accuracy of the forecast against actuals and to setup a collaborative forecasting process, with input from sales, product management, production, procurement, management and customers. It must also be clarified who is committing to the approved forecast.

One common trap when talking to sales must be observed. In most companies, there is a central sales organization in the headquarter, and there are multiple sales organizations, e. g. regional sales offices. The sales representatives create the demand plan for their sales region. The regional plans are merged to one uniform demand plan by headquarter sales. When talking to sales it is important to distinguish between these two sales functions. As most big change programmes are started by the headquarter, it is obvious that project activities focus on headquarter sales. However, it is very important also to involve the sales regions in the APS project from the beginning on, as the sales regions are close to the customers, and by that, have in-depth knowledge about the customers' behaviour and expectations. Further, changes in the forecasting procedures directly affect central sales operations and the sales regions.

12.1.3   Product Management and Engineering

Product management is responsible for the definition and the positioning of the product lines on the markets. Engineering is in charge of designing new products defined by product management. One important aspect of product management and engineering is the product life cycle management. Especially in industries where the product life cycles are short as in the high tech industry, product life cycle management directly impacts the performance of the supply chain. At the beginning and at the end of a product life cycle, supply and demand is difficult to predict, often leading to excess inventory and/or unmet demand. As an example consider the assembly of computers. Disk drives being one of the major components of a computer have an average product life cycle of four months – there are three product generations per year. Product management/engineering must align the product life cycles of their own products with those of the disk drives and make sure that all planning processes that are dependent on the supply of disk drives – e. g. demand planning, master planning, order promising and production scheduling – observe the product life cycles.

Secondly, product management and engineering gives input to postponement strategies (see also Chap. 1). Postponement helps to reduce marketing risk. Every differentiation which makes a product more suitable for a specified segment of the market makes it less suitable for other segments (Alderson, 1957). Thus, differentiation has to be applied as late as possible in order to be able to react to demand from a large variety of market segments.

A third aspect of product management are marketing activities, e. g. marketing events, the definition of special product bundles or special product offers etc. Marketing activities may influence the demand plan by creating additional demand. All planning processes related to procurement, production and order fulfilment must be aligned with the marketing activities.

12.1.4   Procurement

All in-bound supply processes are executed by procurement. In many industries the supplier lead-time is greater than the order lead-time. As a consequence raw materials must be ordered based on the forecast. In order to give the suppliers a forecast of what will be procured in the future, procurement forecasts the future purchasing decisions as part of the master planning process (supplier forecast). In practice the following issues related to the supplier forecast are often apparent:

- *Gap between sales forecast and supplier forecast*: Theoretically, the sales forecast is the direct input to the supplier forecast, as only what can be sold should be procured. However, in many companies there are process gaps between demand planning and master planning, the latter creating the supplier forecast. These gaps may be due to disconnected information systems or due to communication barriers between sales and procurement.
- *No feedback to sales about feasibility of the forecast*: In material constrained industries it is very important to get an early feedback from the suppliers whether they can fulfil the forecasted quantities. Especially in an allocation situation, where material is short in the market, the master plan will be constrained by the supply. In this case, sales should receive information about the supply they can expect.

- *No clear representation of supplier flexibility*: In order to represent the supply capabilities of a supplier, a flexibility funnel can be defined, specifying the lower bound for the quantities that have to be purchased and the upper bound of the quantities to which the supplier is bound to the terms and conditions of the supplier contract. Beyond the upper quantity, the supplier may request higher rates. Figure 12.2 visualizes an example of a supplier flexibility funnel.

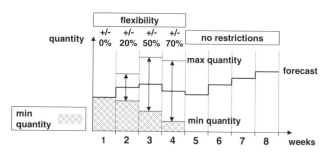

Fig. 12.2. Flexibility funnel of a supplier

- *Accuracy of supplier forecast not being measured*: The supplier forecast accuracy measures the forecasted quantities against the actually procured quantities. The supplier forecast accuracy is a KPI for the procurement processes, as it steers the production of the procured materials at the suppliers' sites.

Besides the supplier forecast the actual purchase orders are issued by procurement. The goal is to fulfil all material requests from manufacturing while keeping inventory levels as low as possible. The interviewer should inquire about the number of inventory turns per year, the average days of supply, the distribution of the inventory age, the on time delivery performance of the suppliers etc. These KPIs give a good overview of the performance of the procurement processes.

12.1.5   Order Management

The management of customer orders gets more important as markets get more competitive. The responsibility of order management is to manage and control customer orders throughout the order life cycle, i. e. from the first customer inquiry to the delivery of an order. The most important planning process order management is involved in is the creation of an initial order promise. Together with sales, order management defines specific allocation policies, allocating the feasible production supply (that is the result of master planning – see Chap. 7 – and is often represented as available-to-promise quantities, ATP – see Chap. 8) to customer segments.

If the supply, the capacity or the demand situation changes, orders have to be rescheduled in order to get a new promise that is based on a feasible plan again. In many organizations, orders are not rescheduled even if the situation is changed – leading to unrealistic order promises. This prevents the impact of the new situation on the customer service level to be assessed – and no action can be taken to inform the customer about the change in time.

As products on global markets get more and more interchangeable due to comparable quality and features, the reliability as a supplier becomes more important – being measured by the customer service level. The customer service level is measured by three KPIs, the on time delivery, the order fill rate and the order lead-time (for a detailled description of these KPIs including a discussion of alternate definitions see Chap. 2). Besides the customer service level, the order volume, the average number of orders per day or week and the peak order entry rate are important measures of the order management processes. Order management must be able to report on these KPIs on a detailed level.

12.1.6   Production

In industries with a complex production process with significant production lead-time, one of the most important performance criteria is the work-in-process (WIP) inventory level. Low WIP inventory levels have a positive impact on many related processes and performance indicators (Goldratt and Fox, 1985):

- *Low WIP reduces production lead-time and on time delivery:* The production lead-time directly depends on the WIP level. The more material sits in the queue in front of a workstation the longer is the average queuing time, leading to a longer production lead-time. Even more serious is that the variability of the production lead-time is increased if the queue in front of a workstation grows. This directly reduces the on time delivery, as it is more difficult to predict the exact production time and confirm orders accordingly.
- *Low WIP improves quality of products:* In most industries production failures leading to quality problems occur in the early production steps, but are detected at later production stages (usually the testing operations). In order to improve the quality of the products, the quality of the whole process must be improved. If the WIP level is high the average lead-time is also high (see previous item). Due to the long lead-time, the test operation at the end of production is often reached a long time after the operation being responsible for the failure has terminated. Often the whole production process changed in the meantime, and the reason for

the quality problems cannot be determined – preventing an improvement of the process. Thus, the lower the WIP, the easier is the detection of quality problems in a complex production environment.

- *Low WIP speeds up time-to-market of new products:* As product cycle time gets shorter and shorter, the importance of the time-to-market of new products grows. If the WIP level is high the production lead-time is also high – leading to a longer time to market. Furthermore, the old products that are still in production can often be sold only for a lower price as soon as the successor product reaches the market. Thus, lower WIP enables a business to bring new products more quickly to the market and to get a higher margin for their products.
- *Low WIP improves forecast accuracy:* The accuracy of the sales forecast depends on the input the sales representatives get from their customers. In many industries an industry specific visibility window has been established: The customers are willing to plan their demand within that window, say for example two months. This standard is often derived from the average production lead-time of this industry – and thus depends on the WIP level. If the production lead-time of a business is below the average purchasing and production get a highly accurate forecast and meet the actual demand of the market. If the production lead-time is above the average the forecast accuracy will be low as sales will not get an accurate demand signal outside the visibility window. Purchasing will procure the wrong materials, production will start the wrong production orders, WIP levels increase and the production lead-time gets even longer.

Besides the WIP level, production controls the manufacturing lead-times, excess capacity, bottlenecks in production and production sourcing decisions (e. g. getting production supply from a contract manufacturer). These are also potential improvement areas for an APS.

12.1.7   Distribution

Distribution can give information about merge in transit operations, physical material flows, inventory levels at distribution centres and the distribution strategy and planning processes (see also Chap. 10). It is important that these processes are synchronized with the demand (i. e. the customer orders) and with the production supply. One of the main issues found in distribution is the synchronization of the supply feeding multiple order line items that have to be shipped together. If the supply is not synchronized unnecessary inventory is build up, and the delivery of the complete order at the due date is jeopardized.

12.1.8   Suppliers, Customers and Competitors

Suppliers and customers are the partners in the supply chain, competitors are potential partners. For example, a manufacturer can join an electronic marketplace together with multiple competitors in order to exchange common procured or intermediate materials. The optimization of the supply chain performance by advanced collaboration techniques (e. g. supplier collaboration, channel collaboration) is beyond the scope of this book (which is focussing on the functionality of APS). Please refer to references like Poirier (1999) and Kilger (2000) for a more detailed coverage of this topic.

12.1.9   Coordination and Integration Technology

One root cause for disconnected planning processes is the extensive use of – department specific or even planner specific – spreadsheets to support the planning processes:

- Spreadsheets maintain data locally; they do not enforce data consisteny and data integrity. Thus, it is highly probable that planners use different data sets, leading to inconsistent planning results.
- Spreadheets are highly flexible; they can easily be adapted to the needs of the individual planners. However, this flexibility leads to a continuous change of the spreadsheets, making it difficult for others to understand the planning process and the planning results.
- Spreadsheets are stored as individual files, limiting the integration with transaction systems, e. g. for loading historic sales, orders on-hand etc. and restricting the capabilities to exploit historic data as input to planning.

Disconnected, spreadsheet based planning processes normally do not consider constraints, leading to planning results without checking feasibility. Due to the sequential execution of the planning processes based on spreadsheets and the non-sufficient decision support functionality of spreadheets planning cycles tend to be long, decreasing forecast accuracy.

The second important aspect of integration technology is the availability of data. Advanced Planning Systems require highly accurate data, including data elements that are normally not maintained within spreadsheets. Even ERP systems like SAP R/3 and J. D. Edwards do not maintain data at a level of detail as required for an APS implementation. For example, the detailed product structure and geographic structure as needed by an APS to support the advanced forecasting functionality is normally not maintained in spreadsheets or ERP systems. But also "standard" data like routings and BOMs are often not maintained in a quality requested by an APS – especially if no planning functionality has been employed that would need this data. The precise review of the available data and the data maintenance processes in place is an important input to make an assessment about the required effort for the APS implementation project.

The third aspect of integration technology that should be reviewed prior to an APS implementation project is the communication between systems.

In organizations where it is common practice to integrate systems via standard middleware products like CORBA, it will be easier to embed an APS into the existing IT landscape, than in an organization, where only disconnected IT islands exist or where only integrated standard software like ERP systems are used. The experience with system integration and the willingness to create and maintain interfaces between systems that are existing in the organization is also an important factor to estimate the effort required for the APS implementation.

12.1.10 Interview Techniques

As SCM is a relatively new area to most industry corporations, it is important to get a good understanding of the experience level related to SCM that is available in the departments. Most people feel that benefits in the way business is done can be achieved, but often they do not believe that improvements are feasible. In many situations, especially if the performance of the supply chain is low, people fear to get critizied and being made responsible for the poor performance and – as a consequence – are not open for cooperation. In order to build a good relationship, questions should be kept open ended and people should have room to talk about their ideas related to supply chain management. The following questions could help to start a discussion (i2, 1998):

- "What is your vision for your business with respect to supply chain management?
- What initiatives are currently started and on-going that move you towards that vision?
- How are your planning processes currently structured?
- What targets are defined for planning process XYZ?
- Who creates the sales forecast, the master plan, the detailed production plan, the distribution plan etc.?
- What would be the impact if your organization would have visibility into the sales forecast, the production plan etc.?
- What obstacles are hindering you to improve the forecast accuracy (or other key performance indicators)?"

In order to make the communication with the supply chain experts in the organization more effective, graphical visualization techniques should be employed. Especially the visualization of the material and the information flows of the supply chain helps in the discussions with the various departments and is a good starting point for identifying constraints and/or improvement areas in the supply chain. To the operation and the material buffer representations of a supply chain flow model, additional information can be attached about specific characteristics like vendor managed inventory, multi-plant sourcing, security stock levels, batch sizes, lead-times etc. If already possible in this step, all constraints in the supply chain should be identified in the model, as well as potential locations of excess inventory. Chapter 2 shows how the SCOR-model can be used to visualize and model a supply chain.

The next step in a supply chain review would be to get an overview of the planning processes, e. g. *sales forecasting, master planning, production planning, distribution planning, detailed scheduling.* A simple process flow notation can be employed, showing sequential relationships between the individual planning processes, the IT systems (decision support systems, transactional systems, ERP systems) supporting the planning processes and the data flows between the IT systems. Chapter 3 gives an introduction to the various planning processes. The most important item to be checked is the integration of the planning processes. In many organizations, planning processes are performed sequentially and disconnected. Planning results of a former process step are not or only partially used as input to the subsequent steps. This leads to non-synchronized process chains and sub-optimal planning decisions.

12.2   Supply Chain Potential Analysis

The motivation of an organization to setup an APS implementation project is to improve business performance. Financial benefits can be measured in three ways. *Net profit* is an absolute measurement of making money. However, if we know that a company earns 20 million $ a year, we cannot tell whether this is a good or a bad performance – as the performance of a company depends on the money that has been invested in the business.

In the business environment at the beginning of the third millenium the performance of a business relative to the invested capital is in the focus of managers and shareholders. The term *shareholder value* is ubiquitous. The *return on investment (ROI)* gives us the performance of a business relatively to the capital that has been invested. The invested capital consists of multiple components, e. g. cash, receivables, inventories, property, buildings, equipment and liabilities. APS implementation projects mainly affect the assets, not the financial components of the invested capital like debts and equity. That is why from a supply chain management perspective the *return on assets (ROA)* is often used as relative business performance measure instead of the ROI.

The third measurement of the financial performance of a business is the *cash flow.* Following Coenenberg (1997), the cash flow is the profit, i. e. sales revenue minus expenses, adjusted by depreciations and financial reserves that can be freely used for investments, repayment of debts and distribution of dividends. As Goldratt and Fox (1985) observe, the cash flow is an on-off measurement: When there is enough cash, it is not important. When there is not enough cash, nothing else is important.

12.2.1   Return On Assets

In the following, we focus on the return on assets as the bottom line performance measure. A common definition for the ROA is as follows (see e. g. Robeson and Copacino (1994)):

$$\text{ROA} = \frac{\text{Revenue} - \text{Expenses}}{\text{Assets}} \tag{12.1}$$

The sales revenue is all the money the customers pay for the offered products and/or services. Expenses is all the money the company spends to turn inventory into sales. This definition follows Goldratt and Fox (1985) and includes all direct costs and those indirect costs that are spent in order to generate sales – all other costs are a waste anyway. Assets include all equipment and material that is involved in turning inventory into sales. In order to improve the ROA by means of an APS implementation project, the ROA components – revenue, expenses and assets – have to be improved. Thus, in order to evaluate the benefits of a planned implementation of an APS, we have to analyze how revenue, expenses and assets will be improved by better planning capabilities provided by the APS. Figure 12.3 gives examples of how poor planning capabilities can reduce the ROA.

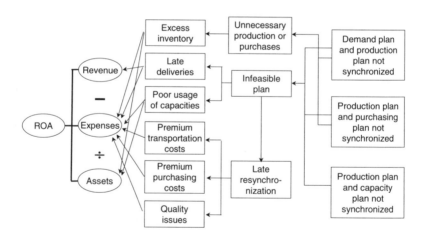

Fig. 12.3. Impact of poor planning capabilities on the ROA

12.2.2   Scenario

Let us illustrate the impact of poor planning capabilities on the ROA by means of an example (adapted from Kilger (1998)). Figure 12.4 shows a supply chain with suppliers, factories, national and regional distribution centres and customers. For example, let us assume that in one factory a machine goes down and due to the service required the machine will be up again in three days. An ERP system would adapt the schedule of that machine accordingly and move out all manufacturing orders that are impacted by the change. But what is the impact of the downtime of that machine on the complete supply chain? In order to answer that question the new situation has to be propagated upstream and downstream:

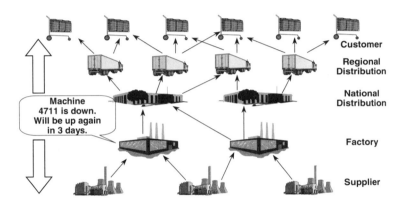

Fig. 12.4. Propagation of changes in a supply chain

- *Upstream:* Due to the machine downtime the raw material of the manufacturing orders that have been moved out will be consumed later. The supplier can peg this material potentially to other customers (factories) and thus make additional revenue.

- *Downstream:* The national distribution centre receiving the finished goods may run into a problem, if the supply that is now delayed is required to fulfil all customer orders on time. This would reduce revenue and increase inventory and expenses.

- *Planning scenario:* In order to assess whether the plan at the national distribution centre can be optimized a planning scenario is created to check the impact on the supply chain if the national distribution centre receives the material from an alternate factory. This potentially can help to ship the orders in time, by that securing revenue.

12.2.3   External Variability

This example indicates that the performance of a supply chain is to a large extent influenced by external disturbances. Thus, in order to assess the potential benefits of an APS implementation project, focus should be laid on the impact of external factors on the ROA components – revenue, expenses and assets. It is interesting to note that transaction systems like Enterprise Resource Planning (ERP) systems (e. g. SAP R/3, J. D. Edwards) focus rather on the internal processes than on the external factors influencing the ROA. For example, the production planning modules of an ERP system help to create an initial production schedule (that is often not feasible) and support the tracking of the material flow on the shop floor – but they do not provide simulation capabilities and problem resolution functions to quickly react to external changes.

In the following, we discuss examples illustrating the impact of external factors on expenses and assets.[1] The impact of the external factors on the revenue is obvious as all sales are generated by customers.

12.2.4   Excess Expenses

Expenses are partially internally and partially externally controlled. In every industry there is a cost segment that is determined by the type of production. For example, computers are assembled in a similar way all over the world: get all components you need and assemble them into the housing, test the device, pack it and ship it. The costs implied by this process are comparable across the computer industry and – more important – there is only a marginal impact of supply chain management techniques on the internal production costs. However, there is a big impact of supply chain management on the expenses determined by external factors, being for example:

- Pay premium air freight fare to get material because of late or short supply by the standard suppliers;
- pay extra production wages for subcontractor manufacturing in order to account for peak load situations due to additional demand or delayed production;
- reschedule the production plan (including the need to pay overtime rates for the workers) because of short term additional demand or delayed supplies of material;
- buy critical components on the spot market (e. g. processors, memory) for a higher price compared to the preferred supplier.

12.2.5   Excess Assets

The total value of assets in a supply chain can be split into "base assets" that are required for the production operations and "excess assets" that are

---

[1] The examples are based on ideas by Sanjiv Sidhu (1999).

being used to shield the supply chain from external variability. For example, excess inventories and safety stocks of raw material, work in progress and finished goods are used to buffer production from the demand variability of the market. These excess inventories may lead to increased material costs due to

- price reductions (e. g. the price of electronic components reduces by 2% per week in the average),
- obsolescences (i. e. components that cannot be sold on the market any longer because a better successor has been introduced to the market for the same price),
- stock keeping costs,
- internal capital costs and
- material handling.

By better controlling the volatility in the supply chain, excess inventory may be reduced and business performance will increase. However, please note that some safety stocks will in most cases be required due to uncertainties that are "inherent" to the supply chain and may not be controlled (Chap. 6 gives an overview of safety stock policies).

Excess capacity is built up in order to have sufficient capacity to cover peak load situations. Due to the interdependencies in a production system – a resource can start a production operation only if all preceding operations have been completed and all required raw material is available – the load variability of a resource increases with the number of preceding operations. Thus, load variability is higher the more downstream the resource is located, and – because of that – excess resources are often build up at the end – downstream – of the supply chain (this is typically the test area). This effect is also referred to as the *bullwhip effect*, see also Fig. 1.5 on page 23. One root cause for the bullwhip effect is a bad synchronization of processes and a lack of visibility and transparency in the supply chain.

12.3   Project Roadmap

ROA, revenue, expenses and assets are financial criteria to measure the performance of a business. In the preceding section we have shown that external factors are responsible to a large extent for the performance level of the financial criteria. Because of advanced planning capabilities APS can quickly react to external changes and by that help to improve the financial performance indicators.

However, having identified improvement potentials based on the financial performance indicators does not necessarily give good hints how to realize these potentials. For example, if revenue is low and shall be increased, what is the root cause? Which levers exist to create additional revenue? What functionality of an APS would help? How should the project be structured in order to get project steps of reasonable size?

In order to answer these questions and to create a roadmap for the project, the financial performance criteria have to be related to concrete improvement activities. The bridge between these financial criteria and the project activities is formed by logistical KPIs. The following steps describe the way to structure a big change programme and to define the project roadmap by a value driven approach:

1. identify improvement potential based on the financial indicators,
2. transform the targeted improvement of the financial indicators to a targeted improvement of the logistical KPIs and
3. assess which functionality of the APS would enable the targeted improvement of the logistical KPIs.

As APS offer a broad range of functionalities – as described in detail in Part II of this book – it is very important to start the definition of an APS implementation project from the value perspective, as indicated by steps 1–3 listed above. Starting the definition of an APS project from the functional perspective bears the risk that the system gets overengineered, i. e. the system would contain many functions that do not necessarily help to improve the business situation.

For example, in the computer industry, order promising and production planning is normally constrained by the material supply and not by capacity. Thus, exploiting the finite capacity planning abilities of APS in order to improve the production scheduling process would not lead to a big business improvement. Following the three steps listed above, one could define the project scope as follows:

1. The main target of the project is to generate additional sales and to increase revenue.
2. Additional sales can be generated by improving the on time delivery. (This value proposition can be backed by industry benchmarks and interviews with the customers; refer to Chap. 2 for additional details.)
3. On time delivery can be improved by an APS by
   - synchronization of purchasing decisions and order promising based on forecast/ATP,
   - creation of feasible master plans considering all constraints and
   - simulation of additional receipts / rescheduling of orders in order to further improve the master plan.

Thus, the focus of the project should be laid on forecasting, master planning and order promising, instead of production scheduling.

In general, the relationships between financial performance indicators, logistical key performance indicators and APS enablers form a complex network. This network strongly depends on the concrete project targets and the

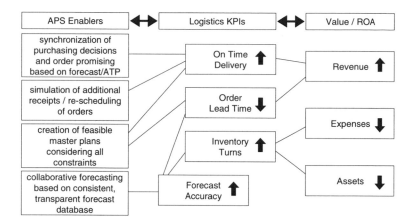

Fig. 12.5. Enabler–KPI–Value network

scope of the change programme. Figure 12.5 shows an Enabler–KPI–Value network based on the example given above.

In the following we briefly describe the main logistical KPIs and discuss how they are related to the financial performance criteria. A detailed description of the KPIs can be found in Chap. 2.

Forecast Accuracy The forecast accuracy relates forecasted quantities to actual quantities. For example, the ratio of the forecast on finished goods level to the actual sales quantities may be used to measure the accuracy of the forecast on finished goods level. The forecast accuracy measures the ability to forecast future demand. By improving the forecast accuracy, inventory levels may be shortened, and the order lead-time may be improved. Thus, forecast accuracy is a *second level* KPI, as it is only indirectly related to the financial performance criteria by further logistical KPIs. Chapter 6 gives an overview of methods to measure the forecast accuracy.

Planning Cycle Time Time between the beginning of two subsequent planning cycles. Long planning cycle times prevent the plan from following the changes in the real world. Thus, purchasing and production decisions are based on old data and therefore do not reflect the actual situation. This may lead to unnecessary production or purchases, increasing inventory and reducing customer service. Please note that setting the appropriate planning cycle time depends on the aggregation level of the planning process and on the planning horizon. Refer to Chap. 3 for an overview of planning processes and their respective horizons.

Customer Service Level Customer service is measured by three KPIs described in the following: on time delivery, order fill rate and order lead-time. Improving the customer service level may improve the positioning of the business in competition and may generate additional sales and increased revenue.

On Time Delivery Percentage of orders that are completely fulfilled at the due date. A low on time delivery indicates that the order promising process is not synchronized with the execution processes, i. e. purchasing, production and transportation. Either orders are promised based on a plan that is not feasible, or the purchasing, production and transportation operations are not executed as planned. Another root cause for bad due date performance can be wrong purchasing, production and transportation decisions based on a non-accurate forecast.

Order Fill Rate Average percentage of completeness of customer orders at the due date. The completeness of an order may be related to the number of line items of that order or to the requested quantities. A low order fill rate might be caused by poor order planning processes or incapability of synchronizing production with order fulfilment. The ability to ship complete orders on the due date can have significant impact on sales revenue.

Order Lead-time Number of days between the order entry and the shipment or delivery of the order, respectively. As product life cycles decrease and demand variability increases, short order lead-times become important in competitive situations.

Inventory Turns The number of inventory turns is the ratio of the total inventory consumption in a time period to the average inventory level in the same time period. High inventory levels are often caused by poor synchronization of demand, supply and capacity. Increasing the number of inventory turns may lead to lower expenses and reduction of assets. Further, increased inventory turns "train" the supply chain to operate on a low inventory level. This enables the supply chain to have the right material at the right time in the right quantity on hand as being requested by the customers – instead of relying on inventories that in many cases will not match the actual demand anyway.

Inventory Age Average time of inventory residing in stock. The age of the inventory is a good indicator for unnecessary high inventory levels. A high variability of the age of inventory indicates potential obsolescences. If the average age of inventory is high inventory has been build up too early as it has not been consumed up to now – and the same service level could have been achieved with lower inventory. Especially in industries where the asset utilization is a key performance measure (like in the steel industry), the age of the inventory indicates whether inventory was build up in order to keep asset utilization high. Inventory age again is a second level KPI, as it helps to identify unnecessary "pockets" of inventory and by that can help to increase inventory turns.

12.3.1   KPI Profile

Having identified a collection of logistical KPIs that have to be improved by the APS implementation project, the next step is to further detail the improvement. This is done by setting up a *KPI profile* for each of the KPIs. A KPI profile consists of five constituents:

1. The first step is to determine the current as-is value of the KPI. This fixes the starting point of the targeted improvement activities and is the base for measuring the success of the project.
2. Then, the targeted to-be value of the KPI has to be set. This gives us the goal we want to reach by the project.
3. In the next step, the time horizon to reach the to-be KPI value is estimated. This can only be a rough estimate as a detailed project plan has not yet been created.
4. From the targeted improvements the enablers of APS that can help to reach the targets have to be determined, as well as additional influencing factors like process restructuring, reshaping the organizational structures, analyzing high-level data requirements etc. Especially process changes are required in most cases to realize the full benefit as expressed by the to-be KPI value.
5. Based on the as-is value, the to-be value, the estimated time horizon and the considered APS enablers, actual project activities are setup and implemented. It is important to note that each of these sub-projects have to generate business value in a given time period, by applying predefined APS enablers.
6. In order to enter a continuous improvement process, one can go back to step 1 and start the cycle again from a higher performance level.

Figure 12.6 visualizes the constituent parts of a KPI profile.

Note that at this point in time, we are still in the definition phase of the project. The KPI profiles helps breaking down the complete project scope into a sequence of sub-projects, each having a clear objective and a well-defined scope. By that we make sure that the definition of the sub-projects is value driven and not driven by the "nice functional features" of an APS – helping to prevent the system to get overengineered. The result of the project roadmap definition phase is a high level project plan, consisting of the identified sub-projects, including preliminary milestones and a first estimate of project resources.

From the APS enablers that are used in the KPI profiles a requirements list for the selection of an APS can be derived. In the next chapter we focus on

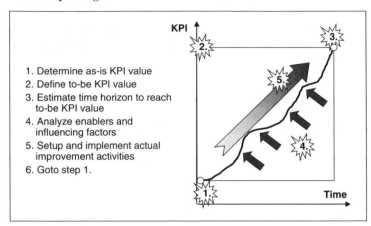

1. Determine as-is KPI value
2. Define to-be KPI value
3. Estimate time horizon to reach to-be KPI value
4. Analyze enablers and influencing factors
5. Setup and implement actual improvement activities
6. Goto step 1.

Fig. 12.6. Continous improvement cycle based on KPIs

the selection process of Advanced Planning Systems – with the requirements list being one major input to the APS selection. However, despite the fact that APS are providing advanced planning capabilities that may help to improve business, it is important to realize that additional measures have to be taken to achieve the full business objectives as documented by the KPI profiles. Especially process changes and the provision of additional data for the APS are required in most cases and should be roughly planned already at this stage.

References

Alderson, W. (1957) *Marketing behavior and executive action*, Homewood, Illinois

Coenenberg, A. G. (1997) *Kostenrechnung und Kostenanalyse*, 3rd edition, Landsberg/Lech

Goldratt, E. M.; Fox, R. E. (1985) *The Race*

i2 Technologies (1998) *Supply chain opportunity assessment*, unpublished

Kilger, C. (1998) *Optimierung der Supply Chain durch Advanced Planning Systems*, in: Information Management & Consulting, Vol. 13, No. 3, 49–55

Kilger, C. (2000) *Supply-based eBusiness: Integration von eBusiness und Supply Chain Management*, in: Dangelmaier, W.; Felser, W. (Eds.) Das reagible Unternehmen, Paderborn, 74–86

KPMG (1995) *Business Performance Improvement Methodology*

Poirier, C. (1985) *Advanced supply chain management: How to build a sustained competitive advantage*, San Francisco

Robeson, J. F.; Copacino, W. C. (1994) *The logistics handbook*, New York et al.

Sidhu, S. (1999) *private conversation*

Umble, M.; Mokshagundam, S. (1995) *Synchronous manufacturing: Principles for world-class excellence*, Boston

13 The Selection Process

Christoph Kilger

j & m Management Consulting GmbH, Kaiserringforum, Willy-Brandt-Platz 6, 68161 Mannheim, Germany

Advanced Planning Systems are a relatively new software technology. One of the first Advanced Planning Systems was OPT that was implemented end of the Eighties (Schragenheim and Ronen, 1990; Silver et al., 1998). OPT is based on the *Theory of Constraints* (Goldratt, 1990), stipulating that the constraints of a production system have to be represented in detail in a planning system in order to exploit and to control the performance of the system.

Since these early days, many other APS have been implemented and installed at many sites. A good overview of the APS market is given by the Gartner magic quadrant which is published quarterly. Gartner groups the vendors along two dimensions: the completeness of the vision and the ability to execute. In the Gartner report from end of 1999 (Enslow, 1999), there is one APS vendor in the leader group having a high ability to execute and a complete vision. The follower group contains approx. 20 APS vendors, being – according to Gartner – visionaries, but with a lower ability to execute. The third group are the niche players, characterized by a lower ability to execute and a more focused vision.

Another good source for information about the APS market are the AMR reports, being published several times a year by Advanced Manufacturing Research. The May 1998 report e. g. gives an overview of the planning capabilities of leading APS (AMR, 1998).

Kortmann and Lessing (2000) give a detailed overview of the APS market as of mid 1999, including a classification scheme for APS and information on the selection of APS.

Beginning of the year 2000, the APS market is growing rapidly, and the systems get more and more mature. The potential user has a large variety of systems to choose from, and in many cases, a clear indication which system to buy and implement is not at hand. Thus, a systematic approach for the selection of an APS is required. There are four steps that can be followed to select an APS:

1. A *short list of Advanced Planning Systems* should be created based on parameters as industry, typical size of companies using the system, licence fees and implementation time and effort.
2. The APS that are on the short list are assessed by the *functional requirements* that have been collected in the definition phase of the APS project (see previous chapter).

3. The detailed implementation plan including a refined estimate of the effort and the timelines for the *implementation and integration* of the APS should match the targeted scope of the project.
4. The *post-implementation tasks* required after the APS has been installed must be assessed.

In the following sections we detail the four steps which in summary provide a practice-proven methodology for the selection of an APS.

13.1   Creation of a Short List

In the early phase of the selection process the "strategic fit" of the APS with the industry within which the supply chain is operating, the size of the companies participating in the supply chain, the budget targeted for the APS implementation project and the planned implementation time may be equally important as the features and functions. The assessment of the APS by these criteria cuts down the number of APS that have to be considered in the subsequent detailed analysis. By that, time and effort for the selection process can be reduced tremendously.

13.1.1   Industry Focus and Experience

The industry is an important selection criteria for APS, as most vendors have expertise in specific industries, supporting the planning processes of these industries better than those in other industries (Enslow, 1998). The manufacturing processes, the used terminology, the business rules, the planning processes, the optimization procedures and the reporting requirements strongly differ across industries (Felser et al., 1999). For a number of reasons, APS vendors often focus on one or two specific industries, for example:

- The engineers that are responsible for the design and the implementation of the system already had experience in these industries.
- The first successful implementations were installed in these industries.
- For strategic reasons the APS vendor is focussing on these industries.

Some of the APS vendors launch implementation initiatives for specific industries, trying to extent the scope of their expertise to a new industry area.

The main improvement areas of an APS implementation strongly depend on the type of industry, resp. the type of the supply chain according to the supply chain typology (refer to Chap. 2). In distribution intensive industries the main potentials are in the optimization of the distribution and transportation operations, including the deployment of supply and the reduction of inventory. In asset intensive industries major improvements are possible by the optimization of the throughput, the detailed scheduling of the capacity bottlenecks and the reduction of change over times. In material intensive

Table 13.1. Industry focus of APS vendors (part 1) (Felser et al., 1999)

Industry	Dynasys	i2 Technologies	Logility	Manugistics	J. D. Edwards[1]
Electronics/High-tech		•	○	•	•
Aviation/Defense	○	•	○		
Automotive	○	•	○	•	•
Mechanical Engineering			○		
Metals	○	•	•	•	
Pharmaceuticals	○	•	○	•	•
Chemicals	○	•	○	•	•
Paper& Print		•	•	•	
Oil, Gas/Energy			○	•	
CPG[2]	•	•	○	•	•
Textile	○	•	○	•	•
Food	•	•	○	•	•
Transport		•	○	•	
Others	Glass		Health care		

•: industry focus according to vendor; ○: installations existing according to vendor
[1] Formerly Numetrix
[2] Consumer Packed Goods

industries forecasting and procurement decisions influence business performance and should be optimized by the APS. Tables 13.1 and 13.2 (originally published in Felser et al. (1999)) give an overview of the industries supported by a range of APS vendors. The data has been collected mid of 1999 based on a questionnaire that has been completed by the APS vendors.

A remark has to be made related to the number of installations. The procedure to measure the number of installations strongly depends on the APS vendor. Some vendors take the number of production sites that are supported by their APS, others count every client installation as a separate installation. Furthermore, some vendors consider any installation, whether productive or in an early implementation stage, whereas others consider only installations where the customer has announced that the system is being used productively. Thus, it should be defined precisely how the number of installations are being measured.

Table 13.2. Industry focus of APS vendors (part 2) (Felser et al., 1999)

Industry	Paragon	Symix Systems	SynQuest	Wassermann	webPLAN
Electronics/High-tech	●	○	○	○	●
Aviation/Defense	●		○	○	●
Automotive	●	○	○	●	●
Mechanical Engineering	●	●	○	○	●
Metals		○	●	○	
Pharma-ceuticals	●	○		○	
Chemicals		○		○	
Paper & Print	●	○	○		
Oil, Gas/Energy					
CPG[1]	●				●
Textile	●				
Food	●				
Transport					
Others			Furnitures		

●: industry focus according to vendor; ○: installations existing according to vendor
[1] Consumer Packed Goods

13.1.2   Typical Size of APS User Companies

Besides the industry focus the size of the companies that are customers of the APS vendors gives first hints whether a specific APS vendor fits to a specific company. Figure 13.1 visualizes the results from Felser et al. (1999). The APS vendors can clearly be classified into those that focus on large organizations as customers (e.g. i2 Technologies and J.D. Edwards) and those that focus on small and medium sized companies (e.g. SynQuest, Wassermann, and webPLAN).

13.1.3   Licence Fees

Typically, the size of the customers of an APS vendor also relates to the licence fees. Whereas APS vendors with larger customers tend to be in the upper price segment, the APS vendors with small and medium sized customers are more often found in the lower price segment. In many cases, the

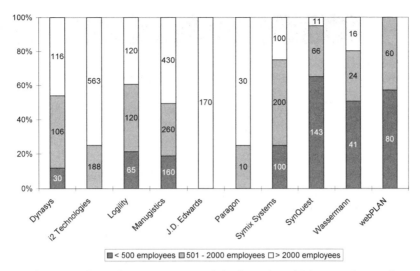

Fig. 13.1. Size of the customers of APS vendors (Felser et al., 1999)

license fees are determined based on the number of users and the expected business benefits created by the implementation the APS – measured by KPI improvements as described in Chap. 12. The license fees should match the expectations and the targeted budget of the APS implementation project. However, it is difficult to get information about the pricing model applied by the APS vendors without entering actual contract negotiations.

13.1.4   Implementation Time and Costs

Besides customer size and implementation costs, the typical implementation time and implementation effort should be considered. From this, an estimate of the implementation costs can be derived, including the use of internal resources as well as external consultants and experts from the APS vendor. The best information source to estimate the time and effort are reference projects in the same industry – or in related industries, as direct competitors most probably will not talk about their experiences. The APS vendors should provide a list with references where projects with a similar scope had been completed and set productive. A visit at one or several reference sites is strongly recommended at an early stage of the selection process in order to learn from the experiences that have been made with the APS vendor and its systems.

13.2   Functional Requirements

The main result of the definition phase of the APS project has been the detailed requirements list (see Chap. 12). The detailed requirements list can

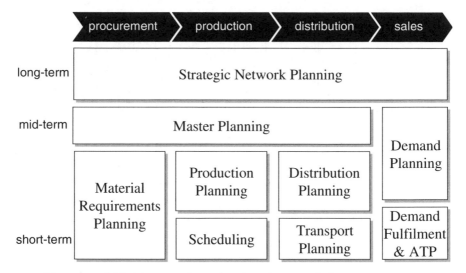

Fig. 13.2. SCP-Matrix as basis for the selection of planning processes

easily contain up to 100 individual requirements; in one APS selection process the author has been involved in, 60 detailed requirements have been selected. In order to be able to handle a large list of requirements the requirements should be grouped according to the planning processes that are in the scope of the envisioned APS implementation project. Figure 13.2 shows the SCP-Matrix as introduced in Chaps. 3 and 4 that can be used to identify the planning processes that are to be supported by the APS, e. g. Demand Planning, Master Planning, Demand Fulfilment and Production Planning and Scheduling. All requirements should be assigned to one of the selected planning processes.

As APS are a relatively new software technology, most systems are only partially developed with respect to the full functional scope announced by the APS vendors. In many areas, the APS have to be further developed, either by adding additional functionality, resolving issues within existing functionality or better integrating the functional modules. The latter issue – lack of integration – is especially a problem for APS vendors that have acquired another APS vendor in order to include the systems of that vendor into their own product suite. To reflect the coverage of the functional requirements and the plans of the APS vendors to further develop their systems, the following assessment scheme has been developed, consisting of five levels:

Level 1 The functionality is not available; there is no plan to develop this functionality.
Level 2 The functionality is not available; it is planned to develop this functionality in the future.
Level 3 The functionality is partially available; there is no plan to develop this functionality further.

Level 4 The functionality is partially available; it is planned to further develop this functionality in the future.

Level 5 The functionality is currently fully available.

There are three options to evaluate the functional requirements according to these five levels. The easiest and fastest way to get an assessment is to hand over the detailed requirements list grouped by the planning processes to the APS vendors and ask them to provide a self-assessment of their respective systems. For requirements being evaluated to be at levels 2 and 4, a date for the availability of the future development must be provided by the APS vendor; for requirements being evaluated to be at levels 3 and 4, details about the degree to which the functionality is currently available must be provided by the APS vendor.

The second option is to ask the APS vendors to demonstrate the required functionality in a live demo. As this takes more time and effort than the first option – on both sides, the potential customer and the APS vendor – only key functionality should be selected for demonstration. Typically, the second option is combined with the first option: Based on the self-assessment of the APS vendor, critical functional requirements are selected to be shown in a live demo. In order to prepare this, the APS vendor can be asked to state for each functional requirements his ability to demonstrate that functionality, according to the following scheme:

Level A The functionality can be demonstrated with an existing demonstration set with less than 24 hours lead-time.

Level B The functionality can be demonstrated, but requires changes to the standard demonstration models (no changes to the software).

Level C The functionality can be demonstrated at another customer's site.

Level D The functionality cannot be demonstrated easily.

The third option is to implement a prototype, to assess in detail to what degree a specific functional requirement can be fulfilled by an APS. This of course creates additional effort and must be carefully planned. The following issues should be clarified before starting a prototype implementation:

- The scope and the target of the prototype must be clearly defined. Only critical functional requirements and interface issues should be prototyped. For example, the integration of the APS into an existing order entry system can be evaluated by implementing a prototype system.
- A detailed project plan for the prototype implementation and a budget (cost and time) must be set up. This includes the decision of what portion of the effort is taken over by the APS vendor.
- In relation to this it must be decided which APS shall be included into the prototype implementation effort. Normally, the number of systems that are prototyped is restricted to one or two. Otherwise, too much effort is invested into development work that cannot be re-used in the real implementation project after the selection process.

Based on the prototype implementation(s) it must be possible to answer all open questions that have been included in the scope of the prototype.

The results of the self-assessment by the APS vendors, the results of the system demonstrations and the results of the prototype implementation are summarized in a report on which the selection decision will be based.

13.3   Implementation and Integration

Besides features and functions, the estimated effort for the implementation of the system and the integration of the APS into the existing IT landscape has to be considered upon the selection of an APS.

13.3.1   Implementation of the APS Functionality

The implementation tasks can be grouped into

- the modelling of the supply chain, including the definition of the locations, sites, material flows, operations, buffers, resources etc.,
- the customization of the planning procedures and the optimization algorithms (e. g. the parameters of a scheduling heuristic) and
- the setup of internal data structures and databases.

Typically, APS use specific modelling techniques and representations of the supply chain and employ system specific planning and optimization techniques. Thus, the implementation approach and the implementation effort strongly depends on the selected APS.

Based on the initial estimate of the implementation effort for each of the APS modules that are in the scope of the project, a rough-cut project plan is created. This is done for those APS that are on the top of the short list; in order to keep the planning effort low the creation of rough-cut implementation schedules should be restricted to the top two or three systems. The plans have to account for the availability of the required APS functionality. If one of the vendors has announced that a specific functionality is available at a certain point in time, all related implementation tasks have to be moved out accordingly. In the next step the functional implementation plan is extended by the required integration tasks.

13.3.2   Integration Technology

The integration approaches for APS range from vendor specific integration techniques to standard middleware systems (see Fig. 13.3 for an overview; a detailed description of integration and communication approaches for supply chain planning is given in Chap. 11). As an example, SAP provides a tight integration of their Advanced Planning System APO into SAP's ERP

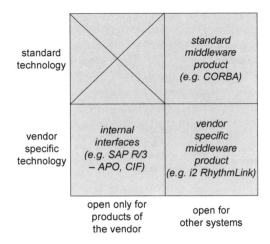

Fig. 13.3. Classification of APS integration technology

system R/3 via internal interfaces. i2 Technologies provides its own middleware product RhythmLink that is open to a large variety of other systems including SAP R/3 and Oracle databases. The trend clearly goes to the use of standard integration technologies like CORBA (Common Object Request Broker Architecture), providing a standardized and uniform interface to all CORBA-compliant systems (Siegel, 2000).

There are advantages and disadvantages for each of the three integration approaches. Internal interfaces like those between SAP R/3 and SAP APO are the easiest to implement. Base data and dynamic data are transferred between R/3 and APO via the internal interface without the need of further interface implementation. However, this holds true only for data *that is already maintained by the ERP system.* Data that is provided by external systems, for example a shop floor control system, requires extra interface programming.

APS vendor specific middleware products are open to external systems. Interfaces between the APS and external systems are customized; programming is normally not required to setup the data transfer. In the case of i2 Technologies' RhythmLink product, so-called *copy-maps* are created, mapping the fields of a data source to the fields of a data target. For example, the source could be the master plan as maintained by the APS, the target could be a table in some ERP system. Standard middleware products provide a similar functionality as APS vendor specific middleware products, with the additional advantage that the system is not proprietary technology of the APS vendor, but is supported by a wider range of applications.

Both APS vendor specific and standard middleware products support the creation of *data interfaces* between a source and a target system very well. But note that data integration is only the first step. In order to fully integrate an APS with other systems, the integration must be extended to the

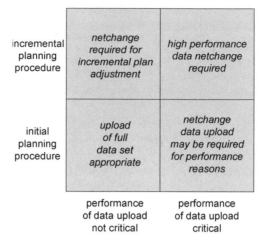

Fig. 13.4. Integration modes dependent on performance and planning process requirements

functional level. Consider as an example the transfer of the master plan from the APS to some ERP system. The transfer of the master plan into some table of the ERP system is just the first step. The full integration requires that appropriate transactions in the ERP system are invoked to further process the master plan data. For example, planned primary demand could be created in order to drive purchasing decisions within the ERP system based on the Advanced Planning System's master plan.

13.3.3   Integration Mode, Performance and Availability

Besides the integration technology, the integration mode has to be assessed. In general, a *full data upload* into the APS system is distinguished from a *netchange of the data* (refer to Chap. 11). The decision whether upload of the full data set is acceptable or whether a netchange interface is required, depends on the planning processes that will be supported and on the performance of the data load (see Fig. 13.4). If an initial plan is created and the performance of the data upload is not critical, a full data upload is appropriate. If performance is critical or if the planning process incrementally maintains a plan, only the changes of the data have to be uploaded into the APS. Many APS create an initial plan and do not support the incremental adjustment of a plan.

For some planning processes, e.g. order confirmation, not only the performance, but also the availability of the interface and the integrated system must be considered. It may be crucial for the business performance that *every order* gets a quote in nearly real-time, i.e. within milliseconds, even in case of system failure. In order to guarantee a high availability of the order promising system, some APS vendors employ highly available transaction systems based on the TIBCO data bus that has been developed for use in highly available, online transaction environments as for example the finance sector Tibco. The mean time between failures can be used as a measurement for the availability of the integrated system.

13.4 Post-Implementation

The fourth step in the selection process is the assessment of the expected post-implementation effort. The efforts – and costs – that is created after the completion of the implementation can be classified into

- the yearly maintenance and support fees requested by the APS vendor,
- the costs for a release update,
- the costs for the system administration and
- the costs for the user support.

Most APS vendors charge a specific percentage of the licence fees per year for the continuous support services they provide to their customers. Typically, the yearly support fees are in the range of 10–20% of the licence fees. However, the availability of the support centres, the languages in which support can be given and the range of the support services differ. Some APS vendors offer the full range of their services online via the Internet, while others rely more on telephone support. It is especially useful if the APS vendor is able to login remotely in the APS in order to detect and resolve issues.

As APS are still evolving very rapidly APS vendors offer several updated and extended releases per year. According to the guiding rule *Never change a running system* one should not follow every release change immediately. However, some APS vendors offer support services only for the latest release. Thus, the APS of these vendors should be upgraded on a regular basis to the latest release (e. g. every second release). In order to get a rough idea about the effort for an upgrade of the system to a new release other customers of the APS vendor should be interviewed about their experience related to release changes. Especially the question whether external support in addition to the support of the APS vendor is required or not has to be answered, as external support would require a higher budget for release changes.

Besides release changes, general administration tasks have to be assessed. Examples of these tasks are

- administration of databases used by the APS,
- rollover of a rolling monthly or weekly plan to the next planning cycle,
- administration of the APS servers on operating system level (in most cases, Unix or Windows NT servers are used),
- extension and/or adaption of the APS, e. g. creation of new reports, installation of new clients, modification of models, user administration etc.

For each of these administration tasks it must be decided whether an internal resource takes over the responsibility or whether the task will be outsourced. In both cases, the skills required and the effort generated have to be assessed for all APS considered.

The fourth post-implementation task that should be evaluated in order to compare APS is user support. In practice a three level support structure is often setup: First level support is given by so-called *super-users*. A super-user is an especially skilled and trained end user, who is able to receive descriptions of issues from other end users, explain and resolve simple issues and transmit a complete description of a complex issue to second level support. Typically, the super-users have already been members of the implementation team and have supported the APS implementation project in a leading role. Second level support is normally embedded into the standard IT support organization. Some issues, especially those related to system administration, will be resolved there. Internal issues of the APS will be forwarded to third level support, i. e. the support of the APS vendor. APS differ in the tools for issue detection and resolution they provide. Again, it might be useful to ask other customers of the APS vendors about their experience with costs and effort related to the end user support for the product of the APS vendors.

References

Advanced Manufacturing Research (1998) *Supply chain planning optimization: Just the facts*, The Report on Supply Chain Management, AMR Inc., Boston

Bond, B.; Dailey, A.; Jones, C.; Pond, K.; Block, J. (1997) *ERP vendor guide – Overview and reference*, Doc. # R-345-129, Gartner Group

Enslow, B.; Gartner Group (Eds.) (1998) *Evaluating a vendor's SCP market strategy*; Integrated logistics strategies, 24 November 1998, Doc. # DF-06-6980

Enslow, B.; Gartner Group (Eds.) (1999) *Supply Chain Planning Magic Quadrant 2Q99 Update*; InSide Gartner Group, 28 April 1999, Doc. #: GG-04281999-02

Felser, W.; Kilger, C.; Ould-Hamady, M.; Kortmann, J. (1999) *Strategische Auswahl von SCM-Systemen*, in: PPS Management Vol. 4, No. 4, 10–16

Goldratt, E. (1990) *Theory of Constraints*, Croton-on-Hudson, N.Y.

Hellingrath, B.; Gehr, F.; Braun, J.; et al. (1999) *Marktstudie Supply Chain Management Software*, Fraunhofer IPA and IML, Stuttgart et al.

Kortmann, J.; Lessing, H. (2000) *Marktstudie: Standardsoftware für Supply Chain Management*, Paderborn

Philippson, C; Pillep, R.; Wrede, P. von; Röder, A. (1999) *Marktspiegel Supply Chain Management Software*, Forschungsinstitut für Rationalisierung, RWTH Aachen

Schragenheim, E.; Ronen, B. (1990) *Drum-buffer-rope shop floor control*, in: Production and Inventory Management Journal, Vol. 31, No. 3, 18–22

Siegel, J. (2000) *CORBA 3: Fundamentals and Programming (OMG)*, 2nd ed., New York et al.

Silver, E. A.; Pyke, D.; Peterson, R. (1998) *Inventory management and production planning and scheduling*, 3rd ed., New York et al.

Tibco (2000) *Homepage*, URL: www.tibco.com, State: June 9, 2000

14   The Implementation Process

Ulrich Wetterauer

j & m Management Consulting GmbH, Kaiserringforum, Willy-Brandt-Platz 6, 68161 Mannheim, Germany

At this stage the decisions about the software and, if required, the consulting partner have been taken. From these decisions a first release of a project plan should result outlining the approach, the time lines and the deliverables for all phases of the project. In this section we will give a brief introduction into the different phases of the project execution based on the experience of several APS impleentation projects. For each phase we will show the necessary organizational tasks and some proven ways to avoid the major pitfalls. The company which has decided to implement the APS will subsequently be called *client* organization.

The implementation process can be broken into five logical phases: *focus, design conceptual solution, design detailed solution, build and test* and *deploy* (KPMG, 2000). Each phase has certain deliverables; the most important ones will be mentioned below.

14.1   Focus

The *focus* (KPMG, 2000) phase is an early period in the life cycle during which project teams are mobilized and project activities are planned in detail for each of the focus areas. Major performance improvement opportunities - based on employee suggestions and on industry best practices - are identified and presented to senior management as potential solution options. Potential changes may address any aspect of the current organization, including process, technology and people. An initial analysis of the costs, benefits, constraints and risks associated with each solution option serves as a foundation for building a *business case* that will support the recommended solution. The organizational tasks in the focus phase are (KPMG, 2000):

- Governance of structure and roles,
- Contractor management,
- Project control and reporting,
- Issue management,
- Risk management.

Governance of structure and roles describes the complete design of a project organization based upon the project's scope, objectives and implementation approach. It defines the roles, responsibilities and skills needed to complete the project, as well as an appropriate project team structure, the position of the project sponsor and the composition of the project management including the project leadership. Establishing the governance of structure and roles also includes defining the initial contractor relationships further documented in the *contractor management plan,* the second task in the focus phase which will be addressed later.

In the following the topics project leadership, contractor relationships and project team structure will be discussed in detail.

An appropriate overall project organization is the prerequisite for every successful project of considerable size. The first topic to be considered is the question of project leadership or, in other words, who has the final responsibility for the success of the project. The project leadership can be divided among the client, the software provider and the consulting firm, although usually not more than two parties are considered. In many projects the team faces a significant resistance against the implementation of a new software, no matter what advantages the new system promises. People could lose influence or would have to give up familiar ways of working. Sometimes this resistance can only be overcome by using internal pressure. In these cases it is very useful if the project leader can use internal politics to build up this pressure which is only effective if the client participates in leading the project.

The following questions should be asked to support a successful implementation of the APS:

- Are internal political problems expected to become a major issue? In this case a leadership of the client will be useful, maybe even necessary.
- Is there experience on the client side in leading a project of this scale and complexity? If an overall leadership of the client is possible, all other parties can be sub-contractors.
- Is the team going to implement a relatively new product with which only the software provider has experience? In this case participation of the software provider in leading the project might be necessary.
- Is the consulting firm experienced in similar projects as far as the scale of the project and the type of software product are concerned? Then a participation in leading the project is possible. Especially if change management is expected to become important, as is usually the case in SCM projects, a participation of the consulting firm in leading the project has shown to be beneficial.

The structure of the project management team usually reflects the distribution of responsibilities among the involved parties, i. e. client organization, software provider and consulting firm. The project management reports to the steering committee which meets on a regular basis, for example every two weeks. The task of this institution is therefore to supervise the whole project based on the project reports, to make decisions about major changes in the project plan and to approve or "sign-off" the project results. The steering committee should be composed of senior management representatives of all involved organizations and departments.

Once the project management has been established a suitable hierarchy of sub-contractors has to be determined. Sub-contractors can be the software provider and the consulting firm, service companies for programming or administrative tasks (administration of hard- and software, databases etc.), freelancers and other third-party resources. Two ways to avoid the major pitfalls in this area are:

- The commitment of the software provider in case of package changes or programming efforts has to be ensured, especially if the software provider does not participate in leading the project.
- The reliability and continuity of freelancers (especially in long-term projects) must be ensured.

The selection of the internal project members is the next step. The implementation of an APS is an inter-disciplinary effort. External experts can be pathfinders providing guidance and support, but only those who live within the organization can carry the project to a successful conclusion. The following criteria should be applied to select the right people:

- Mix of experience: All critical aspects of the project should be covered, e. g. sales, product management, order management, production planning, IT services etc. People with influence in the key areas will be very valuable.
- Mix of skills: Advisers who know the business very well and internal consultants who build up know-how which remains in the client company after the project is finished.

For external resources who are to participate in the project a similar scheme of criteria should be applied:

- mix of experience with modeling and solution procedures and with the software product,
- mix of skills in programming and customization of the software product and in the development of requirement specifications, roll-out activities and training of users.

Especially for long-term projects with the inevitable replacement of team members it is important to insist on a certain level of experience and skills for the external project members. On the other side it is not possible to staff every project exclusively with experienced people; the point is to keep the right balance.

The implementation of an APS usually changes radically the way in which people do their work, communicate and relate to each other. An effective implementation team must therefore represent all constituencies impacted by the project and must possess the capabilities necessary to lead the implementation effort. With the exception of small pilot projects, successful change projects cross organizational boundaries. The most important team members next to the project leader and the leaders of the sub-projects are the so-called coordinators or champions from the client side. Each champion represents a distinct business unit or group affected by the project. Without their participation and buy-in during every single step of the project, an APS project cannot succeed. They have the responsibility to improve the communication between the project team and the client organization, to prepare the organisation for the necessary changes and, in the end, to achieve the final goal of the project. It is therefore essential to keep the motivation of the coordinators at a high level, by monetary or other means. An example for the final project team structure is shown in Fig. 14.1.

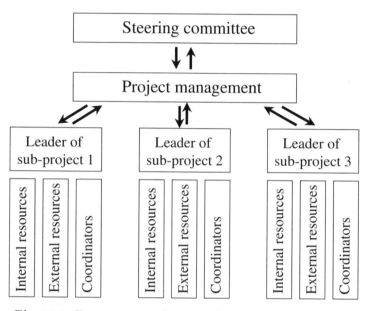

Fig. 14.1. Team structure for an APS implementation project

Besides the core team a project sponsor must be defined on the level of executive management who will support the project from the beginning. The extent of sponsorship and the participation of executive management in leading the APS project influences the extent of change that may be imposed by the project.

Contractor management, the next focus area, deals with the acquisition of resources from outside the organization and the complete management of those contracted resources. Outside resources are members of the project team who do not work directly for the organization. They are contractors hired to perform a specific function or provide a designated set of deliverables, as mentioned above. The contracts may extend throughout the life of the project or merely a specific time frame within it. The hiring of additional outside contractors with specific knowledge provides the client with a team with a broader range of skills to work on the project. Proper management will ensure that the client and all contracted parties have a clear definition of their goals, deliverables and expectations. It also ensures that all contractors adhere to the same procedures and policies as the rest of the project team. Effective management of contractors will reduce the risk of the project.

The importance of *project control and reporting*, the third focus area, can be appraised by the multitude of literature that exists about this topic (see e.g. Kerzner (1997) and Meredith and Samuel (1989)). In this chapter we will give a general introduction and highlight some of the major pitfalls.

The project management has to define the methods, procedures and guidelines used to plan, track, report and control the project and all its deliverables (KPMG, 2000). This is necessary to coordinate project team efforts and to:

- produce deliverables according to standards,
- minimize project risks,
- produce detailed work plans in consistent formats,
- measure, record and report progress,
- identify and address impediments.

Project control and reporting procedures are essential for the effective management of any project, regardless of size or scope. Key aspects of any reporting procedure are timelines and the *early warning* capability. The procedures must effectively deal with project work progress, issues, risks and any other aspects of project management. Control and reporting procedures are necessary to coordinate project team efforts. The project management should ensure that all the methods, procedures and guidelines developed for the project are appropriate and facilitate its effective management and control. In addition it must be sensitive to the steering committee preferences concerning the content and format of various project control reports.

The tasks around the topic project management can be divided into the three domains project plan and controlling, concept of implementation and relations to the end-users. The main tool to control a complex project is the project plan. It should consist of a project master plan for the whole project, with a limited level of detail, and detailed project plans for the different sub-projects. A sub-project may be the implementation of an APS module for a certain facility or the development of an interface between the APS and another IT system like SAP R/3. It is necessary for the project plan to be broken into easily definable phases. Regular updates are mandatory tasks for the project managers, and experience has shown that weekly project management meetings are required to keep the different parts of the project under control.

There are several ways to organize a project plan. Every project manager should consider the difficulty to change the way the advancements of the project are controlled and should therefore carefully choose a suitable kind of method for himself. Most methods are based on monitoring the critical path(s), although the major problem, the combination of unexpected delays and dependencies of tasks, are often not addressed with the right emphasis. Project time requires that everything gets done on time because there are defined completion dates. Also, given the nature of implementation projects, unanticipated tasks will come up that must be completed without revising the deadlines. Communicating this fact of life has a top priority for the project leaders, especially with an unexperienced, temporary project team. Software tools like MS Project have proven to be very helpful to control the project plan, nevertheless the main success factor is simply a painstaking maintenance of the project plan with sufficient detail.

Issue management, the next focus area, provides the approach and necessary procedures to effectively manage and resolve issues arising throughout a project. An issue is a situation, action, problem or question arising during the performance of the project, that team members cannot effectively resolve. Left unresolved, an issue can impede or prohibit a project's progress or development by delaying or suspending work effort (KPMG, 2000). Issues can become "show stoppers", resulting in the termination of the project if they are not resolved in a timely manner. Issue management procedures clearly define the mechanism for issue identification, assignment of responsibility, analysis, tracking, escalation and resolution. It is essential that this process is established, clearly understood by the project management team and then implemented during the early stages of the project to be in a position to deal with issues once implementation takes place.

A very important aspect of issue management is to deal with requirements and expectations. Unrealistic expectations concerning the difficulty of implementing a new concept and a short-term focus can lead to a shift from a planned implementation to "quick fixes" that do not solve the fundamental business problems. These conditions in combination with the lack of a formal process for business requirements often lead to a loss of focus and scope creep, thus drastically increasing the implementation time. This can be avoided by rigidly using a formal process to incorporate user requirements or change of requirements, preferably using the champion to filter out less important requests.

To be able to address potential problems proactively a comprehensive *risk management* programme, the last focus area which will be discussed here, has to be implemented to ensure that the mechanism for identifying, assigning, analyzing and managing risk throughout the lifecycle of the project is in place. Effectively managing potential risks minimizes the impact of unplanned incidents by identifying and addressing them early, before significant negative consequences occur. It is important that the risk management process is proactive, focusing on prevention rather than cure (e. g. timely identificationof project blockers within the client organization). All risks have to be communicated to and well understood by the project team, and periodic risk assessments throughout the project lifecycle should be considered.

14.2   Design Conceptual Solution

This is an early period in the project life cycle during which the high-level design of the proposed solution is refined, adapted to the selected software and presented to senior management for review and (provisional) approval. Best practices (see also Sect. 2.2) and alternative solutions from the previous phase are explored to determine the best fit and converge on the future model. Potential risks and constraints to the implementation (or other gaps and issues) are identified as the business case is refined in more detail. The deliverables of this phase are (KPMG, 2000):

- A complete business solution has been designed.
- The recommended solution, including selected hardware and software, has been validated by employees (and process customers). Any anticipated constraints to implementing the proposed design have been assessed.
- The *business case* and *implementation timeline* have been approved upon "in-principle" by senior management and has been communicated to all affected managers and staff by a proper communication plan.
- Senior Management demonstrates its commitment and buy-in to the proposed high-level solution by giving a "green light" to proceed into the *design solution details* phase and is actively promoting the solution.

The starting point of every project has to be a proper communication of all goals and expected benefits to the relevant people. For this purpose and to create an atmosphere of anticipation and motivation, it is recommendable to start every major step of the project with a carefully organized kick-off workshop. The main goal to be achieved with this workshop is to create acceptance, commitment and enthusiasm within the team, in the environment of the project (shop floors, IT department etc.) and in the supporting management (department managers etc.).

In addition to the kick-off meetings periodical workshops with the users should be organized to show the progress of the project and to preserve and improve their commitment. Especially in long-term projects people tend to forget the goals and expected benefits which might result in discouragement and even resistance.

14.3   Design Solution Details

During this phase the details of the proposed solution are defined. The detailed design is reviewed to gain a full understanding of the implications that implementation of the solution will have on the affected units and on the organization as a whole.

A special emphasis in this phase should be put on the impacts regarding change management tasks and the availability and quality of basic data. These two topics will subsequently be addressed in more detail.

The implementation of an APS almost inevitably requires change to an organization's structure and culture. In addition to the usual problems (resistance to change in general, satisfaction with the status quo, threats to job security and career objectives etc.) there are two more barriers to the implementationof an APS: The acceptance of *automation* and the shift of *responsibility*.

APS are based on problem resolvers and optimization algorithms which help to rapidly respond to changing conditions by generating proposals automatically or even by automated decisions. This has an impact on the daily work of sales people, production planners and other people concerned with the planning process as the responsibility for a successful planning shifts from these people to the software tool (and indirectly to the people concerned with the maintenance of basic data). Resistance against the planning tool is an obvious consequence. This problem can only be solved using an appropriate change management approach (communication plan, involvement of employees,rewards and recognition etc.).

Next to the required organizational changes is the availability and quality of basic data one of the main problems in APS projects. First of all an APS usually has more extensive requirements to the quality of basic data than the old processes and legacy systems which have been evolved on-site and which are therefore more adapted to the current basic data situation. An APS is much more demanding in this respect than the limited legacy systems.

As far as the availability of basic data is concerned the project team will face the problem that SCM is executed across the borders of departments (or divisions or companies). It typically involves the integration of data from diverse application systems on different databases running on multiple hardware platforms. This leads to a very common situation: The people needed to maintain the basic data do not have the overall responsibility. As a result improvement of data quality is a slow and painful process.

Lack of basic data or poor quality inevitably leads to delays in every stage of the project plan: Software development becomes very difficult, professional tests of software releases are almost impossible and a productive use of the completed product is unlikely. To avoid the pitfalls associated with basic data the process for basic data maintenance has to be revised and, if necessary, has to be set up right from the start of the implementation project.

Assuming that the basic data situation is sufficient to continue with the detailed design phase, the next step has to be the development of a realistic pilot. Realistic means that the expected complexity of the final product should be more or less contained in the pilot model using only a small subset of the available data. The effort needed to implement the pilot can be extrapolated to get a feeling for the magnitude of effort needed for the complete project.

14.4   Build and Test

The *build and test* phase is a period in the project life cycle in which key components of the detailed business solution are constructed, tested and documented, often in a parallel operational environment. This phase prepares the terrain for a potential organization wide roll-out. The same reason as for the pilot phase, the complexity of APS projects, holds true for one of most dangerous pitfalls in the build and test phase: scope creep or, in other words, loss of focus. This tendency to insist on the consideration of every detail in the implementation plan, in contrast to the carefully designed solution defined in the previous phases, leads to drastically increased implementation times or even in the failure of the entire project.

The only way to avoid scope creep is to limit the model to the essential input parameters and then to set this solution live. Quite often it turns out that part of the originally indispensable functionality is suddenly not needed any more by the users. Only the part of requirements which still remains after several weeks of testing and validation (by the users, not by the implementation team!) has to be developed and included into the model.

The development activities have to be supported by a well designed testing environment and a defined test base for the validation of software releases and ongoing enhancements. Especially with regard to a final approval by the client management staff it is necessary to implement a formal test-plan management system with a sign-off process.

The next topic in this discussion is documentation. To avoid problems during later stages of the project it is necessary to set up a sufficient documentation system as well as to insist on complete and precise documentation from the start. A professional *document and knowledge management system* benefits the client by providing a standard set of documents for the project (KPMG, 2000). It facilitates the gathering of all knowledge gained during the project to use for future reference. Although this statement seems trivial it is much too often ignored, especially in the first phases of the project where the complexity is still limited and the need for a rigid documentation as well as an extensible documentation system is not coercive, yet. In addition to the technical documentation the minutes of every important or official meeting should be maintained in the documentation system as a future reference.

14.5   Deploy

This is the period late in the project life cycle during which the business solution is made fully operational across the entire organization and performance benefits of the business solution can be measured.

The main topic which will be addressed in this discussion is the user training which has to be performed timely and with sufficient effort, especially in APS implementation projects. This also includes the creation of performance support materials such as desk reference manuals or self paced training exercises that will be used by training participants once the formal training process is completed. A poorly developed user training leads to delays in the project plan and additional costs without meeting the desired learning outcomes (KPMG, 2000). This failure can impede (and in some cases even stop) the progress of the desired business solution.

References

Kerzner, H. (1997) *Project management: A systems approach to planning, scheduling and controlling*, 6th ed., New York et al.

KPMG Consulting GmbH (2000) *Business performance improvement methodology*, internal communication

Meredith, J. R.; Mantel, S. Jr. (1989) *Project management: A managerial approach*, New York et al.

Part IV

Actual APS and Case Studies

15 Architecture of Selected APS

Herbert Meyr[1], Jens Rohde[2] and Michael Wagner[1]

[1] University of Augsburg, Department of Production and Logistics,
   Universitätsstraße 16, 86135 Augsburg, Germany
[2] Darmstadt University of Technology, Institute of Business Administration,
   Department of Operations and Materials Management, Hochschulstraße 1,
   64289 Darmstadt, Germany

This chapter will introduce the APS used in the case studies from *i2 Technologies, J. D. Edwards and SAP*: RHYTHM, Active Supply Chain and APO. As these tools regularly consist of a multitude of software modules and special add-ons, only a brief survey without claiming completeness can be given. Furthermore, different lines of business can use different modules of an APS. It is also possible to use an APS only partially, e. g. without modules for scheduling or only with modules for demand planning and demand fulfilment. For each individual case the composition of modules has to be evaluated and selected (see Chap. 13).

15.1 i2 Technologies – i2 RHYTHM

i2 Technologies, based in Dallas, Texas, with European headquarters in Brussels, offers a broad range of APS software modules through its RHYTHM software suite. i2 was established in 1988, when it offered its first software package called *Factory Planner* which was initially very successful in the metals industry. Today i2 offers a wide range of software modules for optimizing B2B processes in different industries including automotive, consumer goods and high technology. Most recently, i2 has launched a new set of solutions under the brand TradeMatrix which provide software and services necessary to create public and private electronic marketplaces. These developments, in combination with the recent merger in 2000 with *Aspect Development* and partnerships with *IBM* and *Ariba*, indicate the enlargement of i2's software solutions to B2B solutions (see e. g. i2 Technologies (2000)).

15.1.1 i2's Software Modules

Hence, Fig. 15.1 shows only a partial survey of some modules with respect to the case studies of this part of the book (Chaps. 17 and 18). Different modules are integrated by *RhythmLink*. The task of material requirements planning is left to ERP systems.

Supply Chain Strategist supports strategic what-if-analyses across the
   entire supply chain. The optimal combination and location of production

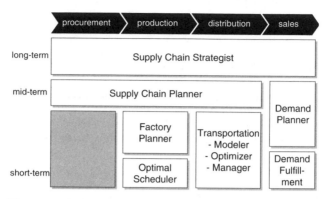

Fig. 15.1. Software modules of i2 Technologies RHYTHM

sites, distribution centres and other entities is determined. Material flows with all related costs as well as constraints can be modelled in different scenarios.

Demand Planner provides statistical methods, inclusion of causal factors and management of multiple inputs of different organizational units. POS data can be integrated and different views on demand data are offered. Furthermore, OLAP tools enable efficient access to relevant data.

The Demand Planner module PRO (Product Relationship Object) supports the creation of dependent forecast. Dependent forecast is used for example in the consumer packed goods industry to derive a forecast for individual finished goods (e. g. shower gel and shampoo) from the forecast for a bundle of finished goods (e. g. shower gel plus a small package of shampoo that is bundled for marketing purposes). PRO is also used in industries like the high-tech industry where a forecast on component level is derived from the forecast on finished goods level to drive purchasing decisions (see Chap. 18).

Supply Chain Planner enables modelling and optimizing supply chains with respect to material, capacity, transportation and customer-service constraints. The *Strategy Driven Planning* (SDP) allows planners to define types of problems and to apply appropriate solvers like Linear Programming, heuristics and genetic algorithms.

Demand Fulfillment generates constraint-driven plans and offers supply chain wide visibility of finished goods, semi-finished products, raw material and resource capacity of all distribution and production sites. It supports definition of complex order-promising strategies based on allocation of ATP to customer groups (see Chap. 8). After delivery dates have been promised, Demand Fulfillment allows order monitoring, and furthermore, maintenance and reassignment of allocations.

Factory Planner generates optimized production plans by scheduling backward from the requirement date, as well as scheduling forward from current date while considering material and capacity constraints. After a first infinite planning step, a finite capacity plan can be determined by i2's proprietary *Constraint Anchored Optimization*. However, the planner can manually interact by analyzing capacity shortages and performing what-if-analyses.

Optimal Scheduler builds sequences and schedules based on genetic algorithms. The decoupling of constraint definition and optimization algorithm allows the handling of a large number of complex constraints. These constraints include shop floor capacities, workload balancing, material availability etc. Additionally, an interactive schedule editor allows manual changes.

Transportation Modeler, Optimizer and Manager are tools for support of distribution planning processes. Transportation Modeler helps an organization to utilize its transportation network efficiently. Real world data are used to perform what-if-analyses. Transportation Optimizer automatically builds and routes loads and determines pick-up and delivery times with respect to delivery, equipment and personnel constraints. Furthermore, cross-docking opportunities can be selected dynamically and grouping constraints can be honoured. The third tool, Transportation Manager, supports activities to execute and manage the transportation process from order management through customer service and financial settlement.

15.1.2 Coordination and Integration of Software Modules

Different software modules of i2's RHYTHM suite can be combined and integrated by *RhythmLink*. This module enables messaging between RHYTHM modules and – by using open industry-based standards (e. g. CORBA) – information can be exchanged with external applications or planning engines.

Data integration is supported by the i2 Active Data Warehouse (ADW). Standard adaptors connect all RHYTHM planning modules (e. g. Supply Chain Planner, Factory Planner, Demand Planner etc.) with the ADW and support the active data exchange between the planning modules. For example, a new forecast that is created using RHYTHM Demand Planner can be automatically transferred via the ADW – and the appropriate adaptors – to the RHYTHM Supply Chain Planner as input to the master planning process.

Additionally, adaptors exist to connect non-i2 systems to the ADW, e. g. SAP R/3. The i2 standard adaptors are RhythmLink applications.

15.1.3 System Integration

RHYTHM tools can be integrated in existing OLTP systems by ADW, ASCII flat files and RythmLink. Flat files can be imported and exported by every software module using import and export files to specify fields and formats exchanged. RhythmLink provides automatic interactions with e. g. SAP

R/3. The special module *RhythmLink for SAP R/3* is based on SAP's standardized interfaces. Changes in R/3 can automatically be propagated to RHYTHM. It is possible to exchange only altered data to reduce transfer amount (netchange).

15.1.4   Software Modules for Collaboration

To enable collaboration of supply chain entities, i2 provides e. g. the modules *TradeMatrix* and *Global Logistics Manager*. TradeMatrix supports procurement services like e-business marketplaces, collaborative planning processes, negotiations and other B2B solutions. Global Logistics Manager is a process modelling and monitoring system. It provides visibility for multi-enterprise logistics operations with different modes. Included functions of this module are: visibility and tracking of orders and inventory, performance measurement, failure warnings and improved customer service.

15.2   J. D. Edwards – Active Supply Chain

J. D. Edwards, founded in 1977 and headquartered in Denver, Colorado, traditionally offers ERP software. In 1999 J. D. Edwards acquired Numetrix Ltd., a Toronto–based provider of APS with more than 20 years experience in supply chain planning and optimization. The former Numetrix/3 APS is in the meantime launched as the *"J. D. Edwards' Active Supply Chain"* (see e. g. J. D. Edwards (2000)).

15.2.1   J. D. Edwards' Software Modules

In the following, the APS software modules of Active Supply Chain are briefly introduced. An overview is given in Fig. 15.2.

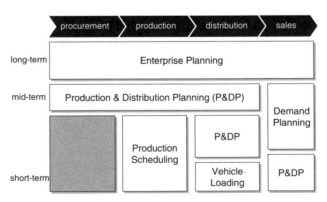

Fig. 15.2. Software modules of J. D. Edwards' Active Supply Chain

Enterprise Planning is intended to be applied on the strategic planning level. Optimization methods of Linear and Mixed Integer Programming (CPLEX; see ILOG (2000)) and special purpose heuristics (e. g. for capital asset management and single sourcing) support the choice of appropriate supply chain structures, simulatively. The most striking feature of *Enterprise Planning* is its visualization. Even complex supply chains can graphically be "designed" without any knowledge of mathematical modelling being necessary. The case study of Chap. 19 will show that *Enterprise Planning* is not restricted to strategic planning, but can also be used for master planning.

Production & Distribution Planning (P&DP) is a versatile tool. Its main focus is the mid-term master planning including procurement, production and distribution planning. Therefore, Linear Programming and some further heuristics are applied. Additionally, a more detailed planning of transportation means is aspired for the Transport Planning software module as already described (see Chap. 4). When looking at the close interdependencies between transportation planning and ATP (see Chaps. 10 and 8) it is not surprising that ATP and CTP functionalities are also addressed by a further component of the P&DP module.

Demand Planning provides statistical forecasting methods, e.g. exponential smoothing and ARIMA, as well as tools to combine theses methods (Bayesian forecasting) and to analyze and incorporate causal factors like promotions and marketing campaigns. Furthermore, the identification of unexpected demand changes, trends, seasonality or correlation and the measurement of forecast accuracy are supported. Additional features are for example product chaining (introduction of new products), cannibalization and simulation/what-if-analysis.

Production Scheduling Two alternative software modules for the short-term production planning are offered. The older one, *Production Scheduling Process*, is one of the rare software tools that is especially designed for continuous production processes common in consumer goods industries or the process industry in general. Its main focus are parallel continuous production lines with up to two stages of production. *Production Scheduling Discrete*, however, is dedicated to multi-stage supply chains with floating bottlenecks and long BOMs which can frequently be met in discrete part production.

Vehicle Loading addresses short term transportation problems, especially the choice of transportation modes, the building of loads and the designation of shipping dates.

Execution-oriented components of the J. D. Edwards' ERP system like *Purchasing, MRP* or *Sales Order Processing* intend to supplement the above APS modules.

15.2.2   Coordination of Modules

The *Integration and Data Flows* (IDF) software component is a graphical tool to constitute and control the data flow between different software modules and to start batch execution of the respective software components. Usually, a common database is kept by IDF for consistent data storage. Both vertical (e. g. between mid-term P&DP and *Production Scheduling*) and horizontal (e. g. between *Demand Planning* and mid-term P&DP) information flows are supported. Some software modules like *Production Scheduling Process* may functionally be adapted to or extended for proprietary requirements by means of the scripting language TCL (see e. g. Ousterhout (1994)). Furthermore, data flows using flat files can be automated by TCL.

15.2.3   System Integration

Certified interfaces to the most common database systems and ERP systems exist. This access is also enabled by the IDF component.

15.2.4   Collaboration Modules

The J. D. Edwards *Distributed Object Messaging Architecture (DOMA)* and the software component *xtr@* facilitate supply chain collaboration over the Internet. Some features supported are:

- multi-user mode and user specific profiles (P&DP),
- decision-making distributed across the whole supply chain,
- real-time information sharing,
- database review and reaction automatically triggered by data changes or
- alert monitoring and messaging.

These functionalities enable ATP/CTP and VMI capabilities, for example. The *Vendor Managed Inventory* component of J. D. Edwards represents a "plug and play" combination of P&DP and *xtr@*, preconfigured to meet the special requirements of VMI.

15.3   SAP – APO

Since 1998 SAP AG (Walldorf/Germany) is present on the APS market. The *Advanced Planner and Optimizer* (APO) is one block of SAP's *New Dimension Products*. Other New Dimension Products are e. g. the *Business Information Warehouse*, a Data Warehouse and the *B2B* application for e-business. This section will provide an overview of selected components. For further information we refer to current APO documentations (see e. g. SAP (2000) and Knolmayer et al. (2000)).

15.3.1 SAP's Software Modules

APO is designed as a fully integrated APS. All modules can be accessed via
the *Supply Chain Cockpit* and have an identical look-and-feel. Presently, SAP
APO has no explicit module for Strategic Network Planning[1] (see Fig. 15.3).
However, it is possible to simulate several scenarios with the APO software
modules and release a final plan. But the evaluation of the results of different
simulated plans and the selection of the best result has to be done manually.

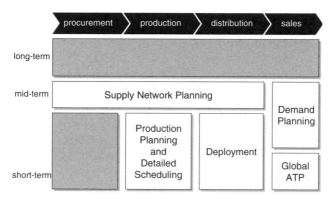

Fig. 15.3. Software modules of SAP APO

Demand Planning offers – besides conventional statistical methods – tools
  for promotion planning, life cycle concepts, what-if-analyses, new product initiation and collaborative prognosis. Reports for accuracy can be
  generated and alerts can be propagated. Furthermore, OLAP tools for
  Data Warehouse integration are provided.
Supply Network Planning provides planning and optimization functionality which considers capacity constraints and costs, for example. Simulation of different supply chain configurations as well as matching of supply
  and demand with respect to alternative production sites, substitution of
  products, preferred customers, durability etc. are supported. Alerts can
  be raised in case of late deliveries, bottlenecks and violation of further
  constraints. Furthermore, Supply Network Planning offers a VMI module.
Global ATP performs a rule based multi-level component and capacity
  check based on current data. It offers methods for substitution of products, selection of alternative sites for production and purchasing and allocation of scarce products and components to customers, markets, orders
  etc.
Production Planning and Detailed Scheduling provides optimization
  methods for detailed capacity and material planning simultaneously. It

---

[1] APO's release 3.0 will provide such a module named *Network Design*.

performs multi-level for- and backward scheduling and forwards changes to each level. Different constraints can be considered in simulations and interactive scheduling is possible by using gantt-charts. Current short-term data are integrated in optimization runs.

Deployment performs the task of the short-term allocation of inventory. *Push* and *pull* strategies, predefined quotas and priority rules control the allocation of materials. For example, results from the Supply Network Planning can be used for defining quotas. Inventory and allocation plans are displayed graphically.

15.3.2   Coordination and Integration of Software Modules

APO provides a graphical user interface, the *Supply Chain Cockpit*, to give an overview of the supply chain modelled and to access all APO software modules. Furthermore, Supply Chain Cockpit provides the *Supply Chain Engineer* to graphically build a macro-model of the supply chain. This model can be shown in detailed views and special information can be reported for each entity. The *Alert Monitor* is also part of this module. APO modules work on a common database. To enable fast access to data for all software modules this database is kept memory resident (so-called *live*Cache).

15.3.3   System Integration

APO provides two different ways for integration of OLTP systems. The *Core Interface* (CIF) allows direct access to SAP R/3's data objects and vice versa. The integration to non R/3 systems is done by so-called *Business Application Programming Interfaces* (BAPIs). Via those BAPIs the objects of APO can be accessed by a kind of programming language. Thus, it is possible to map e. g. ASCII-files to APO data objects. Furthermore, SAP provides the *Business Information Warehouse* for storing historical data. These data can be accessed by APO to receive data, especially for Demand Planning, by predefined queries and OLAP tools.

15.3.4   Software Modules for Collaboration

SAP uses Internet and associated technologies such as XML to enable the collaboration between business partners. Via conventional Internet browsers APO can be accessed on-line. The SAP APO *Collaborative Planning* module enables this collaboration. It supports consensus based planning processes, read-write data access as well as access to planning activities for authorized users via Internet browsers, user configuration of negotiation processes, user defined screens and workplaces, visualization of alerts, the connection to multiple systems and links to partner systems using XML technology.

References

i2 Technologies (2000) *Homepage*, URL: http://www.i2.com, State: August 1, 2000

ILOG (2000) *Homepage*, URL: http://www.ilog.com, State: August 1, 2000

J. D. Edwards (2000) *Homepage*, URL: http://www.jdedwards.com, State: August 1, 2000

Knolmayer, G.; Mertens, P.; Zeier, A. (2000) *Supply Chain Management auf Basis von SAP-Systemen*, Berlin et al.

Ousterhout, J. K. (1994) *Tcl and the Tk Toolkit*, Amsterdam

SAP (2000) *Homepage*, URL: http://www.sap.com, State: August 1, 2000

16 Scheduling of Synthetic Granulate

Marco Richter and Volker Stockrahm

aconis GmbH, Robert-Bosch-Straße 7, 64293 Darmstadt, Germany

This case study deals with a project which has recently been finished in the process industry. It is the first APO PP/DS project that managed to keep up with the difficult scheduling requirements in the field of the chemical and process industries.

This case study is structured in the following sections: First, the general production process of the synthetic granulate in the featured plant is presented. This chapter focuses on the special planning problems which occurred in this example. Subsequently, the modelling of the production process in APO PP/DS is described in detail, and some more information about modelling production processes in APO PP/DS are provided in addition to the general information given in Chap. 9. At the end of this case study the consequences and benefits of this APO implementation are estimated briefly as they are expected today.

16.1 Presentation of the Production Process

The production process dealt with in this case study is the production of synthetic granulate. In technical terms it is a four step hybrid-flow-shop production process. The granulate is widely used in many different industries, especially in the automobile and pharmaceutical industries. About 2000 different products make up the full product spectrum which changes rapidly.

The basic principle of the process (see Fig. 16.1) is melting the undyed granulate in extruders, adding colour substances and perhaps other additives and extruding the coloured granulate again. Depending on the product type, a mixer is used afterwards to create homogenous batches. If the granulate is shipped in bags, an automatic bag filling machine may be used. Otherwise the filling of the granulate in different types of containers is done directly at the extruders or mixer. Depending on the production sequence, transport containers may be needed during a part of the production process. At the end of the production process some more days are needed for the necessary quality checks.

The selection of resources for the production process depends on the product type. For the extrusion process several individual extruders can be used. These resources differ with respect to speed, types of colour that can be added and types of undyed granulate that can be processed. The actual usage of the individual extruder depends on the product type and the lot-size of the

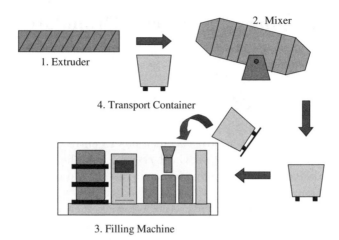

Fig. 16.1. Production process

production order. Generally speaking, for each product there are several extruders with different priorities that can be used for the extrusion process. As there is a high variety of products with very different chemical and physical characteristics, the scheduling of orders on the extruders is very critical. Depending on the sequence of the production orders, setup times for cleaning the extruders vary between nearly no setup time and up to five hours.

Products with special quality requirements by the customer have to be mixed afterwards to create batches with homogeneous characteristics. For this part of the production process several mixers with different capacities are available. The selection of the mixer is lot-size dependent. Also the setup times on the mixers depend on the sequence of production orders, but the scheduling is less critical, as the setup times are shorter and the mixer is usually not a bottleneck. Granulates which are shipped in bags can be packed in two different ways. The first alternative is packing directly at the extruder or mixer which requires no additional resources. This procedure is chosen for production orders with small lot-sizes. Large production orders are packed with a special automatic filling machine which has to be planned separately. The setup times are sequence dependent as well, but less problematic than setup times on extruders. A further resource group, the transport containers, is needed, if a product needs the mixer or the filling machine or both of them. As the automatic filling in bags does not take place directly at the extruder, the transport containers are used to transport the loose granulate from extruder to mixer and further on to the filling machine. Since the number of available transport containers is limited, they must be considered as a relevant resource. The last resource group is the personnel required to operate the machines. Several different qualification groups can be distinguished, all of them have to be considered for production planning. If several workers are not present, use of certain machines might not be possible and production must be rescheduled.

16.2   Special Planning Problems

As mentioned before, the sequencing of production orders is the critical task in the planning process to avoid setup times and costs. This and as many different resource combinations for the products must be considered makes it hard for the production planner to generate feasible and economical plans in a short period of time. Especially the setup problems usually have been solved by building large standardized campaigns of similar products. Moreover, the plans once generated could not be changed easily when machines broke down or special short-term orders had to be fulfilled. This situation has been tackled by allowing buffer times in the production schedule. If this buffer time was not needed, the production capacities were not exploited to their maximum. So there has been the clear demand for an intelligent production planning and scheduling solution. This and as the integration with SAP R/3 should be as seamless as possible led to the decision to implement SAP's *Advanced Planner and Optimizer (APO)*.

16.3   Modelling the Production Process in APO PP/DS

Within this section of the case study not only the actual modelling of the production process in APO is described, but also some general principles of modelling processes in APO for production planning and scheduling in addition to the general description in Chap. 9. Of course, not all options of modelling with APO can be presented here.

16.3.1   General

In Chap. 9, the groups of data needed for planning have been defined. Especially the necessary structural data will be explained in this chapter.

To use the PP/DS module of APO for planning and scheduling in industry, basically the following groups of structural data must be maintained in the system:

- locations,
- products or parts,
- resources,
- Production Process Models (PPMs),
- setup matrices and
- supply chain models.

Additionally, situation-dependent data (e. g. sales orders, planned orders, inventories and setup states of resources) will be needed for planning. As the APO is using a standard R/3 basis system to maintain the system functionality, it uses a relational database of its own to maintain structural and situation-dependent data. Therefore, data are not handed over using flat ASCII files which are read by the system on start unlike most other advanced planning systems. Considering this, some information about filling the system with data will be provided:

Usually, a special interface provided by SAP will be used to connect the APO system to an R/3 system. This interface generates the structural data by an initial upload and communicates the situation-dependent data as soon as they are changed by one of the systems. This guarantees the fastest and most recent data transmission. Nevertheless, other interfaces to non-R/3-systems may be used as well.

16.3.2   Locations

The *location* is the first step, when creating a model. As APO is an integrated supply chain planning tool, it is important that all the subsequent data can be assigned to individual locations. Although for the *supply network planning* there are several kinds of locations (supplier, production plant, distribution centre and customer), for the PP/DS only the production plants are relevant. This makes up one location – a production plant – for this production process.

16.3.3   Products

For every product which is to be planned in APO (final product or raw material) a set of *product master data* has to be generated. The APO philosophy for the selection of the "relevant" products suggests that only critical materials should be planned in APO. So, one will usually plan the final products and some of their critical components in the APO system. Thus, only a portion of the materials contained in the complete bill-of-materials (BOM) is transferred to APO. In this particular case, the final products – the coloured granulate – and the undyed granulate are planned in APO, although the BOMs in R/3 contain many additional components like some additives. But these are no critical components and are not planned in APO. The complete BOM is exploded in R/3 and the additional components are generated as secondary demands, when a generated or changed order is retransmitted to the ERP system.

A lot of the settings and product properties are not relevant for PP/DS planning and are not presented here. The important values for PP/DS are

- basic unit of measurement,
- alternative unit of measurement,
- lot-size calculation,

- planning method and
- procurement method.

The *units of measurement* are taken over automatically from the R/3 system, depending on the product. It is usually "unit" or "kg" for this production process. Regarding the *lot-size calculation* APO offers the following options: fixed lot-size, lot for lot with a maximum/minimum lot-size and lot-for-lot without maximum/minimum lot-size. For the lot-for-lot calculation a rounding value can be defined. In our case, all the products use lot-for-lot with maximum/minimum lot-size. All these individual values are taken from the R/3 system.

The *planning method* describes how APO will react, when a demand is transferred. If the planning method is "automatic planning", the system checks the availability and – if the check is negative – creates a planned order or a purchase proposal (depending on the procurement method). If "manual planning with check" is selected, the system checks the availability and creates an alert in the *Alert Monitor*, if the check is negative. But it creates no orders of any kind. The third alternative "manual planning without check" always assumes that there is enough material to fulfil the demand. The *procurement method* determines, what APO will do if a demand cannot be fulfilled using stored materials. The procurement method offers the settings "in-house production", "external procurement" or "in-house production or external procurement". The last option is "direct procurement from other plants".

When "in-house production" is selected, the system creates a planned order for the product, considering resource capacity availability and material availability simultaneously. When "external procurement" is selected, the system creates a purchase proposal. In case of "in-house production or external procurement" the cheaper alternative is selected, so costs for production and external procurement have to be maintained. For highly integrated production processes taking place in different plants, the last option "direct procurement from other plants" can be selected. In case a product is needed for production in one plant, but it is produced in another plant, a planned order for this product is placed directly in the other plant. Anyway, if the procurement method is set to "in-house production", but no suitable PPM (see following section) is found, the system will create a purchase requisition as well.

The planning method "automatic planning" and the procurement method "in-house production" has been selected for coloured granulates (the final products). So, automatically planned orders are created and sent back to R/3, if a sales order cannot be fulfilled using stored materials or work-in-process. The undyed granulate status is set to "manual planning with check". So, if there is not enough material for production, a warning in the Alert Monitor is created. The reason for this is that the undyed granulate production which takes place in another plant of the same company is not yet integrated in the PP/DS planning process. As soon as this integration is done, it will be possible to check the availability of the corresponding undyed granulate and create a planned order for it immediately in the other plant together with a transportation order to the plant, where the coloured granulate is produced. To implement this functionality, the "direct procurement from other plants" option will have to be used for the undyed granulate. Figure 16.2 shows the actual planning process and communication between APO and the ERP system.

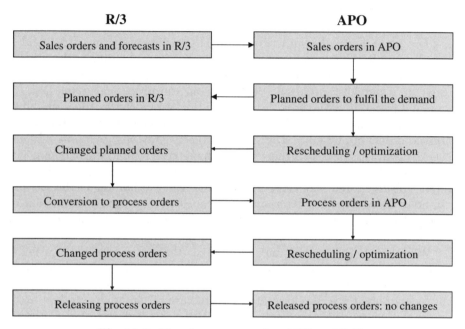

Fig. 16.2. Planning process using APO and R/3

16.3.4   Resources

APO uses several different types of *resources* for different planning requirements. For PP/DS *single* or *multi-activity resources* are used. Planning on these resources is not based on periods. They use a continuous time stream, and orders are scheduled using seconds as time units.

Single-activity resources always have the capacity of 1 without any unit of measurement. They represent a machine that can only process one order at the same time. Multi-activity resources are used to model either groups of identical machines which lead to a capacity of more than 1 without a dimension or single machines which can process more than one order at the same time and every order requires a certain amount of capacity. For example, an oven can have a capacity of 10m^3, and every order processed in the oven at the same time requires some volume of the oven. Several orders can be processed in the oven at the same time as long as the sum of their individual capacity requirements does not exceed 10m^3.

Not only different capacity types can be distinguished in APO, also the *usage* of a resource is indicated. The resource types "production", "transportation", "storage" and "handling" are possible, but only the production resource is relevant for PP/DS.

Capacities can be defined in multiple variants in APO. In this way one can model different capacities for e.g. different shifts or reduced capacities for breakdown times. Besides the amount of capacity there is the possibility to indicate, when the capacity of a resource can be used. While the *factory calendar* describes on which days the resource can be used or not because of e.g. weekends, holidays etc., the *resource calendar* describes the working times for the working days. So, for the working days, the start time and end time of resource availability are specified. Additionally the resource usage can be defined to allow buffer times or reserve capacity for some reasons. This resource usage is measured in percent. Further settings concerning properties of resources can allow some overlap of orders without creating an alert. For each resource a flag can be set whether the actual capacity load should be considered during scheduling (*"finite planning"*) while another flag indicates whether the resource is a *bottleneck*. If the bottleneck flag is set, the system schedules an order first on the bottleneck resource and then the other activities of this order on the other (non-bottleneck) resources. To model sequence dependent setup times, a *setup matrix* must be created and assigned to the resources where these setup times occur. The setup times automatically reduce the resources' capacity.

The setup times and costs are the only relevant factors to build lots on the resource and activity level as it is done in PP/DS. When using the optimizing algorithms to reschedule an initial plan, activities are planned on the resources in an order which creates the fewest losses by setup times and costs while concerning lateness, production costs and makespan simultaneously.

The classic lot-sizing which regards the trade-off between setup, transportation and storage costs has to be done in the mid-term planning, using the *Supply Network Planning*.

For the granulate production process, the following resources have been created in the APO system:

- a single-activity resource for each extruder,
- three multi-activity resources for the three personnel groups,
- one single-activity resource for the filling machine,
- one single-activity resource for each mixer and
- one multi-activity resource for the transport containers.

The extruders have been marked as bottleneck resources. So the system first schedules the extruders, as there is the biggest planning problem. All the resources, except the quality testing, are available for 24 h on work days, the quality testing department works for ten hours. Although the quality testing is in fact just a dummy resource – there is no finite planning – the exact working times are necessary to model that the quality testing takes three days. Quality testing always starts at the beginning of a shift (6 a.m.) and ends always at the end of a shift (4 p.m.). The use of a dummy resource is necessary in APO, as waiting times without a resource cannot be modelled. If a resource shows a variable capacity, an additional capacity can be defined for each shift to represent the actual number of available workers or transport containers. If no specific capacity is given for a shift, the standard capacity for that resource will be used.

The following Table 16.1 shows the individual resource properties, i. e. the detailed definition of the resources. In fact there are some more fields which can be used in APO, but only the essential ones are described here.

Table 16.1. Modelling the resources

Name	Type	Start	End	Usage	Matrix	Bottleneck	Finite	Capacity	Unit
PERS_1	Multi	00:00:00	24:00:00	90%			X	0-2	
...	...	...	...	...	...	...	...	...	...
PERS_N	Multi	00:00:00	24:00:00	90%			X	0-12	
FILLING	Single	00:00:00	24:00:00	90%	SHORT		X	1	
MIXER_1	Single	00:00:00	24:00:00	90%	SHORT		X	1	
...	...	...	...	...	...	...	...	...	...
MIXER_M	Single	00:00:00	24:00:00	90%	SHORT		X	1	
EXTRUDER_1	Single	00:00:00	24:00:00	90%	LONG	X	X	1	
...	...	...	...	...	...	...	...	...	...
EXTRUDER_O	Single	00:00:00	24:00:00	90%	LONG	X	X	1	
QUALITY	Single	06:00:00	16:00:00	100%				1	
TRANSPORT	Multi	00:00:00	24:00:00	90%			X	30-40	

For the synthetic granulate process two setup matrices (SHORT and LONG) have been defined. They both contain the same setup keys, but different setup times for the individual product combination. The matrix with the longer setup times is assigned to the extruders, the one with the shorter setup times to the mixers and the filling machine. The matrix with the shorter entries can be regarded as a copy of the first matrix with all entries divided by a constant factor. The huge number of products can be reduced for the setup matrices as a product in different shipment containers is represented by individual product numbers. The actual setup matrices contain about 700,000 entries each. The generation of the setup matrices could not be handled manually, so a special ABAP/4 programme in APO generates the setup times, using physical and chemical characteristics of the products.

16.3.5   Production Process Models

The *Production Process Model (PPM)* is the most essential element of an APO model. As presented in Chap. 9, it represents both the routing and the

BOMs. So, here it is determined which resources are used for what time and which components enter or leave the production process. This is indicated at activity level. So the production step, when a component is needed or ready, is described precisely. Also the temporal relations between single production steps are defined. APO is the first APS which actually uses the complete PPM concept, while most other systems work with separated routings and BOMs.

According to Chap. 9, a PPM is a hierarchical structure of elements which together form the production process. The elements of a PPM are:

- *Operations* which describe a group of production steps which take place on the same resource without interruption by other production orders;
- *Activities* as the single steps of an operation, e. g. setup, production, wait, tear down;
- *Activity relationships* which determine the sequence of the activities and their relative position in time;
- *Modes* which describe the resource or the alternative resources an activity can use and their duration;
- *Capacity requirements* for the primary and secondary resources of each mode;
- *Logical components* which serve as containers for groups of physical products (inputs or outputs) and are attached to activities;
- *Physical components* which describe the groups of real products represented by the logical components;
- The list of products which can be produced using this PPM (which may be all or just a part of the output components) and the lot-size ranges for which the PPM is valid.

As mentioned at the beginning in the description of the production process, many different routings through the process exist depending on the product. Here is presented the "maximum" PPM for a product which uses the extruder, the mixer, the filling machine, the transport containers and several personnel resources. First, the general modelling possibilities and principles for the elements of a PPM are presented, immediately after each element. A practical example is given by showing how the synthetic granulate process was modelled in this step.

For every production step which takes place on another resource an *operation* is defined, as long as this resource is not only needed as a *secondary resource*, parallel to the primary resource (e. g. a worker who is needed to operate the machine). If sequence dependent setup times shall be used, the *setup key* which identifies the manufactured product in the setup matrix is specified in the operation. As there can only be one setup activity per operation the setup key is not specified in the setup activity. Regarding the granulate production process, there is a maximum of five operations. The transport containers cannot be modelled as secondary resources for reasons to be explained later. Therefore they require an operation of its own. The naming of the location is necessary because the location is needed to identify the setup key. Using a graphical representation, the PPM structure is described in Fig. 16.3.

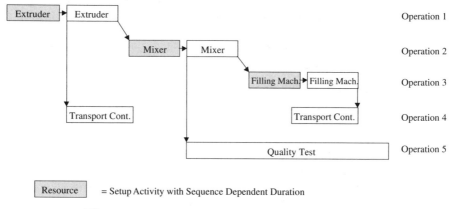

Fig. 16.3. PPM structure of the production process

The complete list of operations for this example is shown in Table 16.2.

Table 16.2. Modelling the operations

Operation key	Description	Setup key	Location
0010	Extruder	SETUP_KEY	GRANULATE_PLANT
0030	Mixer	SETUP_KEY	GRANULATE_PLANT
0050	Filling machine	SETUP_KEY	GRANULATE_PLANT
0070	Transport container		
0090	Quality test		

Every operation possesses at least one *activity*, usually the production activity. In many cases more than one activity will be defined in one operation, to model a single production step. The standard types of activities are "setup", "production", "wait" and "tear down" which all can be used only once in one operation. The activities are marked by an "S", "P", "W" or "T" accordingly. Only the setup activity can have a sequence dependent duration which says the duration is looked up in the setup matrix. If this feature is to be used, the flag for sequence dependent setup must be set. This flag makes it impossible to enter a duration for the setup activity later on in the modes. Another field in every activity determines the percentage of scrap which occurs during this activity. This scrap percentage is used to determine the order size which is necessary to produce the quantity ordered. All of the first three operations in this example have the same activity structure (see Table 16.3).

Table 16.3. Modelling the activities

Activity key	Description	Type	Sequ. dep. setup flag
0010	Cleaning	S	X
0020	Producing	P	

The transport container and quality test operations do not require a setup activity. So the quality test operation has only one activity type "production", the transport operation has two activity types: "production" and "wait". These activities represent the start and the end of the container usage. APO always lays a so-called cover chain around the activities which belong to the same operation. This guarantees that no activity of other production orders which are also processed on this particular resource is scheduled in between these activities.

The activities for the transport and the quality test operations can be described as shown in Tables 16.4 and 16.5.

Table 16.4. Transport activities

Activity key	Description	Type	Sequ. dep. setup flag
0070	Container start	P	
0080	Container end	W	

Table 16.5. Quality test activitiy

Activity key	Description	Type	Sequ. dep. setup flag
0090	Quality test	P	

Every activity must have at least one *relationship* to another activity. APO does not automatically connect the orders and activities in the way they are numbered or sorted in the tables. This provides a high amount of flexibility in modelling production processes. There are several types of activity relationships already introduced in Chap. 9 which are also used by APO:

end-start, start-start, end-end and start-end. For every relation between activities a minimum and maximum time difference can be maintained. The *resource connection flag* at each activity relationship can be used to force APO to use the same primary resource, even if the activities belong to different operations. If the activities belong to the same operation, APO uses the same primary resource anyway, as there is not much sense in doing the setup on one machine and the production on another. The *material flow flag* must be set for every activity relationship which represents an actual flow of material. APO uses this path from input activity to output activity to calculate the total percentage of scrap which occurs during the whole production process.

Generally speaking, all the activities in this example which belong to extruder, mixer or filling machine have simply been connected with end-start relationships and no minimum or maximum time constraints. So they are processed one after the other, and the material can be stored for an infinite time. In fact the system will not let the waiting times between the activities of one operation become too long, as the order would consume transport container capacity while waiting. This would lead to a longer makespan, as other orders have to wait for the containers. This way the optimizer keeps the gaps short and no maximum time constraint is required. Activity relationships are shown in Table 16.6.

Table 16.6. Activity relationship

From	To	Type	Resource flag	Min. deviation	Max. deviation
Produce extr.	Setup mixer	end-start		0	0

The activities of the transport container operation have been connected to the other activities in a slightly different way. The "container start" activity has a start-start relationship to the activity "produce with extruder" with a minimum and maximum deviation of zero. So, the containers are occupied once production begins. The "container end" activity has an "end-end" relationship also with no time deviation allowed with the last production activity (mixer or filling machine). The quality test activity has simply been connected to the last production activity as well.

Every activity must have one or more *modes*. A mode is a primary resource or a combination of a primary resource and one or more secondary resources which are used simultaneously. So when using alternative resources each of these resources represents one mode. But even if all of the primary resources require the same secondary resource it must be named separately for each mode. Every mode can be given a *priority* from A (first selection) to Z (only manually selectable). This priority influences the resource selection during incremental scheduling and optimization. Actually, the priorities represent penalty costs. If no priorities are used, the system always tries to use the fastest machine first. The mode also contains the information about the activity duration – depending on the resource the mode represents. Selecting the mode with the fastest machine therefore leads to the shortest activity duration. So, in APO the production speed and power of a resource can differ, dependent on the PPM which uses the resource. The resource speed is not maintained with the resource, but with the actual product/resource combination. The activity duration in the mode can be defined with a *fixed* and a *variable* part which grows with the order size. If the activity is a sequence dependent setup activity, the activity duration is taken from the matrix, and the fields in the mode are ignored. The fields "break" and "in shift" determine the activity which can be interrupted by a break, and the activity must be completed within one shift.

For every mode there are the *capacity requirements* of the resources defined in a separate table. Here also the names of the secondary resources for the specific mode are given. A secondary resource is always covered as long as the primary resource with the same start and end times. The primary resource which is also given in the mode definition is always the so-called *calendar resource*. This says that the times of availability of this resource affect the availability of all the secondary resources in this mode. As mentioned in Sect. 16.3.4 an activity on a single activity resource always has the capacity requirement of 1. On multi-activity resources, capacity requirements other than 1 will occur and have to be defined here. Like the activity duration the resource consumption can be defined using a *fixed* and a *variable* part. But if the activity duration already uses order size depending values, the resource consumption cannot contain order size depending values additionally. This is one of the reasons, why the transport containers had to be modelled in a separate operation. Modelling the transport containers as secondary resources would require both variable activity duration and variable capacity requirements. In the Tables 16.7 and 16.8 an example is given for the modelling of modes and capacity requirements.

Table 16.7. Modes

Activity	Mode	Resource	Dur. fixed	Dur. variable	Break	In shift	Pirority
Produce extr.	1	Extruder 1	0	1.5 h			A
Produce extr.	2	Extruder 5	0	2.75 h	X		C

As the last part of the PPM the *components* (inputs and outputs) are maintained. The entries are made for the activity, where the input or output occurs. It is defined whether the material enters or leaves the production

Table 16.8. Capacity requirements

Activity	Mode	Resource	Cap. req. fixed	Cap. req. variable	Calendar
Produce extr.	1	Extruder 1	1	0	X
Produce extr.	1	Worker	0.5	0	

process at the begin of the activity, at the end of the activity or continuously. APO distinguishes between *logical components* and *physical components*. A logical component represents one or more physical components which may be time dependent. So the logical component "processor" for a PC production may have the entries "Pentium-III-500" valid from 2000-01-01 to 2000-05-31 and "Pentium III-600" which is valid from 2000-06-01 to 2000-12-31. In this way the BOMs are integrated into the APO PPM, as BOMs can be time dependent in R/3 as well. As every activity may have inputs and outputs, complex production processes with several inputs and outputs at different production steps can be described by a PPM.

16.3.6 Supply Chain Model

Finally all the elements described above must be added to a *model*. A model allows actual planning with the system. Without creating a model the locations, products, resources and production process models cannot be used yet. Using the model philosophy one can create completely separated planning environments in the same system with the data in the same storage device (*live*Cache). Every model can have several *planning versions*. This says that several copies of the transaction data of the model are used to simulate different scenarios and to answer what-if questions. Only one planning version – the active version – is relevant for transferring the planning results back to the connected OLTP system and for receiving new planning data.

16.4 Consequences and Benefits of the APO PP/DS Implementation

The implementation of APO PP/DS proved to be very successful. Since the system has been implemented a few weeks before this paper was prepared, only preliminary results can be presented.

Early planning results show that the quality of the generated plans is not worse than the plans the planners have been creating before with their expert knowledge. The difference between the plans created manually and those created by APO is the speed and the flexibility in planning: Previously, it took several planners for more than one day to create a production plan which was fixed for several weeks. Now, APO plans the same amount of orders in an optimizer run taking about one hour. The fixed horizon could be reduced from about one week to one or two days. Especially when an important machine breaks down, a new plan can be created with APO immediately. The integration with the R/3 system is seamless: no additional steps are necessary to transfer planning results and new orders between the systems.

The quality of the created plans can be measured in terms of production time consumed for a certain amount of orders. In this case, the production plan generated by APO usually has a makespan less than the manually created plan. This results mainly from the excessive reserved buffer times which are not needed anymore.

A very important factor is the acceptance by the user. This new planning tool has been fully accepted by the production planners as it is no additional burden for them to work with this tool. They see that they have a powerful system to help them in their daily routine work and make the production more flexible and profitable.

16.5   Outlook – Supply Network Planning with APO

After this first APO project has been finished, the use of APO modules in the company will increase further. There are several production plants that also want to use PP/DS locally. Besides further PP/DS implementations, a prototype, modelling the whole production network in the supply network planning module has been created. This is the first step to coordinate the whole supply chain using the Demand Planning and Supply Network Planning modules of APO.

17 Semiconductor Manufacturing

Lorenz Schneeweiss[1] and Ulrich Wetterauer[2]

[1] KPMG Consulting GmbH, Olof-Palme-Straße 31, 60439 Frankfurt a.M.,
Germany
[2] j & m Management Consulting GmbH, Kaiserringforum, Willy-Brandt-Platz 6,
68161 Mannheim, Germany

17.1 Introduction

The semiconductor industry has one of the longest and most complex manufacturing processes and supply chains. Yet the fast changing market and the
continous price decrease in the semiconductor industry imposes increasing
pressure on the manufacturers to decrease production lead-time, while keeping costs low. As a result superior planning capabilities across the corporate-
wide supply chain become more and more vital to meet the challenges of this
industry.

This chapter provides some insight into the implementation of the RHY-
THM Supply Chain Planner (RHYTHM SCP) from i2 Technologies (see
Chap. 15) for a large semiconductor manufacturer. The goal of this APS
project was to unify the planning processes throughout the organization and
to achieve a significant reduction of the planning cycle time.

After introducing the main characteristics of the semiconductor supply
chain and the APS model typology a case study is described which investigates the possibility of using the software product RHYTHM Factory Planner
(RHYTHM FP) from i2 Technologies instead of RHYTHM SCP for the detailed short-term planning.

17.1.1 Description of the Supply Chain

The structure of the semiconductor supply chain is influenced by several
characteristics. For one thing the ratio of value to volume of the product is
very high. This means that transportation even over long distances by plane
is not an issue. On the other side the equipment necessary for production is
expensive and difficult to transport and install. Furthermore the production
process can be split over several locations, e.g. front end facilities (wafer
fabrication and wafer-test/sawing) in Europe and back end facilities (die
bonding, wire bonding, moulding and chip-test) in Asia. The production sites
for the different stages of the production process can therefore be chosen
all over the world to achieve goals like reduction of costs for real estate,
equipment or wages.

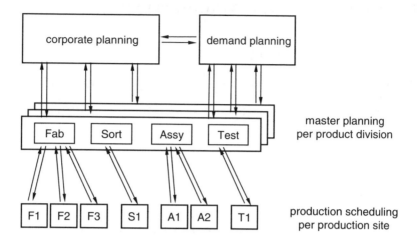

Fig. 17.1. The semiconductor industry supply chain

Another characteristic is that the customers are usually resellers or large industry corporations with considerable influence on the manufacturers as a consequence. It is for example not uncommon that a customer demands the fabrication of a logic component in a special production site or even on a special machine.

The semiconductor industry is at the beginning of a complex supply chain leading to a large demand variability with a corresponding uncertainty of demand forecasts. Usually a manufacturer offers a variety of products, mainly in the areas communication, automotive and industrial, wireless solutions, chip card & security and memory products. The organization of the manufacturer used for the case study is divided into product divisions according to these areas (see Fig. 17.1).

Table 17.1 shows the classification of the semiconductor industry according to the supply chain typology (see Chap. 2).

17.1.2   The Architecture of the Planning System

As mentioned before the goal of the APS implementation project was to unify the planning processes and to reduce the planning cycle time. This should be achieved by using an integrated planning system with a top-down approach for the product structure (from aggregated to detailed) and coordinated shared facility capacity through aggregated capacity groups (see below for details). The planning processes which had to be considered in this planning system were:

- demand/forecast planning,
- long-term production and distribution planning (corporate planning),

Table 17.1. Supply chain typology for the semiconductor industry

Functional attributes	
Attributes	Contents
products procured	highly specific
sourcing type	single or double sourcing
organization of the production process	job shop and flow shop
repetition of operations	batch production
distribution structure	one and two stages
pattern of delivery	dynamic
deployment of transportation means	unlimited
availability of future demand	forecasted
product life cycle	several months
products sold	highly specific
portion of service operations	low
Structural attributes	
Attributes	Contents
network structure	mixture
degree of globalization	global
location of decoupling point(s)	deliver-to-order and make-to-order
legal position	inter- and intra-organizational
direction of coordination	mixture
type of information exchanged	orders

- mid-term master planning (divisional planning) and
- short term production sheduling (facility planning).

A graphical representation of these planning processes is given in Fig. 17.2 and will be explained subsequently.

Demand/forecast planning is used to generate accurate forecast values and as a tool for marketing to manage volume and revenue planning. The results are used as input for corporate planning and master planning.

Corporate planning tasks (see Fig. 17.1) comprise financial/budget planning, product aggregation to gather future demand and allocation of capacity to business units (divisions) with the focus on key equipment. This long-term planning is done once or twice a year with a time horizon of three years. The results of corporate planning are based on the interaction with the demand planning and master planning and include an investment plan for additional capacity, capacity checked forecast (forwarded to demand planning) and capacity allocations per division, product group and production site (forwarded to master planning).

The interface between corporate planning and divisional planning (or master planning) are the aggregated capacity groups where the capacity per division and product group is modelled as a single resource. Divisional planning

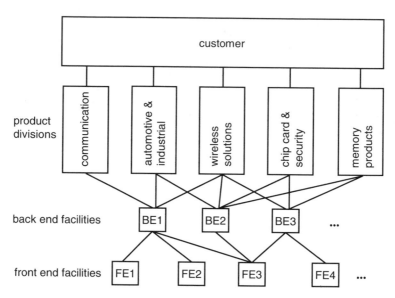

Fig. 17.2. Model architecture in the semiconductor APS implementation project

is done to quote and confirm orders, to determine the demand for the different production facilities (forwarded to production scheduling), to receive the feedback of the facilities and reconcile the master plan to the changes and finally to conduct early warnings in case of planning problems (late or short orders) within the planning horizon (12 months in case of the semiconductor company considered in this case study).

The results of the short-term production scheduling (or facility planning) are the generation of a dispatch list for the line control and a detailed scheduling on key resources. These informations are based on the demand taken from the master plan and work in process information from the shop floor control system. If orders can only be planned late or short an early warning message should be generated. The planned quantities and dates are reported back to the divisional planning.

In the APS implementation project the three parts of the planning system corporate planning, divisional planning and production scheduling (facility planning) were carried out with the software tool RHYTHM SCP while demand planning was done using the RHYTHM Demand Planner from i2 Technologies, respectively. The integration with the Oracle database was done using the software RhythmLink from i2 Technologies. The actual scheduling process is supported by the shop floor control system Workstream by Consilium (see www.consilium.com).

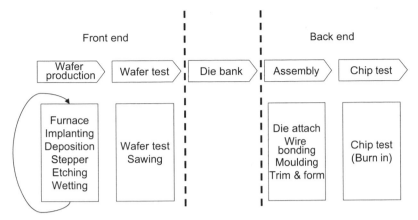

Fig. 17.3. The semiconductor production process

17.1.3 Production Process

The production process of semiconductors consists of two stages each divided into two phases. The two stages are called *front end* and *back end* and are separated by a die bank. The front end consists of the *wafer production* and the *wafer test* phases whereas the back end is represented by the two phases *assembly* and *chip test* (see Fig. 17.3).

17.1.4 Wafer Production

Starting point of every chip production is a round silicon disc. The so-called wafer does not represent a functional element of the future chip but serves as the basis and carrier for the functional elements to be implemented, see Fig. 17.4. Layers of conductive and isolating material are spread on the wafer in several repetitive processes. After each layer a photo chemical layer is spread on the top layer and exposed with a mask carrying the circuit information of each layer. This film is then developed to etch the circuits in an acid bath. Afterwards the photo chemical layer are removed and the next conductive or isolating layer can follow.

This process cycles six to twelve times per wafer depending on the complexity of the chip architecture. A number of several hundred small multi-layer circuits and transistors can be developed on a single wafer. All wafers are processed in lots of up to 50 pieces. The maximum lot-size is defined by technical restrictions of the racks used to carry the material. The lot-size can also be less then 50 pieces if necessary to reduce the number of intermediate parts in the inventory, but it is tried to maintain the maximum lot-size over the whole process.

The wafers run through these repetitive process steps in four to six weeks. The constraint is a machine called "stepper", responsible for the positioning

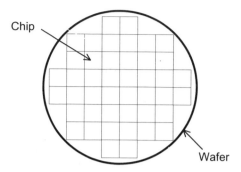

Fig. 17.4. Structure of a silicon wafer

of the wafers and exposing the layers according to the mask. This process has to be conducted with great accuracy to avoid wasted material.

Subsequently the intermediate product can be used to produce different finished goods. The production lead-time of this process is again four to six weeks weeks. At the end of this process the wafers are ready to be shipped to the wafer test.

17.1.5   Wafer Test

The production process of the wafer test starts with the output of the preceding production step. This process is constrained by the availability of testing capacity. The testing capacity is usually a constraint to the complete semiconductor supply chain.

After testing, the wafers are sawed to separate the single chips. The yield factor of the testing procedure depends on the quality of the production process and on the number of chips per wafer. Consecutively, the chips are shipped to the customer or stored in a finished goods stock.

17.1.6   Back End

The back end operates in a make-to-order mode. In the assembly the chips are supplied from the central ware house and are connected to the platforms, bonded and sealed in plastic. The production process is finished with the final quality control, where the finished element is aged artificially with high temperatures. The back end processes are not part of this case study.

17.1.7   Case Study

As mentioned before the software product RHYTHM SCP from i2 Technologies was used for the detailed short-term production planning in the actual APS implementation project. This case study investigates the possibility of using the software product RHYTHM FP instead of RHYTHM SCP for the production planning in the semiconductor industry. For this purpose the two front-end production sites of the supply chain, the wafer fabrication and the wafer test, have been simulated in two separate models using the RHYTHM FP. Furthermore, a two-way communication between the two models was established:

- the wafer test site calculates material demand (requests) for the wafer fabrication based on orders, work in process and basic data like yield, cycle time and lot-sizes.
- the wafer fabrication calculates the material flow to the wafer test site based on these requests as well as work in process and basic data.

A detailed description of the two models will be given later.

The goal of this case study was to understand the consequences of using RHYTHM FP for the short-term production planning in the semiconductor industries instead of RHYTHM SCP and to investigate whether all relevant details of the production process could be included in the model.

17.2   The Modelling Concept of i2 RHYTHM Factory Planner

This section describes the procedure of creating a model of a production process using i2 RHYTHM Factory Planner (FP). First the basic data structure will be explained in order to get an impression of the modelling philosophy. In the following the most important elements of a model will be introduced, the basic model. Any additional modelling is case specific and will be explained subsequently in detail.

17.2.1   The Data Structure

The whole data model of FP is based on flat files (ASCII) of two different types, spec files and data files. Spec files are used to structure and define the content of the data files. They provide the framework of the model whereas the data files build it.

Spec Files

The *standard spec file*, provided with each release of FP, contains the standard definition for all possible ASCII data files that may be input to and output from FP. A *spec file* contains a subset of the definitions specified in the standard spec file. Each data file in the customer data directory must be defined either in the standard spec file or in the implementation specific spec file. The type and class of each field in the definition must match the corresponding field in the data file. Table 17.2 shows the field definitions of an example spec file.

Table 17.2. Definition of an example spec file

std_spec_file: (here: demand order record)

demand_order_data	name of the data file to be read or written
mode: read	indicates the mode of the data file (other: readwrite, write)
optional: True	indicates if this file is essential or not (this value influences the error messages)
Demand_Order_Record	name of the record, defined by the following fields:
order	unique identifier of the order (first entry in the data file)
sales_due_date	desired due date (second entry in the data file)
part_number	the end product to requested by this order
part_quantity	the ordered quantity of the end product
priority	etc.
category	etc.
customer	etc.

Data Files

The data files contain records matching the structure defined in the spec files. A record is one line in the data file. In a record the field information is separated by a delimiter. The following text is an excerpt from a larger data file that corresponding to the spec file definition of Table 17.2:

```
Demand_Order_Data
Order 1,03APR1999120000,Part A,20,,,Customer 1
Order 2,03APR1999120000,Part B,70,,,Customer 1
Order 3,03APR1999120000,Part B,40,,,Customer 3
Order 4,03APR1999120000,Part C,40,,,Customer 3
Order 5,03APR1999120000,Part C,50,,,Customer 2
```

In this example the fields *priority* and *category* are not populated and will be filled with the defaults in FP. One may want to change the default for a certain field to reduce the amount of data to be read in. This might be crucial dealing with big data volumes. Therefore the default can be defined in the spec file, as shown in the following example:

```
demand_order_data:
....,
customer = Customer 1,
....;
```

In this example the company has only one customer, Customer 1, and the field will not be considered in the data files anymore.

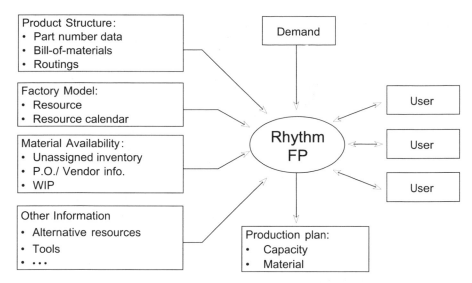

Fig. 17.5. Modelling data classification of i2 RHYTHM Factory Planner

Table 17.3. Description of basic FP model data

part_number_data	definition of all parts and products
bill_of_materials_data	the bill-of-materials for all products
routing_data	description of the operation plans
resource_data	defines all resources and their properties
resource_calender_data	availability calendar of the defined resources
unassigned_inventory_data	contains the unassigned inventory at any time
purchase_orders	planned and scheduled material receipts
supplier_part_data	vendor information
wip_data	work in process quantities

17.2.2 Building a New Data Set

The I/O data model of the planning process with FP is displayed in Fig. 17.5 (see also Table 17.3 for explanation of input data). On the input side the basic model and the additional modelling features are shown. The basic model consists of data files describing the product structure, the factory model and the material availability. The dynamic part of every basic model is represented by the demand. FP in interaction with the users creates a material and capacity feasible plan as output (refer to Fig. 17.5).

There is a minimum of data files necessary to build a basic model in FP which can be extended using other modelling features (see Fig. 17.6 and Table 17.3).

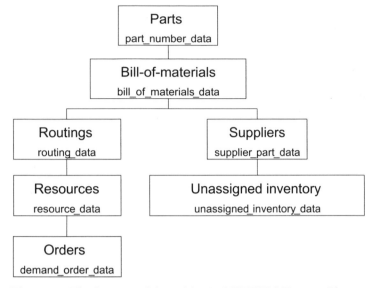

Fig. 17.6. The basic model used by i2 RHYTHM Factory Planner

17.3 Modelling

17.3.1 Wafer Production

The wafer production model considers three products (wafer A, wafer B, wafer C, see Fig. 17.7). A relaxation will be used in the model that aggregates for each product all the process cycles mentioned before to one operation in order to keep the model simple. The machine is loaded from 2 hours (6 cycles) to 4 hours (12 cycles) per lot, depending on the production process of the wafer. This modelling is sufficient to create a rough capacity plan. The detailed scheduling of the process cycles will be done by a shop floor control system. The lead-time of the non-constraining processes can be modelled as a fixed set-up time, for example.

As regards to modelling the following requirements have been identified:

- lot-sizing
- safety stock on intermediate parts

After a common understanding of the requirements the aggregation of the modelling has to be defined. As a principal rule it can be said that only (potential) constraints have to be planned for. Therefore the aggregation level of the model concentrates on the two constraining operations.

Like in all implementations the modelling has to start with the basic model described above. So, all parts, bills of material, resources, routings, suppliers, inventory and demand have to be specified according to the model

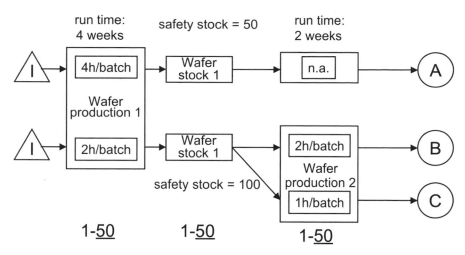

Fig. 17.7. The production process model of the phase *wafer production*

and spec file definitions. Then the model can be extended with additional features and functionalities.

Lots can be defined using the following two data files populated accordingly. It would be sufficient to populate only the batch_size_data file if the lot-size definition was unique for one resource. But in case of different operations on the same resource it is necessary to identify a certain batch_type with every different operation. The batch_size_data has the following structure:

resource	type	max.	min	ideal	run_time	run_time_uom
wafer production 1	Typ A	50	0	50	4	HOURS
wafer production 1	Typ BC	50	0	50	2	HOURS
wafer production 2	Typ B	50	0	50	2	HOURS
wafer production 2	Typ C	50	0	50	1	HOURS
wafer production A2		50	0	50	2	HOURS

The batch_type_data file is structured as follows:

routing	operation	primary
routing A1	preprocessing A	Typ A
routing B1	preprocessing B	Typ BC
routing B2	postprocessing B	Typ B
routing C2	postprocessing C	Typ C

The wafer production A2 represents a dummy resource with a machine load time 0 but a wait time greater than 0. Therefore the resource does not cause capacity problems in the capacity planning.

In contrast to time based safety stock a simple quantity based safety stock on intermediate parts is not supported explicitly by FP.

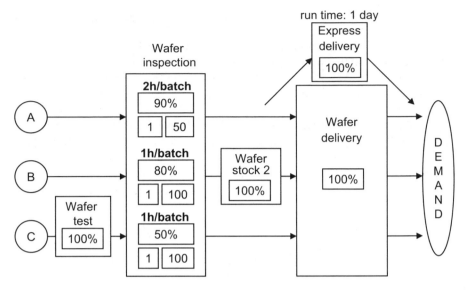

Fig. 17.8. The production process of the phase *wafer test*

17.3.2   Wafer Test

The planning model is represented in Fig. 17.8. In this model the rule can be extended that not only the potential constraints have to be modelled but also every process the planner needs to have detailed information about in order to be able to create reports or to take a decision. In this case FP is to take a decision about the delivery service used thought it is not a constraint. A specialty of the semiconductor production are the low yield factors at the beginning of the use of a new production process (about 5%) which increase in the course of time to up to 95% with the learning curve effect. Consequently the following requirements have to be considered:

- ramp up/yield,
- lot-sizing and
- alternative resources.

The modelling starts again with the basic model.

In order to model ramp up and yield, time dependent bills of material are used to refer to different routings. The first record of the bill_of_materials_data is valid until 6/1/99 because then a new record is added (A) describing the same relationship and the former record is deleted (D) from the list of records. However, the new record references a different routing with a different base yield factor. Yield can therefore be modelled in a time dependent step function.

The following is an excerpt of the bill_of_materials_data:

```
produced_part    routing    consumed_part      ecn_code ecn_date
produced_part_A  routing 1  consumed_part_A
produced_part_A  routing 2  consumed_part_A  A          6/1/99
produced_part_A  routing 1  consumed_part_A  D          6/1/99
```

The routing_data file is structured as follows:

```
routing      operation     resource    run_time     uom     yield
routing 1    OP1           Res1        2            HOURS   0.8
routing 2    OP1           Res1        2            HOURS   0.9
```

Lot creation is modelled in the same principal way as presented before. Alternate resources can be specified in the operation_resource_data. By assigning a different resource to the same operation in a routing an alternate resource can be created. The time factors of the alternate resource reference the time factors of the primary resource.
The operation_resources_data file is structured as follows:

```
routing    operation      resource         runtime    cooldown_time
delivery   chip_delivery  fast delivery    1          0.3333
```

The decision to use an alternate resource is often linked with higher costs. Financial figures are not considered by the decision rules in FP though they can be displayed. Therefore the alternate resource can be chosen either automatically or manually if higher costs are involved in the planning decision.

17.4 Model Communication

A communication link between the two models was setup, leading to a collaborative planning process. The two models exchange data and enable the planners responsible for wafer production and wafer test to react to changes in the plans, based on data provided by the other model. One loop is shown in Fig. 17.9. This iterative planning process can be run as often as required until all severe planning problems are resolved.

The wafer test model creates a plan for the demand orders that were accepted. It therefore creates procurement recommendations anticipating the capacity and the behaviour of the supplier (wafer production model). The wafer production model now plans for the demand imposed on it by the consumer (wafer test model) and generates deliveries for the requested material. The deliveries are imported by the wafer test model to generate a new plan based on the new supply information. Here the loop may stop or start again until an acceptable result is found.

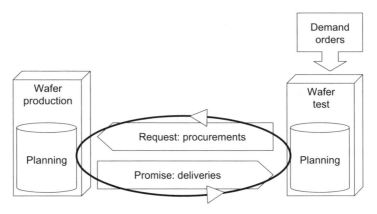

Fig. 17.9. Model communication

17.5   Lessons Learned

FP models are easy to develop and can be understood quickly and intuitively. The data required to create a FP model is sourced from flat files or from the i2 RHYTHM Active Data Warehouse. The flat file modelling is normally used to identify the data requirements in an early phase of an APS implementation project.

FP has been developed continously and improved by i2 over more than 10 years, based on a large variety of real life implementation projects. The FP product embodies an enormous variety of modelling features and can be employed in many industry branches. But of course there are still a number of cases where the modelling functionality is not sufficient to properly reflect the real planning problem. In most cases work arounds can be developed – extending the standard planning functionality of FP, at the cost of increased maintenance effort of the solution.

The FP on-line help function provides information about the modelling concepts and helps to solve most modelling problems. Still a lot of aspects are not completely described in the documentation though included properly in the programme.

The user has access to a variety of useful information on the user interface (the FP client user interface is usually Windows based) and can customize reports according to the planning workflow. Two effects of the implementation of an intelligent planning tool have to be lined out here. First, automated decisions are taken by the tool according to a committed set of business rules so the planner can concentrate on relevant aspects and exception handling which increases the planner productivity. Second, the planner is forced by the tool to plan according to the pre-defined rules which guarantees a stability in decision-making (see also Chap. 14).

18 Computer Assembly

Christoph Kilger

j & m Management Consulting GmbH, Kaiserringforum, Willy-Brandt-Platz 6, 68161 Mannheim, Germany

The computer industry is a typical example of a *material constrained* supply chain. The main bottleneck of demand fulfilment is the availability of the electronic components, e.g. disk drives, processors, memory etc. This case study is based on an actual APS implementation project at a large international computer manufacturer. Four modules of the APS system RHYTHM by i2 Technologies are implemented, supporting the demand planning process, the master planning process, the demand supply matching process and the demand fulfilment process. The following sections describe in detail

- the computer assembly supply chain,
- the scope and the expected benefits of the APS implementation project,
- the planning processes being supported by the APS system, i.e. demand planning, master planning, demand supply matching and demand fulfilment and
- the integration of the applied i2 planning modules with the existing SAP R/3 system.

18.1 Description of the Supply Chain

18.1.1 Computer Industry Supply Chain

The typical supply chain in the computer industry consists of five main stages: suppliers, computer manufacturers, logistic service providers, deployment partners and customers. Fig. 18.1 depicts the complete computer industry supply chain.

The suppliers supply electronic and mechanical components for the system board and computer assembly, external units like printers and monitors, accessories like keyboard and mouse, software, manuals etc. In many cases, there are multiple sources for one type of components like disk drives and memory (disk drives supplied by one supplier may be substituted by disk drives from an alternate supplier if these are qualified for the corresponding configuration). The computer industry is a material intensive industry. In general approx. 15–20 suppliers constitute 80% of the procured value, 30–40 suppliers represent 95% of the procured value. Some suppliers provide simple assembly services. In the supply chain shown in Fig. 18.1 the housing supplier receives power supplies from two alternate sources and assembles the power

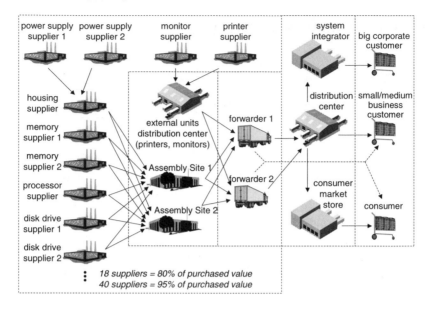

Fig. 18.1. Overview of the computer industry supply chain

supplies into the housings before shipping the housings to the computer assembly site.

The computer manufacturing process itself consists of two main parts: the assembly of the system board and the assembly of the system unit. There are three options to organize this part of the supply chain:

1. System board assembly and system unit assembly are done in the same assembly site.
2. System board assembly and system unit assembly are done in separate assembly sites, but belong to the same legal entity.
3. System board assembly and system unit assembly are done in separate assembly sites and belong to different legal entities.

In this case study we assume option 1, as depicted in Fig. 18.1. Typically, the computer manufacturer runs a separate distribution centre for external units like printers and monitors that are procured from external suppliers.

The transport between assembly sites and the deployment partners is executed by logistic service providers. There are three kinds of deployment partners: logistics service providers (forwarders) running a distribution centre, system integrators and consumer market stores. In most cases products are shipped by a forwarder from the assembly site and from the distribution centre for external units like printers and monitors directly to a distribution centre, where the separate line items of a customer order a merged. From there, complete customer orders are shipped.

There are three cases for the shipment of customer orders, depending on the type of customer:

- Orders by small and medium business customers are shipped directly from the distribution centre to the customer's site.
- Big corporate customers like banks and insurance companies typically place orders with a volume of up to several thousand PCs (e. g. in order to equip all offices in a specific region). These big orders are often executed by a system integrator, who takes over responsibility for the procurement and the installation of the computing devices (PCs, servers, monitors, printers, networks, modems etc.).
- For the consumer market, department stores and consumer market stores place big orders (in the range of 10 000 to 20 000 units) that are shipped to their distribution centres and are distributed from there to the individual outlets.

As indicated by the dashed arrows in Fig. 18.1 additional direct distribution paths from the computer manufacturer to the consumer market and to small and medium businesses will be established, supported by e-business strategies.

18.1.2 Product Structure

The product portfolio contains consumer PCs, professional PCs, servers and notebooks. Within these product families, two types of products can be distinguished. *Fixed configurations* have an individual material code that can be referred to in customer orders. Normally, fixed configurations are made to order. However, in order to offer very low lead-times to the market (for example two days) a make-to-stock policy can be applied. This requires a very good understanding of future demand of these market segments, i. e. a high forecast accuracy.

Open configurations can be freely configured by the customer (configure-to-order). An open configuration is identified by the *base unit*, specifying the housing and the system board. The customer can then choose from a selection of processors, disk drives, network, video and sound controllers and can define the size of the main memory. During the configuration process specific configuration rules have to be fulfilled. Examples of hard configuration constraints are "the number of controller cards may not exceed the number of extension slots of the system board" and "the selected processor type must be compliant with the system board." An example of a soft constraint is "The number of selected CD-ROM drives should not exceed one." Only the base unit and the components have individual material codes. The complete configuration is either identified by the material code of the base unit (this requires a hard pegging of production orders to the customer order) or a new material code is generated as final step of the configuration process.

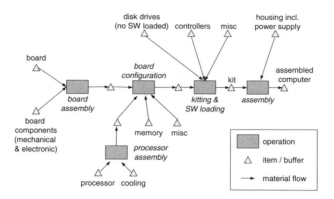

Fig. 18.2. Detailed computer assembly supply chain (Part 1: Assembly processes)

18.1.3   Computer Assembly Process

The computer assembly process is divided into two main parts (as shown in Figs. 18.2 and 18.3):

- the assembly operations and
- the testing and packing operations.

The first step is the assembly of the system board. Boards are assembled in batches of 100 to 1 000 pieces. The board assembly lead-time for one batch is roughly half a day. There are approx. 20 different system boards for PCs and another 20 for servers. The system boards for notebooks are procured.

The second step is the configuration of the board. In this step, the processor assembly – consisting of the processor and the cooling – and the memory are put onto the board.

The third step is the kitting and the loading of the disk drive with the selected software. The kitting operation collects all selected components – disk drives, controller cards for network, video and sound etc. – into a box that is called the kit. The kit, the housing and the power supply – which are not part of the kit – are used in the fourth step, the actual assembly of the computer.

If the customer has special requests – e. g. specific controller cards that have to be assembled into the computer – a separate customization step follows the computer assembly operation. After that, the computer is tested and packed. In the final packing operation the keyboard and accessories as mouse, manuals, software, cables etc. are added.

The complete lead-time is 24 - 28 hours. The most time consuming operations are the software loading and the test operations. There are two production types: Small batches (usually below 200 PCs) are assembled in a job shop, large batches (above 200 PCs) are assembled in a flow shop. Please note that kitting takes place only for the job shop production type. In the flow

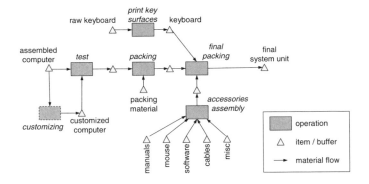

Fig. 18.3. Detailed computer assembly supply chain (Part 2: Test & packing processes)

shop, the material for the complete batch is provided along the production line.

Table 18.1 summarizes the classification of the computer industry according to the supply chain typology introduced in Chap. 2.

18.2   Scope and Expected Benefits

The target of the APS implementation project described in this case study is to improve the business performance of the computer manufacturer. For this purpose the business performance is measured by three key performance indicators (see Chaps. 2 and 12):

- The forecast accuracy shall be improved from 65% to 75%.
- The on time delivery shall be improved from 75% to 90%.
- The inventory turns shall be improved from 20 to 40.

The following planning processes are in the scope of the project and shall be supported by the APS RHYTHM by i2 Technologies:

- demand planning (on finished goods level and component level),
- forecast netting,
- master planning,
- allocation planning,
- demand supply matching, and
- order promising.

The following modules of i2 RHYTHM have been implemented:

- Demand Planner (DP) including PRO (Product Relationship Object, a module of demand management to support the component planning process) supporting the demand planning processes,

Table 18.1. Supply chain typology for the computer industry

Functional attributes	
Attributes	Contents
products procured	standard and highly specific
sourcing type	multiple sourcing
organization of the production process	flow shop and job shop
repetition of operations	batch production / single product
distribution structure	two and three stages
pattern of delivery	dynamic
deployment of transportation means	individual links
availability of future demand	forecasted
products life cycle	several months
products sold	fixed and open configurations
portion of service operations	products and services
Structural attributes	
Attributes	Contents
network structure	mixture
degree of globalization	several countries
location of decoupling point(s)	configure-to-order and make-to-order
legal position	inter- and intra-organizational
direction of coordination	mixture
type of information exchanged	demand and supply (forecast and orders)

- Factory Planner (FP) supporting the demand supply matching process,
- Supply Chain Planner (SCP) supporting the master planning process,
- Demand Fulfillment (DF) supporting the forecast netting, the allocation planning and the order promising processes,
- RhythmLink (RL) and
- Active Data Warehouse (ADW).

The i2 RHYTHM modules are integrated with the existing SAP R/3 system, i. e. MM Materials Management, SD Sales and Distribution and PP Production Planning. Figure 18.4 summarizes the supported processes and the data flows between them.

By the time this book was written, the demand planning process for units and the demand supply matching process were used productivly. The demand planning process for components was in the parallel phase (four weeks prior to the productive use). The implementation of the master planning and demand fulfilment processes had started. The project started in 1999, the total implementation time was scheduled for 18 months, including a two months

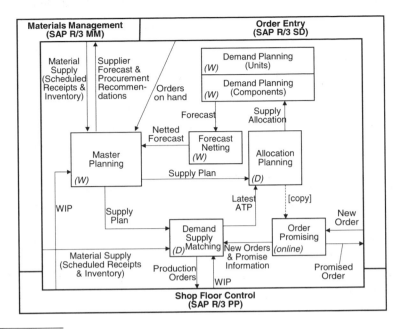

(D) daily planning cycle; *(W)* weekly planning cycle; *(online)* online process

Fig. 18.4. Computer assembly planning processes

phase in which the APS implementation project had been defined and the APS software was selected.[1]

18.3   Planning Processes in Detail

18.3.1   Demand Planning

The demand planning process is running weekly. It determines the forecast on unit level (i.e. finished goods) and on component level. The implementation was structured into three steps. Step 1 covered unit planning for a subset of all products, i.e. planning of complete computer systems (units), Step 2 extended unit planning to all products and Step 3 supports component planning.

The goal of the implementation of i2 Demand Planner is a more accurate forecast: The forecast accuracy shall be improved from 65% to 75%.

The following technical "enablers" of i2 Demand Planner help to improve the forecast accuracy:

---

[1] Chapters 12 and 13 contain additional information on the definition and selection phases of APS implementation projects in general.

Table 18.2. Structure of the geographic and product hierarchies

Level	Geographic Hierarchy	Product Hierarchy*
1	All_Geo (1)	All_Prod (1)
2	Area (6)	Prod_Segment (4+10)
3	Region (> 40)	Prod_Group (10+20)
4		Prod_Family (20+50)
5		Model_Line (40+100)
6		Sub_Model_Line (80+200)
7		SKU (200+400)

* The number of instances on that level are given in parentheses. The product hierarchy includes the instances used for the unit planning process and those used for the component planning process, denoted as $(a + b)$, where a is the number of units on that level and b is the number of components.

1. i2 DP provides a common database to maintain all input and output data of the demand planning process.
2. i2 DP supports a collaborative planning process, where all departments participating in the demand planning process find their own planning results and are supported in the integration of the various plans to one collaborative demand plan.
3. All needed actual data like shipments and orders are maintained within i2 DP and can be used within the planning process.[2]
4. All groups participating in the demand planning process can define their own views on the data, independently from the other groups.
5. Forecast accuracy is measured based on the i2 DP database, using a well defined uniform method that has been defined within the project.

Unit Planning

Table 18.2 shows the levels of the geographic and the product hierarchies used in the demand planning process. The numbers given in parentheses specify the number of instances on that level.

All_Geo is the root of the geographic hierarchy. The area level represents geographically defined areas in the world, e.g. Europe, Middle East and Africa (EMEA); Americas; Asia Pacific. The regional level represents sales regions within an area, e.g. Germany, France and the UK are regions within the EMEA area.

All_Prod is the *root* of the product hierarchy. The *product segment* level divides the product hierarchy into sub-hierarchies for PCs, servers, notebooks

[2] In fact, because of the integration of all actual data and the daily update of the actuals, i2 DP is also used as a management reporting tool.

and the planned components (see next subsection). On the *product group* level each sub-hierarchy is split into multiple product groups, e. g. the PC sub-hierarchy is split into consumer PCs and professional PCs and the server sub-hierarchy into small servers and large servers. The next level is the *product family* that groups products which are in the same performance class (low-end consumer PCs vs. high-end consumer PCs). The *model line* groups PCs and servers by the type of the housing. The *sub model line* groups PCs and servers within one model line by the type of the system board. The *SKU* level is normally not planned for units (refer to the next section about component planning for explanation why the SKU level is in the product hierarchy).

The time dimension is structured into Year, Quarter, Month and Week. The weekly level is not used for the unit planning, but for the component planning. The time horizon starts two years before the start of the current fiscal year and covers 12 months into the future. Thus, it is possible to maintain two years of historic data in the i2 DP database. This provides a good basis to setup stochastic forecasting methods including seasonal patterns. However, two years of historic data are currently not available. The average product life cycle is about five months. Thus, a large manual effort is required to define the historic substitution rules that are used to map historic data of products that have reached their end of life to living products.

The following data rows have been defined and are maintained in the i2 DP database:

- *Actual data*: Three types of actual data are maintained: Shipments (quantities related to shipment date), orders (quantities related to customer requested date) and confirmed open orders (quantities related to confirmed date).
- *Budget plan*: The budget plan is updated yearly and is valid for the current fiscal year.
- *Sales forecast*: The sales forecast is created monthly and covers six months. The database contains four separate rows for the sales forecast, representing the current planning round and the last three planning rounds.
- *Plant forecast*: The plant forecast is created weekly by the planners in the production sites. The database contains four separate rows for the plant forecast, representing the current planning round and the last three planning rounds.
- *Collaborative forecast*: The collaborative forecast is determined monthly by a collaborative process in which sales, product management, procurement and the production sites participate.

There is a yearly, monthly and weekly planning cycle as shown in Fig. 18.5. Once per year, the budget plan is created, covering the next fiscal year (12 months horizon). Every month, the sales planners update the sales forecast. For that purpose, i2 DP has been installed in all regional sales offices (approx. 50). In the second step, the sales forecast is reviewed by the planners in the plants; the result of this step is the plant forecast. In a final step, a

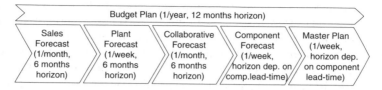

Fig. 18.5. Planning processes supported by i2 Demand Planner

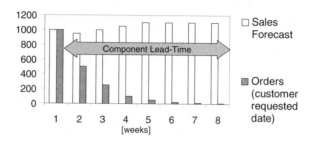

Fig. 18.6. Order lead-time vs. component lead-time

collaborative forecast is created based on the sales and the plant forecast. All three types of forecast cover six months.

The collaborative forecast is adjusted every week by the planners in the plants, resulting in a weekly plant forecast. The weekly plant forecast is the basis for the weekly component planning, that is described in the next subsection.

Component Planning

The main purpose of the monthly and weekly forecasting processes is the creation of an accurate component forecast. As the order lead-time is much shorter than the material lead-time, the component forecast is an important input into purchasing decisions. The typical order lead-time ranges from two days to three weeks, whereas the typical component lead-time is in the range of one week to several months (see Fig. 18.6). Out of the approx. 2 000 components, 400 components are being planned. The planned components belong to the material groups processors, memory, disk drives, controllers, housing and power supply.

An important aspect of component planning in the computer industry is the specification of particular components by large customers. For example, a large customer makes a contract (forecast) of 5 000 PCs which are configured to meet the IT-requirements of that customer and shall be delivered over five weeks (1 000 PCs a week). In this case, a component forecast can automatically be derived from the collaborative forecast by exploding the bill-of-materials of the particular configuration. On the other hand side, the standard case is that a PC is configured during order entry – in this case the sales forecast does not specify a particular configuration.

In order to meet these two requirements – fixed specification of components vs. on-line configuration of components at order entry – the following procedure is applied to derive a component forecast from the collaborative forecast:

1. The collaborative forecast has to be split into (1) forecast related to fixed configurations and (2) forecast related to open configurations (that are still to be configured).
2. For forecasting fixed configurations, the bill-of-materials of the fixed configuration is being exploded.
3. For forecasting open configurations, the following steps are followed:
   (a) So-called mappings are defined that map some planned instances on finished goods level (e. g. a model line) onto planned components (e. g. disk drives, processors etc.). A mapping is established between a planned item A on finished goods level and all components C that can be configured into products of type A.
   (b) The distribution of the forecast on some planned item A on finished goods level over all components related to A by some mapping is defined by attach-rates (i. e. distribution factors). The actual planning process is to determine these attach-rate factors.
4. The total component forecast of a component is derived by adding the forecast from Step 2 and Step 3.

This component planning procedure is supported by i2 RHYTHM PRO (Product Relationship Object).

18.3.2   Operational Planning

Operational planning consists of the master planning process and the demand supply matching process.

Master Planning

The demand planning process generates the forecasts for all products and components. This forecast is updated weekly and is netted against the actual orders received (forecast netting process, see Fig. 18.4). The netted forecast is created on end item level for fixed configurations and on component level for open configurations. The master planning process receives the netted forecast and creates a fulfilment plan for the netted forecast and the orders on hand. Master planning is executed once per week, directly after the weekly demand planning process has been completed.[3]

The master plan serves two purposes:

---

[3] Refer to Chap. 7 for more information on the master planning process in general.

1. The master plan is the basis for purchasing decisions.
2. The master plan is transformed into so-called ATP in the allocation planning process and forms then the basis for the order promising process.[4]

Thus, the master plan is the common source for purchasing and order promising. By that, the purchase orders are synchronized with the promises of the customer orders. Given that the computer industry is material constrained, the synchronization of purchasing and order promising drastically improves the due date performance. Please note that the due date performance is – within certain limits – independent of the *accuracy of the master plan*. However, if the master plan accuracy is low, the orders do not match the master plan. As a consequence, the procured material does not match the material requirements of the orders and orders will receive a late promised date. Thus, the inventory turns, the order lead-time and customer service level will improve, if the master planning accuracy increases.

During the master planning process, the planners

- decide about sourcing options (sourcing from multiple suppliers, sourcing from multiple plants, use of alternate parts),
- generate supply requirements based on the netted forecast, including safety stock management decisions,
- generate a constrained demand plan on forecasted item level based on the netted forecast and the actual customer orders on hand and
- generate production requirements for make-to-stock forecast.

The master plan defines the minimum purchasing volume that is to be ordered during the next week, based on the constraints, i. e. demand (netted forecast and actual customer orders), material supply and capacity. The capacity model that is applied to master planning is quite simple, as it is based on the number of computers that can be assembled per day. On the other hand side, the weekly master plan is the basis for the creation of the ATP. Thus, the master plan captures the maximum order volume that can be promised during the week.

The master planning process is implemented based on i2 RHYTHM Supply Chain Planner. Only planned components, planned configurations on end item level and finished goods for which orders are existing are represented in the master planning engine.[5]

Demand Supply Matching

In addition to the master planning process there is a more detailed planning process on factory level that is running daily (see Fig. 18.4). This process is

---

[4] Refer to Chap. 8 for a detailed description of the allocation planning process.
[5] Purchasing decisions for non-planned components are taken in the SAP MRP run.

Fig. 18.7. Customer hierarchy used for allocation planning

called the *Demand Supply Matching Process (DSM)*. The DSM process plans all orders and the net forecast based on the complete bill-of-materials as being maintained by SAP. Thus, DSM checks the demand and supply situation for all parts – whereas master planning only checks parts that are planned by the demand planning process as described above.

The DSM process is executed twice per day by a group of planners, representing purchasing, order management and production. These planners review the current demand supply situation, check options to resolve late order problems, try to improve the supply situation by moving-in scheduled receipts in coordination with the suppliers, and simulate the impact of moving-in of orders. The result of that planning process is a new demand supply plan which is then used to update the ATP once per day. For that purpose, the new demand supply plan is send to the allocation planning process which then updates the ATP.

The demand supply matching process is implemented based on i2 Factory Planner.

18.3.3   Demand Fulfilment

The master plan is input to the allocation planning process that allocates the master plan quantities to the customer hierarchy (see also Chap. 8). The customer hierarchy is a sub-hierarchy of the geographic hierarchy used in the demand planning process. Currently, the customer hierarchy contains the root top_seller and one node for each sales region (Fig. 18.7).

The allocation planning processes allocates the quantities represented in the master plan (these quantities are called ATP, Available-to-promise) to the nodes of the customer hierarchy, according to the following rules:

- The quantities planned in the master plan for pre-defined fixed configurations are allocated to the sales regions according to the sales forecast. The following table shows an example for one weekly time bucket (using the allocation rule *per committed*, refer to Chap. 8):

	Total	Germany	France	UK
Sales Forecast	10 000	5 000	3 000	2 000
Master Plan	8 000			
Allocations	8 000	4 000	2 500	1 000

- The quantities planned in the master plan for open configurations are allocated on component level at the root of the customer hierarchy (top_seller).

The allocations are called *allocated ATP (AATP)*. The AATP is created in a batch planning run and is then provided to the order promising process and given as feedback to the demand planning process (Fig. 18.4). Thus, the demand planners have the overview of the ATP quantities that are allocated to them compared to what they have forecasted. This information can be used to direct demand according to the ATP situation, e. g. by suggesting alternate products to the customers driven by availability.

The orders come into the system through the order entry process and are promised by the order promising process. Again, one must distinguish between fixed configurations and open configurations:

- Let us assume an order is received from a customer in France for x units of fixed configuration f with a request date for week w. The order promsing process checks the quantity for the fixed configuration f that is allocated to France in week w; let us call this a. If the ordered quantity x is less than the allocated quantity a the order receives a due date in week w. If this is not the case, i. e. $x > a$, then additional ATP is searched in the succeeding weeks – even if ATP is available in week w at other nodes of the customer hierarchy, e. g. Germany and the UK. This promising policy ensures that quantities that have been planned by some region are reserved for orders coming from customers out of that region.
- Orders for open configurations are quoted based on the ATP for components. The order promising process searches the best ATP for each of the components required for the order. The latest ATP is assigned as due date to the complete order.

An order can be quoted in milliseconds (below 100 ms per order, more than 10 orders per second can be quoted). Given that currently 800 orders per hour have to be quoted in peak load situations, the i2 Demand Fulfillment architecture scales well with an increasing number of orders – supporting even aggressive business growth strategies.

In a second step the demand fulfilment solution will be migrated to i2's High Availability architecture that is based on the TIBCO message bus system (refer to www.tibco.com). This architecture supports 24x7 (24 hours a day, seven days a week) order quoting even in case of server or network failures.

18.4   Integration of i2 with SAP R/3

The i2 planning engines – RHYTHM Supply Chain Planner, RHYTHM Demand Fulfillment, RHYTHM Factory Planner and RHYTHM Demand Planner – closely interact with the SAP R/3 system, particularly with the SAP

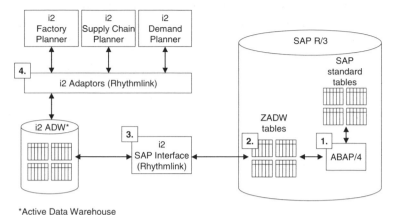

*Active Data Warehouse

Fig. 18.8. Integration of the i2 planning modules with SAP R/3

modules MM Materials Management, PP Production Planning and SD Sales
and Distribution. In this case the SAP R/3 release 3.0f was installed.

Figure 18.4 shows the interfaces between the SAP system and the i2 modules. There are two classes of interfaces: The first class contains all interfaces
except the order entry interface. These interfaces exchange static and dynamic data in a batch mode. The second class consists of the order entry
interface. This interface transfers a new order from SAP SD to i2 Demand
Fulfillment and gives the order quote back to SAP SD. The order entry interface is an online interface.

18.4.1   Batch Interfaces

Figure 18.8 shows the architecture used for the interfaces operating in batch
mode. In the following we describe the data flow from SAP to i2. The data
flow back is implemented in the same way. We use the interface between SAP
and the master planning process as example to illustrate the ideas.

1. The master planning process represents only planned materials, i. e. those
   materials that are also used in the demand planning process. Furthermore, all orders and the net forecast are imported, as well as WIP quantities, scheduled receipts, inventory etc. The selection, filtering and aggregation of the SAP data according to the data requirements of the master
   planning process are executed by a collection of ABAP/4 functions. These
   functions have been developed specifically for the project.
   Please note that the filter and aggregation functions applied represent the
   actual business logic on which the design of the master planning process
   is based. Thus, using a pre-defined standard interface between SAP and
   some APS Master Planning Module would constrain the design of the

process and the interface – potentially preventing that a best-in class master planning process is achieved.

2. The ABAP/4 functions write the filtered and aggregated data for the master planning process in user-defined tables that have been created in the SAP database. These tables – called ZADW tables – have the same data schema as the master planning tables that exist in the i2 RHYTHM Active Data Warehouse (ADW).

3. The contents of the ZADW tables is transferred into the tables of the ADW, using the i2 standard SAP interface. This interface is based on the middleware module i2 RhythmLink. RhythmLink has a specific module – the SAP-Listener – that is responsible for the technical data transfer between SAP and RhythmLink. Data streams are opened by RhythmLink copy maps that transfer the data from SAP (via the i2 SAP-Listener) directly into the corresponding ADW table.

4. After the complete data has arrived in the ADW the standard i2 adaptors are used to provide the data for the i2 RHYTHM Supply Chain Planner engine that is running the master planning process. The i2 adaptors are standard software components that are shipped with each i2 module. The adaptors provide all required interfaces between the i2 module and the ADW (in both directions). Technically, the adaptors are based on RhythmLink.

18.4.2 Order Entry Interface

The order entry interface is an online interface. When an order is received by the order entry system SAP SD, the order is transferred to i2 RHYTHM Demand Fulfillment to be quoted. The quoted order is then sent back to SAP SD.

Technically, the order entry inferface is based on the RHYTHM Optimization Interface. This interface consists of a collection of predefined ABAP/4 functions that have to be plugged into the order entry transaction as an user exit. The RHYTHM Optimization Interface then transfers the order to i2 Demand Fulfillment and receives the quote. The quote information is written into the SAP order, and the transaction is closed. In this project the RHYTHM Optimization Interface is combined with i2's high availability architecture that is based on the TIBCO message bus system (for further details on that please refer to www.i2.com and www.tibco.com).

19 Food and Beverages

Michael Wagner, Herbert Meyr

University of Augsburg, Department of Production and Logistics,
Universitätsstraße 16, 86135 Augsburg, Germany

Everyone knows the situation: You go shopping in your favourite supermarket and all the items on your list are available, except for one. Therefore, you have to drive to the next store and hope that you can get the product there.

Situations like that decrease customer satisfaction quite noticeably and affect both retailer and producer. That is why customer service has become the main objective of consumer goods supply chains. However, too often higher customer service is accompanied by higher investments in inventory. State-of-the-art Advanced Planning Systems are basic tools for achieving both contradictory management goals, high customer service, *and* low stock levels.

This chapter provides some insights into the implementation of the *J. D. Edwards Active Supply Chain* APS (see Chap. 15 and J. D. Edwards (2000)) for the food and beverages division of a large European consumer goods company. The aim of the project was to build the infrastructure for more flexible, accurate and faster planning processes.

After introducing the most important attributes of the supply chain in Sect. 19.1, the planning architecture for the company's German food branch is described (Sect. 19.2). Furthermore, model-building with the J. D. Edwards Master Planning module *Enterprise Planning* is specified (Sects. 19.3 and 19.4). This model served as a template for the whole division and therefore had to integrate requirements of other product lines of the company, too.

19.1 Description of the Supply Chain

The supply chain under consideration consists of production plants, a distribution network and some key suppliers. Each of the three production sites produces up to 20 different products, but only a few products can be made in all three plants.

19.1.1 Procurement

The material procured for food production can be divided into two classes.

The first type of materials are the raw materials and ingredients which the food is prepared from. They are usually bought on the free market and therefore the ordering decision noticeably depends on the current market price. Packaging and labeling material on the other hand is usually single or double sourced. For those items yearly basic agreements are made with the suppliers. Therefore, the ordering decision neither causes additional costs nor depends on the order size or the price.

19.1.2 Production

The production process consists of three consecutive stages: pre-blending, blending and packaging. The first one is physically separated from the others and only available at plant 3 (see Fig. 19.1). From plant 3 all plants are supplied with pre-blend just-in-time. The pre-blend process comprises a complex production network consisting of batch processes. As more than one product is based on the same pre-blend, the number of pre-blend types is less than the number of end products.

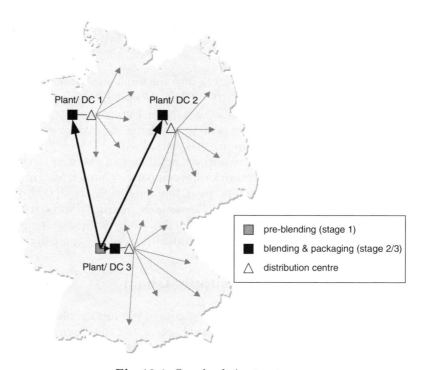

Fig. 19.1. Supply chain structure

If the production equipment has to be switched from one product to another, significant sequence-dependent changeover costs and times occur on the first and second stage. In each production plant more than five blenders/ packers (dedicated to a specific range of products) operate in parallel. A fixed 1:1 relationship usually holds between blenders and packers, but it is also possible that one blender feeds two packers (simultaneously or alternatively).

As the pre-blending stage supplies the blenders just-in-time, there are only small buffers for storage of one day's demand at the most. Between stages two and three there are no buffers, as there are fixed pipes which connect both stages (Fig. 19.2). While most products are produced once per week, a few are set up every second week (cyclic schedule). Therefore, the reorder lead-time for the distribution centres equals one to two weeks, depending on the product.

The regular working time in the plants is based on a three shift pattern (24 hours) on five days per week. This regular time can be extended by one to three shifts overtime on Saturdays, resulting in additional costs for higher wages.

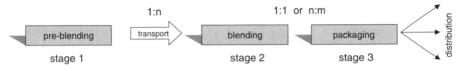

Fig. 19.2. The production processes

19.1.3   Distribution

After packaging, the products are transported to the distribution centre (DC) next to each production site. Those items which are not available at the local factory are supplied by one of the other two plants. Each customer is served from the next DC either directly or via cross docking in one to two days (three-stage distribution system). Therefore, each DC has the whole assortment of products available. Only if stock-outs are impending, emergency transports between the DCs are initiated to balance the stocks.

19.1.4   Sales

Most products are made to stock and only a few items are made according to customer orders. These make-to-order products are supplied exclusively for one customer under his own brand name. The customer service level is determined by matching orders and available stock at the DC daily. The "customer" ordering the product is usually not the consumer, but mostly a retailer (chain) which operates the retail outlets. Even though the sales for some products are quite constant over time, most of the products are influenced by seasonality and promotional activities. Storage of finished products is limited in time due to shelf-life restrictions.

This type of supply chain has already been introduced in Chap. 2. The food and beverages case considered here is additionally summarized in Table 19.1.

Table 19.1. Typology for the food and beverages supply chain

Functional attributes	
Attributes	Contents
products procured	standard (raw materials) and specific (packaging materials)
sourcing type	multiple (raw materials) single/double (packaging materials)
organization of the production process	flow line
repetition of operations	batch production
distribution structure	three stages
pattern of delivery	dynamic
deployment of transportation means	unlimited, routes (3rd stage)
loading restrictions	chilled and non chilled transports
relation to customers	stable
availability of future demands	forecasted
products life cycle	several years
products sold	standard
portion of service operations	tangible goods
Structural attributes	
Attributes	Contents
network structure	mixture
degree of globalization	Europe
location of decoupling point(s)	deliver-to-order
legal position	intra-organizational
direction of coordination	mixture
type of information exchanged	forecasts and orders

19.2 The Architecture of the Planning System

The architecture template had to take into account the specific requirements of different production processes in the whole food and beverages division. Furthermore, the existing planning systems and the IT-landscape needed to be integrated into the new architecture. But obsolete spreadsheet solutions which had been developed by the planners only for their specific purposes should be replaced by the Advanced Planning System of J. D. Edwards.

In the first phase of the project it was decided to focus on the following planning processes (for a description of general planning tasks in the consumer goods industry see also Chap. 3):

- long-term production and distribution planning,
- mid-term master planning (production and distribution) and

- short-term production scheduling.

For demand planning and short-term distribution planning proven third-party systems already existed before implementing *Active Supply Chain*. As these modules have tight connections to the new Active Supply Chain modules, they needed to be integrated accordingly (see Fig. 19.3). Procurement processes were only integrated if they had been identified as potential bottlenecks.

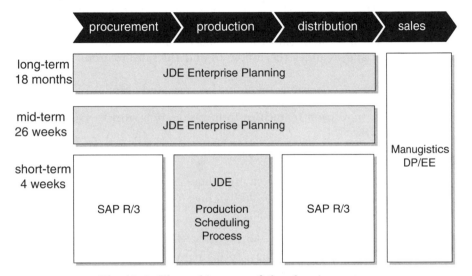

Fig. 19.3. The architecture of the planning system

19.2.1   Long-term Production and Distribution Planning

Long-term planning tasks in the food and beverages business comprise a time horizon between one and five years. In this range strategic decisions on the product programme to be offered, the opening or closing of production lines or plants and the distribution network are made. But in case of the company described here, the long-term production and distribution planning is restricted to 18 months, as in this time horizon production lines can be built up or moved from one site to another. Furthermore, changes in the shift-pattern have to be coordinated with the works committee and therefore need to be initiated months in advance.

This planning task is based on monthly time buckets and aggregated products and resources. The Enterprise Planning module is utilized to simulate different scenarios. The software calculates a capacity-constrained, optimized flow of goods and the respective costs for the 18 months horizon. Therefore, the planning process consists of the following steps, iteratively executed:

1. evaluate the status quo,
2. change the network structure manually, e. g. close a line, allow three instead of two shifts etc. and
3. evaluate the new model.

19.2.2   Mid-term Master Planning (Production and Distribution)

The Master Planning module integrates all decisions on materials and capacities concerning the whole network of plants and DCs. Therefore, the connecting material flows between the different locations need to be planned on this level. The more detailed Production Scheduling module considers only local resources and assumes the inflow to and the outflow from the site as being given.

The Master Planning decisions taken in this case study are:

- weekly transportation quantities from production sites to DCs and between the DCs,
- weekly material requirements (i. e. packaging material) which have to be ordered from suppliers,
- necessary overtime on the production lines,
- assignment of products to production lines per time bucket and
- weekly inventory levels in DCs.

As the number of product types is relatively small in this application, the products and resources do not have to be aggregated. The time horizon of half a year is divided in 26 weekly time buckets.

Enterprise Planning was selected as the premier solution for this task, because it provides easy to use graphical modelling capabilities and an powerful optimization engine (CPLEX; see ILOG (2000)). The model has tight data integration to the short-term Production Scheduling module via the J. D. Edwards Integration and Data Flows component and an Oracle database (see Oracle (2000)) which holds all relevant planning data.

The objective of the Master Planning model is to minimize all costs which are influenced by the decisions described above. Therefore, transportation costs, production costs, costs for overtime and storage costs have been considered.

19.2.3   Short-term Production Scheduling

The production scheduling   task is implemented using the J. D. Edwards *Production Scheduling Process* module. It covers both the lot-sizing and the scheduling task and therefore integrates the modules Production Planning and Scheduling (see Chap. 4). Production Scheduling only has to plan stages two and three of production, as the first stage is decoupled by transport and therefore can be planned independently by an additional scheduling model.

The objective is to create a cost-optimized schedule for the production facilities of a single factory. Inventory holding costs, setup costs and penalty costs for not meeting the desired minimum inventory levels form the objective function.

The model covers a planning horizon of four weeks rolled forward once a week. However, the plan may even be revised daily on an event-driven basis. These events are caused by machine breakdowns or impending stock-outs. As some materials and pre-blend have to be ordered two days in advance, the frozen horizon only covers the next two days. The "demand" (requirements) which drives the scheduling model is calculated considering

- updated daily forecasts,
- actual and planned shipments to all DCs,
- safety stocks which have to be held at the DCs,
- actual inventory levels at the DCs, in transit to the DCs and at the plant and
- a "sourcing-matrix" which states the quota to be sourced from a specific plant (calculated from the results of Master Planning; see Sect. 19.4).

19.3   Model Building in J. D. Edwards Enterprise Planning

Models built in Enterprise Planning do not use any mathematical notation. A production and distribution system is modelled graphically (e. g. by means of drop down menus) and interactively within the system. An Enterprise Planning model consists of the following basic elements (see e. g. Günther et al. (1998), Kolisch (1998) and Numetrix (1998)):

- time periods,
- commodities,
- nodes and
- arcs.

Their most important properties will now be introduced.

Time Periods

An optimization model considers a certain planning horizon that may be subdivided into several time buckets. Since the model structure has to be the same in all periods, it has to be graphically defined only once. This structure is then copied for each period to be considered and the period-specific data (e. g. demand varying over time) have to be filled in each copy. In an optimization run all periods are considered simultaneously. Thereby, each period is linked with the preceding one by the stock that is held at the beginning of the period (of course being equal to the stock at the end of the previous period).

Commodities

Two different kinds of "commodities" may occur. First, commodities denote distinct types of *(physical) goods* like raw materials, work-in-process or final products – no matter in which stage of production they are. In this case study the various kinds of pre-blend and packaged goods are examples for such goods. Secondly, commodities represent the *time* spent in production, transport or storage processes. For example, the commodities *regular blending time* or *blending overtime* may be used to distinguish between the cheaper and the more expensive variant of the blending process.

Nodes

"Nodes" represent the processes themselves, e. g. all activities supplying, storing, consuming, transforming or simply controlling any type of commodity. Therefore, nodes model the critical components and constraints of a production and distribution system, but not the material flow within the system. Different kinds of nodes have been launched to represent different types of activities. Generally, nodes can have several input and several output commodities. Nodes without either input or output commodities are available as well. However, nodes of the same kind share common input and output characteristics.

A few kinds of nodes – later on used in this case study – shall illustrate the function and dominant role of nodes. For sake of clarity only the main attributes of each kind of nodes are presented:

Supply node: A *supply node* supplies a single commodity (usually of the physical goods type) and therefore does not have any input commodities. Upper and lower bounds of the amount to be supplied can be specified as given data. Also unit costs for supplying the commodity can be particularized in order to consider total costs of supply. The result of an optimization run is the amount of the commodity actually (and optimally) to be supplied.

Machine node: A *machine node* has a quite similar function, but is intended to supply the commodity *machine (or personnel) time*. Therefore, the capacity and unit costs of a machine have to be specified. The optimal run length of a machine (of both regular time and overtime, depending on the type and costs of the commodity supplied) results.

Process node: A *process node* transfers input commodities (goods and/or time) into output commodities and therefore may have several input and output commodities. This transformation is done with respect to fixed rates of input and output. For example, two units of intermediate product, one tub and two seconds machine time are combined in a packaging process to obtain one unit of a final product.

Batch node: *Batch nodes* restrict the flow of a commodity. A batch node can e.g. be used to specify a *minimum run length* of a process or a *minimum lot-size* – depending on the type of commodity considered. Note, by this a binary decision is implied: either nothing or more than the minimum lot-size have to be produced. As Chaps. 7 and 22 show, a model containing batch nodes is quite hard to solve because the underlying optimization problem has changed from a simple LP to a more complex combinatorial MIP. The user should therefore utilize a batch node only if it is absolutely indispensable to represent reality correctly. Other types of integer/binary decisions like *batch sizes* (predefined amounts of commodities with only integer multiples being allowed) or *setup times* can be modeled by a batch node, too.

StorageCoverLocal (SCL) node: The *StorageCoverLocal node* calculates the desired stock level of a commodity (physical good) at the end of the time period considered. This calculation is due to the inventory balance equation:

stock at the end of the current period =
= stock at the end of the previous period + inflow - demand.

Thereby, the *demand* (e.g. market demand for a final product) is not computed within the model but has to be pre-specified. *Inflow* and *stock levels* (except for beginning inventory) are results of an optimization run. The inflow is an input commodity of the SCL node whose amount is usually further restricted by another node, e.g. a process node representing some production process.

The resulting amount of stock is influenced by three types of (increasing) "target" stock levels: the minimum, safety and maximum stock level. While minimum and maximum stock levels usually are hard constraints that must not be violated, the safety stock level is a soft constraint which will be punished by penalty costs if fallen short of. These stock levels have to be specified by the number of periods of future demand, they are expected to cover. Each stock keeping unit – independent of the stock level – is priced with actual per unit holding costs.

Monitor node: A *monitor node* takes different types of commodities as input and limits the total number of (stock keeping) units consigned. This is useful for modelling the storage capacity of a warehouse where stocks of distinct products share a common inventory space. For example, the total stock held in several SCL nodes can jointly be controlled by a single monitor node.

Arcs

Arcs connect nodes, thereby carrying exactly one commodity, each. Therefore, arcs represent the material or time flows within a production and distribution network. The amount of the commodity to be carried is a decision variable.

It can be restricted by predefined upper and lower bounds (e. g. minimum or maximum transport capacities if the commodity denotes deliverable goods). Again, the unit cost of the commodity can be specified.

For aesthetic purposes and sake of clarity a further kind of nodes, a *working node*, has been introduced in Enterprise Planning. It bundles arcs connecting two bipartite set of nodes, but carrying the same commodity. So an $n : m$ relation of nodes is replaced by an $n : 1 : m$ relation, thus reducing the number of arcs significantly.

After analyzing the decision situation (see Sect. 7.1), the elements of the Enterprise Planning model have to defined and the necessary data (e. g. resource capacities, production rates, costs) have to be filled in. This may either be done graphically and interactively or via import files. A trial solution run has to be started, checking whether predefined solver parameters are set adequately or refinements have to be made.

These may especially be necessary if a MIP model has been defined, for example by use of some batch nodes. In the most lucky case such a refinement just requires some changes in the parameters of the solver heuristics that Enterprise Planning provides for MIP problems. In the worst case a redefinition of the optimization model is necessary, possibly inducing serious modifications in the design of the planning module (see Chap. 3).

19.4   The Master Planning Module

19.4.1   Model Structure

In the following section the elements of the mid-term Enterprise Planning model and the solution approaches actually used in this project are described. The model covers the food supply chain from some important external suppliers to the final distribution centres. Master Planning is usually done every Thursday starting with the following week over a rolling horizon of 26 weeks. Four different groups of commodities are considered: raw/ packaging material, intermediates, finished products and time. All nodes and arcs utilized in the model are described in the following subsections. A graphical overview of the node structure is given in Fig. 19.4.

Procurement

Procurement processes are implemented in Master Planning only if the supply of material is restricted in some manner. This applies to the internal supply of pre-blend from plant 3 and to some critical suppliers of packaging material whose weekly production (or supply) capacities are known. As already mentioned, the production processes of pre-blending are not explicitly considered in the Master Planning model, but their capacities are restricted and therefore have to be modelled as material bottlenecks.

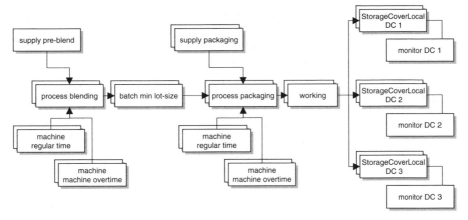

Fig. 19.4. Overview of the Enterprise Planning Model

In Enterprise Planning the internal and external suppliers are represented as supply nodes. For each material and supplier a respective supply node is needed (only a small section of the procurement part is shown in Fig. 19.5).

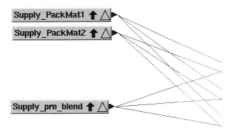

Fig. 19.5. Example of procurement processes in the Enterprise Planning Model

The fields of the node are filled with the data described in Table 19.2. The costs in the supply node are required only if a specific material is double-sourced or the prices are changing over time. Cost have to be filled in for all materials, since the objective function calculates the whole procurement costs in this case.

Table 19.2. Supply node data fields

Data field	Case specific input
Max	Maximum material supply (of pre-blend or packaging materials)
Costs	linear costs per unit procured

The supply nodes are connected with process nodes representing the blending stage. If transportation costs for the transports to the plants occur (esp. for pre-blend from plant 3 to plants 1 and 2), these are modeled as a linear cost rate penalizing the flow on the arc.

Production

Since both production stages, blending *and* packaging, are potential bottlenecks, they cannot be considered as a single planning unit. Furthermore, the production model has to guarantee minimum lot-sizes on the production lines. For each production line and product a single process node is needed (see also Fig. 19.6). The blending process node combines the commodities pre-blend and (regular and over-) time for producing the intermediates. Therefore, the input rates are modelled as follows:

- pre-blend: quantity (in tons) needed for production of one ton intermediate product,
- time: capacity (in hours) needed for production of one ton intermediate product.

Arcs connect the blending process nodes with the batch nodes which ensure that either nothing or more than the minimum lot-size is produced per week. This is the only kind of node in the model which induces integer variables (more precise: semi-continuous variables). This additional complexity (for further information see Chaps. 7.2.2 and 22) has to be balanced carefully against the higher accuracy achievable by considering the minimum lot-sizes. The field "min-run-length" is filled with the minimum lot-size (in tons) which

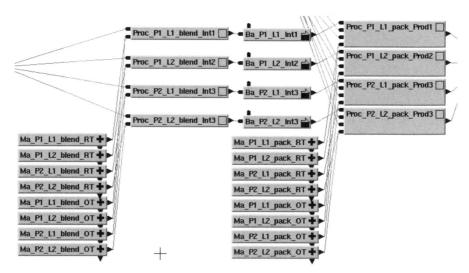

Fig. 19.6. Example of production processes in the Enterprise Planning Model

is given by technical restrictions of the machines. The arc (intermediate product) leaving the batch node is directly connected to the packaging process node. Variable production costs (excluding costs for material supply and personnel taken into account otherwise) are modelled as a cost rate on the arc. Input rates of these process nodes are set according to:

- intermediate product: quantity (in tons) required for one ton of finished products,
- packaging material: quantity (in units) needed for one ton of finished products,
- time: capacity (in hours) needed for the production of one ton of finished products.

Both types of process nodes (blending and packaging) consume capacity (time) which is supplied by *machine nodes*. For each process node two machine nodes are required: one provides regular capacity (RT) and the other overtime capacity (OT). Both machine nodes are connected with the process node. Table 19.3 shows the field entries which have to be made in machine nodes and arcs. The maximum capacity is calculated by reducing the total capacity (e. g. five days × 24 hours per day = 120 hours) per week by an efficiency factor. This value is retrieved from historical data by considering the following components: start-up/ shut-down time, changeover time, maintenance and repair time.

Table 19.3. Capacity model data fields

	Data field	Case specific input
Machine RT	Max	regular maximum capacity (in hours) available for production on a respective blending or packaging machine
Machine OT	Max	maximum overtime capacity (in hours) available for production on a respective blending or packaging machine
Arc	Costs	linear personnel costs per hour

Distribution and Sales

Each production site is able to serve all three DCs. Therefore the necessary transports from packaging to warehousing are modelled by arcs connecting the packaging process node with the SCL node. As in some cases an n:m relationship between production lines and DCs exists, a working node merges the flows from different production lines producing the same product (see e. g. lines 2 and 3 in Fig. 19.7). This also enables quick access to the overall production quantity of a specific plant/ product combination (e. g. plant 1/

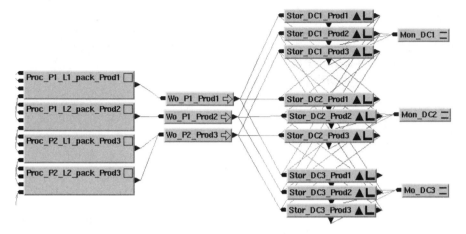

Fig. 19.7. Example of distribution and sales processes in the Enterprise Planning Model

product 1). The transportation arcs carry linear transportation costs which are calculated from price lists of the third-party carriers.

The SCL node stays abreast of inventory tracking and demand fulfilment. Limits on inventory levels are modelled as *stock covers* (number of periods of future demand covered by stock-on-hand), as it is common practice in the consumer goods industry. Here, all stock limits (min, safety and max) were modelled as soft constraints (with penalties) in order to ensure feasibility of the optimization model which could be endangered if the forecasted demand in the first week is much higher than stock-on-hand plus available production capacity. The minimum stock (min cover), the model has to guarantee, is calculated by summing the following components:

- Lot-sizing stock (cycle stock): As most products are produced each week, the lot-size equals approximately the demand of one week. Therefore, the mean lot-sizing stock is half of the weekly demand.
- Transit stock: The delivery lead-time from the plant to the DC is about one day. As the stock for this transport is not considered on the arc, the minimum stock in the DC has to be increased by this amount.
- Quarantine stock: All products have to be kept at the plant for 24 hours. This quarantine time is added to the minimum stock cover at the DC.

Since violation of minimum stocks is punished by very high penalty costs (under costs), the safety cover is only penalized by a lower unit cost (safety cost). The safety cover is calculated by adding the min cover and some further cover buffering against demand uncertainty. Table 19.4 summarizes the SCL node options. All SCL nodes for one product are connected to each other to enable emergency shipments between DCs. These transports should be avoided as they lead to additional administrative effort. Therefore, these shipments are

Table 19.4. StorageCoverLocal node data fields

Data field	Case specific input
Min cover	Minimum stock cover for lot-sizing, transport and quarantine
Safety cover	Additionally buffering against demand uncertainty
Max cover	Maximum stock cover: this bound ought to avoid large inventory build-ups which could result in obsolescence
Under cost	Cost for falling below the minimum stock level (penalty!)
Safety cost	Cost for falling below the safety stock level (penalty!)
Over cost	Cost for exceeding the maximum stock level (penalty!)
Inject	Beginning inventory position of the next week (first planning bucket)
Cost	Inventory holding costs calculated mainly from interest on bound capital
Demand	Forecasted demand of each week

only performed in the short run if stock-outs impend. The respective cost fields of the arcs are filled with penalties and not with real transportation cost rates.

Monitor nodes are connected to all SCL nodes of one DC to constrain the maximum inventory level.

19.4.2   Solution Approaches

An optimal solution can be calculated if minimum lot-sizes are not taken into account. Therefore, the model can be solved using one of the LP procedures offered by the optimization engine (*primal and dual simplex, barrier*) of Enterprise Planning. The optimal solution is retrieved in a few seconds or minutes.

However, if the batch nodes are taken into consideration, solution time increases up to several hours. For this kind of integer variables (min run length) special purpose heuristics guide the solution process. In general, optimal solutions cannot be computed anymore.

19.4.3   Data Flows

All supply chain planning modules of this case study are connected to a common database (Oracle). This database stores all static and dynamic data required for planning. The planning software itself does not prepare database connectivity and therefore needs to be integrated by a middle-ware product. This is enabled by J. D. Edwards *Integration and Data Flows* (see Fig. 19.8: IDF Data Flows) which retrieves data from the Oracle database and converts it to flat files which are accessible for the planning tools.

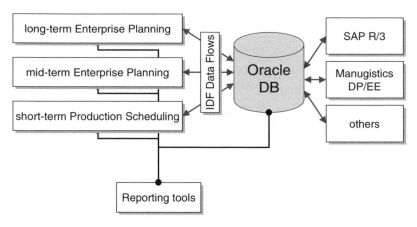

Fig. 19.8. Integration Data Flows

Enterprise Planning is able to generate the model from a flat file describing each node and arc. Therefore the Enterprise Planning model is created from scratch once per week. This automatic procedure bases on the data file generated by the J. D. Edwards *Integration and Data Flows* component. In addition, an update of dynamic data is possible upon request of the planner. In this case the following data flows are necessary:

- update of forecasts from Demand Planning (SCL node),
- calculation of beginning inventory positions for the first planning bucket (SCL node),
- import of planned production quantities from Production Scheduling within the fixed horizon (arc between packaging process node and working node).

Input to the database is gathered from planning output of further J. D. Edwards modules and from the ERP-system SAP R/3 (see SAP (2000)), the demand planning solution Manugistics DP/EE (see Manugistics (2000)), and some others. Reporting capabilities are necessary for two reasons: First of all the planner needs transparency of data available and all planning results. Therefore, the Enterprise Planning reporting capabilities (*smart graphs*) are used to get overviews in tabular form. These smart graphs can be customized and permit simple calculations on data available in nodes and arcs (e. g. calculation of seasonal stock from minimum stock and planned stock level). High-end reporting tools are also required, because the overall success of the project is measured by some core key performance indicators (KPIs). Every participant of the crew needs up-to-date information on these figures. The KPIs are based on planning *and* actual data which is only available in the database. Therefore, standard database reporting tools are used to build customized reports for this purpose.

19.5 Concluding Remarks

The Enterprise Planning model described above and the Production Scheduling model are live since more than half a year now. To identify major mistakes in the implementation, both the new APS and the old planning system ran in parallel for just a few weeks. Since then the planner is able to save 30% of the planning time he required before applying the APS.

At this point in time usually the question on benefits arises. The most important improvements measured are:

- *Reduced inventory levels:* Without affecting customer service, it was possible to avoid buffers which were used to hedge against planning inaccuracy and uncertainty.
- *Reduced overtime:* The bottleneck production lines are identified early and if necessary, production can be shifted to alternative sites.
- *Less emergency transports between DCs:* More accurate planning balances production and transports in advance.

The software template described so far is currently being used for fast implementation of J. D. Edwards Active Supply Chain in other food-divisions of the company. This is possible since the template is based on intensive, collaborative analysis of different food and beverages supply chains covering the whole food-branch of the enterprise.

References

Günther, H. O.; Blömer, F.; Grunow, M. (1998) *Moderne Softwaretools für das Supply Chain Management*, Zeitschrift für wirtschaftlichen Fabrikbetrieb, Vol. 93, No. 7–8, 330–333

ILOG (2000) *Homepage*, URL: http://www.ilog.com, State: August 1, 2000

J. D. Edwards (2000) *Homepage*, URL: http://www.jdedwards.com, State: August 1, 2000

Kolisch, R. (1998) *Linx*, ORSpektrum, Vol. 20, No. 1, 1-4

Manugistics (2000) *Homepage*, URL: http://www.manugistics.com, State: August 1, 2000

Numetrix Ltd. (1998) *Enterprise Planning 5.0 User's Guide*, Toronto et al.

Oracle (2000) *Homepage*, URL: http://www.oracle.com, State: August 1, 2000

SAP (2000) *Homepage*, URL: http://www.sap.com, State: August 1, 2000

Part V

Conclusions and Outlook

20   Conclusions and Outlook

Hartmut Stadtler

Darmstadt University of Technology, Institute of Business Administration, Department of Operations and Materials Management, Hochschulstraße 1, 64289 Darmstadt, Germany

The preceding chapters have shown the different steps of introducing an APS in industry, starting with an analysis of a given supply chain, its redesign and subsequently modelling the supply chain from long-term to short-term decision levels. The integration of all planning tasks relating to the order fulfilment process will result in a new era of enterprise wide and supply chain wide planning.

Thereby an APS yields improvements not only on the three crucial factors of competitiveness, namely costs, quality and time, but it will also allow to

- make processes more transparent,
- improve flexibility and
- reveal system constraints.

Widely available information from all over the supply chain results in a *transparent* order fulfilment process. It enables companies and supply chains to provide customers with accurate information about the order status and provides alerts in case an unexpected event causes a delayed delivery of an order. However, before this happens a decision-maker can find and check alternative ways to fulfil the customer order, either by a shipment from another warehouse, from another production site or by offering parts with the next higher grade. Additionally, transparent processes will reduce waste along the supply chain, because waste, e. g. resulting from excessive inventories or resources with low utilization rates, will be recognized quickly and measures for its improvement may be introduced. More importantly, due to its optimization capabilities, an APS will keep waste to a minimum right from the beginning.

With markets and customer expectations changing quickly, supply chains have not only to respond but to anticipate new trends. In some cases this may be achieved by integrating key customers in the supply chain. On the other hand *flexibility* comes into play which can be discussed along two dimensions. One is to be able to cope with changes in actual demands given the current inventory position, equipment and personnel. The second aspect of flexibility is a supply chain's ability to adapt to changing markets over time (sometimes called agility, see Pfohl and Mayer (1999)). An APS supports both dimensions. As an example, the ATP module can show ways to use existing inventories in the most effective manner. Also Production Planning and Scheduling allows to reoptimize a new mix of orders quickly. Flexibility is further enhanced by an APS, due to a significant reduction of the frozen (firmed) horizon (as an example see Chap. 16). Finally, mid-term Master Planning should not only coordinate the decentralized decision units, but also plan for a reasonable degree of flexibility over time.

In order to improve competitiveness the *revelation of system constraints* is a crucial part of a continuous improvement process (see also Goldratt (1999)). System constraints may be detected at different levels of the planning hierarchy. For example, mid-term Master Planning will not only provide an optimal solution for a given situation, it also shows which constraints are binding, i.e. prevent a higher level of our objectives. Looking for ways to lift the system's constraints, e. g. by a more flexible employment of the workforce, will further improve competitiveness. This will give rise to defining several scenarios to choose from. Compared with former times, defining a scenario and getting an answer is now a matter of hours, not weeks. So, management and planning staff can work together more closely and effectively than before.

Some of the above statements may be regarded as visions. But as our case studies have shown, there are already implementations of APS in industry showing impressive improvements. In order to extend these success stories to a wider range of companies and supply chains, three main topics have to be addressed carefully:

- Improving modelling and solution capabilities of APS,
- extending the applicability of APS to polycentric supply chains and
- providing special training for managers, employees and consultants.

Due to the fact that most APS are rather new, additional features are expected to be introduced in the near future. However, the standard architecture of modules should remain stable. Experiences with some modules have shown that there may still exist some restrictions in modelling a given (production) process adequately. Given that supply chains have to adapt to new market trends quickly, modelling should be easy to learn and fast to implement. Likewise, one should expect a similar modelling language for all modules provided by an APS vendor (unfortunately this is not always the case).

Furthermore, we experienced that not all models generated have been solvable within reasonable time limits or have shown a satisfactory solution quality. However, minor changes in the model have improved solvability significantly. Hence, enhanced modelling capabilities and more robust solution procedures solving large problem instances are still looked for.

So far APS are best suited for supply chains with centralized control, e. g. exercised by a focal company. Although information exchange – in principle – is no problem for APS implemented in a *polycentric supply chain*, the willingness to operate on the basis of "open books" (e. g. regarding costs and available capacities) cannot always be assumed. Several options have been proposed in this respect recently, like considering "auctions" or "agents" on the interface between two adjacent units of a supply chain (Kutanoglu and Wu, 1999; Ottaway and Burns, 2000). However, we have not seen any options for this case in APS.

In order to use APS effectively, managers and employees must have *special training*, enabling them to interpret solutions, to recognize interactions with other parts of the supply chain, to set up scenarios and to react to alerts appropriately. In addition to project management, the mastery of change management and basics of information science, consultants must now have knowledge and experience in generating adequate models of the supply chain for the different modules of an APS. These models, neither being too detailed nor too rough, have to support decision-making and must be solvable with reasonable computational efforts. Inadequate models may even deteriorate the position of the supply chain instead of improving it.

Introducing an APS is not just adding another software package to those already existing in a company. On the contrary, it will replace many individual software solutions formerly "owned" by individual employees. Also, some types of decisions which formerly required several employees – like creating a detailed schedule for the shop floor – will now be made automatically. Consequently, some of the employees have to change to other positions, which may result in some resistance to change. On the other hand optimization capabilities of APS will yield better plans than before with the additional option of checking alternatives interactively, thus giving those involved a greater satisfaction.

Last but not least, one should bear in mind that introducing APS changes the way an organization or supply chain works. The definition of processes fulfilling the needs of different market segments will have to be reflected within the organizational structure. For legally separated firms or profit centres within a single firm covering only a portion of a given process an effective reward system has to be installed, in order to achieve the best solution for a supply chain as a whole and not being trapped in isolated sub-optima (see e. g. Fleischmann (1999)).

As stated in the introduction, SCM and APS are closely related to new developments in information and communication technology. Now, since business via the internet is growing rapidly, new challenges with respect to the order fulfilment process arise. Topics like "customer relationship management" have to be reconsidered for this new sales channel. Also, one can expect that future SCM will not only concentrate on the order fulfilment process alone, but will incorporate neighbouring processes like the product design or recovery process.

References

Fleischmann, B. (1999) *Kooperation von Herstellern in der Konsum-güterdistribution*, in: Engelhard, E.; Sinz, E. J. (Eds.) Kooperation im Wettbewerb. Neue Formen und Gestaltungskonzepte im Zeichen der Globalisierung und Informationstechnologie, Wiesbaden, 68–196

Goldratt, E. M. (1999) *Theory of constraints*, Croton-on-Hudson.

Pfohl, H.-Ch.; Mayer, S. (1999) *Wettbewerbsvorteile durch exzellentes Logistikmanagement*, Logistik Management, Vol. 1., No. 4, 275–281

Kutanoglu, E.; Wu, S. D. (1999) *On combinatorial auction and Lagrangean relaxation for distributed resource scheduling*, IIE Transactions, Vol. 31, 813–826

Ottaway, T. A.; Burns, J. R. (2000) *An adaptive production control system utilizing agent technology*, Int. J. Prod. Res., Vol. 38, No. 4, 721–737

Part VI

Supplement

21   Forecast Methods

Herbert Meyr

University of Augsburg, Department of Production and Logistics,
Universitätsstraße 16, 86135 Augsburg, Germany

In Chap. 21 we will show how demand planning can be done when seasonality and trend are given. For a comprehensive and ostensive introduction to forecasting in general the reader is referred to Hanke and Reitsch (1995) or Waters (1992).

21.1   Forecasting for Seasonality and Trend

This section introduces *Winters' method* which is appropriate for multiplicative seasonal models (see Chap. 6). In Sect. 21.2 the parameters of Winters' method are initialized. This incorporates the introduction of *linear regression*, too. A working example illustrates the explanations.

21.1.1   Working Example

Figure 21.1 shows the sales volume of a supplementary product of a large German shoe retailer. The data are aggregated over the whole sales region and comprise a time horizon of four weeks. In our working example we use the first three weeks (days -20, ..., 0) as input and – starting with day 1 – try to estimate day by day the sales of the fourth week.
Two observations are striking when analyzing the data:

- There seems to be a common sales pattern with weekly repetition. Saturdays usually show the highest, Sundays the lowest sales volume of a week. So weekly seasonality can be assumed with a cycle length of $T = 7$ days.
- Sales per week appear to be continuously increasing. This is obvious when all four weeks are considered. But even within the first three weeks a (weaker) trend of growing sales is visible.

Since the amplitude of seasonality is increasing, too, a seasonal multiplicative forecast model seems justified. All subsequent explanations will be demonstrated by use of this working example.

21.1.2   Modelling Seasonality and Trend

As already shown in Sect. 6.2 a multiplicative seasonal model is characterized by the parameters a and b describing the trend and the seasonal coefficients

Observed Sales

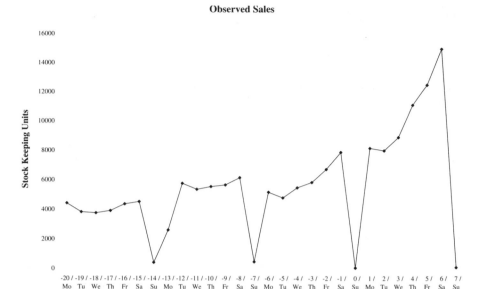

Fig. 21.1. Sales volume of a supplementary product of a German shoe retailer

c_t modelling the seasonality of period t. Figure 21.2 makes clear that the trend is expressed by the linear function $a + b \cdot t$ with t denoting periods of time (e. g. days in our working example).

A sales volume x_t observed in period t is modelled by

$$x_t = (a + b \cdot t) \cdot c_t + u_t \qquad (21.1)$$

with the seasonal coefficients c_t in- or decreasing the trend. Please note, if all seasonal coefficients are equal to 1, seasonality disappears and the model reduces to a simple trend model (see e. g. Silver et al. (1998, pp. 93)). The erratic noise u_t makes things difficult. Because of the randomness that is represented by u_t the other parameters cannot be measured exactly, but have to be predicted. In the following the superscript ˆ is used to differ between an observation (no superscript) that has been measured and its forecast being estimated without this knowledge.

Let $\hat{a}_t, \hat{b}_t$ and $\hat{c}_{t-T+1}, \ldots, \hat{c}_t$ denote the forecasts of $a., b.$ and the seasonal coefficients $c.$ that are valid in period t. Then (21.1) can be engaged to estimate the sales volume $\hat{x}_{t+s}^t$ of all subsequent periods $t + s$ $(s = 1, 2, \ldots)$. For example, the sales volume of the next seasonal cycle is predicted in period t by

$$\hat{x}_{t+s}^t = (\hat{a}_t + \hat{b}_t \cdot s) \cdot \hat{c}_{t+s-T} \quad (s = 1, \ldots, T). \qquad (21.2)$$

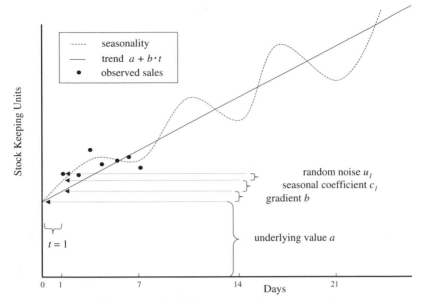

Fig. 21.2. Modelling seasonality and trend

The method of Winters described in the next subsection iteratively computes the sales estimation of only the subsequent period $t+1$. For this reason we can use the simpler notation $\hat{x}_{t+1}$ instead of $\hat{x}_{t+1}^t$.

21.1.3 Winters' Method

The method of Winters (1960) basically builds on (21.2) and the principle of exponential smoothing which has been introduced in Chap. 6. Since sales are predicted indirectly via $\hat{a}.$, $\hat{b}.$ and $\hat{c}.$ in (21.2), these three types of parameters have to be estimated by means of exponential smoothing instead of the sales volume itself (as it has been done by (6.5) for models without trend and seasonality). Remember the generic principle of exponential smoothing:

$$\text{new forecast} = sc \cdot \text{latest observation} + (1 - sc) \cdot \text{last forecast}. \qquad (21.3)$$

The *new forecast* of the current period estimating the subsequent period(s) can be calculated by smoothing the *latest observation*, i.e. the observation in the current period and the *last forecast* that has been made to predict the current period's observation. The smoothing constant $sc \in (0; 1)$ determines the weight the new observation has. The higher the smoothing constant the more importance is given to the latest observation. Table 21.1 summarizes how Winters applies exponential smoothing in period $t + 1$ to estimate the parameters $\hat{a}_{t+1}$, $\hat{b}_{t+1}$ and $\hat{c}_{t+1}$ determining the sales forecast $\hat{x}_{t+2}$ of the subsequent period (21.2).

Table 21.1. Exponential smoothing applied in Winters' method

new forecast	smoothing constant sc	latest observation	last forecast
$\hat{a}_{t+1}$	α	$x_{t+1}/\hat{c}_{t+1-T}$	$\hat{a}_t + \hat{b}_t \cdot 1$
$\hat{b}_{t+1}$	β	$\hat{a}_{t+1} - \hat{a}_t$	$\hat{b}_t$
$\hat{c}_{t+1}$	γ	$x_{t+1}/\hat{a}_{t+1}$	$\hat{c}_{t+1-T}$

These three types of equations become clear when looking at our working example. We start our computation at the end of day $t = 0$. Table 21.2 further illustrates this proceeding:

1. **Initialization**:
   In order to get things work initial values $\hat{a}_0$, $\hat{b}_0$ and $\hat{c}_{-6}, \ldots, \hat{c}_0$ (seasonal coefficients for each weekday) have to be given. Subsections 21.2.2 (for $\hat{c}.$) and 21.2.3 (for $\hat{a}_0$, $\hat{b}_0$) exemplarily show how these values can be computed from the sales observations of the first three weeks (day -20, $\ldots$, 0). For the moment we will accept in blank the values $\hat{a}_0 = 5849.0$, $\hat{b}_0 = 123.3$ and $\hat{c}_{-6} = 1.245693$ that are used in Table 21.2.[1]

2. **Estimating the sales volume of period $t + 1$**:
   Applying (21.2) we can estimate the sales volume $\hat{x}_1$ of period 1:

$$\hat{x}_1 = (\hat{a}_0 + \hat{b}_0 \cdot 1) \cdot \hat{c}_{-6} = (5849.0 + 123.3) \cdot 1.245693 = 7440$$

   The linear trend $(\hat{a}_0 + \hat{b}_0 \cdot 1)$ does not consider any seasonal influences and will therefore be called *"deseasonalized"*. Since sales on Mondays are (estimated to be) about 25 % higher than average weekly sales ($c_{-6} = 1.245693$), the trend has to be increased accordingly. Please note that at the end of day 0 sales of day 2 (Tuesday) could roughly be estimated to amount to $(\hat{a}_0 + \hat{b}_0 \cdot 2) \cdot \hat{c}_{-5} = 6798$. However, a more accurate forecast of $\hat{x}_2$ can be given at the end of day 1 because the sales observation x_1 of day 1 offers further information.

3. **Observation in period $t + 1$**:
   In day 1 sales x_1 of 8152 stock keeping units (SKU) are observed.

4. **Using the latest observation to update trend and seasonal coefficients**:
   The latest observation x_1 improves the forecast of the trend and Monday's seasonal coefficient. So the smoothing constants $\alpha = 0.8$, $\beta = 0.8$ and $\gamma = 0.3$ are applied to the three exponential smoothing equations defined in Table 21.1:

---

[1] Note that the initial seasonal coefficients $\hat{c}_{-6}, \ldots, \hat{c}_0$ are printed with two additional digits in order to indicate that high precision floating point arithmetic – commonly used in APS, programming languages and spreadsheets – is applied throughout the working example.

Table 21.2. Forecasting the fourth week using Winters' method

t	weekday	x_t	$\hat{x}_t$	$\hat{a}_t$	$\hat{b}_t$	$\hat{c}_t$
-6	Monday					1.245693
-5	Tuesday					1.115265
-4	Wednesday					1.088853
-3	Thursday		Initialization			1.135378
-2	Friday					1.178552
-1	Saturday					1.229739
0	Sunday			5849.0	123.3	0.006520
1	Monday	8152	**7440**	**6429.8**	**489.3**	**1.2523..**
2	Tuesday	7986	**7717**	7112.3	643.9	1.1175...
3	Wednesday	8891	8445	8083.6	905.8	1.0922...
4	Thursday	11107	10206	9624.0	1413.5	1.1410...
5	Friday	12478	13008	10677.6	1125.5	1.1756...
6	Saturday	14960	14515	12092.8	1357.3	1.2319...
7	Sunday	81	88	12628.5	700.0	0.0065...

(a) The underlying value $\hat{a}.$ of the trend is updated as follows:

$$\hat{a}_1 = \alpha \frac{x_1}{\hat{c}_{-6}} + (1-\alpha)(\hat{a}_0 + \hat{b}_0) = 0.8 \cdot \frac{8152}{1.245693} + 0.2 \cdot 5972.3 = 6429.8$$

Thereby, the "deseasonalize" sales volume $\frac{x_1}{\hat{c}_{-6}}$ of day 1 serves as a new observation for the underlying value, while $(\hat{a}_0 + \hat{b}_0 \cdot 1)$ was the forecast of the deseasonalized sales of day 1 which has been obtained in period 0 (21.1).

(b) Using $\hat{a}_1$, the new gradient $\hat{b}_1$ can be calculated:

$$\hat{b}_1 = \beta(\hat{a}_1 - \hat{a}_0) + (1-\beta)\hat{b}_0 = 0.8(6429.8 - 5849) + 0.2 \cdot 123.3 = 489.3$$

Between day 0 and day 1 the underlying value $a.$ has been increased from $\hat{a}_0$ to $\hat{a}_1$. Since $\hat{a}_1$ is based on the latest sales observation x_1, this is interpreted as the "new observation" of the gradient $b.$ which again has to be exponentially smoothed.

(c) The same procedure is applied to the seasonal coefficient $\hat{c}_1$:

$$\hat{c}_1 = \gamma \frac{x_1}{\hat{a}_1} + (1-\gamma)\hat{c}_{-6} = 0.3 \frac{8152}{6429.8} + 0.7 \cdot 1.245693 = 1.2523$$

$\hat{c}_{-6}$ was the last forecast of the Monday's seasonal coefficient. The new observation of the seasonal influence of a Monday, however, is achieved by dividing the observed sales volume x_1 (including seasonal influences) by $\hat{a}_1$ (deseasonalized).

5. **Stepping forward in time:**
   Now we can go one day ahead (increasing t by 1) and repeat the steps (2) to (5). At the end of day 1 the sales volume $\hat{x}_2$ of day 2 is estimated by

$$\hat{x}_2 = (\hat{a}_1 + \hat{b}_1 \cdot 1) \cdot \hat{c}_{-5} = (6429.8 + 489.3 \cdot 1) \cdot 1.115265 = 7717$$

and so on...

Table 21.2 shows the results of Winters' method when applied to the days 2 to 7.

Figure 21.3 illustrates the consequences of a variation of the smoothing constants α and β of the trend. Generally, smoothing constants $\alpha \in [0.02; 0.51]$,

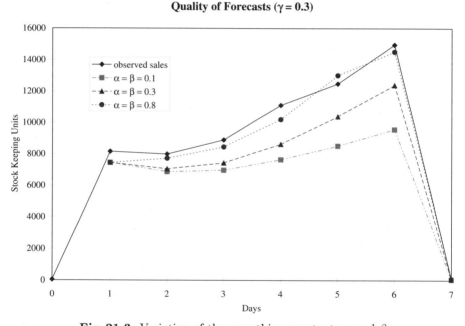

Fig. 21.3. Variation of the smoothing constants α and β

$\beta \in [0.005; 0.176]$ and $\gamma \in [0.05; 0.5]$ are recommended (see Silver et al. (1998, p. 108)). In our working example, however, $\alpha = \beta = 0.8$ perform best, i. e. the few latest observations get a very high weight and smoothing is only weak. Thus, the forecast is able to react quickly to the progressively rising sales of the fourth week.

21.2   Initialization of Trend and Seasonal Coefficients

Until now we have not shown how the trend and seasonal coefficients can be initialized using the information that is given by the sales volume of the first three weeks. The next subsection demonstrates how the data basis can be improved if additional information is considered. Sections 21.2.2 and 21.2.3 finally present the initialization of the seasonal coefficients $\hat{c}.$ and the trend parameters $\hat{a}.$ and $\hat{b}.$

21.2.1   Consideration of Further Information

When looking at the data of the first three weeks (see Fig. 21.1) two phenomena seem to be contradictory to the assumption of a linear trend with seasonality:

1. Sales on Monday -13 are unexpectedly low. In weeks 1 and 3 sales on Mondays are clearly higher than sales on Tuesdays.
2. While the trend of weekly increasing sales is obvious, sales on Sunday 0 are much lower than sales on the respective Sundays of the first two weeks (days -14 and -7).

We want to know whether these inconsistencies are purely random or due to an identifiable actuator and get the following information:

1. In some parts of Germany Monday -13 was a holiday. Therefore, 58 % of the stores of the shoe retailer were closed this day.
2. Usually, shoe stores have to be closed on Sundays in Germany. Some few cities, however, granted a special authorization for sale. Starting with the third week $93\frac{1}{3}$ % of these cities do not grant such an authorization any more.

We can now improve our data basis by exploiting this information about special influences in our further investigations. Therefore, the sales volume of day -13 is increased by 138.1 % $(x_{-13} = 2600 \cdot \frac{100}{100-58} = 6190.4761)$ and sales on Sundays -14 (410 SKU) and -7 (457 SKU) are decreased by $93\frac{1}{3}$ % so that $x_{-14} = 27.\bar{3}$ and $x_{-7} = 30.4\bar{6}$. In the next two subsections original sales are replaced by these corrected sales.

21.2.2   Determination of Seasonal Coefficients by the Ratio-to-Moving Averages Decomposition

The ratio-to-moving averages decomposition (see e. g. Makridakis et al. (1983, pp. 137)) is exemplarily used to determine the initial seasonal coefficients of Winters' method. In Sect. 21.1.3 we already applied the equation:

observed sales in t = (deseasonalized sales in t) $\cdot$ (seasonal coefficient of t).

In other words, if we want to isolate seasonal coefficients, we have to compute

$$\text{seasonal coefficient of period } t = \frac{\text{observed sales in } t}{\text{deseasonalized sales in } t} \qquad (21.4)$$

where the *deseasonalized sale in period t* is a sales volume that does not contain any seasonal influences. But how to determine such a value?

Considering our working example, the sales volume of a full week is apparently not influenced by daily sales peaks. So the most intuitive way to obtain sales data without seasonal influences is to compute daily sales averaged over a full week. This leads to average daily sales $\frac{4419+...+27.\overline{3}}{7} = 3544.6$, 4951.6 and 5122.4 SKU for the weeks 1 to 3 (see Table 21.3). Thereby, the Thursday is settled in the middle of each week.

But we can employ the same procedure for each other time period of seven days, e. g. day -19, ..., -13, and assign the average daily sales 3797.7 to the medium Friday -16. By doing so we compute moving averages over a full seasonal cycle of 7 days for each day -17, ..., -3 which represent deseasonalized daily sales volumina. Table 21.3 illustrates the whole procedure.

In a next step we apply (21.4), thus setting the observed sales x_t in *ratio to* the deseasonalized *moving averages* (remember the name of the algorithm). The result are multiple observations of seasonal coefficients $o_{weekday}^{week}(t)$ for each day of the week (three for a Thursday and two for each other weekday) which still contain the random noise u_t.

In order to reduce this randomness, now we compute the average seasonal coefficients $o_{weekday}^{aver}$ of each weekday (Table 21.4). For example, for the Thursday we get

$$o_{Thursday}^{aver} = \frac{o_{Thursday}^{week\,1}(-17) + o_{Thursday}^{week\,2}(-10) + o_{Thursday}^{week\,3}(-3)}{number\ of\ weeks} =$$
$$= \frac{1.1031 + 1.1188 + 1.1377}{3} = 1.1199$$

If a pure trend without any seasonal influence is given, one would expect all seasonal coefficients to equal 1 (see Sect. 21.1.2), thus summing up to 7 for a weekly seasonal cycle. As we can see in Table 21.4, the sum of our average seasonal coefficients $o^{total} = \sum_{day=Monday}^{Sunday} o_{day}^{aver} = 6.9045$ falls short of 7. To reflect the trend correctly we have to normalize our o^{aver} by multiplying them with the constant $7/o^{total}$. The resulting final seasonal coefficients for *Monday ... Sunday* are already known as $\hat{c}_{-6}, ..., \hat{c}_0$ from Table 21.2.

21.2.3   Determining the Trend by Linear Regression

Finally it will be shown how the trend parameters a and b can be determined. When "deseasonalizin" the observed sales by dividing through c_t one can see from (21.5) that the trend $a+b\cdot t$, distorted by some random noise $\frac{u_t}{c_t}$, results:

$$d_t = \frac{x_t}{c_t} = \frac{(a + b \cdot t) \cdot c_t + u_t}{c_t} = a + b \cdot t + \frac{u_t}{c_t}. \qquad (21.5)$$

Table 21.3. Ratio–to–moving averages decomposition

week	day	weekday	(corr.) x_t	moving aver. (ma_t)	$o_{weekday}^{week}(t) = \frac{x_t}{ma_t}$
1	-20	Monday	4419		
1	-19	Tuesday	3821		
1	-18	Wednesday	3754		
1	-17	Thursday	3910	**3544.6**	1.1031
1	-16	Friday	4363	**3797.7**	1.1489
1	-15	Saturday	4518	4074.0	1.1090
1	-14	Sunday	$(27.333\bar{3})$	4302.3	0.0064
2	-13	Monday	(6190.4761)	4535.1	1.3650
2	-12	Tuesday	5755	4719.0	1.2195
2	-11	Wednesday	5352	4951.1	1.0810
2	-10	Thursday	5540	**4951.6**	1.1188
2	-9	Friday	5650	4804.1	1.1761
2	-8	Saturday	6143	4664.6	1.3169
2	-7	Sunday	$(30.466\bar{6})$	4680.6	0.0065
3	-6	Monday	5158	4721.8	1.0924
3	-5	Tuesday	4779	4873.8	0.9806
3	-4	Wednesday	5464	5120.8	1.0670
3	-3	Thursday	5828	**5122.4**	1.1377
3	-2	Friday	6714		
3	-1	Saturday	7872		
3	0	Sunday	42		

Table 21.4. Reducing randomness of seasonal coefficients

week	Mo	Tu	We	Th	Fr	Sa	Su	$\sum$
1				**1.1031**	1.1489	1.1090	0.0064	
2	1.3650	1.2195	1.0810	**1.1188**	1.1761	1.3169	0.0065	
3	1.0924	0.9806	1.0670	**1.1377**				o^{total}:
$o_{weekday}^{aver}$	1.2287	1.1000	1.0740	**1.1199**	1.1625	1.2130	0.0064	**6.9045**
$\hat{c}.$	1.2457	1.1153	1.0889	1.1354	1.1786	1.2297	0.0065	7.00

The parameters a and b can be estimated by means of *linear regression* (see Wood and Field (1976, pp. 76)). As Fig. 21.4 shows, appropriate estimators $\hat{a}$ and $\hat{b}$ are computed by minimizing the (squared) vertical distances between $d_t = \frac{x_t}{\hat{c}_t}$ and the trend line $\hat{a} + \hat{b} \cdot t$. This useful way of eliminating the random noise is also applied in causal forecasts and has already been introduced in Sect. 6.2.2.

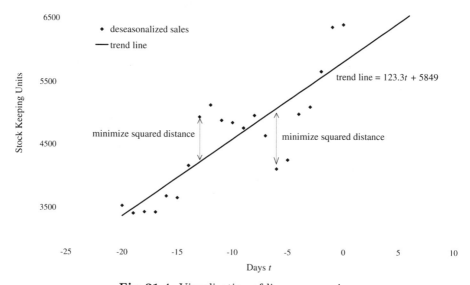

Fig. 21.4. Visualization of linear regression

Table 21.5 and Equations (21.6) and (21.7) illustrate how the trend parameters $\hat{a}_0$ and $\hat{b}_0$ have been calculated by linear regression to initialize Winters' method in Sect. 21.1.3:

$$\hat{b}_0 = \frac{\sum_t (t - \bar{t})(d_t - \bar{d})}{\sum_t (t - \bar{t})^2} = \frac{94943}{770} = 123.3 \qquad (21.6)$$

$$\hat{a}_0 = \bar{d} - \hat{b}_0 \cdot \bar{t} = 4616 - 123.3 \cdot (-10) = 5849. \qquad (21.7)$$

At this $\bar{t} = \frac{1}{21} \cdot \sum_t t = \frac{-210}{21} = -10$ and $\bar{d} = \frac{1}{21} \cdot \sum_t d_t = \frac{96936}{21} = 4616$ represent the average values of t and d_t over the first weeks of our working example.

Please note that similar deseasonalized sales have been obtained through the moving averages computation in the last subsection. These could also be used to estimate $\hat{a}$ and $\hat{b}$ by linear regression. In this case, however, only 15

Table 21.5. Calculation of linear regression

week	day	(corr.) x_t	$\hat{c}_t$	$d_t = \frac{x_t}{\hat{c}_t}$	$(t - \bar{t})^2$	$(t - \bar{t})(d_t - \bar{d}_t)$
1	-20	4419	1.2457	3547	100	10686
1	-19	3821	1.1153	3426	81	10709
1	-18	3754	1.0889	3448	64	9347
1	-17	3910	1.1354	3444	49	8206
1	-16	4363	1.1786	3702	36	5484
1	-15	4518	1.2297	3674	25	4710
1	-14	$(27.333\bar{3})$	0.0065	4192	16	1695
2	-13	(6190.4761)	1.2457	4970	9	-1060
2	-12	5755	1.1153	5160	4	-1088
2	-11	5352	1.0889	4915	1	-299
2	-10	5540	1.1354	4879	0	0
2	-9	5650	1.1786	4794	1	178
2	-8	6143	1.2297	4995	4	759
2	-7	$(30.466\bar{6})$	0.0065	4673	9	170
3	-6	5158	1.2457	4141	16	-1901
3	-5	4779	1.1153	4285	25	-1655
3	-4	5464	1.0889	5018	36	2413
3	-3	5828	1.1354	5133	49	3620
3	-2	6714	1.1786	5697	64	8646
3	-1	7872	1.2297	6401	81	16068
3	0	42	0.0065	6442	100	18256
$\sum$	-210			96936	770	94943

instead of 21 observations for deseasonalized sales would have been available, thus preparing a noticeably smaller sample to overcome randomness.

References

Hanke, J. E.; Reitsch, A. G. (1995) *Business forecasting*, 5th ed., Englewood Cliffs et al.

Makridakis, S; Wheelwright, S. C.; McGee, V. E. (1983) *Forecasting: Methods and applications*, 2nd ed., New York et al.

Silver, E. A.; Pyke, D. F.; Peterson, R. (1998) *Inventory management and production planning and scheduling*, 3rd ed., New York et al.

Waters, C. D. J. (1992) *Inventory control and management*, Chichester et al.

Winters, P. (1960) *Forecasting sales by exponentially weighted moving averages*, Management Science, Vol. 6, No. 3, 324-342

Wood, D.; Field, R. (1976) *Forecasting for business: Methods and applications*, London et al.

22 Linear and Mixed Integer Programming

Hartmut Stadtler

Darmstadt University of Technology, Institute of Business Administration, Department of Operations and Materials Management, Hochschulstraße 1, 64289 Darmstadt, Germany

Linear Programming (LP) is one of the most famous optimization techniques introduced independently by Kantarowitsch in 1939 and by Dantzig in 1949 (Krekó, 1973). LP is applicable in decision situations where quantities (variables) can take any real values only restricted by linear (in-) equalities, e. g. for representing capacity constraints. Still, LP has turned out to be very useful for many companies so far. LP is used in APS e. g. in Master Planning as well as in Distribution and Transport Planning. Very powerful solution algorithms have been developed (named solvers), solving LP models with thousands of variables and constraints within a few minutes on a personal computer.

In case some decisions can only be expressed by integer values, e. g. the number of additional shifts for a given week, LP usually will not provide a feasible solution. Similarly, logical implications might be modelled by binary variables. As an example consider the decision whether to setup a flow line for a certain product or not: A value of "0" will be attributed to a decision "no" and a value of "1" to "yes". Still, the corresponding model may be described by linear (in-) equalities. In case the model solely consists of integer variables, it is called a pure *Integer Programming* (IP) model. If the model contains both real and integer variables a *Mixed Integer Programming* (MIP) model is given.

Thus, both LP and MIP comprise special model types and associated solution algorithms. Numerous articles and textbooks have been written on LP and MIP (e. g. Martin (1999), Winston (1994) and Wolsey (1998)) representing a high level of knowledge which cannot be reviewed here. In order to give an understanding of LP and MIP, only the basic ideas will be provided in the following by means of an example.

First, an LP model is presented and solved graphically (Sect. 22.1). This model is then converted into an IP model and solved by Branch and Bound (Sect. 22.2), where for each submodel a LP model is solved graphically. Finally, a few remarks and recommendations regarding the effective use of LP and MIP complements this chapter (Sect. 22.3).

22.1 Linear Programming

A hypothetical production planning problem is considered here, where two products A and B can be produced within the next month. The associated production amounts are represented by (real) variables x_1 and x_2 measured in ten tons. Both products have to pass through the same production process. The available capacity is 20 days (on a two shift basis). The production of ten tons, or one unit, of product A lasts 5 days, while the respective coefficient for product B is 4 days. This situation is represented by inequality (22.2). LP model:

$$\text{Max!} \quad 19x_1 + 16x_2 \qquad (22.1)$$

subject to

$$(1) \qquad\qquad 5x_1 + 4x_2 \le 20 \qquad (22.2)$$
$$(2) \qquad\qquad -x_1 + 2x_2 \le 5 \qquad (22.3)$$
$$(3) \qquad\qquad 2x_1 + 5x_2 \ge 10 \qquad (22.4)$$
$$(\text{NNC}) \qquad\qquad x_1 \ge 0,\ x_2 \ge 0 \qquad (22.5)$$

Inequality (22.3) represents the demand constraints, stating that only sales of product B are limited. However, we might increase sales if we also offer product A: For every two units of product A we can extend sales of product B by one unit (the reason may be that one has to offer a complete product range to some customer groups in order to sell product B). Although we aim at maximizing our revenue (22.1), we also want to make sure that a contribution margin of at least ten thousand \$ is reached within the next month (22.4). Note, the dimension "one thousand" is scaled down to "one" for the contribution margin constraint. Obviously, one cannot produce negative amounts which is reflected by the non-negativity constraints (NNC, see (22.5)).

This small LP model can be solved algebraically by the simplex algorithm (or one of its variants, see Martin (1999)). However, we will resort to a graphical representation (Fig. 22.1). Variables x_1 and x_2 depict the two dimensions. Inequalities restrict the combination of feasible values of variables. The limits of the corresponding set of feasible solutions are illustrated by a line (see Fig. 22.1). Whether the set of feasible solutions lies below or above a line is depicted by three adjacent strokes being part of the set of feasible solutions.

The intersection of all the (in-) equalities of a model defines the set of feasible solutions (shaded area in Fig. 22.1). For a given objective function value the objective function itself is an equation (see dashed line in Fig. 22.1, corresponding to a value of 76 [\$ 000]). Since we do not know the optimal value of the objective function we can try out several objective function values. An arrow shows the direction in which the objective function value can be increased. Actually, we can move the dashed line further to the right. The maximum is reached once it cannot be moved any further without leaving the set of feasible solutions. This is the case for $x_1 = 20/14$ and $x_2 = 45/14$ resulting in a revenue of 78.57 [\$ 000]. The optimal solution has been reached at the intersection of inequalities (1) and (2). It can be shown that it suffices

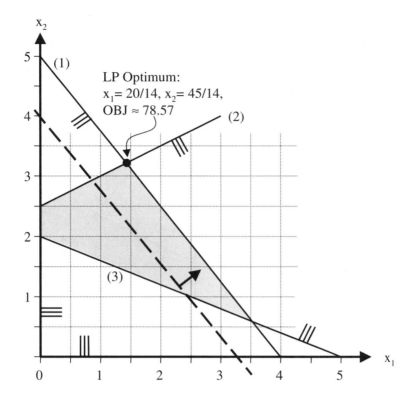

Explanations: ░ region of feasible LP solutions

— — constraint relating to a given level of the objective function

OBJ maximum objective function value

⋯⫶⋯ grid (as a guidance for recognizing solutions)

●   LP Optimum

Fig. 22.1. Graphical representation of an LP model

to look for an optimal solution only at the intersections of (in-) equalities limiting the set of feasible solutions or, graphically speaking, at the "corners" of the shaded area.

The simplex algorithm (and its variants) carries out the search for an optimal solution in two phases, namely

- creating an initial feasible solution and
- finding an optimal solution.

In our example a first feasible solution may be $x_1 = 0$ and $x_2 = 2$ with a revenue of $2 \cdot 16 = 32\,[\$\,000]$. Now, the second phase is started, probably generating an improved second solution, e. g. $x_1 = 0$ and $x_2 = 2.5$ with a revenue of 40 [\$ 000]. In the next iteration variable x_1 will be introduced, resulting in the optimal LP solution.

However, an initial feasible solution may not always exist. As an example, assume that a minimum contribution margin of 22 [\$ 000] is required (see inequality (3') in Fig. 22.2). The set of feasible solutions is empty and thus no feasible solution exists.

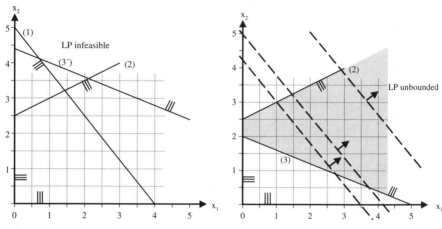

Fig. 22.2. An infeasible LP model   **Fig. 22.3.** An unbounded LP model

Now consider the situation where there is no production constraint (i. e. eliminating inequality (1)), resulting in an unrestricted shaded area (Fig. 22.3) and an unbounded objective function value. This case will also be detected in the first phase. Actually, an unbounded solution indicates that the model or the data have not been created correctly.

We would like to point out that an LP solution does not only provide optimal values for the decision variables. It also shows the *dual values* associated with the (in-) equalities of an LP model. As an example consider the production capacity (22.2). If we were able to increase the number of working days from 20 to 21, the optimal objective function value would rise from 1100/14 to 1154/14. Thus an additional capacity unit has a dual value of 3.86 [\$ 000]. Management now may look for options to extend capacity which are worth further revenues of 3.86 [\$ 000] per working day. Note that only inequalities which are binding in the optimal solution may have a positive dual value. Although dual values have to be interpreted with caution, they are a fruitful source for finding ways to improve the current decision situation.

As has already been stated at the beginning of this chapter, very powerful solution algorithms and respective standard software exist for solving LP models (e. g. CPLEX (ILOG CPLEX Division, 2000) and XPRESS-MP (DASH Associates, 2000)). However, users of an APS do not have to deal with these solvers directly. Instead, special modelling features have been selected within APS modules for building correct models. Still, care should be taken regarding the numbers entering the model. If possible, appropriate scaling should be introduced first, such that the coefficients of variables are in the range from 0.01 to 100 to avoid numerical problems.

22.2   Pure Integer and Mixed Integer Programming

Now let us assume that a product can only be produced in integer multiples of ten [tons], since this is the size of a tab which has to be filled completely for producing either product A or B. Then the above model (22.1)–(22.4) has to be complemented by the additional constraints

$$x_1 \in N_0 , \quad x_2 \in N_0 \qquad (22.6)$$

The set of feasible solutions reduces drastically (see the six integer solutions in Fig. 22.4). Still, in practice the number of solutions to consider before an integer solution has been proven to be optimal may be enormous.

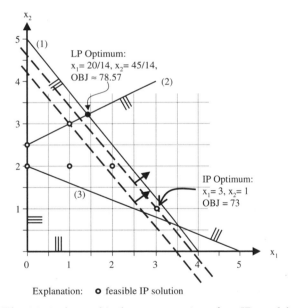

Fig. 22.4. A graphical representation of an IP model

As can be seen from Fig. 22.4 a straightforward idea, namely rounding the optimal LP solution to the next feasible integer values ($x_1 = 1$, $x_2 = 3$ with a revenue of 67 [$ 000]), does not result in an optimal integer solution (which is $x_1 = 3$, $x_2 = 1$ and with a revenue of 73 [$ 000]).

Anyway, an intelligent rounding heuristic might be appropriate for some applications. Hence, some APS incorporate rounding heuristics which usually require much less computational efforts than Branch and Bound which is explained next.

Four building blocks have to be considered describing a *Branch and Bound* algorithm, namely

- relaxation,
- separation rules,
- search strategy,
- fathoming rules.

The two building blocks *separation rules* and *search strategy* relate to "branch" while *relaxation* and *fathoming rules* concern "bound". These building blocks will now be explained by solving our example.

Although solving the associated LP model directly usually does not yield an optimal integer solution, we can conclude that the set of feasible integer solutions is a subset of the set of feasible LP solutions. So, if we were able to cut off some parts of the non-integer solution space, then we would finally arrive at an integer solution.

Consequently, we first *relax* the integer requirements (22.6) in favour of the non-negativity constraints (22.5). The resultant model is called an *LP relaxation*. If we solve an LP relaxation of a maximization problem, the optimal objective function will be an *upper bound* for all integer solutions contained in the associated set of feasible (integer) solutions. Hence, if the solution of an LP relaxation fulfills the integer requirements (22.6), it will be an optimal integer solution for this (sub-) model.

Next, submodels are created by introducing additional constraints, such that a portion of the real-valued non-integer solution space is eliminated (see Fig. 22.5). Here, the constraint $x_1 \leq 1$ is added resulting in submodel SM^1, while constraint $x_1 \geq 2$ yields submodel SM^2. Now, we have to solve two submodels with a reduced set of feasible solutions. Note that the union of the set of feasible *integer* solutions of both submodels matches the initial set of feasible integer solutions, i.e. no integer solution is lost by *separation*.

Submodel SM^1 results in a first *integer* solution ($x_1 = 1$, $x_2 = 3$ with a revenue of 67 [$ 000] representing the local upper bound of SM^1). Subsequently, we will only be interested in solutions with a revenue of more than 67 [$ 000]. Thus, we set the global lower bound to 67 [$ 000] (OBJ = 67). The term "global" is used in order to refer to our original IP model. Since submodel SM^1 has resulted in an *integer solution* (and cannot yield a better solution) it will be discarded from our list of open submodels, i.e. it is *fathomed*.

The second submodel has a local upper bound of 78 [$ 000] which is clearly better than our current global lower bound, but its solution is non-integer valued ($x_2 = 2.5$).

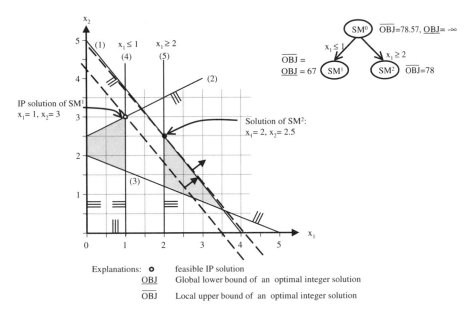

Fig. 22.5. A graphical representation of the first and second submodel

The search for an optimal solution can be represented by a *search tree* (see right hand side of Fig. 22.5). Each node corresponds to an LP (sub-)model.

Now an unfathomed submodel has to be chosen for further investigations. However, only submodel SM^2 is unfathomed here. Subsequently, one has to decide on the non-integer-valued variable to branch on. These two choices make up the *search strategy* and may have a great impact on the number of submodels to solve and hence the computational effort.

The only variable which is non-integer valued in the optimal solution for submodel SM^2 is x_2. Two new submodels are created, submodel SM^3 with the additional constraint $x_2 \leq 2$ and submodel SM^4 with the additional constraint $x_2 \geq 3$. Note that all additional constraints that have been generated on the path from the origin (SM^0) to a given submodel in the search tree have to be taken into account (here $x_1 \geq 2$).

Since, there *is no feasible (real valued) solution* for submodel SM^4 (see Fig. 22.6) it may be *fathomed*. For submodel SM^3 a non-integer valued solution with an upper bound of 77.6 [\$ 000] is calculated. Since this local upper bound exceeds the global lower bound (i. e. the best objective function value known) submodel SM^3 must not be fathomed.

It now takes three further separations until we reach submodel SM^9 (Fig. 22.7), where the LP relaxation yields an integer solution with an objective function value of 73 [\$ 000].

Usually, there will be some unfathomed submodels which have been generated in the course of the search. An unfathomed submodel has to be selected

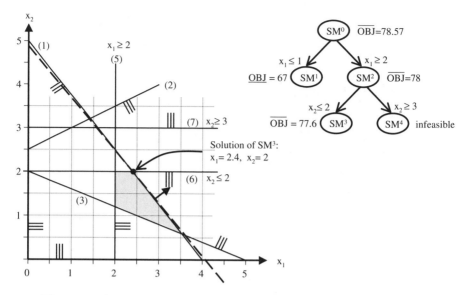

Fig. 22.6. A graphical representation of the third and fourth submodel

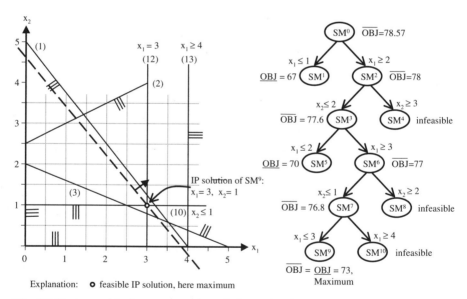

Explanation: ○ feasible IP solution, here maximum

Fig. 22.7. A graphical representation of the optimal integer solution and the complete search tree

for a further separation until all submodels are fathomed. Then the best feasible integer solution found will be the optimal one for the initial IP model.

In our example, the search ends once it has been found out that submodel SM^{10} has no feasible solution. Now we have proven that the solution to submodel SM^9 is optimal.

Finally, we would like to add that the Branch and Bound scheme is almost the same for MIP models. As an example consider that only x_2 has to take integer values. Then we would start separating on variable x_2 (i.e. $x_2 \leq 3$ and $x_2 \geq 4$). Only constraint $x_2 \leq 3$ results in a feasible solution for the LP relaxation. Since it is also feasible with respect to the mixed integer constraints it is the optimal solution, too.

22.3 Remarks and Recommendations

Although the examples presented are rather simple, they have illustrated the differences in solving an LP model and a MIP model. Generating an optimal solution for an LP model requires "some" simplex iterations leading from one "corner" of the feasible solution space to the next and finally to the optimal one. However, solving a MIP model by Branch and Bound incurs solving an LP (sub-) model for each node of the search tree – and there may be several thousand nodes to explore until an optimal solution has been proven.

One way to reduce the number of submodels to investigate is to *truncate the search effort*. For example, the user may either set a certain time limit for the search or indicate that the search has to be stopped once the k-th feasible integer solution has been found. However, the problem with truncation is that one does not know in advance at which point in time a feasible or good solution will be found.

Another option to limit the computational effort of Branch and Bound is to specify in advance that the search for an improved solution should be stopped, once we are sure that there is no feasible integer solution which is at least $\delta\%$ better than our current best solution. This allows us to calculate an aspiration level in the course of Branch and Branch, simply by multiplying the objective function value of the current best solution by $(1 + \delta\%)$. The question whether there exists a feasible integer solution with an objective function value no less than the aspiration level is known from the maximum upper bound of *all* unfathomed submodels. If the maximum is less than our aspiration level the search is stopped.

In our example (see the search tree in Fig. 22.7) we now assume $\delta = 10$. Having generated the first integer solution ($\underline{OBJ} = 67$) the aspiration level is 73.7 [$\$\,000$]. Since the maximum of the upper bounds of unfathomed submodels is 78 [$\$\,000$] (submodel 2) the search will continue. Having reached the second integer solution with an objective function value of 70 [$\$\,000$], an aspiration level of 77 [$\$\,000$] is calculated. In this example the search stops once the maximum upper bound of all unfathomed submodels falls below 77 [$\$\,000$] which is true after having generating submodel 8.

The number of submodels to solve largely depends on the relative difference between the objective function value of the LP relaxation and the optimal integer solution, named *integrality gap*. For our example the integrality gap is rather modest (e. g. (78.57-73)/73 = 0.076 or 7.6%). The smaller the integrality gap is, the greater is the chance to fathom submodels and thus to keep the search tree small. Today much effort is invested in deriving additional *valid inequalities (cuts)* to yield small integrality gaps for each submodel generated within Branch and Bound (see Wolsey (1998)).

A further option applied by advanced MIP solvers to reduce the search effort is *preprocessing*. Here one investigates the interactions of the model's constraints in order to restrict or even fix the values of some integer variables before starting Branch and Bound. For our example, one might conclude that the set of feasible integer values for x_1 will be restricted to $\{0,1,2,3\}$ and to $\{1, 2, 3\}$ for x_2. Preprocessing is very similar to the ideas of Constraint Programming (Chap. 24).

In any case the user should use integer or binary variables carefully – a MIP model incorporating (only) one hundred integer variables may already turn out to require excessive computational efforts.

References

DASH Associates (2000) *Homepage*, URL: http://www.dash.co.uk, State: May 12, 2000

ILOG CPLEX Division (2000) *Homepage*, URL: http://www.ilog.com/products /cplex, State: May 12, 2000

Krekó, B. (1973) *Lehrbuch der Linearen Optimierung*, Berlin

Martin, R. K. (1999) *Large scale linear and integer optimization: A unified approach*, Boston et al.

Winston, W. L. (1994) *Operations Research: Applications and algorithms*, 3rd ed., Belmont, California

Wolsey, L. A. (1998) *Integer Programming*, New York et al.

23 Genetic Algorithms

Robert Klein

Darmstadt University of Technology, Institute of Business Administration, Department of Operations Research, Hochschulstraße 1, 64289 Darmstadt, Germany

23.1 General Idea

Many optimization problems of the type arising in scheduling and routing (see Chaps. 9 and 10) are of combinatorial nature, i. e. solutions are obtained by combining and sequencing solution elements. When solving such problems to optimality, the number of solutions to be examined exponentially grows with the problem size. For example, for n solution elements $n!$ different sequences exist.

Recently, *genetic algorithms* (GA) have become increasingly popular as a means for solving such optimization problems heuristically, i. e. for determining near-optimal solutions within reasonable time. One of the main reasons for this popularity is the relative ease of programming at least a simple genetic algorithm. Furthermore, many researchers have observed empirically that already basic versions of GA will give very acceptable results without excessively finetuning them for the problem on hand. Finally, since GA work on a representation (coding) of a problem (see Sect. 23.2), it is possible to adapt existing procedures to modified problem versions quite easily or to write one general computer programme for solving many different problems. GA were initially developed by Holland and its associates at the University of Michigan and the first systematic but rather technical treatment was published in Holland (1975). For comprehensive descriptions from a more practical point of view, we refer to Goldberg (1989), Reeves (1993) and Michalewicz (1994). Surveys on successful applications of GA for solving combinatorial optimization problems are, for example, given in Dowsland (1996) and Reeves (1997).

According to the biological evolution, GA work with *populations* of *individuals* which represent feasible solutions for the problem considered. The populations are constructed iteratively through a number of *generations*. Following the idea of Darwinism ("survival of the fittest"), each individual of the current generation "contributes" to the subsequent one according to its quality which is measured by a *fitness value*. This is achieved by *selecting* individuals randomly with the probability of choosing a certain individual depending on its fitness value. In order to obtain the next generation from the individuals selected, two basic operations exist. Using a *crossover*, the features of two (parent) individuals are *recombined* to one or more new (child) ones. By *mutation*, some features of an individual are modified randomly. A template for a single iteration of a genetic algorithm is depicted in Fig. 23.1. Usually, GA are executed until a prespecified stopping criterion is fulfilled, e. g. a certain number of generations has been evaluated or a time limit is reached.

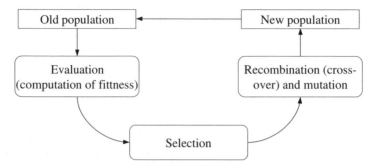

Fig. 23.1. Template for a single iteration of a genetic algorithm

In the following, we discuss the different aspects of GA in more detail. To ease presentation, the following *production scheduling problem* is considered. A number n of jobs has to be processed on a single machine (with concurrent execution being impossible). Each job $j = 1, \ldots, n$ has a fixed processing time (duration) of d_j periods and preemption is not allowed. Furthermore, job j cannot be started before its release date rd_j and should be terminated until a due date dd_j. In case it is finished later than dd_j, a penalty cost c_j for each time unit of tardiness arises. Hence, the problem consists of finding a schedule, i. e. a starting time s_j for each job, such that the total tardiness costs are minimized. The data of an example with $n = 8$ jobs are given in Table 23.1.

Table 23.1. Data of an example problem

j	1	2	3	4	5	6	7	8
d_j	5	4	7	8	3	2	6	4
rd_j	0	2	4	16	18	28	25	28
dd_j	17	10	13	28	22	31	36	36
c_j	3	2	5	3	4	1	3	4

23.2   Populations and Individuals

As stated before, a population consists of a set of individuals. Each individual is *represented* by a vector (*string*) of fixed length in which the corresponding solution is coded by assigning specific values to the vector elements (*string positions*). In order to obtain the solution associated with an individual, the respective string has to be *decoded*. Both the dimension (length) of the string as well as the domains (sets of feasible values) of the string positions depend on which representation is chosen for coding the solution.

In our example, a solution can be represented by a sequence S of jobs. That is, the string consists of n positions and each position can take one of the values $1, \ldots, n$ (with all positions having different values). For decoding the string, we proceed as follows. The jobs are considered in accordance to the sequence S. The job j in turn is started at the smallest possible point in time $s_j \geq rd_j$ at which its execution does not overlap with a job already scheduled. After having scheduled all jobs, the total tardiness costs can be computed. Consider the string $S = \langle 1, 2, 3, 4, 5, 6, 7, 8 \rangle$ for our example. By decoding this sequence, the solution shown in the Gantt chart of Fig. 23.2 is obtained. The numbers within the bars denote the job numbers and the tardiness of the jobs, respectively. The lengths of the bars correspond to the processing times.

Job 1 can be started at the earliest. Scheduling job 2 results in $s_2 = 5$ due to the processing of job 1 which does not allow for a smaller starting time. After terminating job 2, job 3 can begin at $s_3 = 9$, hence, finishing three periods after its due date $dd_3 = 13$. The jobs 4 and 5 are scheduled subsequently. Job 6 cannot be launched earlier than $s_6 = rd_6 = 28$. Finally, the jobs 7 and 8 are considered with the latter terminating after 40 periods. The total tardiness costs are $3 \cdot 5 + 5 \cdot 4 + 4 \cdot 4 = 51$.

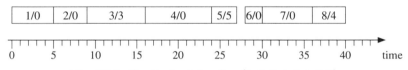

Fig. 23.2. Gantt chart for $S = \langle 1, 2, 3, 4, 5, 6, 7, 8 \rangle$

Note that we have chosen the above representation, because it is well suited for a large number of scheduling and routing problems and, hence, is used by a large number of GA for such problems (Reeves, 1997). Most commonly, GA are described using a representation where problems are coded in a bitwise fashion, i. e. each string position can take either the value 0 or 1. However, for most combinatorial optimization problems this representation is not appropriate.

Choosing an efficient representation for coding solutions is important for the performance of the genetic algorithm to be developed. The representation should be designed such that both the decoding does not require too much computational effort as well as the operations crossover and mutation can be performed efficiently. Within our example, an alternative representation of solutions could consist of using a string with n elements, where each position

$j = 1, \ldots, n$ defines a priority value for job j. This representation can be decoded in two steps. First of all, a job sequence S is obtained by sorting the jobs according to, e. g. non-decreasing priority values. Subsequently, a feasible schedule can be constructed as described above for the sequence based representation. Obviously, the sorting step results in an additional effort which is not justified unless the representation has some other advantages, e. g. it would allow for more efficient crossover and mutation operators. When using a representation where each string position denotes the starting time s_j of a job j, the implementation of the crossover and mutation operations becomes difficult. As already stated earlier, a mutation consists of modifying a string randomly (see Sect. 23.4 for details). Simply changing the starting time of a single job randomly may result in an infeasible schedule due to processing jobs in parallel. The problem of infeasibility is even more difficult to resolve when recombining individuals.

In any application of GA, an important question consists of choosing an appropriate *population size* P, i. e. the number of individuals considered in each iteration. If the population size is too small, the search space of feasible solutions may only be evaluated partially, because just a few existing individuals are recombined in each iteration and these individuals increasingly resemble each other with each additional generation. Otherwise, in case of a too large population size, also rather poor individuals may be considered for recombination and, hence, the search will only proceed slowly towards high-quality solutions. In the literature, most successful applications of GA propose an even-numbered population size of $P \in [50, 100]$ (Reeves, 1997).

Finally, an *initial population* has to be determined before starting a genetic algorithm. Most commonly, the corresponding individuals are obtained by randomly assigning values to the string positions. In our example, sequences of jobs may be constructed randomly. Alternatively, simple heuristics, such as randomized priority-rule based approaches (e. g. Drexl (1991)), may be applied in order to start the search with promising solutions.

23.3   Evaluation and Selection of Individuals

As stated previously, individuals contribute to the next generation with a probability depending on their fitness value. For this purpose, a *gene pool* consisting of P copies of individuals is constructed. For those individuals with a high fitness value, several copies are included in the pool, i. e. the individuals are selected several times, whereas for those with low values no copy may be contained at all. This reflects the analogy to biological evolution. The best individuals should contribute to the next generation the most often, i. e. their positive features are reproduced in many of the new individuals. By way of contrast, the worst ones with a low selection probability should be discarded and, hence, "die off".

In the most simple form, determining the fitness values v_i for the individuals $i = 1, \ldots, P$ consists in computing the objective function values f_i of the corresponding solutions.

For maximization problems, the selection process often used within GA can be subdivided in the following two steps. In the first step, a roulette wheel with $i = 1, \ldots, P$ slots sized according to the fitness values $v_i = f_i$ is constructed. For this purpose, the total fitness of the population is computed by $T = \sum_{i=1}^{P} v_i$. Subsequently, each individual i is assigned a selection probability of $p_i = v_i/T$ as well as a cumulative probability $q_i = \sum_{h=1}^{i} p_i$. In the second step, the roulette wheel is spined P times. In each iteration, a single individual is selected, i. e. a copy is included in the gene pool, as follows. After generating a random float number $\beta \in [0, 1]$, the individual $i = 1$ is chosen in case of $\beta \leq q_1$. Otherwise, the i-th individual with $q_{i-1} < \beta \leq q_i$ is picked.

The above selection process bears the difficulty that if the objective is minimization instead of maximization as in our example, a transformation of the objective function values has to be performed. One simple transformation consists of defining an upper bound F which exceeds all possible objective function values and subsequently using the fitness value $v_i = F - f_i$. Another difficulty is that the scale on which the values are measured may not be considered appropriately. For example, values of 1,020 and 1,040 are less distinctive than values of 20 and 40.

Therefore, two possible alternatives for designing the selection process have been proposed in the literature. When using a *ranking* approach, the individuals are ordered according to non-deteriorating fitness values with r_i denoting the rank of individual i. Subsequently, a selection probability is computed by, e. g. $p_i = 2r_i/(P \cdot (P + 1))$. In this case, the best individual with $r_i = P$ has the chance of $p_i = 2/(P+1)$ of being selected. This is roughly twice of that of the median whose chance is $p_i = 1/P$. With the values p_i on hand, the selection can be performed by spinning the roulette wheel as described above.

The other possibility is the *tournament selection*. In this approach, a list of individuals is obtained by randomly permuting their index numbers $i = 1, \ldots, P$. Afterwards, successive groups of L individuals are taken from the list. Among these individuals, the one with the best objective function value is chosen for reproduction and a copy is added to the gene pool. Then, the process is continued with the next L individuals until the list is exhausted or the gene pool contains P copies, whatever comes first. In the first case, the tournament process is continued to determine the missing members of the gene pool after determining a new list randomly.

Except for the tournament selection, the above approaches have in common that there is no guarantee that the best of all individuals is selected for reproduction. From the optimization viewpoint this may not be efficient. Therefore, the concept of *elitism* has been introduced which consists of putting a copy of the best individual into the gene pool by default and applying the roulette wheel and ranking approaches only $P - 1$ times. In generalized versions, a larger number of individuals is chosen by default.

23.4   Recombination and Mutation

For the *recombination* process, a pair of individuals is chosen from the gene pool either randomly or systematically. A *crossover* is carried out with a certain probability γ, i. e. the pair is recombined into two new individuals. In case that no recombination is performed, the original individuals become part of the new population with a probability of $1 - \gamma$. This process is repeated until P individuals have been considered and, hence, a new population with P individuals has been obtained. In the literature, different values for γ have been proposed with values of $\gamma < 0.6$ not being efficient (Reeves, 1997).

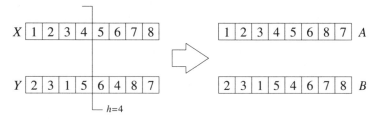

Fig. 23.3. 1-Point crossover for sequence representations

In the following, we describe the simple *1-point crossover* which is the one most commonly used. In general, it is defined for strings with length n as follows. For each pair of parent individuals X and Y, a *crossover point* $h \in [1, n - 1]$ is determined randomly. Afterwards, a first individual is obtained by concatenating the first h string positions of X with the $n - h$ last positions of Y. The second individual is obtained just the other way round. Unfortunately, this definition does not work for every possible representation of solutions. For our example problem, such a crossover results in individuals with feasible solutions when the representation based on priority values is applied but fails for the representation relying on sequences. In the latter case, it yields individuals with some jobs occurring twice and others being discarded.

Therefore, a different approach is used for sequence based representations, the principle of which is depicted for two possible strings of our example problem (Fig. 23.3). After selecting a crossover point $h \in [1, n - 1]$ randomly, the first h string positions of the parent individual X are copied into the child one A. Subsequently, the remaining $n - h$ positions are filled up with those elements which have not been considered yet in the order in which they are contained in individual Y. The second child B is constructed accordingly now starting with the first h positions of individual Y. Note that in our example both individuals obtained by the crossover yield better objective function values than their parent ones. The total tardiness costs of the schedules represented by X and Y are 51 and 93, whereas for A and B we obtain 47 and 29, respectively.

In addition to recombination, *mutation* is applied for some of the new individuals to diversify the search, i. e. to avoid that the same set of solutions is examined repeatedly through a number of consecutive generations. For this purpose, a probability δ with which each individual is mutated has to be specified. According to the selection process, the decision whether to mutate an individual or not can be made by randomly generating a number from the interval $[0, 1]$. The usual approaches for determining δ are either to choose a very small value, e. g. $\delta = 0.01$ or to use a value $\delta = 1/n$, because there is some theoretical and practical evidence that this is a reasonable value for many problems (Reeves, 1997). In general, mutation consists of randomly altering the value at a random string position. In order to preserve the feasibility for sequence based representations, two more versatile mutation possibilities are distinguished. Within an *exchange* mutation, two string positions are randomly selected and the corresponding elements are interchanged. In our example, the positions three and six may be selected for individual A resulting in the mutated sequence $A' = \langle 1, 2, 6, 4, 5, 3, 8, 7 \rangle$. A *shift* mutation consists of randomly choosing a single string position and moving the corresponding element a random number of positions to the left or right. After selecting position six of individual B and left shifting the element by three positions, we yield $B' = \langle 2, 3, 6, 1, 5, 4, 7, 8 \rangle$.

23.5   Conclusions

The previous expositions aim to review the basic ideas of GA in the context of solving combinatorial optimization problems. They also show that a large variety of design possibilities exist when implementing GA for particular problems. This includes choosing a representation of solutions, a selection mechanism as well as efficient recombination and mutation strategies. Fortunately, as stated at the beginning, already basic versions of GA are robust in the sense that they are able to yield satisfying results for many problems. However, depending on the problem to be solved, it may be difficult to consider constraints appropriately, i. e., to avoid that infeasible solutions are obtained throughout the solution process. Within production scheduling, such constraints may be due to generalized precedence relationships among jobs or to time windows for their execution. In order to overcome such difficulties, several concepts have been developed. The most common one is to modify the objective function by a penalty term such that infeasible solutions are assigned a low fitness value. For more comprehensive discussions we refer to Reeves (1997).

References

Downsland, K. A. (1996) *Genetic algorithms – A tool for OR?*, Journal of the Operational Research Society, Vol. 47, 550–561

Drexl, A. (1991) *Scheduling of project networks by job assignment*, Management Science, Vol. 37, 1590–1602

Holland, J. H. (1975) *Adaption in natural and artificial intelligence*, Ann Arbor

Goldberg, D. E. (1989) *Genetic algorithms in search, optimization, and machine learning*, Reading/ Massachusetts et al.

Michalewicz, Z. (1994) *Genetic algorithms + data structures = Evolution programs*, 2nd ed., Berlin et al.

Reeves, C. R. (Ed.) (1993) *Modern heuristic techniques for combinatorial problems*, Oxford et al.

Reeves, C. R. (1997) *Genetic algorithms for the operations researcher*, INFORMS Journal on Computing, Vol. 9, 231–250

24 Constraint Programming

Robert Klein

Darmstadt University of Technology, Institute of Business Administration, Department of Operations Research, Hochschulstraße 1, 64289 Darmstadt, Germany

24.1 Overview and General Idea

Constraint programming (CP) represents a relatively new technique for computing feasible (and optimal) solutions to combinatorial decision problems like those typically arising in scheduling and routing (see Chaps. 9 and 10). In the mid eighties, it was developed as a computer science technique by combining concepts of *Artificial Intelligence* with new programming languages. In the meantime, it has received considerable attention in practice as well as in the *Operations Research* (OR) community, in particular, since it has successfully been included into commercial software systems (e. g. ILOG OPL Studio). The basic idea of CP consists of providing an integrated framework for formulating and solving decision problems based on a single programming language. For the latter purpose, generalized solution procedures are included within CP systems, the application of which can be controlled by the user. Hence, in contrast to classical OR techniques such as mixed integer programming, the user of CP does not only specify the decision problem to be solved but also determines how the search for corresponding feasible solutions should be performed.

For solving decision problems, CP does not rely on mathematical optimization problems but on constraint satisfaction problems which, basically, consist of variables, domains as well as constraints (Sect. 24.2). For each variable, an associated *domain* defines a set of feasible values which need not necessarily be real or integral. The variables are related to each other by *constraints* describing restrictions that have to be observed by feasible solutions. In general, constraints need not be simple expressions, in particular, they need not be linear inequalities or equations as common in mixed integer programming. Possible examples involving two variables x_1 and x_2 are $x_1 \neq x_2$, $x_1 \cdot x_2 < 10$ or $x_1 > 3 \Rightarrow x_2 > 7$. The corresponding *constraint satisfaction problem* (CSP) is to assign a value to each variable of its domain such that each constraint is satisfied. Obviously, a CSP differs from a classical optimization problem by not considering an objective function. That is, solving a CSP aims at finding feasible solutions to a real-world problem rather than an optimal one. However, a possible objective function can be represented within CSPs by particular constraints and optimized by solving several CSPs consecutively.

In order to compute feasible solutions to a CSP by CP, constraint propagation techniques are usually combined with special purpose search algorithms. *Constraint propagation* provides an effective mechanism to systematically reduce the domains of variables by carefully analyzing the constraints for the problem data on hand and resolving inconsistencies (Sect. 24.3). The *search algorithms* applied within CP are based on systematically enumerating all feasible solutions of a CSP (with reduced domains) using a backtracking approach (Sect. 24.4).

Among the major advantages of CP are the ease of application and the flexibility to add new constraints to existing problems. This is due to the rich set of possible constraint types and to the search algorithms employed being rather general. A disadvantage may be the rather poor performance with respect to solution quality and computation time (Brailsford et al., 1999).

In the following, we describe the different components of CP in more detail. To ease the presentation, we use the example and the notation of the production scheduling problem introduced in Chapt. 23. For recent introductions and surveys on constraint programming see, e. g., Brailsford et al. (1999) as well as Lustig and Puget (1999).

24.2   Constraint Satisfaction Problems

As stated in the previous section, a CSP considers a set of n *variables* $x_1, x_2, \ldots, x_n$. Associated with each variable $x_j (j = 1, \ldots, n)$ is a finite *domain* (set) D_j of possible values. In our production scheduling example, the variables x_j may denote the start times of the jobs $j = 1, \ldots, n$. Assuming that all jobs have to be terminated until a common deadline of T, i. e. T periods after the beginning of the planning horizon, the domain of a job j is $D_j = \{rd_j, \ldots, T - d_j\}$, because it cannot begin before its release date rd_j and has to start d_j periods before T the latest. Note that in general the values of D_j need not be a set of consecutive integers. Furthermore, they even need not be numeric, e. g. they can correspond to elements of some general set. However, in case that the domains are not finite like in linear programming problems, the solution techniques described in the following sections have to be modified.

The variables are related by a set of *constraints*. Formally, a constraint C_{ij} between two variables x_i and x_j corresponds to a feasible subset of all possible combinations of the values of x_i and x_j, i. e. $C_{ij} \subseteq D_i \times D_j$. If $(x_i, x_j) \in C_{ij}$, the constraint is said to be *satisfied*. For example, if $D_1 = \{1, 2\}$ and $D_2 = \{3, 4\}$, then the constraint $x_1 + 2 = x_2$ is equivalent to the subset $\{(1, 3), (2, 4)\}$ of the set of all possible combinations $\{(1, 3), (1, 4), (2, 3), (2, 4)\}$. For constraints referring to a larger number of variables, the definition can easily be extended.

In practice, the programming languages of CP systems provide more efficient approaches for representing constraints. For our production scheduling problem we obtain the following CP formulation when omitting the objective function:

$$x_i + d_i \leq x_j \text{ or } x_j + d_j \leq x_i \text{ for } i = 1, \ldots, n, \ j = 1, \ldots, n,$$
$$\text{and } i < j \tag{24.1}$$
$$D_j = \{rd_j, \ldots, T - d_j\} \text{ for } j = 1, \ldots, n \tag{24.2}$$

The first set of constraints is commonly called *disjunctive* constraints. It says that for two jobs i and j, either job i must finish before job j starts or job j must terminate before job i begins. This type of constraints plays an important role in many production scheduling problems, where two jobs are not allowed to be processed simultaneously on a single machine, as this is e. g. the case in our example or in a flow-shop or job-shop environment. Note that such a straightforward formulation of disjunctive constraints as in (24.1) is not possible in a mixed integer programme where binary variables have to be introduced for this purpose. This is also true for a large number of further types of constraints (Williams and Wilson, 1998). Another typical example of a constraint which can easily be defined within CP but is difficult to express in a mixed integer programme is the following. Each of the five variables $x_1, x_2, \ldots, x_5$ is to be assigned a different value from the interval $[1, \ldots, 5]$.

Obviously, a *feasible solution* to a CSP is an assignment of a value to each variable from its domain such that all constraints are satisfied. Basically, we may be interested in computing just one or all feasible solutions of a CSP with no preference as to which one. In case an optimal (e. g. a minimal) or at least a good solution for some objective function has to be determined, several CSPs have to be solved consecutively. For this purpose, an objective variable is additionally defined which corresponds to the objective function value. After finding a first feasible solution, a modified CSP is obtained by introducing a new (objective) constraint which specifies that the value of the objective variable has to be smaller than in the initial solution. That is, an upper bound on the objective function value is established such that only solutions with smaller values are considered feasible when solving the modified CSP. This process is continued by tightening the upper bound each time a new feasible solution has been determined until a CSP is obtained for which no feasible solution exists. Then, the last solution found represents a minimal one. In case that the process is terminated prematurely, e. g. due to limited computation time, only a heuristic solution is determined.

For our example, we define $y = \sum_{j=1}^{n} c_j \cdot max\{x_j + d_j - dd_j, 0\}$ as objective variable. When the solution depicted in Fig. 23.2 with total tardiness cost of 51 is to be improved, a CSP consisting of the constraints (24.1), (24.2) and $y < 51$ has to be solved.

24.3   Constraint Propagation

The basic idea of *constraint propagation* is to "propagate" the effects of modifying a variable's domain to any constraint that interacts with that variable. By analyzing each of these constraints, possible inconsistencies resulting from the modification are discovered and subsequently resolved by removing inconsistent values from the domains of the remaining variables participating in the affected constraint. This step is usually referred to as *domain reduction*.

In the following, we describe the principle of domain reduction for constraints which only concern two variables, such as the disjunctive constraints discussed in the previous section. In this case, the variables and the constraints can be depicted in a constraint graph with the nodes representing variables. Arcs are introduced between two nodes, if a constraint C_{ij} is defined between the corresponding variables x_i and x_j. Furthermore, the arc (x_i, x_j) is called *(arc) consistent* if for every value $a \in D_i$, there is a value $b \in D_j$ such that the assignments $x_i = a$ and $x_j = b$ do not violate the constraint C_{ij}. Any value $a \in D_i$ for which this is not true, i.e. no corresponding value b exists can be removed from D_i, because it cannot be contained in any feasible solution. By treating all such values from D_i accordingly, consistency for the arc (x_i, x_j) is obtained. This is best illustrated by an example. Consider two variables x_1 and x_2 with domains $D_1 = \{1, \ldots, 5\}$ and $D_2 = \{1, \ldots, 5\}$. The constraint to be observed is $x_1 < x_2 - 2$. By examining the variable x_1, we see that due to $x_2 \leq 5$ the constraint can not be satisfied for the values $x_1 \in \{3, 4, 5\}$ and, hence, the values can be removed from D_1 resulting in $D_1' = \{1, 2\}$. Subsequently performing the same check for x_2 yields $D_2' = \{4, 5\}$ due to $x_1 \geq 1$. In general, a constraint considering more than two variables is called consistent when for each possible value from the domain of a variable affected an assignment to all other variables from their domains can be made such that the constraint is satisfied. Furthermore, a CSP is consistent when this is true for all its constraints.

Within a constraint programming system, constraint propagation is usually applied iteratively to make the domains of each variable as small as possible, while making the entire CSP consistent. For this purpose, a number of algorithms have been developed among which the predominant one is called AC-5 (Van Hentenryck et al., 1992).

In the above example, evaluating the constraint $2x_1 = x_2$ for the initial domains $D_1 = \{1, \ldots, 5\}$ and $D_2 = \{1, \ldots, 5\}$ leads to the reduced domains $D_1'' = \{1, 2\}$ and $D_2'' = \{2, 4\}$ which guarantees consistency of the corresponding arcs. Now, if the results for the domain reduction applied to the constraint $x_1 < x_2 - 2$ have been propagated, the reduced domains $D_1' = \{1, 2\}$ and $D_2' = \{4, 5\}$ can be used in the evaluation. Then, we yield $D_1'' = \{2\}$ and $D_2'' = \{4\}$ which represents the only feasible solution to the CSP on hand.

Though for the small example constraint propagation seems to be rather simple, it may be much more complicated in case of more complex constraints. Therefore, a typical constraint programming system allows the user to define new propagation and domain reduction algorithms. Fortunately, state-of-the-art systems such as OPL provide large libraries of predefined constraints, including disjunctive ones as in our example. Therefore, it is often not necessary to create new constraints and to develop specialized propagation algorithms.

24.4 Search Algorithms

In general, algorithms for solving CSPs systematically enumerate all possible assignments of values to variables. By verifying for each combination of values whether it corresponds to a feasible solution or not, the algorithms are guaranteed to either determine a feasible solution, if one exists, or to prove that the problem is unsatisfiable. The most simple and common approach applied for this purpose is backtracking. To increase its performance, several extensions have been proposed among which forward checking and maintaining (arc) consistency seem to be most promising (Brailsford et al., 1999).

By *backtracking*, a multi-level enumeration (search) tree is systematically constructed. Each node of the tree corresponds to a partial solution in which values have been determined for a subset of variables. In each node on the current level of the tree, a yet unconsidered variable is selected. Subsequently, it is assigned a value from its domain thereby defining a node on the next level of the tree. If for this value, any of the constraints between this variable and those already considered is violated, a *dead end* is detected. In this case, the assignment is abandoned and a new neighbouring node is obtained by examining the next value of the variable's domain. Otherwise, if the assignment is feasible, the next variable for which no value has been determined yet is chosen and treated in the same fashion. As soon as all values of a variable have been examined, the search backtracks to the previous level and assigns a new value to the corresponding variable. For a CSP, the search can stop when a complete consistent solution has been obtained, i. e. a value has been determined to each variable such that all constraints are satisfied. If no feasible solution exists, the search is terminated after examining all possibilities of assigning values to variables.

Figure 24.1 shows a part of the search tree obtained for our production scheduling problem. On the root level of the tree, variable x_1 is selected. After assigning the value $x_1 = 0$, the variable x_2 is considered on the subsequent level of the tree. However, the values $x_2 \in \{2, \ldots, 4\}$ are not feasible due to the constraints (24.1) which prevent that jobs are executed in parallel and, hence, lead to dead ends (black nodes). For $x_2 = 5$, the search may continue with selecting e. g. variable x_3. After having examined all possible values of $x_2 \in D_2$ for $x_1 = 0$ as well as the possible assignments for the remaining variables on the subsequent levels of the tree, the search backtracks to the root node and the next value for x_1 is examined. Then, for $x_1 = 1$ all values $x_2 \in D_2$ have to be evaluated again etc.

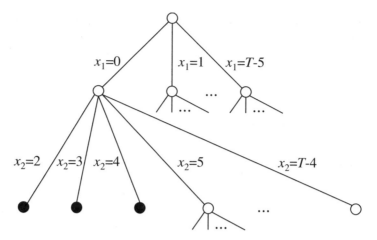

Fig. 24.1. Partial search tree for the example problem

Backtracking as described above only verifies the constraints between the current variable on a level of a tree and the variables considered on the previous levels. Within *forward checking*, after assigning a value to the current variable, all constraints affecting this variable are examined and values in the domains of yet unconsidered variables conflicting with this assignment are temporarily removed. If for one of these variables, the corresponding domain becomes empty, no feasible solution can be obtained by completing the current partial solution and, hence, the current variable value is infeasible and backtracking is performed. In case of *maintaining (arc) consistency*, additionally all available constraint propagation techniques are applied each time a variable has been assigned a value to temporarily reduce domains of the unfixed variables. That is, also inconsistencies in constraints which do not contain the variable just fixed itself but are affected indirectly are detected.

Obviously, the order in which variables are selected has a considerable influence on the size of the search tree. In particular, this is true if fixing the values of some variables also allows for reducing the domains of others. In this case, to keep the search tree as small as possible, those variables should be selected first the fixing of which lead to the largest domain reductions. Therefore, CP systems usually offer the possibility to determine the order in which variables are chosen (Van Hentenryck, 1999, Chap. 7).

24.5   Concluding Remarks

The previous sections show that CP for which a number of modern and easy-to-use software packages exist compares favourably with classical OR techniques in terms of modelling combinatorial decision problems. This is mainly due to the ease of defining logical constraints such as e. g. disjunctive constraints which often arise in production scheduling problems (Sect. 24.2). The formulation of such constraints is difficult within mixed integer programming (for further examples see Williams and Wilson (1998)). However, the performance of CP systems still seems to be rather poor with respect to solution quality and computation time (Brailsford et al., 1999). For a CP approach to be competitive to modern OR methods such as highly developed branch and bound procedures or meta-heuristics (e.g. genetic algorithms), the constraints of the problem to be solved should be rather restrictive, like this is e.g. true in production scheduling in case of tight due dates. Then, after fixing a single variable, constraint propagation allows a large number of reductions in the domains of other variables. In general, when CP is applied to solve problems optimally, it may benefit from OR by including bounding techniques as well as more versatile techniques to evaluate the search tree (see e.g. Klein and Scholl (1999)). If CP is used for determining heuristic solutions, it is promising to incorporate ideas from local search. Simple approaches of this type are e.g. discussed in Nuijten and Aarts (1996).

References

Brailsford, S. C.; Potts, C. N.; Smith, B. M. (1999) *Constraint satisfaction problems: Algorithms and applications*, European Journal of Operational Research, Vol. 119, 557–581

Klein, R.; Scholl, A. (1999) *Scattered branch and bound – An adaptive search strategy applied to resource-constrained project scheduling*, Central European Journal of Operations Research, Vol. 7, 177–202

Lustig, I. J.; Puget, J.-F. (1999) *Program != Program: Constraint programming and its relationship to mathematical programming*, Working Paper, URL: http://www.ilog.com, State: August 1, 2000

Nuijten, W. P. M.; Aarts, E. H. L. (1996) *A computational study of constraint satisfaction for multiple capacitated job shop scheduling*, European Journal of Operational Research, Vol. 90, 269–284

Van Hentenryck, P. (1999) *The OPL optimization programming language*, Cambrige/Massachusetts et al.

Van Hentenryck, P.; Deville, Y.; Teng, T. M. (1992) *A generic arc-consistency algorithm and its specializations*, Artificial Intelligence, Vol. 57, 291–321

Williams, H. P.; Wilson, J. M. (1998) *Connections between integer linear programming and constraint logic programming – An overview and introduction to the cluster of articles*, INFORMS Journal on Computing, Vol. 10, 261–264

Index

AATP (allocated ATP), 140, 242, 294
- customer hierarchy, 141
activity, 37, 154
advanced planning, 16
aggregation, 61, 128
alert, 77
- monitor, 192, 246, 248
allocation, 201, 203
- planning, 144, 285
allocation rule
- fixed split, 143
- per committed, 143
- rank based, 143
alternative-generating algorithm, 90
alternative-selecting algorithm, 90
AMR (American Manufacturing
  Research), 217
anticipation, 118
APO PP/DS model, 253
APS (Advanced Planning System), 18,
  60
- assessment, 223
- enabler, 198, 212, 215, 287
- implementation, 224
- industry focus, 218
- integration, 186, 224, 295
- licence fees, 220
- number of installations, 219
- post-implementation, 227
- prototype, 223
- release change, 227
- selection, 217
- super-user, 228
- system administration, 227
- user support, 228
- vendor, 218, 220
- vendor support, 227
APS implementation project
- definition phase, 197, 221
- functional requirements, 221
- implementation costs, 221
- implementation time, 221
- selection phase, 217
APS module

- (Material Requirements Planning),
  76
- coordination, 184
- Demand Fulfilment and ATP, 76, 135
- Demand Planning, 76, 97
- Distribution Planning, 76, 167
- interaction, 184
- Master Planning, 76, 117
- Production Planning, 76, 149
- Scheduling, 76, 149
- Strategic Network Planning, 76, 79
- structure, 75
- Transport Planning, 76, 167
arc consistent, 356
arc-based formulation, 88
architecture of planning system, 268
ARIBA, 241
ARIMA, 105, 245
Aspect Development, 241
assembly process, 284
asset turns, 35
assets, 208
ATP (available-to-promise), 66, 136,
  137, 170, 245, 293
- consumption, 146
- dimension, 145
- granularity, 138
- product dimension, 138
- retained, 143
- search rule, 145
- time buckets, 139
automotive industry, 171
availability of data, 205

B2B (business-to-business), 15, 193,
  241, 246
B2C (business-to-consumer), 15, 193
back end, 272
backorders, 109
base-stock-system, 193
basic data, 236
batch interface, 295
batch production, 298
beer distribution game, 21

beginning inventory, 312
Benders Decomposition, 90
best practice, 37, 43
BOM (bill-of-materials), 154
BOM explosion, 76
bottleneck, 65, 118, 121
Box-Jenkins-method, 105
BPI methodology, 238
Branch and Bound, 340
build and test phase, 237
bullwhip effect, 21, 22, 67, 211
business
– case, 229, 235
– performance, 207, 285
– process, 37

calculation scheme, 31
calendar, 156
cannibalization, 245
capacity allocation, 269
capacity planning, 65, 68, 76
cash flow, 207
cash-to-cash cycle time, 35
causal factor, 245
causal forecasting, 102
change management, 236
change programme, 197
changeover, 66
– costs, 70
channel research, 19
choice of partner, 12
client organization, 229
collaborative forecasting, 98, 100, 101
communication, 15
– plan, 235
– technology, 205
complexity, 127
component planning, 290
computer industry, 100
configuration, 283, 294
configure-to-order, 139, 283
constraint propagation, 354, 356
consulting firm, 230
consumer goods industry, 67, 245, 297
continuous improvement, 215
continuous review system, 114
contract, 66
contractor management, 232
cooperation, 20, 64

coordination, 9, 20, 67, 69
coordination of APS modules
– Demand Fulfilment and ATP, 185
– Demand Planning, 185
– Distribution and Transport Planning, 186
– MasterPlanning, 185
– Production Planning and Scheduling, 185
– Strategic Network Planning, 185
CORBA, 225, 243
core process, 37
corporate planning, 269
CP (constraint programming), 344, 353
CPLEX, 302
crossover, 345, 350
CSP (constraint satisfaction problem), 353
CTP (capable-to-promise), 66, 139
customer
– service, 10, 297
– service level, 203, 214, 299
customer hierarchy, 141
cycle stock, 171, 176, 177, 310

data
– exchange, 188
– transfer, 188
data mining, 190
decoupling point, 11, 169
delivery performance, 33
demand fulfilment, 135, 293
demand planning, 97, 200, 269, 285, 287, 301
– geographic dimension, 141
– geographic hierarchy, 288
– product hierarchy, 288
– time dimension, 289
demand supply matching, 285, 293
demand wave, 136
dependent forecast, 242
deployment, 169, 177
deployment phase, 238
design phase, 235
die bank, 271
disaggregation, 128
distribution, 204, 299, 309
– paths, 169
– structure, 63

– type, 48
distribution planning, 65, 68, 69, 76, 167, 301
divisional planning, 270
documentation, 237
domain reduction, 356
downstream, 209
dual value, 132, 338
due date, 158
duties, 84
DW (Data Warehouse), 186
– APS integration, 190

e-business, 77, 193, 244
EDI (electronic data interchange), 15
emergency transport, 299, 313
enabler-KPI-value network, 213
engineering, 200
ERP (enterprise resource planning), 59, 60
– system, 76, 205, 210
event-oriented planning, 59
every-day-low-price, 64
excess
– assets, 140, 211
– capacity, 140, 211
– expenses, 140, 210
– inventory, 211
executive management, 198
expenses, 208
exponential smoothing, 103, 245, 325
external resources, 232
external variability, 210
extrusion process, 251

facility planning, 270
fill rate, 114
financial measures, 207
finite planning, 257
firmed, 160
first-come-first-served, 140, 141, 143
fitness value, 345
fixed, 160
– configuration, 283, 294
– split, 143
flexibility funnel, 202
flow lines, 161
flow shop, 284
focal company, 14

focus phase, 229
food and beverages industry, 297
food industry, 101
forecast
– accuracy, 110, 202, 204, 205, 213, 245, 285, 287
– collaborative, 289
– component, 290
– error, 99, 110
– netting, 285
– sales, 289
forecasting, 69
– seasonality and trend, 323
forecasting model, 57
FP (Factory Planner)
– alternate resource, 279
– BOM (bill-of-materials), 278
– data files, 274
– model, 276
– routing data, 279
– spec files, 273
front end, 271
frozen
– horizon, 121, 160, 165
– period, 59, 303, 312
functional attribute, 47

GA (genetic algorithm), 243, 345
gain, 1
gantt-chart, 158
Gartner Group, 217
gene pool, 348
generation, 345
geographic dimension, 141

heuristic, 59, 127, 311, 345
hierarchical (production) planning, 25
hierarchical planning system, 60
House of SCM, 9
hybrid-flow-shop, 251

i2 Technologies, 241
– Active Data Warehouse, 286, 296
– adaptor, 243, 296
– ADW (Active Data Warehouse), 243
– Constraint Anchored Optimization, 243
– Demand Fulfillment, 242, 286, 294

- Demand Planner, 242, 269, 270, 285, 287
- Factory Planner, 241, 242, 267, 273, 286, 293
- Factory Planner modelling, 273, 276
- Global Logistics Manager, 244
- High Availability, 294
- Optimal Scheduler, 243
- PRO (Product Relationship Object), 242, 285, 291
- RHYTHM, 241
- RHYTHM Optimization Interface, 296
- RhythmLink, 225, 243, 270, 286, 296
- RhythmLink for SAP R/3, 244
- SAP Listener, 296
- SDP (Strategy Driven Planning), 242
- software modules, 241
- Supply Chain Planner, 242, 267, 270, 286, 292
- Supply Chain Strategist, 241
- TradeMatrix, 241, 244
- Transportation Modeler, Optimizer and Manager, 243
IBM, 241
ILOG, 302
implementation
- costs, 221
- process, 229
incremental planning, 158, 226
indicator, 29
- functions of, 30
- system of, 31
individual, 346
ingredients, 297
initial plan, 226
initial population, 348
Integer Programming, 335
integer variable, 308, 311
Integrated Supply Chain Benchmarking Study, 42
integration, 9, 67, 69
- mode, 226
- of APS, 186
integration and coordination, 50
interaction of APS modules, 184
interface, 225
interview techniques, 206

inventory
- age, 214
- days of supply, 35
- level, 203
- system, 20
- turns, 214, 285
issue management, 234
IT (information technology), 14

J. D. Edwards, 205, 210, 244
- Active Supply Chain, 244, 297
- arc, 305, 308, 309, 312
- commodity, 304
- Demand Planning, 245, 312
- Distributed Object Messaging Architecture, 246
- Enterprise Planning, 245, 297, 301–303, 306, 307, 311–313
- Integration and Data Flows, 246, 302, 311, 312
- Master Planning, 297, 302, 306
- model building, 303
- Production & Distribution Planning, 245
- Production Scheduling, 245, 302, 312, 313
- Production Scheduling Discrete, 245
- Production Scheduling Process, 245
- Vehicle Loading, 245
- xtr@, 246
judgmental forecast, 98, 106
just-in-time, 64, 298

KDD (knowledge discovery in databases), 190
knowledge management system, 237
KPI (key performance indicator), 11, 33, 197, 198, 212, 213, 312
- as-is value, 215
- asset turns, 35
- cash-to-cash cycle time, 35
- customer service level, 203, 214, 299
- delivery performance, 33
- forecast accuracy, 213, 287
- inventory age, 214
- inventory days of supply, 35
- inventory turns, 138, 214
- master plan accuracy, 138

– on time delivery, 135, 137, 144, 203, 214
– order fill rate, 214
– order fulfilment performance, 33
– order lead-time, 138, 214
– order promising lead-time, 144
– perfect order fulfilment, 33
– planning cycle time, 213
– procurement, 202
– production flexibility, 34
– profile, 215
– supply chain responsiveness, 34
– to-be value, 215
– total logistics management cost, 34
– value-added employee productivity, 34
– warranty cost, 34

lead-time offset, 164
leadership, 14
life-cycle-management, 63, 112
linear regression, 104, 332
load variability, 211
local search, 59
location, 154
location-allocation, 91
logistics, 17
lost sales, 109
lot-size, 271, 273, 276
lot-sizing, 66, 69, 76, 123, 156, 302
lot-sizing stock, 70, 173, 310
LP (Linear Programming), 59, 84, 124, 177, 242, 245, 305, 311, 335
LSP (logistics service provider), 167

machine scheduling, 66, 69, 76
make-to-order, 138, 169, 283, 299
make-to-stock, 66, 69, 138, 169, 283, 299
management-by-exception, 192
Manugistics
– Demand Planning, 312
marketing, 201
master data, 188
master plan, 150
Master Planning, 168
– data, 123
– decisions, 121
– model adjustment, 133
– model building, 125
– objectives, 122
– planning horizon, 120
– results, 124
master planning, 68, 117, 136, 137, 245, 270, 285, 291, 302
master production scheduling, 65, 68, 76
mean absolute deviation, 110
mean absolute percentage error, 110
mean squared error, 110
method of Winters, 104, 112
metrics, 29, 37, 42
mid-term personnel planning, 76
mid-term sales planning, 76
middleware, 205, 225
minimum lot-size, 305, 308, 311
minimum run length, 305
MIP (Mixed Integer Programming), 80, 124, 245, 305, 306, 335, 339
model, 57, 153
monitor node, 311
moving average, 103
MRP (material requirements planning), 46, 60, 65
multi-activity resource, 256
multi-dimensional forecast, 99
multi-echelon, 82
multi-objective decision problem, 58
multicommodity, 82
mutation, 345, 351

nervousness, 159
net profit, 207
netchange, 226
– data, 188
network flow model, 177
network organization, 13
Numetrix, 244, 303
– Numetrix/3, 244

objective function, 57, 303
objectives, 157
OLAP (online analytical processing), 190, 242, 247
OLTP (online transaction processing), 186
on time delivery, 33, 135, 137, 144, 203, 214, 285

open configuration, 283, 294
operating instruction, 154
operation, 154
operational planning, 58
operations research, 18, 59
OPT, 217
optimization
– model, 57
– problem, 345
– stochastic, 80
optimizer, 127
Oracle, 270, 302, 311
order
– entry interface, 296
– fill rate, 33, 203, 214
– fulfilment lead-time, 33
– fulfilment performance, 33
– initial promise, 202
– lead-time, 135, 203, 214, 290
– life cycle, 202
– management, 202
– matching, 299
– promise, 135
– promising, 135, 144, 285, 294
– promising (MRP logic), 136
– promising lead-time, 144
– quote, 135
– quoting, 135
ordering of materials, 76

part, 154
path-based formulation, 88
penalty costs, 131, 310
per committed, 143
perfect order fulfilment, 33
performance measures, 29
periodic review system, 114
personnel planning, 65, 67
phase-in/phase-out, 112
physical distribution structure, 76
pick-the-best option, 111
piecewise linear approximation, 90
pilot phase, 237
planning, 57
– cycle time, 213
– horizon, 57, 75, 120, 301–303
– interval, 149
– module, 60
– scenario, 209

– section, 77
planning-profile, 127
plant location, 63, 76
population, 345, 346
– size, 348
POS (point-of-sale), 24
postponement, 19, 201
PPM (Production Process Model), 154,
    258
– elements, 259
preemption, 159
priority rules, 156
process, 37
– category, 39
– element, 41
– organization, 161
– orientation, 15
– term, 37
– type, 38
procurement, 201, 297, 306
procurement type, 47
product
– life cycle, 200, 289
– management, 200
– programme, 62
– quality, 203
– structure, 283
product master data, 254
production, 203, 298, 308
– flexibility, 34
– lead-time, 203
– planning, 301
– process, 251, 271
– schedule, 149
– scheduling, 270, 302
– scheduling problem, 346
– system, 63
– type, 48
Production Planning and Scheduling,
    149
project
– champion, 232
– control and reporting, 233
– coordinator, 232
– leadership, 230
– management, 230
– management team, 230
– members, 231

- mobilization, 229
- organization, 229, 232
- phase, 229
- plan, 233
- roadmap, 211
- sponsor, 232
- team, 231
promise, 202
- date, 135
- reliable, 144

quarantine stock, 310
quote, 135

rank based, 143
ratio-to-moving averages decomposition, 329
recombination, 350
reference model, 37
regression analysis, 104
resource group, 163
revenue, 208
risk management, 234
ROA (return on assets), 207
ROI (return on investment), 31, 207
rolling horizon, 59, 303, 306
routing, 154, 156, 176
rule scheme, 31
rule-based forecasting, 108

safety stock, 64, 65, 69, 97, 113, 117, 123, 176, 177, 276, 303
safety stock management, 292
sales, 200
- ATP consumption, 143
- central, 200
- forecast, 201, 289
- planning, 62, 64, 66, 68
- regions, 200
- type, 49
SAP, 246
- *live*Cache, 248
- APO's software modules, 247
- Alert Monitor, 248, 255
- APO (Advanced Planner and Optimizer), 225, 246
- BAPI, 248
- Business Information Warehouse, 246, 248
- CIF, 248
- Collaborative Planning, 248
- Data Warehouse, 246
- Demand Planning, 247
- Deployment, 248
- Global ATP, 247
- modelling philosophy, 254
- modelling technique, 253
- New Dimension Products, 246
- planning method, 255
- Production Planning and Detailed Scheduling, 247, 251
- Production Planning and Scheduling, 253
- R/3, 205, 210, 225, 244, 295, 312
- Supply Chain Cockpit, 247, 248
- Supply Chain Engineer, 248
- Supply Network Planning, 247, 257
SCC (Supply-Chain Council), 37
scheduling
- backward, 248
- forward, 248
SCM (Supply Chain Management), 18
- building blocks, 9
- definition, 9
- project, 197
scope creep, 234, 237
SCOR (Supply Chain Operations Reference)-model, 36
- application, 44
- best practice, 43
- deliver, 39
- levels, 38
- make, 39
- metrics, 42
- plan, 38
- source, 39
- standard terminology, 37
- Supply Chain Scorecard, 44
SCP-Matrix (supply chain planning matrix), 62, 75
search algorithms, 354
seasonal coefficient, 104, 112, 324
seasonal stock, 68, 118, 124, 312
seasonality, 68, 102, 104, 245, 299, 323
selection of an APS, 218
semiconductor industry, 267
service level, 35, 114

368   Index

setup time, 298, 305
– sequence dependent, 54, 69, 163, 298
shop floor control, 66, 76
short-term sales planning, 76
sign-off, 231
simulation, 98, 132, 158, 245
– model, 57
single sourcing, 90
single-activity resource, 256
smoothing constant, 103, 325
software
– component, 75–77, 246
– module, 62, 75–77
– provider, 230
sporadic demand, 109
spreadsheet, 205, 300
statistical forecasting, 98, 101
steering committee, 14, 230
stepper, 272
stock cover, 310
Strategic Network Planning, 168
strategic planning, 58, 245
strategic sales planning, 76
structural attribute, 49
sub-contractors, 231
sub-project, 233
super-user, 228
supplier
– contract, 202
– flexibility, 202
– forecast, 201
– lead-time, 201
– selection, 64
supply chain, 7, 267, 281, 298
– demand constrained, 140
– material constrained, 281
– potential analysis, 207
– process, 62, 75
– responsiveness, 34
– review, 198
– supply constrained, 140
– type, 76, 299
support process, 37
synthetic granulate industry, 251
system of indicators, 31

tactical planning, 58

target scheme, 31
task, 37
TCL, 246
team, 230
– structure, 232
test environment, 237
theory of constraints, 217
TIBCO, 227, 294, 296
time bucket, 121, 162, 301, 303
time-series-analysis, 101
time-to-market, 204
topography of a supply chain, 49
total logistics management cost, 34
training, 238
transaction system, 76
transactional data, 188
transfer price, 83
transit stock, 172, 177, 310
transport planning, 66, 167
transshipment point, 167
trend, 101, 104, 245, 323
truncation, 343
typology, 299

upstream, 209

value driven APS implementation, 212
value-added employee productivity, 34
vehicle
– loading, 170, 179
– scheduling, 171, 179
virtual market, 193
VMI (vendor managed inventory), 55, 64, 169, 192, 246, 247

wafer production, 271
wafer sawing, 272
wafer test, 272, 278
warehouse replenishment, 66
warranty cost, 34
what-if-analysis, 98, 245
Winters method, 104, 112
Winters' method, 325
WIP (work-in-process), 203
workshop, 235

yield, 273, 278

About Contributors

Prof. Dr. Bernhard Fleischmann holds a chair for Production and Logistics at the University of Augsburg. 1978-1991 he was a professor of Operations Research at the University of Hamburg. 1971-1978 he worked in the Operations Planning department of Unilever Germany. His research interests include the development and application of systems for production planning, transportation and distribution planning and inventory management. He can be contacted at ⟨bernhard.fleischmann@wiso.uni-augsburg.de⟩.

Prof. Marc Goetschalckx is Associate Professor in the School of Industrial and Systems Engineering of the Georgia Institute of Technology. His research interests are in the areas of analysis and design of material flow networks, ranging from the design of global supply chains to the dispatching of vehicles to pick orders in a warehouse. He has written numerous articles, is a frequent speaker at international meetings and short courses, consults, and has developed decision support software in these areas. He can be contacted at ⟨www.logisticsCAD.com⟩ or ⟨marc.goetschalckx@isye.gatech.edu⟩.

Dr. Christoph Kilger is managing director of j & m Management Consulting, Mannheim. He is responsible for supply chain management and electronic commerce. From 1996–1999 he was a consultant and project manager at KPMG Consulting. He has in-depth experience from several APS implementation projects in the high tech industry. He holds a PhD in computer science from the University of Karlsruhe. He can be contacted at ⟨christoph.kilger@jnm.de⟩.

Dr. Robert Klein is a research assistant at Darmstadt University of Technology where he received a doctoral degree in business administration in 1999. He has published many articles on quantitative methods and their application to production and logistics in international journals, like International Journal of Production Research, European Journal of Operational Research, and INFORMS Journal on Computing. He can be contacted at ⟨rklein@bwl.tu-darmstadt.de⟩.

Dr. Herbert Meyr has been working at the department of Production and Logistics at the University of Augsburg since 1994. After finishing his PhD thesis about *"Simultaneous Lotsizing and Scheduling for Continuous Production Lines"* in 1999 he changed his research interest to model building and integration aspects of supply chain planning. He can be contacted at ⟨herbert.meyr@wiso.uni-augsburg.de⟩.

Marco Richter is consultant at aconis GmbH, Darmstadt, a company specialized in the field of supply chain management solutions and optimizing logistic processes. He studied business administration and engineering. Since graduation from Darmstadt University of Technology, he is involved in consulting projects dealing with SAP APO and is specialized in the PP/DS module. He can be contacted at ⟨m.richter@aconis.de⟩.

Jens Rohde works on his PhD thesis at the department of Operations and Materials Management at Darmstadt University of Technology. His research domain is the anticipation of short-term production and distribution planning decisions in mid-term master plannig to provide more accurate targets. Since his graduation in business administration and computer science in 1999 he also was involved in projects concerning analysis of supply chains and implementation of APS. He can be contacted at ⟨rohdej@bwl.tu-darmstadt.de⟩.

Lorenz Schneeweiss is working for KPMG Consulting in Frankfurt, Germany, since 1999 in the field of production planning and demand fulfillment in the supply chain management group. He studied business administration, management and engineering at Darmstadt University of Technology and specialized in production and material management. He can be contacted at ⟨lschneeweiss@kpmg.com⟩.

Prof. Dr. Hartmut Stadtler is professor of Business Administration at Darmstadt University of Technology since 1990. From 1987–1990 he was employed as a consultant in the field of production management. He has published numerous articles about operations and materials management in international journals like International Journal of Production Research, Management Science, and Production and Operations Management. He can be contacted at ⟨stadtler@bwl.tu-darmstadt.de⟩.

Volker Stockrahm is managing director of aconis GmbH, Darmstadt. He is responsible for the competence center Supply Chain Management and Optimization. Since his graduation in business administration and management 1996 he was involved in many development and implementation projects for optimization and APS projects in the process industry. Moreover, he works on his PhD thesis at the department of operations and materials management at Darmstadt University of Technology. He can be contacted at ⟨v.stockrahm@aconis.de⟩.

Christopher Sürie is currently working as assistant at the department of Operations and Materials Management at Darmstadt University of Technology, Germany. He studied industrial engineering at Darmstadt University of Technology and graduated in 2000. In addition to Supply Chain Management where his focus is on Production Planning and Scheduling, his areas of interest include lot-sizing and scheduling algorithms. He can be contacted at ⟨suerie@bwl.tu-darmstadt.de⟩.

Michael Wagner works on his PhD thesis at the department of Production and Logistics at the University of Augsburg. His research concentrates on the integration of production and distribution planning. Since the completion of his study of business administration in 1998 he also was involved in projects concerning inventory management and implementation of APS. He can be contacted at ⟨michael.wagner@wiso.uni-augsburg.de⟩.

Dr. Ulrich Wetterauer is a senior consultant at j & m Management Consulting, Manheim. From April 1998 - May 2000, he was a consultant at KPMG Consulting. He worked as a technical implementor, solution architect, and project manager in a large, international APS implementation project in the high tech industry. He holds a PhD in physical chemistry from the University of Heidelberg. He can be contacted at ⟨ulrich.wetterauer@jnm.de⟩.